# Driftwood

# DRIFTWOOD

A NOVEL BY

RAY BENTLEY

*Driftwood* is a work of fiction. Characters, names, places, and incidents are either the product of the author's imagination or are used fictitiously. Any resemblance to actual persons, events, or places is completely coincidental.



Published in the United States by Five Count Publishing LLC.
www.fivecountpub.com

Library of Congress Control Number: 2015909902

ISBN: 978-1-943706-00-6 (Hardcover)
ISBN: 978-1-943706-01-3 (ebook)

Printed in the United States of America.

Cover & Logo designs by Gwynn Olds.
Book design by Ritch Bentley.
Author photo courtesy of Alaina Creswell.

*For Jodi,*

*the love of my life who waited patiently for over 20 years for me to finish the damn thing.*

## Acknowledgements

The idea for this book was originally hatched back in my playing days with the Buffalo Bills. I was injured at the time, as was my good buddy and teammate, Mike Hamby. We started thinking about our football mortality and I mentioned I wanted to write a book from the perspective of a grizzly old linebacker which I hoped to one day be. My boy Hamby said "Yeah, old Driftwood." And then he drew up and awesome picture of what Driftwood would look like. The seed was planted! Thanks, "Hambone."

Many people helped me throughout the long process of getting this pig up on skates. My son, Ritchard, turns out, is a damn good editor. No nepotism here, folks, just the truth. My baby-boy, Jake, has a good eye and ear for what works, what's real. They were the ultimate, final reason we finished the book. (Personally, I think it could use another hundred or so edits.) They both quit their jobs and started a publishing company. Guess who their first author was? Yes, me. So I had to finish, and as you can see, I did – and only six months late!

Many others are worthy of plaudits for assisting me in this venture. I know I will forget to mention somebody here, so please allow me to pre-emptively apologize if you belong on this list and are left wanting. Just know, in my heart, I truly appreciate your help.

One particular group, essentially my initial test-audience, was incredibly inspirational to me while writing the first draft of the manuscript. I would finish a chapter and straightaway email it to them and receive immediate encouragement and instant useable feedback – except from Lou Rossi. He fed me useless information, per usual. Thanks, "Lewis." This group also helped inspire several characters in the book, although any specific reference is purely coincidental and the characters and their actions are exclusively a product of my imagination. They are Joe Vizzi, the aforementioned Lou Rossi, Rudy Klawiter, Rahn Bentley and Jake Bentley. Furthermore, both Viz and "Lewis," along with Ryan Gallo, made themselves available to answer any question I had regarding the city of Buffalo, whenever and wherever they came up. After vicious arguing and a volley of tasteless, personal insults, I always got an answer, and occasionally even a consensus. Thanks, guys.

I also received a great piece of advice from Jamie Turner, a longtime journalist and editor in the Cleveland area who saved me a lot of potential heartbreak and conflict. Thanks, brother. The cover art and various logos were done by Gwynn Olds, who did a fantastic job! Thanks, Gwynn.

During the extended process of putting this together I received positive feedback and copious encouragement from many. My usual partners on my ESPN College Football telecasts, Mark Neely and Dave LaMont, both took the time to read the manuscript and provide feedback and continually inquire about my progress. It's been a true blessing being paired with these two great guys.

This book has been something of a Bentley family project. Each of my five children has had input and helped me immensely in the writing process somewhere along the way. Cousin RJ Bentley would even make copies of all 400+ pages for me to review and share with his various resources. My sister Judy Dawn Schroeder was very helpful and encouraging in the process. The oldest fruit of my loins, my daughter Alaina was especially helpful in guiding the decisions regarding the artwork of the book and read early drafts providing valuable input all along. My son TJ went over the final version with a fine-tooth comb and caught several things that had escaped all eyes, which was very helpful. Two of my most immediate and reliable resources were my wife Jodi and youngest daughter Morgan. While doing the final edit, I would ask them myriad questions about punctuation, grammar, and spelling. Although I occasionally received a blank, glazed-over stare before getting a response, they always gave me valuable input. I would run sentences by them constantly, and they helped me every single time. That is pretty amazing. They are the best! The true goal was achieved when I watched them enjoy reading it. After all, that's why we do whatever it is we do.

"The snow's piled high on the highway tonight,
I'm a ship lost at sea on this ocean of white,
Eighteen wheels anchored somewhere out of Dover-
I wish I could hold her-
Instead of huggin' this old, cold shoulder."

(Kent Blazy, Kim Williams, Garth Brooks)

# Prologue

Through a frosted seventh-floor window of the Brylin Mental Hospital, Jack Driftwood gazed out at the tip of the iceberg of the furious blizzard ravaging the city of Buffalo, New York. It was the perfect Christmas Eve to be wrapped in a blanket sipping a totty in front of the fireplace. No doubt, that would have been Jack's preference; anything was better than his current status as an involuntary inmate in a mental institution. The powerfully disruptive storm raging outside served as a fine metaphor for the awakening mind of the deeply troubled linebacker.

Jack pressed his broad, scarred nose through the bars and onto the icy-cold pane of security glass. He shivered as he peered into the night at the drifting sea of white which had once been the hospital parking lot. A fierce wind rocked the streetlights below, making them appear as lighted buoys bobbing on an angry surf of blowing snow. Jack closed his eyes to shut it all out, yet the storm continued to roil – outside the window, inside his skull.

*What the hell happened, anyway? Why am I in this goddamn looney bin?*

His memory was sketchy but his gray matter was heating up and the details of his ill-timed demise were sliding back into focus, albeit fuzzy around the edges. The ringing headache he'd endured since regaining consciousness an hour or so earlier was beginning to subside. He felt hungover, like he'd been on an old-school type of bender, like back in the day when he would play all day and run all night. But those days were long gone; at the ripe, old age of thirty-nine, he paid dearly for such sins.

*What the hell day is it, anyways?*

Jack shuffled slowly away from the window. Just looking out at the raging snowstorm had given him the chills. He stopped and bent at the waist, struggling to touch his toes which were covered in light-blue paper booties the hospital staff had issued him.

Stretching his stiff muscles, he tested his body by doing a quick inventory of the damage. He gingerly fingered the stitches above his right eye. Other than that he had a few bruises and sore spots, but there were no significant injuries. He wasn't concerned; he always recovered quickly from a beating. That was his business. You don't play pro football in the NAFA for eighteen years if you can't deal with a good ass-whipping from time to time.

Jack knew his body would recover soon enough; his main issue was getting out of this damn cuckoo's nest. After that, he would set things right, making whoever put him in this place pay dearly for it. He was confident it would happen soon enough. In fact, he was fairly certain the cavalry was already locked and loaded and would soon be on the way.

He shuffled to a nearby table, sat down, and picked up the deck of playing cards lying on the table. After giving them a quick shuffle, he dealt himself a hand of solitaire. Perhaps a little game would expedite the clearing of his mind. At the very least it would kill some time, because apparently time was one of the few things Jack Driftwood had left.

# Chapter One

The seagulls from nearby Lake Erie circled the neatly lined practice fields at Fredonia State University like a squadron of B-52's marshalling for a critical mission. The gulls were locked and loaded with a capacity payload of creamy shit-bombs manufactured from the feast they had culled during the previous day's double-session. There was never a shortage of good seagull chow at a Buffalo Blizzard training camp; several concession stands pumped out hot dogs, popcorn, cotton candy, and other goodies at capacity the entire three weeks the team practiced on the small Western New York campus. Any seagull worth its salt knew the training camp fare was far better than a Burger King dumpster during lunch hour.

The team was orderly assembled across the field in formation for their pre-practice stretching routine. The offense, in white jerseys, had been assigned the near side; the defense, in blue, had taken the longer walk gathering on the far side. As usual, such arrangements catered to the offense.

Even though it was only 8:30 in the morning, the campus grounds were teaming with Blizzard fans jockeying for the best vantage points behind the temporary fencing enclosing the practice fields. They came from all over Western New York and beyond to watch their team prepare for the upcoming season. The place was always a carnival of energy, but things were especially amped up this particular morning, and with good reason: this was the first day of full pads. The Blizzard was going to play some real football again.

Jack Driftwood, in his eighteenth NAFA training camp, had seen more than his share of hotshot rookies and lowly free agents come and go. To this point he had survived on know-how, twenty-inch guns, and what he considered to be good looks. He maintained an even-keeled approach and was self-aware enough to know the primary reason he was back for yet another campaign was the high-priced, prima donna, pretty-boy rookie stretching in front of him. His primary role was to groom the lad and expedite the process of making him a pro, if not a Star-Bowler.

Another savior had arrived to lead the Buffalo Blizzard back to the Promised Land – the NAFA championship game known as the Mega Bowl. Steven Stark, Buffalo's first-round draft pick, chosen fifth overall the previous spring, had inked a lucrative, five-year deal the night before and was in uniform. The team had traded up on draft day to select Stark, an inside linebacker by trade, and he had immediately been anointed as a franchise-type player by the media and fans alike, even though he had yet to take a single snap in professional football. The local media championed him as the defensive stopper Buffalo desperately needed to get over the hump and back to the playoffs. His acquisition had spurred open talk amongst the fan base of a realistic shot at a return to the playoffs after a sixteen-year hiatus. Praise God Almighty! The long drought was about to end and today was its genesis. A true Blizzard fan wouldn't miss this occasion for all the chicken wings in the Southtowns.

Driftwood relished the thought of being Steven Stark's mentor. The game had been passed down to him over the years and it was a matter of pride to return the favor. He hadn't had a rookie prospect of Stark's magnitude his entire career. It was time to unlock the vault of sacred knowledge and spoon feed the golden boy.

Anticipation of the season's initial full-contact hitting session made patience no longer a virtue. An overzealous fan, barebacked with his face painted in the Blizzard team colors – red, white, and powder blue – clung to the top of a fifteen-foot high fence separating the practice field from bleachers packed with Blizzard faithful. He cried out to his new hero.

"Steven Stark! Yer the best, man! Yer gonna kick ass all the way to the Mega Bowl!"

The crowd cheered and rocked the fence, nearly flinging the painted fan to the ground. A young, hot chick in a low-cut Blizzard tank top yelled, "We love you, Steve Stark!" which set off a round of high-pitched screams usually reserved for rock stars.

Driftwood hadn't seen a training camp crowd this worked up since Ben Brady, the team's quarterback, had arrived as a top draft pick three years earlier.

"What the hell, Stark," Driftwood called out, "you bring your whole family of webbed-footers down here just to watch you practice?"

Stark turned and looked at Driftwood as if he were covered in fresh feces. "They sure as hell ain't the Driftwoodies, no bikers, sleazebags, or druggies."

The Driftwoodies were the Jack Driftwood Fan Club. And Stark was exactly right; they were one sorry-ass collection of humanity. Jack wouldn't have had it any other way.

"You got that right, dickhead," he shot back, "the real people appreciate Jack Driftwood."

He laughed and snapped on his helmet as he headed for the linebacker's drill area when the whistle blew. His rookie had a lot to learn but the kid definitely had some spite. Spite could be good, especially in this business, as long as you could back it up.

The team went through a strictly monitored fifteen-minute agility period, which was basically no more than a thorough warmup before the 9-on-7 segment started. This was where the fur would begin to fly.

The 9-on-7 drill was just that, nine guys on offense against seven on defense using only running plays. This drill was where the ground game was to be honed to perfection through live blocking against full-speed defenders. More importantly, it would separate the men from the boys. Only wide receivers and defensive backs were kept out of the action. Those faint-hearts worked on one-on-one pass coverage drills on the opposite field.

Howard Ivy, the octogenarian Buffalo head coach, brought the team up for his customary chat prior to the first live, physical contact of the season. Coach Ivy was a highly educated man and felt it was important his team understood why things were being done a certain way, believing this knowledge would maximize the results. That was his style and at the age of eighty-two he was too damn old to change it now.

"Alright, fellas," the venerable coach began, "this is the initial full-contact drill of the year so be sure to protect yourselves at all times. No hitting the quarterbacks, no chop blocking, no live tackling. Just thud the ball carrier and then let him run on. We are working together. Any questions?"

"Yeah, how the hell are we supposed to have any fun?" Driftwood asked.

There was muffled, nervous laughter, but the coach's only response was a quick smile displaying some expensive dental work and a chirp of his whistle.

Upon that whistle, Bo-Bo Karpinski, the Blizzard's 345-pound nose tackle, held up both arms and screamed at the top of his lungs.

"Huddle!"

Instantly the defensive huddle formed around the mammoth hulk like an odd shapes and sizes puzzle. Driftwood stood with Steven Stark poised to call the defense in front of the assembled mass of humanity. But first, Lester Faber, the Blizzard's defensive coordinator, had a few words for his troops.

Coach Faber looked around ponderously and then pulled the signature, unlit, chewed-up, soggy cigar out of his mouth and spat on the ground.

"Men, this is our drill. Now, I don't give a shit what they say on the other side of the ball. Never have, never will. We are on defense and they are on offense, you have to hate those communist cocksuckers! We are out here for one thing and one thing only…to win! So let's kick us some asses and let them worry about taking the names."

Coach Faber's little speech achieved the desired effect as the grown men began screaming out profanities and pounding on one another. Indeed, they were ready for some football.

Driftwood made the defensive call and, after breaking the huddle, snagged Bo-Bo Karpinski by the face mask.

"Grab the Tank and don't let that sumbitch off the line," he growled.

Bo-Bo's fat, red, freckled face was ablaze and spittle flecked the corners of his mouth. His face and eyes were bulging out of what appeared to be a two-sizes-too-small helmet. In short, Bo-Bo looked to be a small step from requiring the strict constraints of a straitjacket and the confines of a padded room, perhaps for an extended stay.

Bo-Bo didn't like being told anything, but he trusted Jack Driftwood. The "Tank" was the Blizzard's Star-Bowl left guard, Jeremy Patton, the man likely to block Driftwood on the first play. Bo-Bo finally comprehended the situation and nodded slowly. He smiled sickly and slapped Driftwood upside the helmet hard enough to make his ears ring.

Ben Brady took the NAFA's top-ranked offense from the previous year out of the huddle and to the line. The Buffalo attack, nicknamed the "BB-Gun Offense" after Brady's initials, had kept many a NAFA defensive coordinator awake at night. Initially the term BB-Gun Offense was meant in a derogatory fashion, as the Blizzard attack had been about as lethal as a BB-gun Brady's first two seasons. However, after last year's explosive production, the joke was on Buffalo's opponents and the nickname stuck. But this was a controlled drill with no tricks or hurry-up, no-huddle tempo, just straight-ahead, dick-in-the-dirt, smash-mouth football.

Brady cozied up under the center and called out the cadence. He took the snap, reversed out and handed the ball to Earl Johnson, the team's Star-Bowl running back, on a simple zone play over the left guard. Upon the snap, Bo-Bo nimbly stepped to his right and grabbed the surprised Tank. Driftwood took advantage and shot through the resulting gap, smashing Earl Johnson in the backfield for a two-yard loss. The collision sounded like a train wreck with no survivors. The crowd loved it!

Earl Johnson, not so much. He jumped up and threw the ball at Jack.

"What the fuck is wrong with you, dickwood? This ain't the goddamn Mega Bowl!"

"Golly gee, Earl, I am truly sorry," Jack said. "I didn't hurtcha did I, little fella?"

"Fuck you, wood-dick."

Offensive line coach Mike Pelosi broke up the party. He went after the Tank like a howitzer for letting Bo-Bo grab him. The Blizzard's season of destiny had officially begun.

Back in the defensive huddle, Stark was impressed. "Not bad for an old man."

Driftwood limited his response to a grunt and made the next huddle call. He was all business. As the huddle broke he grabbed Stark by the arm.

"They are coming your way, asshole, outside," he said and roughly pushed the rookie away.

Stark started to protest but Brady and the offense were already lined up. Earl Johnson took the pitch and headed around the end toward Stark's side. Stark got there and stopped the play for no gain, riding Johnson out of bounds. The rowdy crowd went crazy and began chanting "Stee-ven Star-ark."

*Not bad,* Driftwood thought. *Maybe this kid is the real deal. Maybe the fucker can play.*

Only time would tell.

They took a brief water break after the 9-on-7 period. Stark filled a cup with water and offered it up to Driftwood, flashing his big, goofy grin.

"You called every play out there," he said.

Driftwood downed the water, crumpled the paper cup and threw it at Stark, beaning him in the forehead.

"They do the same shit every year, rook. Tomorrow they'll install the trap and ol' Bo-Bo will get ear-holed a few times, get madder than hell and start a fuckin' fight. Same shit every year." The simplicity of it made Jack smile.

Buffalo's General Manager, Donald Allen Fegel Jr., appeared out of nowhere bearing a cup of water for Stark. "Great job out there, Steven."

Fegel made a grand gesture of lightly delivering the water with his pinky flared out wide and a slight bow in posture.

"Old habits die hard, huh, Feegs," Driftwood said, smiling wide. "Don't forget to pick up the kid's shitty jock after practice and give it a good wash."

Fegel's ears turned crimson with anger and resentment. "Very funny, Driftwood – by the way, you look a step or two slower. Is it old age or are you just carrying a little extra weight for camp?"

"If it's the weight, it sure as hell ain't in my back pocket, your bean counters gave all the dough to this here blue-chipper." Jack poked Stark in the ribs, making him spill the cup of water. "But don't worry, Feegs. I'll make sure you get your money's worth."

"See that you do, Mr. Driftwood, or you won't be here long enough to cry about it." Fegel turned his focus back to Stark, beaming up at him. "You just keep up the good work, Steven. If you need anything, and I mean anything, just let me know."

Fegel left but not before shooting one last menacing look at Driftwood. They had both been with the franchise the previous seventeen years, and that entire time there had been nothing but animosity between them. Yet here they were, fighting like hell for the same thing: to bring a NAFA title to the Queen City on the Niagara. So far, somehow, they had managed to coexist.

"Hey, rook," Jack called after Fegel slunk away. "Don't listen to that douche. You got a stupid question, ask me. I love stupid questions."

"You do?"

"No! So quit asking stupid-ass questions. But seriously, we are heading out for a few pops in the metropolis of Dunkirk tonight after the meetings. Prepare to be dazzled."

"Ooh! I can hardly wait!"

Jack wasn't sure if the kid was serious or just being a smart ass – probably both. He didn't have time to mull it over, though. Coach Ivy blew his trusty whistle and they were off and running to the next drill.

The hot blonde spinner folded her arms around her large bodice and pouted. Ben Brady leaned in and mashed his face into her cleavage and blew like you would on a baby's tummy. The resulting sound was akin to Bo-Bo Karpinski breaking wind, which he did with an alarming frequency. Everybody laughed and Brady came up for air, shouting to the bartender to fetch another round before turning his attention back to the doubly-blessed lass. He whispered something into her ear and she pretended to take offense, slapping his arm lightly before giggling like a little school girl.

Jack smirked at the wide-eyed expression on Steven Stark's face and handed his rookie another ice-cold draft from the bar.

"Brady gets more ass than a toilet seat," he told Stark. "Hang around long enough and you might be in line for some sloppy seconds or a runner-up or two. I've been down that dirt road of regret a few times myself, pards. It ain't worth it, but I can see you're gonna have to learn that lesson the hard way."

"Nothing wrong with a little trial and error," Stark replied. His eyes were glued to the blonde's chest. Apparently several tall drafts from Coughlin's Olde Irish Pub in downtown Dunkirk were beginning to have an effect on Stark's gonads. "Damn! Those are some Tig ol' Bitties"

"No denying that. Ol' girl is rackin' it out. You want to meet that little monster?" Jack asked.

"I'd like to meet 'em both," Stark laughed, swilling down the rest of his draft.

Jack slid off his barstool and pushed through the crowd to where Brady was holding court. He leaned in and shouted over the din into the quarterback's ear.

"My rookie over there has taken a profound liking to your well-endowed friend. The kid's got a taste for tots."

Brady broke into his best backwoods grin as he spotted Stark making his way over. He held up his hand for a high-five to which Jack obliged.

"No problem, bro," Brady replied. "The kid looks like he could use a serious spit shine."

Brady put his arm around the blonde and pointed toward the approaching Steven Stark and whispered into her ear again, eliciting another round of giggles.

Jack smiled contentedly as he scoped out Coughlin's from his usual seat at the end of the bar. Not much had changed in this place over the years; there were dartboards hanging on the back wall, cheap beer signs randomly hung about, and Christmas lights strung limply around the etched mirror behind the long, oak bar. It also appeared the same collage of patrons packed the place.

Locals made up nearly half of the sizable crowd crammed into the main room. Then there were the Blizzard fans who stayed in town long after practice to quench their thirsts and hopefully rub elbows with some Blizzard players. The main attraction was the various women that come from every nook and cranny of the surrounding area dressed for battle in the dive bar. It was as if Prince Charming was holding a ball and every ugly step-sister from the countryside had received an invitation. There was always plenty of slop at the trough and hay in the loft at Coughlin's during the annual Blizzard Training Camp, but seldom was there any princess material.

Until Cinderella walked in, that is.

Driftwood saw her coming through the door. She was an earth-angel, a vision of beauty. Her dark hair glistened, even in the dim light, as it framed her aristocratic face. Her skin glowed, highlighting her high cheek bones that shone despite the fact she wasn't caked in make-up like the other lady warriors battle-clad in the dingy bar. She was dressed conservatively in a blue jacket and pants with a white lacy blouse that ruffled at the collar. She was obviously a damsel in distress, dangerously out of her element at Coughlin's Pub.

Jack wove through the crowd to the rescue without taking his eyes off of her. She spotted him coming a mile away and flashed a faint smile before looking around as if plotting an escape.

*Too late, princess. Jack Driftwood's in the house.*

"Excuse me, Cinderella, but aren't you a little late for the ball?"

"I like to make an entrance," she said. She gazed around the crowded saloon looking for somebody – anybody – to rescue her from what was bound to be a lame come on from the quintessential meathead. Then she stared Driftwood straight in the eyes and said with unmistakable disdain, "I can see Prince Charming isn't here yet, either." It sounded like eye-thur.

Driftwood's hearty laugh was drowned out by the louder roar that filled the room. Steven Stark was dancing up on the bar with the blonde bombshell and Brady had reached up and torn her buttoned blouse wide open. Her lacy, black bra was losing the battle of the bulges and the crowd was hungry for the kill. Stark's hands were in search of the Holy Grail as he ran them all over the writhing girl.

"Ah, but you are mistaken, that's Prince Charming right there," Driftwood said. "You'll have to forgive his youthful protuberance."

"Youthful protuberance?"

"Um, no. Exuberance. I'm pretty sure I said exuberance," Driftwood said. "Anyways, what brings her Highness to such a humble establishment?"

She pulled back and looked more carefully at Jack Driftwood. He looked like a cowboy from an old cigarette commercial, ruggedly handsome with a deeply tanned face. She saw a broad nose, scarred at the bridge, and a strong jawline. His big, light-blue eyes carried a hint of laughter. His smile was disarming and showed dimples on both cheeks. His neck was massive and his shoulders incredibly thick. His hair was full and the color of gold but too long for her tastes, although she was instantly jealous of his natural curls. He'd have to lose the Fu Man Chu, but overall he looked pretty much like his photo in the 2015 Buffalo Blizzard Media Guide.

"I'm here on royal business," she said, slightly flustered by the intensity of his gaze.

Jack nodded. "I see. Well, Miss Cinderella, I'd love to buy you a drink and hear all about it." He paused to tap his watch. "But I'm about to turn into a pumpkin. Curfew. But maybe I can get your number and, I don't know, maybe give you the royal business some other time?"

"I'm afraid that's not a good idea," she said. "There is always trouble when royalty mixes with commoners."

"What about protuberances?" he asked, but he was drowned out as the bar crowd erupted again.

The blonde's bra had lost the battle and Brady was swinging it around like an old fashioned slingshot. He let it go and it sailed across the room right at them. Driftwood instinctively reached up and snatched it out of the air. He started to bring it to his nose but saw she was mortified. Maybe it was the look on her face, maybe not, but something made him stop. He turned the garment around to read the tag.

"Frederick's."

"Excuse me?" She asked.

"Frederick's of Hollywood, quality stuff," he said holding it out for her inspection.

She recoiled in utter disgust, totally grossed out and not wanting it to touch her skin anywhere. She was ready to just turn around and walk out of the place when he took a step back, almost as if in retreat, and flashed a sheepish look. Without a word he slightly bowed, turned, and began to work his way back through the crowd. She watched as he threw the bra back at Brady who immediately brought it to his face and inhaled deeply. Thoroughly disgusted, she headed for the door but couldn't resist taking one last gander at Jack Driftwood. He had grabbed Prince Charming off the bar by the legs, thrown him over his shoulder, and was heading for the back door.

But then he stopped and turned to look at her one last time. When they locked eyes he smiled wide and held her gaze. Then he winked at her and turned and headed out the door with his drunken buddy hanging over one shoulder. She couldn't help but smile, if only at the absurdity of such a scene.

# Chapter Two

One of the many things Jack Driftwood hated about training camp was the endless meetings, with the lone exception being the nightly team gathering following dinner. Simply stated, he loved to listen to his head coach, Howard Ivy, orate. The nightly show began at 7 p.m. sharp with the esteemed Professor Ivy at the dais in the Fredonia State University Center. The agenda was relatively consistent; Coach Ivy made general announcements, read portions of the team's hefty playbook, and occasionally wove hypnotic anecdotes to his captive audience. The man could tell a story.

Jack was anything but a diligent student, yet he always took careful notes in Coach Ivy's meetings. He also kept a dictionary in his backpack to decipher the "big" words liberally sprinkled throughout Coach Ivy's monologues. Over the years Jack had collected some doozies from the Harvard-educated coach. Jack had no doubt most of the people in the room where ignorant to the subtlety and nuance of the coach's full eloquence; they didn't get the details of what the hell the old boy was really trying to say. Jack took notes to hold his coach polysyllabically accountable, to keep him honest and to make sure he wasn't slipping. So far, so good on all accounts. Many times back in the day, Jack had either complimented or questioned the man in these regards and they both had come to enjoy those occasions.

As the ninety-man squad filtered into the meeting room, Jack sat in his usual spot at the back near the door and busted out a fresh can of wintergreen chewing tobacco. He thrummed the tin a few times to pack the tobacco nice and tight and spun the lid off. He proceeded to cram nearly a quarter of its contents into the well-worn flap of his lower lip. Immediately he began to spit into an empty plastic bottle.

"Here ya go, chawer-dawg," he mumbled through a mouthful of tobacco, flipping the can to Stark. "This'll keep your dumb ass busy."

Steven Stark hesitantly fingered the can of dip and then popped it open. He clumsily shoved a decent-sized pinch between his cheek and gums. Some of the tobacco stuck to his lips and the kid smeared it across his cheeks and chin with a careless swipe of his sleeve. Driftwood shook his head, a gesture totally lost on the rookie.

"Now, will you tell me the Cinderella story again? Pretty please, Uncle Jack?"

Driftwood had recounted his close encounter with royalty from the night before all day to anyone who would listen and to some who wouldn't. He had yet to tire of the exercise but was in the minority in that regard. And if young Stark wanted to hear it again, he was more than happy to oblige.

"Why, it would be my pleasure, son. There I was drinking a beer, just minding my own business when it happened. I was sittin' there thinkin' this is the same old shit, you know, just a different year, when suddenly I felt a disturbance in the Force, man. I'm not kidding, it was like the whole fuckin' world had just come to a screeching halt and the Earth had stopped spinning. Under mysterious control, my eyes were drawn to the door when Whump! There she was! She glowed in the dimly lit, smoke-filled room. She was a beautiful princess and a damsel in distress who was so hot, sweet, and innocent. My heart was fluttering and my bladder physically ached – in fact, it still hurts to piss. But Jack Driftwood don't shy away from neither greatness nor beauty, so I went in for the kill."

"Then what happened—"

"Calm down, douchebag. I'm getting to it. So, as I was saying, my rap was dialed up way past eleven, dawg. I mean, I was sweeping her out of her glass slippers when out of nowhere we came under attack. Some asshole threw a lacy, black brassiere right at her but I protected my princess and reached up and intercepted it. Problem was, the fuckin' thing scared my little princess away."

Stark was wobbling a bit in his chair and had turned a whiter shade of pale. Still, he managed to smile. "Was it from Frederick's, Uncle Jack?"

"Yes, as a matter of fact it was, Mr. Stark," said a woman's voice from the doorway behind them. Stark and Driftwood scrambled around to see who had spoken. Jack about shit his pants.

"I'll be damned," Jack said, finally recovering enough to talk, "Cinder-fucking-rella."

"Actually, my name is Geraldine Wainscott."

In an occurrence as rare as a Blood Moon, Jack Driftwood's jaw went slack and he had nothing to say.

"Holy shit," Stark croaked, wiping a dribble of tobacco juice from his lower lip.

Geraldine Wainscott, the owner's daughter and lone heiress to his untold fortunes, turned and examined Stark like some sort of biology specimen.

"It's a pleasure to formally meet Prince Charming," she said. "I saw your act at Coughlin's last night. I hope you are as much of an animal on the field."

"Yes, ma'am, I definitely am," Stark said.

He involuntarily flashed a toned-down version of his big, goofy grin, which was quickly becoming his trademark. The tobacco flecked his teeth and was smeared on his lips and chin. He looked like Beetlejuice.

"Sweet Jesus," Jack said, shaking his head at the fading rookie. "You'll have to excuse the kid here, Geraldine—"

"Ms. Wainscott, please."

"Oh, ok. Ms. Wainscott then, but the kid don't chew tobacco all that often and he tends to get a little messy and intoxicated. But you look fabulous. It sure is a pleasure to see you again."

Standing there not sure what to do, Jack extended a large, scarred hand.

She didn't deign to acknowledge the gesture. There was a disturbing intensity to him as their eyes locked. She quickly looked away, pulling her eyes from his grasp.

"Perhaps, you had better control *your* youthful protuberance, Mr. Driftwood."

Stark busted out laughing and spit tobacco all over the desk and down the front of his shirt. Ms. Wainscott recoiled and quickly distanced herself from Driftwood and his sickly counterpart. She split tail for the safety of the front of the room.

Jack was stunned and barely noticed the green-around-the-gills rookie wobble out the door. He was too busy watching Cinderella flee, wondering what the hell had just happened.

Howard Ivy stood at the front of the meeting room beaming with pride as he patiently waited to call the meeting to order. He held a deep and abiding love for his owner, Gerald Wainscott III. And why wouldn't he? Who else but a like-minded, stubborn, old geezer would hire a man of nearly eighty-three years of age to coach his NAFA team? But they shared a long, storied history together, these two; they had built a team that had gone to four consecutive Mega Bowls back in the late '90s. Together, they had fallen short, losing all four times.

Coach Ivy had hung around for a few years after their last Mega Bowl loss but left unceremoniously shortly thereafter. When broadcasting turned out to be less than fulfilling he drifted through life for a while, though the itch to coach never left him. He made it known he was ready, willing and still able to take the helm of a NAFA team, but the message was collectively ignored. The response was universally, "Thanks but, uh, no thanks," with his age as the unspoken deterrent.

As the years piled up, Howard began to lose hope. Meanwhile, the Blizzard had stumbled around for well over a decade, not making the playoffs even once since he had departed. They had spun the coaching wheel half a dozen times over the previous thirteen years until Gerald Wainscott had seen enough. He made a call to his former coach and before they knew what happened Howard Ivy had been hired back as head coach of the Blizzard, for which he was eternally grateful.

The atmosphere in the meeting room was electric, filled with energy and excitement as the gravity of the evening's proceedings was not lost on the team.

They were eager to hear from their highly respected owner. Coach Ivy moved behind the podium, signaling the official start of the meeting.

"Men, I don't have to tell you how fortunate we are to have Mr. Wainscott as our owner. The exigencies and vicissitudes of pro football make for a mighty challenge, which, in our case, is infinitely more manageable under such a benefactor as our beloved owner.

"Now, I am sure you have all heard the various rumors and innuendo regarding the fate of this storied franchise. Well, as Mark Twain once said, 'Rumors of our demise have been greatly exaggerated.' We have a darn good football team and everything else is in place for us to achieve our lofty goals. This is not happenstance; rather, it is the culmination of the unrelenting efforts of a man of great vision. Therefore, it is my inestimable pleasure to turn this meeting over to that very man. He has put us all, you and me, and this entire franchise on the precipice of incredible success. Gentlemen, I humbly present your owner, the only owner in the history of the Buffalo Blizzard, Mr. Gerald Wainscott III."

The room exploded as the players rose in unison to give their owner a rousing standing ovation. To a man, they loved and respected Wainscott, especially those who had been around for any length of time and had been personally touched by the man's grace and sincere favor.

Wainscott was no spring chicken at the ripe, old age of ninety-three and was battling occasional health issues that come with such longevity. Being a realist, as well as a prudent businessman, he was putting his house in order. Wainscott had seen brutal fights for the control of too many NAFA franchises over the years. He'd be damned if he was going to have his baby torn asunder in a similar manner. His intentions were to gracefully hand his team down the family line to the next generation.

Wainscott was one of six original Continental Football League owners; "The Ridiculous Six," as they had been known. He had persevered through the lean, early years and had been an integral factor in the league's merger with the NAFA in the mid-'60s and in its rise to an all-time high in fan interest and revenue.

The crown jewel of his franchise was Buffalo's brand-spanking-new retractable-roof stadium which would host the landmark Mega Bowl 50 culminating this season. That was to be the final piece of the enduring legacy of Gerald Constantine Wainscott III, not a franchise embattled in a custody fight destined to be torn from Buffalo and relocated upon his death.

Wainscott was visiting his team to share his succession plan with them. The old dog still had a few new tricks. Throughout his tenure as an owner in the NAFA he had displayed an uncanny knack for pulling things from the fire in what often appeared to be the darkest hour. Tonight, he would continue in that vein and put an end to the rampant speculation regarding who would control the franchise once he was out of the picture.

He basked in the ovation, not able to suppress his smile or emotions. Finally, he raised a liver-spotted hand and almost instantly the room went silent.

"I can't put into words what this team and what you fellas have meant to me. When I put down twenty-five thousand dollars to buy this franchise way back in 1959 I had no idea it would become such a part of me and such a part of my family. I consider every player who ever came through those doors to be part of that family. I could name 'em all for you if you had the time to listen, although that would likely bore you all to death."

The room filled with polite laughter, but it was true. His mind was still as sharp as a razor and he loved his team; he always had.

"But let me get right to the point, boys. Let's not fool ourselves, we all realize I am not too far from pushing up daisies myself – but I won't go without a fight. And I also won't go without first taking care of this football team and its future. I am sure you have all heard the talk and speculation about who will own this team after I am gone and what will become of this franchise. Well, I am here to tell you, in person, that a Wainscott will own the Buffalo Blizzard long after I am gone!"

Wainscott pounded his fist on the podium for emphasis upon making the declaration. There was confusion in the room as it was widely known Wainscott had no heir other than a little-known daughter who lived abroad and was reportedly not at all interested in the business of football.

"I can see by the looks on some of your faces I may have confused you, so please bear with me a moment. Now, I know none of you have ever met this beautiful lady seated up here to my right. Gentlemen, please allow me to introduce to you my daughter, Gerry Wainscott. Unbeknownst to her, she has been in a little training camp of her own. After graduating with honors from the University of Michigan, she moved across the pond to London and has been managing my business affairs over there for the past fourteen years. And I can tell you, fellas, in all honesty, she's way better at it than I am.

"Well, after some lengthy family discussions and gentle persuasion on my part, she has decided to come home. More importantly, she has graciously agreed to join me in the football business as part of the ownership of this football team. The Blizzard is staying where it belongs, right here in Buffalo, and it is staying in the Wainscott family!"

The room erupted into cheers of celebration. For years the specter of the franchise being relocated had hung over their collective heads like the axe of an executioner. Even the building of their new stadium hadn't guaranteed the team would stay in town under new ownership. Many considered it a hell of a gamble and a foolish waste of money and resources. Everyone in the room understood the debilitating effect moving the Blizzard out of Buffalo would have on the Western New York community, not to mention the immediate uncertainty and upheaval it would create in their own lives. After the initial outburst the players quieted and settled back down and Wainscott continued.

"But, before I turn things over to Gerry, I do have one request for each of you." He paused dramatically and looked purposefully around the room, attempting to make eye contact with every individual seated before him. "As you are all aware, Mega Bowl Fifty will be played in Buffalo following this season in our new stadium. Hot damn, boys, that gets this old-timer's juices flowing! Never in the long and storied history of the NAFA has the host team made it to the Mega Bowl. I don't know about you, but I think it's about darn time that happened. We are pulling out all the stops, as they say, this year. That's why I brought Coach Ivy back; he knows how to get us there.

"But to accomplish this we need everybody in here to come together. Come together to sweat, bleed, and sacrifice for the team. Come together to consistently give great effort. Come together to love one another, to do it for each other. Come together...do that, men, do that and I'll do my part and we will get this thing done. Every single thing we do, every decision we make must be with our end goal in mind. If we go about our business in that manner there is no doubt in my mind we will be playing for all the marbles right here in Buffalo at the season's end. All I am asking is for you all to come together. Because only together can we win it all!"

There were shouts of agreement filling the room that smoldered with emotion. Wainscott paused again to let his words sink in. Eventually the room went deathly still as each man contemplated the request and silently vowed to do his part.

At that, Wainscott bowed slightly to the assembly. "Thank you. I am greatly excited by the prospect of working with my daughter Gerry to make this happen. I also look forward to seeing her interact with you all. She has my backing one hundred percent. When you address me, you are addressing her, and vice versa. I know she will bring an incredible passion and an undeniable will to win to this organization. And now it gives me great pleasure to introduce the new co-owner of the Buffalo Blizzard, Ms. Geraldine Wainscott."

There was an enthusiastic response to the introduction, though the only ones standing and yelling were Jack Driftwood and Steven Stark, who had made his way back to the room. Seemingly oblivious, they continued whistling and applauding after most of the clapping had died down.

"Well, I know why Mr. Stark is so excited; we just made him a very wealthy young man," she said. "But what about you, Mr. Driftwood?"

"Must be my youthful protuberance, er, I mean exuberance, ma'am."

She couldn't help but smile as muffled laughter filled the room, but she ignored the comment and plowed into her speech.

"I'm going to be brief as I know you all have a lot going on right now. I am very glad to be here as well and extremely excited to learn from each and every one of you and support you both on and off of the football field. With the help of Mr. Fegel and the rest of the staff, I expect to catch on to this business very quickly. However, I can tell already that football is way different than the real world."

This observation drew much laughter and she paused until it died back down.

"It may take a while but I will get accustomed to how things are done. All I ask is that you give me a chance to prove myself to you all. I am not my father, but I am my father's daughter. He raised me with the same qualities we all admire and love in him: honesty, compassion, toughness, intelligence, dedication, motivation, humility, and, most of all, undying loyalty. These are the qualities that make my father the leader he is. My hope is to follow his lead and work with you all in the same way. I do know it takes everybody working together to be successful. We will find enough things in common, that we can agree upon, to build something special.

"Another way I am very much like my father is I like to win. I like it a lot. When I agreed to do this I told my father I wanted it all. Now I am telling you – I want it all. And together, we will get it!"

She happened to be looking directly at Jack Driftwood when she made her final declaration. She received a standing ovation from the team as she made her way back to her seat. Gerald Wainscott was beside himself with joy. He could have died and gone to heaven right then and not known the difference.

# Chapter Three

Jack was bordering on nostalgic as he packed up his few remaining possessions scattered about the smallish, cinder-block dorm room that had served as his home the past twenty-three days. He couldn't believe he had made it through yet another NAFA training camp. He felt pretty good, all things considered. They had lost their first two preseason games, but he felt like things were coming together.

They had their final preseason game in Detroit coming up in a couple of days and he expected better results. After going through so many camps, Jack had a pretty good idea how this current team stacked up and was greatly encouraged. How many camps had it been, eighteen? The number blew his mind.

*Eighteen of these bad boys down and how many more to go? How about none.*

It was true; this was it, the end of the line. He was done. Kaput. Stick a fork in his ass because the cold, hard reality was this would be Jack Driftwood's swan song. When he thought in those terms, that this was his final season, it was a bitter pill to swallow. There were still days where he felt pretty damn good and would fantasize about one or even two more years, which would give him an even twenty.

But that was a bunch of bullshit and he knew it, though he preferred not to think about it. Football had been his life for so long he had no idea what he would do with himself when it was finally over. Jack had never been one to worry too much about such things, though. He figured it would all get sorted out, one way or another.

He tucked the last of his things into his suitcase and sat heavily onto the squeaky, hammock-like, university-issued bed. Sitting frozen, Jack stared out the window, his mind drifting back through the years.

*What the hell had happened? Where did all the time go? And how did it last so long and yet almost be over so soon?*

His mind was reeling as emotions and memories flooded his stream of consciousness. It seemed like just yesterday he had quietly slipped into town with little or no fanfare for his first Blizzard training camp. Arriving as an anonymous, undrafted, rookie free-agent out of Northwest Missouri State, he was given little to no chance of making the team. But he had made it, though mostly out of dumb luck. Several players ahead of him on the depth chart had been injured during that training camp, which moved Jack up the ladder. But he had earned his spot just like the other fifty-four players on that squad that season.

Initially he had made his mark by making a splash on special teams. Jack smiled ruefully at the memory of the first kickoff he had covered almost two decades earlier in his first appearance in a NAFA game. They were playing the St. Louis Arches in Buffalo. This was before the Arches had moved to Arizona and changed their name to the Roadrunners and before St. Louis received its current incarnation known as the Nighthawks.

He could still feel himself lining up ready to cover the opening kickoff of the season in front of a sold-out home crowd. He had been so hyped up with fear, excitement, and intensity he developed the dangerous syndrome known in the business as tunnel vision. He had run almost blindly down the field as fast as he could and was right on track to blow up the return man, a Star-Bowler by the name of Etu Mondrake.

He should have known better, that it couldn't be this easy. Because it wasn't; similar to life, just when he thought he had it made, the Reaper showed up. And he showed up bigtime on that play. At the last instant, when Jack was sure he was going to make the tackle, he saw a flash of movement to his left. Too late! He got blindsided by another special teams Star-Bowler for the Arches, Roger Wolfson, in a clean but brutal block.

Driftwood got knocked a winding; "Ass over apple cart," is how Coach Ivy had described it in the film session the next day. But that wasn't the end of the story. Somehow, after rolling over twice from the force of the blow, Driftwood had popped up to his feet, staying alive. He was seeing double when a pair of Mondrakes cut back toward him. He shuffled a step, crossed over and dove, somehow managing to flip the foot of one of the four legs he saw churning past him. Mondrake stumbled and fell, thus Driftwood's first career tackle had been of the touchdown-saving variety.

Driftwood made it to the sideline a little woozy from the big hit and the celebratory pounding administered by his teammates. He also had a deep, burning sensation in his left shoulder but was otherwise pretty much intact.

They had to stop the action on the field as Wolfson had given himself a concussion from hitting Jack so hard. In a rare occurrence at that point in NAFA history, the Arches' medical staff took Wolfson's helmet away. He sat on the bench the rest of the afternoon asking the same question over and over, "Did I get him?"

Yes, Roger, you got him.

Meanwhile, Driftwood had been escorted to the Blizzard locker room where the doctor stuck a needle filled with Xylocaine and cortisone deep into the AC joint of his left shoulder to deaden the pain and lessen the accompanying inflammation from the grade 2 separation.

"Welcome to the North American Football Association, kid," was all the Doc had said.

The old linebacker shook his head as he absently rubbed the bony lump atop his left shoulder, a souvenir from the episode; there were so many memories. And so many things he wanted to forget. Like his ill-fated marriage. Toward the end of his rookie season he had fallen in love with a lovely young lady named Linda Smith.

He had met sweet, little Linda in a dark, grimy strip club off of Route 5 in Lackawanna. She had a couple of friends pressing her to join them in working at the club. Linda was at somewhat of a crossroad, seriously considering taking her big shot on the small stage. Jack had stopped into the place for a quick drink and little look-see after a practice. She was gorgeous and something in her sad, big, brown eyes grabbed ahold of his soul. He talked her out of stripping in public and managed to get her to do it for him in private. He was smitten, while she had found her golden ticket out of a life of poverty, boredom, and, most likely, whoredom.

It all had happened so fast. Jack cringed at the thought of it. What a dumb, young tool he had been. She buzzed through his meager rookie salary and playoff bonus money like a beaver through bark. It was only right she have the things the other player's wives had in abundance: clothes, jewelry, cars, a house, and other finery the wealthy possess. Through going to parties and other team functions she met a lot of the movers and shakers in town. The new Linda Driftwood was a social climber, to say the least.

She ended up leaving Jack after eight months. She hooked up with an older, wealthy attorney who left a wife and three kids for the proverbial younger woman. Jack had just been a stepping stone along the way. Another rueful smile passed his face. In truth, that lawyer was the best damn thing that had ever happened to him. The guy had handled the entire divorce himself and it had hardly cost Jack a thing.

He recalled his brief exchange with the man.

"You know, I fell in love with that girl the first time I met her," Jack had told him.

"Well, that's one thing we have in common, Jack," the man had replied. "And I can promise you I will take good care of her. I know it sounds shallow coming from the bastard that just left his wife and three kids but I mean it."

Jack had looked the guy in the eye and was convinced he meant it.

"You know," the man had continued, "this whole thing is going to cost me an arm and a leg because I'm going to take care of my previous family as well. But you know why divorce is so goddamn expensive, don't you, Jack?"

Jack remembered looking earnestly into the man's eyes and asking, "No, why?"

"Because it's fucking worth it," the lawyer had replied, laughing raucously at his own joke.

Jack laughed himself at the memory. It had hurt for a while, but he learned his lesson the hard way. He hadn't really had a close call since but he was fond of saying he was always looking for the next ex-Mrs. Jack Driftwood.

As a rookie, Jack had played in Mega Bowl 33. It was the fourth and final of four consecutive appearances in the ultimate game for Buffalo. They had gotten killed by the Seattle Stealth 42-10 in that one. That was nearly seventeen years ago. At the time, Jack had figured going to the Mega Bowl was a natural born right for the Buffalo franchise; might as well put it on the schedule. He could hardly fathom they had not been back. Not only had they not been back to the Mega Bowl, but Buffalo hadn't even made it to the playoffs since then. He was dumbfounded at the very idea of it.

*Better get 'er done this year.*

So much had happened since his first and only trip to the Big Game. He had lost his parents in a tornado that had ripped through northern Missouri and into Kansas on April 19th, 2002, leaving death and devastation in its wake. A total of twenty-two people had died as a result of the epic storm, which had also caused billions of dollars of damage across the plains.

The killer tornado had taken a hard right turn when it closed in on the 250-acre Driftwood family farm, heading straight for the hundred-year-old farmhouse that had been handed down through three generations. It was an EF-4 with winds topping out at over 190 miles per hour. Even hunkered down in the basement storm shelter his folks hadn't stood a chance. Miraculously, their bodies had been found together, still locked in a loving embrace, under a huge pile of rubble over one hundred feet from where the house had stood. Big Ed and Erma Driftwood were barely into their sixties, their golden years, when they had gone to meet their Maker.

Driftwood's eyes misted over as he twisted his father's Big Seven Football Championship ring, a keepsake from Big Ed's playing days at Kansas. Jack rarely removed it from his left ring finger. This was a tough one for their orphaned and only son to reconcile. He knew in his heart his mom and dad were eternally happy but he wrestled with the "why?" Why did it happen to the two best and most honorable people he had ever known? Why were they taken from him? He knew in his mind God had a good answer or it would have never happened, but it tortured his heart. It tested his faith every time he thought about it. He knew he would get an answer one day, straight from the Top. And it would be a damn good one, it had better be. Still, over a decade later it hurt; it hurt badly. It made him feel terribly alone, if not lonely.

April 19 was a day that would forever live in infamy in the life of Jack Driftwood – it was also the day his divorce had become final in 1999. Every few years when April 19 came around he would hunker down, usually with a couple of bottles of Crown, and lay low, absorbed in the self-pity of depression. But when the day passed he put it out of his mind and moved on. Life was too short to constantly dwell on your misery.

So here he was, thirty-nine years old, divorced, his parent's dead and gone; he was virtually alone on the planet. That was why his football family, the Buffalo Blizzard, was so close to his heart. They were, in reality, the only family he had left. He did have his father's twin brother, his Uncle Jack, whom he was named after, and several cousins, but they all lived back on the family farm in Missouri. They had taken over and rebuilt the place after the twister tragedy, although Jack still owned it. But Jack had sworn to never go back to the ranch on the day he buried Erma and Big Ed and had stuck to the vow.

Sure, he had had his share of problems and tough times, but for the most part Jack realized what a highly blessed and fortunate man he was. It was hard to fathom he had been able to play in the NAFA for so long, especially for the same team. This was his eighteenth year in the league, all of them with the Blizzard. Honestly, who did that?

He had been pretty fortunate as far as his body was concerned. He had missed the entire 2003 season with a torn ACL ligament in his left knee which had required reconstructive surgery, and he had missed the last half of the 2005 season with a bad back. Other than that he had remained relatively healthy throughout his career. It also helped that he had been a backup for the first three years of his career and again on and off the past three years, leading to less wear and tear on his body.

But so far he was in the starting lineup this year; he was being given one more shot at glory, one more run at going back to the Mega Bowl. That in itself was downright amazing.

He finally broke from his reverie and rose from the sagging bed to look around the room one last time. He felt a little silly for getting so emotional. He caught a glimpse of himself in the cheap, chipped mirror as he lugged his suitcase to the door and paused, wiping at his eyes.

*Well, at least I'm still one good-lookin' sumbitch,* he thought, winking at his reflection.

He laughed at himself and walked out of dorms of the State University of New York at Fredonia for what was most assuredly the final time.

# Chapter Four

The Blizzard had lost their first two preseason games quite handily, which doesn't always mean a whole lot, except they hadn't looked particularly good in doing so. The reality was they had "stunk it up," at least according to the Buffalo News, getting beat by a combined point total of 72-21. As expected, the slow start had brought about grumblings from the fan base and the local media. The team had not been to the playoffs since the 1998 season, but that never seemed to dampen the expectations of each new season. The Blizzard faithful were among the most optimistic, die-hard, if not delusional, fan bases in the country. This inevitably led to their collective heart being broken year after year. Yet, irrationally, they still believed the next season would most certainly be the one.

Every year the combination of off-season free-agent acquisitions, coaching changes, the incoming draft class, and the preseason propaganda gave the illusory promise of certain success. Blizzard fans were so hungry for a long-awaited return to the playoffs they were duped year after year. Gorging on the hype, they were fattened for the kill like so many turkeys which, like the Blizzard, were also slaughtered shortly before Thanksgiving.

The previous season had started quite promisingly in Buffalo with five straight wins to open the campaign and a sporty 9-3 record heading into their bye week. By all accounts they appeared a sure bet to break the drought and finally return to the post season.

That's when the wheels had come off. Injuries totally decimated the defense and the youthful Ben Brady began to try to do too much to compensate. He had thrown 32 touchdown passes, but his interception count had ballooned to a NAFA-high of 25. The Blizzard ended up losing their final four games of the season to finish with a 9-7 record, missing out on the playoffs. Even though it was the team's first winning record in a dozen years, the collapse was devastating. Gerald Wainscott III had seen enough. He fired his coach and reached deep into the past in a last gasp effort to right the ship. He brought in his old friend and three-time NAFA Coach of the Year, Howard Ivy, to try to recapture the magic that had once enraptured Blizzard Nation.

Howard Ivy was confident he could still manage the rigors of being a head coach in the NAFA despite being in his early eighties. Moreover, the man had unfinished business in Buffalo. He had always kept tabs on his former team and was more than familiar with the roster, having paid close attention the previous season.

Howard had an inkling the perfect storm could be brewed in Buffalo. The ingredients were in place. The team possessed a talented, young QB, an outstanding stable of running backs, a deep group of talented receivers, and a veteran offensive line. The Blizzard offense had led the NAFA in total yards the previous year. There was a nice, solid cast of veterans and good, young talent on that side of the ball. After adding a few pieces via free agency, he felt this unit could mirror that of yesteryear when the Blizzard were on the cutting edge of offensive innovation and production in the NAFA.

The defense would need more help but there was a tangible toughness to the core group that Howard really liked. One of the biggest assets on that side of the ball was the defensive coordinator, Lester Faber. Lester's style fit Howard's plan to a tee and gave him hope for the defense. He had been in the league for forty years; twelve as a player and twenty-eight as a coach. But more importantly, with his innovative zone blitz schemes and uncanny knack for putting people in the right places to make plays, a Faber-led defense would give them a chance.

Of course, there was more to the game than just offense and defense. Nobody believed that more than Howard. An essential ingredient to any Howard Ivy football team had always been special teams play. He was compulsive about this underrated aspect of the game. Most coaches gave lip service to special teams, but he walked the walk. Building a core group of special teamers had always been a top priority to him. He had learned that lesson early in his career when he was hired as one of the first special teams coaches in NAFA history.

The fact he had never led the Blizzard to a Mega Bowl victory was an ulcer in Howard's underbelly. It was the monster under his bed that woke him up and made him shiver in the deepest, darkest hours of the night. That failure had driven him to stay sharp and in shape, proactively maintaining his health for the prospect of another shot for which he had fervently prayed. Many times Howard had doubted whether he would get his shot at redemption; yet, in a small, vibrant place, deep in his heart, he believed his day would come. This faith had finally been rewarded. Now that he had been given the chance, he was bound and determined to make the most of it. The old coach knew there was no other place he would rather be than right here, right now.

The Blizzard's preseason finale pitted them against the Detroit Muscle at Mustang Field in the Motor City. Because the construction of their new stadium had not yet been completed, Buffalo was forced to play all three of their exhibition games on the road. Crews were working around the clock on their new home, Seneca Stadium, on the downtown waterfront of Lake Erie. The modern marvel, nicknamed the Wigwam, was expected to be ready for their home opener in less than three weeks. The Blizzard would start the regular season on the road in Georgia before coming home to christen the Wigwam against the defending World Champion Pittsburgh Brawlers on Sunday Night Football in front of a national television audience.

But no football team ever wanted to get ahead of itself and Detroit looked to pose a stiff test coming off a playoff win the previous season. The Muscle took the opening kickoff and flexed their way smartly down the field. In a matter of just six plays they had advanced to the Buffalo three-yard line where they were facing 2nd and goal when the winds of change blew through Mustang Field.

Standing in front of the Buffalo huddle, Driftwood was gasping for breath waiting for Coach Faber to shoot him the signals. Driftwood wasn't in game-shape yet and this opening drive had him sucking serious wind. This sure as hell was not the start the Blizzard had hoped for and if somebody didn't do something, and fast, it could turn into one long-assed evening.

Detroit broke the huddle with 23 personnel – two running backs and three tight ends. It was an obvious running situation and the Muscle had loaded up with big bodies for the occasion. The Blizzard aligned in their standard seven-man front, goal line defense. Coach Faber had called "57 Strong Charlie," meaning Buffalo was blitzing the strong-side corner off the edge with man-to-man coverage across the board. The call was a risk against the pass but stout against the highly anticipated run.

Something didn't quite sit right with Driftwood as Detroit lined up for the play. The very fact all things pointed to the run made the contrarian in him think pass. A lightbulb switched on in the recesses of his brain – he recalled the Muscle had run a play-action pass to the fullback in a similar situation in their playoff game the previous season. An urgent sense of panic hit him as he was cock-sure they were going to try it again. He felt it in his bones and what little cartilage he had left separating them. The simplicity of the ruse was almost insulting.

Stark was playing the Mike, or strong-side inside linebacker position, but not for long. Just before the Muscle's quarterback began his cadence Driftwood grabbed Stark and pulled him towards his side yelling, "Switch, switch!" Stark wasn't sure what the hell was going on but there was no time to argue as Detroit was about to snap the ball.

Detroit did snap the ball and both the fullback and the tailback headed away from Stark towards the strong side in an obvious fullback lead play, just as he had expected. Stark shuffled hard to the play side and readied himself to launch over the pile. Just as he left his feet he realized the tailback didn't have the football. It was too late to do anything but smash into the guy, so that's exactly what he did.

Meanwhile, Driftwood had widened his alignment so he could get outside to the flat faster and deeper; he was playing pass all the way. He got a little depth to stay out of the QB's line of sight and clear any bodies that might impede his path to the outside. The fullback widened his course as he faked into the line before releasing on his route toward the corner of the end zone. Leroy Clarkson, the blitzing corner, saw the fake and redirected toward the quarterback, forcing him to throw the ball a tick sooner than he wanted. Just as he was getting shellacked by Clarkson, the QB hung the pass towards the corner of the end zone.

It appeared the Buffalo defense had been fooled and an easy Detroit touchdown was in the offing. The pass floated out to the flat toward the waiting fullback when Driftwood seemingly came out of nowhere. Slashing in front of the Detroit fullback, he snagged the ball out of the air and started humping it the other way.

All Driftwood had in front of him was air and opportunity and he was sucking up the air awfully fast. The race was on as the crowd moaned and screamed for somebody to kill the guy with the ball. Driftwood had taken off like a shot but fatigue from the long drive set upon him quickly. He felt like he was churning through quicksand with cement boots lumbering up the sideline.

The quarterback had popped up off the turf and was pursuing at an angle to cut Driftwood off near midfield. Driftwood saw him approaching out of the corner of his eye and lurched to a stop. He swatted the QB, who flew helplessly past him into the Blizzard bench area.

Unfortunately, this pause allowed the Detroit pursuit to gain precious ground. A big offensive tackle caught Jack from behind at the Buffalo 45-yard line where he was grinding somewhere between third and an elusive fourth gear. The guy didn't just tackle Driftwood, he clobbered him. It was as if a piano had suddenly been dropped on Jack's back as he went down hard right in front of the Buffalo bench.

The crowd groaned again as several Muscle players piled on late, which elicited a flurry of flags from the officials. Stark had been gaining ground on Driftwood during the return and was frantically yelling for the ball. He stopped at the pile ready to bitch at him for not lateralling the ball when he heard the unmistakable giggle of his linebacker partner coming from the bottom of the heap of humanity.

When Driftwood finally did get untangled from the pile he was jerked off the ground by a jubilant Stark, who, in his youthful exuberance, hugged Driftwood and bounced him up and down like a dancing bear. Bo-Bo Karpinski came roaring up to the celebration and slapped Driftwood across the head so hard his ears rang until halftime. Nearly everyone on the Buffalo bench came over to lay hands on their grizzly old leader. A new powerful and infectious spirit of energy flowed through the team. Everybody was cranked up.

As Driftwood had anticipated, his teammates began to mock him for being caught from behind by a "three-hundred-fifty-pound, club-footed behemoth." At least that is what Coach Faber called the Muscle's tackle during film review the next day. This ridicule was what brought about his giggling from the bottom of that pile; he knew he'd never hear the end of it.

The offense took the field with renewed energy, and three plays later Ben Brady hit his favorite target, Shady Solomon, down the sideline for a 15-yard touchdown strike. Just like that, the tide had turned and the Blizzard had that good vibration. Stark intercepted a pass of his own on the next series and the Buffalo offense turned it into another six points. Detroit fumbled away the ensuing kickoff return and the blizzard of points intensified for Buffalo when Miles Bradley, one of their newly acquired special-teams demons, scooped the ball off the turf and took it to the house.

Coach Siglar, the special teams coach, was apoplectic. He sprinted into the end zone and jumped up to chest bump Bradley and promptly got knocked flat on his ass. A video clip of the collision was shown repeatedly all week on every news station in Buffalo.

It was now 21-0 Buffalo with 4:23 still remaining in the first quarter. The Blizzard bench was all abuzz. Not a single player was sitting down; they raged up and down their sideline screaming and pounding on each other.

Even Coach Ivy found his "happy place," but you couldn't tell by looking at him. He patrolled the sidelines like a highly-decorated field general. He poured on the steam, continually lambasting the officials and cajoling his players and assistant coaches as if the score were reversed. He finally had his new machine up and running on all cylinders and wanted to see what she could do. He kept the pedal to the metal, making sure no one let their guard down. He needed his team to handle and harness their success. They needed to know they had this gear for when they would most certainly need it further down the road. Coach Ivy knew this collective spiritual experience could become ingrained into the fabric of his team's psyche; winning could become second nature, habitual even. He'd seen it morph before his eyes previously, and if those old eyes could still be believed, he was starting to see it again. They were coming together just as Mr. Wainscott had so passionately requested.

The Blizzard led 34-0 at the half. Despite the commanding lead and the fact this was only a preseason game, Coach Ivy gave a stern lecture at halftime about playing hard for 60 minutes, regardless of the score. But in reality, everyone in the locker room knew this one was in the bag and there was going to be one hell of a party back in Buffalo later that night.

However, Coach Ivy pressed on, determined to make his point. He told the starters to be ready to not only start the second half but play the whole game, if necessary. He didn't want to see a single sign of a letdown. They needed to learn to play the game to a certain standard, irrespective of their opponent or what they tried to do.

He needn't have worried. After the first team offense drove the length of the field for another touchdown on the opening drive of the second half, this one a 28-yard scamper by Earl Johnson, the defense knocked Detroit backwards seven yards in a three-and-out series. At that point, even Coach Ivy had seen enough and emptied the bench. The backups continued riding the wave of intensity and Buffalo romped over the Muscle, 51-3.

Jack sat in front of his locker and began the struggle of removing his equipment. It was a battle not easily won because of his tightly-tailored number fifty-seven jersey. He felt claustrophobic being wrapped so snugly in the damn thing, but you couldn't leave any slack cloth for an offensive lineman to grab onto. Stark came to the rescue and helped him wriggle free from the stranglehold the garment had on him. He looked like a giant snake molting out of his old skin. With a tremendous final jerk from Stark the jersey came off.

"Hey, asshole," Stark said, throwing the jersey at Jack, "thanks for stealing my other interception. I knew they were gonna pass on the goal line so don't ever pull that 'switch' shit again, got it?"

Jack tried to poke the rookie in the balls with the shoe he was holding, but Stark was learning and had already moved out of range.

"You're right, I should have left you there, but then Detroit would have been up six-zip and the entire season would be lost."

"Actually, we would have been up six-zip because I'd never let a fat-ass, offensive lineman catch me. When I get the rock, I go to the house!" Stark struck a fairly decent Heisman pose.

Jack halfheartedly defended himself. "Hey, he never would have come close if I hadn't slowed down and juked the jock off of the quarterback. And that big dude was fast!"

"Yeah, right. You may be smart, old man, but you damn sure are slow. If you ever make another interception, which I doubt, you need to immediately look behind you. I'll be there for the lateral and I'll rock that bitch to the hizzy!"

"Shit, you'll be so far out of position I'd get creamed waiting for you. Unless, of course, I had already told you where to go… again."

"Let me tell you where to go—"

Lester Faber walked over for a word, causing Stark to choke on his words. Lester stood in front of his linebackers with a shit-eating grin. He had the usual nasty, spit-soaked, unlit cigar firmly clenched between his teeth and what looked like a piss-stained Gatorade towel hanging around his thick neck.

"What in the hell am I going to do with you two?" he asked. "One of you doesn't know what the hell he's doing and the other is so slow you have to time him with a goddamn sundial. If I could put his brain," he jabbed the cigar at Jack, "into your body," he nodded to Stark, "then I might have an average high-school linebacker. And I can't believe you both caught the damned ball. I guess the sun does shine on a dog's ass every once in a while."

Coach Faber didn't wait for a reply. He just chuckled, obviously pleased with himself, and wheeled around and walked away.

"I hope you choke on that dog turd," Jack yelled after him.

Stark grabbed a towel and headed for showers when Jack stopped him in his tracks.

"Hey kid, I got that Crown, so save me a seat on the bus, unless you ain't thirsty—"

"Oh no," Stark said. "No, no, no, I am. Thirsty, I mean. I am thirsty. I'm very thirsty. Hey, that could be my new nickname – Thirsty Steven."

Jack clambered onto the fourth and final bus in the Blizzard caravan and slogged his way down the whole aisle before squeezing into the open seat next to Stark.

"Why the hell did you pick this bus, you douche? This is the last bus where all the shoe clerks and knob polishers sit. You were supposed to get on the first bus where all the pampered superstars ride, dumb shit."

"A bus is a bus, man. Who gives a fuck what bus you're on," Stark said. "Jesus, just give me a shot of that juice. Thirsty Steven damn near died of thirst waiting for you."

"Jesus…Juice? Funny you should ask. I just happen to have an entire bottle of the stuff right here."

Jack fished into his oversized man purse and dug out the familiar, blue-clothed bottle of Crown Royal. He pulled it from the sack, snapped off the cap, and handed it over to Stark. Without a word the young linebacker put the bottle to his lips and took a long, hard pull. He wiped his mouth with the back of his hand and handed it back to Jack without so much as a grimace. His bland expression never changed and his eyes never watered or blinked.

"You've got a fuckin' problem there, *mejo*," Jack said.

Stark didn't argue the point. Just as Jack tipped the bottle to take a little nip for himself Stark elbowed him in the ribs.

"Feegs!" He whispered the urgent warning to Jack.

The Stark elbow hit Jack directly in the diaphragm and he involuntarily spewed a fine spray of the precious amber liquid. Normally Jack would have considered this a minor tragedy, if not an epic waste of precious resources.

But in this case, the finely spewed mist had caught Donald Fegel head-on in his approach to the back of the bus. He was steeped in it, wearing it like a cheap cologne. Fegel froze from the blast, blinking his burning eyes while trying to assess the damage. Jack quickly slipped the bottle inside the breast of his jacket.

"Hey, Mr. Fegel," Stark said, "how about that ballgame!"

Fegel wiped a fine layer of Crown Royal off of his red power tie and threw his shoulders back as if nothing had happened.

"That was a great game, Steven! You made some serious progress tonight. That interception of yours really turned the game around, hell, maybe the season. You guys were so pumped up. I haven't seen that kind of intensity around here in a long time. You keep it up and we just might have a chance to do something."

"Thanks," Stark said, "but it was Jack's interception that really got things going."

"Really?" Fegel questioned, eyeing Jack disdainfully. "Was that before or after the piano fell out of the sky and landed on his back?"

The two of them laughed like old drinking buddies. Jack just smiled and let them have their fun.

"No kidding," Stark said, "it was like he hit a brick wall at midfield."

Fegel snorted, truly enjoying Stark's revelry. "Well, that was a damn fine win. You just keep it up, son. Next week it's for real. And you be sure to let me know if you need anything this weekend."

He made a little clicking sound as he winked at Stark and stuck out his fist to get a bump. He turned and headed back to his seat at the front of the bus still wiping the whiskey from his suit. Fegel sat back down next to Gerry Wainscott who instantly wrinkled her nose.

"Geez," she said, "you smell like the town drunk."

Fegel just grunted and slumped lower in his seat.

At the back of the bus Jack and Stark were carrying on like a couple of high school kids who had just punked the principal. The bottle of Crown had been reopened and was making its way back and forth between them in time with the steady rhythm of their conversation and laughter.

"I still can't believe you sprayed him with the Crown," Stark said. "I almost pissed my pants."

"Hey, the fucker had it coming, sneaking up on us like that," Jack said. "I hope he learned his lesson. But I doubt it."

# Chapter Five

The strong, late-August sun beat down through the fifth-floor windows of the Blizzard's immaculate headquarters built into the west side of Seneca Stadium, their new 1.2-billion-dollar home. The calm, smooth waters of Lake Erie shimmered as a handful of sailboats were catching the light, westerly winds. Several speedboats careened across the flat surface of the Buffalo Harbor heading out onto the Great Lake. Gerry Wainscott's corner office was spectacular in both view and décor. The west and south-facing walls were floor-to-ceiling glass. To the west was a breathtaking view of the mouth of the Niagara River, the Peace Bridge to Canada, and the northern-most tip of Lake Erie. To the south lay they rest of Lake Erie and the Buffalo Harbor. On a clear day she could see beyond the old Bethlehem Steel mills all the way into the Southtowns.

The interior walls were adorned with poster-sized, tastefully framed aerial photos of the Blizzard in game action. One depicted the 1995 Eastern Conference Championship game at Blizzard Stadium in Orchard Park, where they had pounded the Boston Revolution 37-3 to go to their first Mega Bowl. Another was from Veterans' Memorial Stadium, nicknamed the "Gravel Pit," as it was built into an old hole in the ground left over from a mining operation. It had been the original home of the franchise. The picture captured the on-field celebration after they had won their second consecutive Continental Football League title in the early '60s, a couple years before the merger with the NAFA and the first Mega Bowl. The final picture was of their new stadium, the Wigwam, empty with the roof open on a glorious summer day taken just a week earlier. Her office walls held the photographical history of the high points from each the Blizzard's home fields.

It was in this setting that Gerry Wainscott took a deep breath and tried to recount how she had come to be sitting in this place. It had been a whirlwind last month or so and she had had little time to reflect on how she had gotten there.

She had never been overly impressed by the hype and excitement of pro football growing up, but she had witnessed how much the game, its players, coaches, and office personnel all meant to her father. Times could be tough, but that always seemed to bring the best out of the football world and make for more special memories and relationships. Although intrigued by the football life, she knew there was a great big world out there. She had sensed, correctly, once she took the football road there was no turning back. She decided it was best to stay away and go see the world first. The Blizzard would always be there.

That's primarily why she had gone to London after college to control and grow her father's interests in Europe and beyond. She had done extremely well, too. In fourteen years she had helped grow his warehousing and real estate businesses many times over. Her gift was an ability to create a consensus and get people to work together despite their personal differences. But she had begun to feel the pull of her familial ties, especially after losing her fiancé in a tragic auto accident two years prior. The biggest lure for her return was her beloved father.

Both Gerry and her father were realists; they knew Gerald's days were becoming numbered. After several in-depth conversations with her dad and some serious soul-searching, Gerry decided to come home to be with her father and learn the ropes of how to actively own a sports franchise. There was no reason to believe she couldn't be as successful as she had been in her other endeavors. She would approach it with the same passion she had seen in her father over the years. The next thing she knew, here she was, back in the States, up and running on the pro football treadmill.

Gerry was lost in these thoughts while enjoying her view when Donald Fegel rapped on her partially open door and then walked right in.

"Hello there, Ms. Wainscott, I just wanted to make sure you have everything you need up here and officially welcome you to our new palace."

"Please, Donald," she said, "call me Gerry. And yes, everything here is perfect. I'm well on my way learning the ins and outs of the football business."

"Well, Gerry, I just want you to know that I am at your service. I'm available to answer any questions you might have, any time you might have them. On that note, I was hoping to have lunch with you today to talk personnel. We have to make our final cuts and send the roster in to the league offices by four o'clock tomorrow afternoon. There is also a briefing later today with Sully about salary cap implications before the big meeting with Coach Ivy."

Sully was David Sullenberger, the team's "capologist." His sole responsibility was crunching the numbers to keep the Blizzard under the NAFA salary cap, which had ballooned to 155 million dollars for the upcoming season. Sully was a numbers guy to the core and could produce immediate answers pertaining to the salary cap implications concerning any scenario regarding the makeup of the Blizzard's final roster. He was an integral, if not indispensable, asset, especially this time of year when the roster was still undecided.

Despite only being with the franchise for a few weeks, Gerry had a pretty solid understanding of the political structure within the office. Sully was one of Donald's guys. Once Fegel had taken over the GM position, he had begun to fill the organization with his "people" to assert control. Gerry knew all this from her father, who claimed he was well aware of what was going on and had no reason to doubt the loyalty of Donald, and, by extension, anyone he brought into the fold.

"Lunch would be nice."

"It's a date, then!" Donald said. "Ms. Wainscott – I mean Gerry, I want you to know that Mr. Wainscott is like a father to me. He is a great man and I would do anything for him. And I can't tell you how happy I am he is keeping the team in the family by bringing you home. I look forward to developing a great partnership with you. Your father has spoken glowingly about you and what an asset you will be to the franchise. It truly is an honor."

With that he bowed slightly and left the room. Gerry was touched; she felt a full measure of sincerity in his statement. Her father had spoken fondly of Donald Fegel, but she had heard many differing opinions regarding the man from others within the organization, not all of them particularly flattering. Some claimed he was a conniver, power hungry and someone to be wary of. He would stab you in the back in a heartbeat if it would benefit him in the least. He sucked up to the owner but spoke maliciously behind his back. The word was her father had a blind spot for Donald and Mr. Wainscott's strong sense of loyalty had impaired his judgment regarding the gopher-turned-executive.

On the other side, Donald appeared to be a shrewdly effective businessman. Since he took on the role of GM, the organization had seen a sharp increase in profitability. According to what Gerry could gather, he was primarily responsible for the funding and building of the Wigwam that had solidified the franchise's position in Buffalo and quieted much of the talk of the team moving out of town.

He was either one hell of an actor or people were just jealous of his meteoric rise through the ranks of the organization. Either way, the man was an enigma and he had definitely made an impression on her.

No expense was spared in putting together the Blizzard's new Board Room. It consumed nearly a quarter of the fifth floor, complete with its own connecting kitchen. A massive fifty-foot mahogany table straight out of Valhalla was the centerpiece. The tremendous tableau was surrounded by seemingly countless plush, leather reclining chairs. The drapes, custom made with an original Blizzard logo design, were partially open, allowing natural light into the room. This place was already affectionately known as the War Room and would be the home to many contentious discussions regarding every facet of the business of running a NAFA franchise. Today's personnel meeting was just another of many more to come.

Assembled in the War Room was the Buffalo Blizzard brain trust. Donald Fegel sat at the head of the table with Gerry Wainscott immediately to his right. Next to her was Bob Johnson, the team's director of pro-player personnel. Rounding out the trust side was David Sullenberger and Colin Meade, the assistant general manager.

Across the way were Howard Ivy, his personal assistant, Gary Chuckles, head trainer Alvin Kaplan, and both coordinators, Lester Faber representing the defense and Jerry Sturm the offense. Both men also had assistant head coach titles next to their names.

Gary Chuckles, perhaps the most beloved man in the organization, was close to many of the players and was a favorite of pretty much everyone else inside the office walls. He had been with the Blizzard since before Howard's first tenure as the team's head coach. He was an invaluable resource to Howard, providing a direct conduit between the past and the present. He was the ears and eyes of the institution and seemingly nothing happened within the ranks that escaped Chuckles' ubiquitous scrutiny.

Buffalo's head trainer, Alvin Kaplan, had been with the Blizzard the past twenty seasons and was present to answer any questions regarding potential health concerns of the players. He knew their bodies and medical histories better than most did themselves. Alvin and Gary were two of the very few people still with the organization from Howard's previous stint. Having both in the fold with their ears to the ground had made re-acclimating to the politics of being a head football coach much easier for Coach Ivy.

Howard had been given final say over personnel decisions as part of his deal to return to Buffalo. However, this did not mean the rest of this group was a collection of yes-men signed on to simply rubber stamp the coach's recommendations. The NAFA was a complicated business and the dollars and cents had to make sense. Every person in the room was expected to be prepared to battle for their opinions, the very reason for which they all were handsomely compensated.

Regardless, Howard's main concern was to create and nurture the elusive and ethereal quality often referred to in the business as team chemistry. He knew well the delicate nature and balance of the team dynamic which too often swung on the whims and behavior of powerful, young millionaires. Things had changed while he was away from the game and he knew that could be considered a weakness, if only perceived.

That was one of the myriad reasons the coach favored older, veteran players. Those men already knew how to play the game; they just had to be motivated and pointed in the right direction. Plus, once he got the vets to buy in, they would help his cause with the new generation of younger players.

Howard knew what he wanted and he planned on getting it. He had already met with his coaching staff and together they had hashed out where the players ranked across the board. He knew who he planned to keep and to let go. This meeting, in his mind, wasn't much more than a formality, although it was an important exercise in checks and balances. The group needed to learn how to work together under his leadership. Having also met with Sully, he knew his roster would fit under the salary cap and still leave a reasonable cushion for possible trades or in-season signings required due to injury or other unforeseen circumstances. There was even room to extend the contracts of some of their younger players to effectively keep them from hitting the free-agent market once their current deals expired.

The meeting moved at a fast, almost furious, pace. Howard had steamrolled through his selections at each position with barely an objection. He was quite pleased as his well-informed staff substantiated his opinion at nearly every turn.

Howard pushed his chair back away from the table after finalizing the fifty-five-man roster, not anticipating any further business. "I believe we are done here then, unless there is anything else anybody feels we need to address…"

"Well, Coach, I like it," Donald said, "I like it a lot. It all looks good, but I have to tell you, I am still concerned about our linebacker depth situation. We are solid on the outside with Beeson and Gallop, backed up by Killings and Thrill. But inside we may have some issues."

Howard slid his chair back under the table. He should have known it wouldn't be that easy. But he wasn't upset in the least, not yet, anyways. One of the reasons he had been upbeat and optimistic about working with the young GM was the man's attention to detail. Despite some of the negative feedback he had encountered before returning to the Blizzard, one comment had been consistent; Donald Fegel would never be outworked and was one sharp customer when it came to the business of football.

"To be honest, Donald," Howard said, "I have some concerns with the depth there as well. Stark is coming along fine and Driftwood somehow is still making plays – not to mention he is a coach on the field – but after that we have some work to do. We can check the waiver wire and see what's out there tomorrow after cuts are made."

"I totally agree that Steven Stark is exactly who I thought he was when I made the move up the board to pick him first last spring," Donald said.

Howard raised his eyebrows. He had been equally, if not more, instrumental in making the deal to acquire Stark, but he let it slide as Donald continued.

"But I am concerned about Driftwood on several fronts. First off, he doesn't respect authority. I caught him with a bottle of whiskey on the bus ride to the airport in Detroit, and after what happened in Baltimore last year that's the last thing we need."

He was referring to the horribly tragic and senseless car crash that had claimed the lives of two Baltimore Avenger players the previous season. The NAFA had long ago prohibited the serving of alcoholic beverages by its teams to players, but those two had smuggled a couple of bottles onto the plane and were plastered by the time they landed in Baltimore. The driver, who had wrapped his SUV around a telephone pole, had a blood alcohol level of .26, the passenger registered a .29.

Howard grunted at the news. The old coach liked to knock back a few after games himself. Besides, Jack Driftwood came from a different era. When Jack had begun his career the teams provided beer for their players as they got onto the plane and hard liquor once they were airborne. He was not the least bit concerned about Jack over doing it. He was, however, concerned Donald hadn't brought the issue to his attention, immediately and privately. Now that it had come to light, Howard was obligated to act upon it.

Right on cue, Colin Meade spoke up. "Another problem is Driftwood is damaged goods. He's had several knee surgeries, a bad back, has broken nearly every one of his fingers, not to mention numerous concussions. He's also the oldest player in the NAFA."

There was a lengthy silence as Howard mulled what was beginning to shape up as a coordinated challenge to Jack Driftwood's place on the team.

"What is your opinion, Alvin," he finally said, "will Jack hold up physically?"

He hated asking the question almost as much as he knew Alvin hated answering. This was a violent game where every play could be your last. Men who looked indestructible would miss action because of turf toe, yet others with torn ACL's, pulled muscles, or broken bones would still be on the field. You just never knew. But one thing they all knew, for a fact, was Jack Driftwood had already proven he would do whatever it took to stay on the field. He'd done as much time and again over the years. The guy was a throwback who would play with pain, even injury, and would take the needle when necessary.

"Obviously, I don't have a frigging crystal ball," Alvin said, a bit more irritably than intended. "But I can tell you he is cleared to play. He's got some miles on him, no doubt, but he is at no more risk for injury than anyone else at his position. Historically, he is a fast healer and will play with pain. He'll do whatever it takes to get on the field and he's in excellent shape. I think the shortened preseason was a big plus for him."

It was Donald's turn to grunt. But he still had more ammo to unload regarding the matter.

"Well, regardless of his health, I don't like his influence on Steven Stark. He was sitting with Steven on the bus when he was drinking his whiskey. And the bottom line is this game may have passed him by. With all of the wide open offenses using three and four and even five wide receivers these days he can't keep up. Face it, he's too slow to cover receivers in space and you can't match him up on a running back consistently, either. He is a flat out liability verses the pass."

This is where Howard strongly disagreed. But what really got his goat was Donald overstepping his boundaries. The field of play was his domain. The man was clearly crossing a red line.

"I think you are stepping over the line here, Donald. Was he a liability when he made that game-changing interception in Detroit? What he lacks in speed he more than makes up for with knowledge and instinct. From my viewpoint, he has been a tremendously positive influence on Stark. He has literally taught the young man the nuance of the position and gets him lined up properly every play. Arguably, he is the primary reason Stark is ready to start." He paused and nodded at Lester Faber. "All due respect, Coach."

Coach Faber nodded back and held up his hands. You wouldn't hear him argue against Jack Driftwood.

"Furthermore," Howard said, "you could not be more incorrect regarding his ability to play the pass. As I am sure you are well aware, Lester's defense deploys multiple looks featuring myriad variations of the zone blitz. It is true, we do employ our fair share of man-to-man coverage, but our calling card is confusion. This confusion must be on the part of our opponents, not us, and the only one who grasps our defense as well as Lester is Jack Driftwood. The fact of the matter is, Driftwood is as effective as any linebacker in the NAFA against the pass. He recognizes patterns instantly and is rarely found out of position. At this point and time he is an essential piece of the puzzle within our scheme."

"That is even more reason to bring in some veteran help," Donald said. "We need another guy around with his knowledge. That's why I took the liberty of calling Orlando earlier today. Don Schwantz took over as their defensive coordinator a couple years ago. He learned Coach Faber's defense while serving as our linebacker coach here and took it to Orlando. They even use the same terminology. Schwantz stole Lester's scheme right down to the smallest detail. But you all knew that. However, what you may not know is Orlando is loaded at inside linebacker and looking to move Billy Brogan. I think we can get him in here for a fifth-round draft pick. This would give us a nice little insurance policy in case Driftwood goes off the rails or gets himself hurt."

Howard shifted in his chair. "Off the rails?"

"You know what I mean," Donald said before quickly changing the focus by bringing Sully into the discussion. "Sully, what are the financial implications?"

Sully pushed his glasses up on his nose and shrugged as if his answer was common knowledge. "Brogan is due to make a base salary of two million this year. He is in his fifth and final year of his rookie deal and will become an unrestricted free agent after this season. His bonus package is minimal, tops out at another couple hundred thousand. We can fit him in without a problem."

Howard Ivy knew an ambush when he stumbled into one. He was angry but refused to give Donald the pleasure of showing it. More importantly, he was intrigued. He had seen Brogan play in college at Northwestern while living in Chicago during his hiatus from coaching and had taken a liking to the young man. Howard looked over at Bob Johnson, Director of Pro Player Personnel, who would have the rundown on Brogan.

"Bobby, I suspect you have checked Brogan out?"

"Yessiree, Coach. He graded out pretty high, over ninety percent, in a ten-game breakdown from last year. He's physical against the run and shows great speed and instincts in the passing game. The kid can flat get after the quarterback. He started all sixteen games last year and led the team in tackles. He is married – to his agent, no less – with two kids, has never tested positive for any drugs or PEDs, and has a spotless record in the community. Smart guy, too, his IQ is one twenty-six and he was in the top ten in his draft class on the Wonderlic test at the combine. He is on the cusp of becoming a Star-Bowl type of player. Billy Brogan is a keeper, Coach, almost too good to be true."

Howard nodded in response and wondered if everybody in the organization was in on Donald's covert plan to hijack his authority. He doubted his trusted trainer was involved but nothing would surprise him. Might as well find out.

"How about his health record, Alvin?" It sounded more like an accusation than an inquiry.

Kaplan's normally pale skin turned bright red. However, it was hard to tell for sure, as he lowered his head, appearing to inspect the stack of papers in front of him.

"He had a separated shoulder as a rookie but other than that he checks out healthy, Coach," he said, almost apologetically.

"Hmm. Well, it looks like you *all* did your homework," Howard said. "But I guess that's what you get paid for. How soon can Mr. Brogan get here?"

"We can have him in here first thing tomorrow," Donald said, lamely attempting humility.

Another good inside linebacker who also played well on special teams would certainly help their cause. Howard was angry about Donald's blatant efforts to conceal the matter from him, but he would get over it as long as it didn't become a habit. He didn't believe it was a matter of Donald not trusting him. More likely it had to do with his hatred for Driftwood and his insecurity manifesting in a need to garner credit and credibility amongst the inner sanctum of the club's decision makers. But his tactics were divisive and cut Coach Ivy's legs right out from under him.

Howard decided to move on. He was confident the day would come when he would address the issue with the man, but ultimately there was nothing to be gained by going after him in the current setting.

"All right, who do we cut to make room for Brogan?"

"I was thinking Robbie Ferguson, but that is totally your call, Howard," Donald replied.

Both Colin Meade and Bob Johnson were smiling at this point. An uncomfortable silence settled over the room.

Howard finally nodded in assent. "Let's do it, then. This meeting is over, unless there is something *else* you all have been working on?"

"No, Howard."

As he got up to leave the room he noticed the same sly smile forming on Donald Fegel's face.

*Go ahead, smile now, sonny-boy. But what goes around comes around.*

The meeting broke up and everyone hurried out of the room intending to avoid the potential wrath of Howard Ivy. They also had no time to waste as they were on to the next chore in their steady stream of endless work. Gerry remained seated, waiting for the room to clear. Finally, she was alone in the War Room with Donald.

"What's up?" Donald asked. He was in high spirits, almost giddy in the aftermath of the coup.

"First off, I wouldn't make a habit of blindsiding Howard like that. He has final say on all roster moves, correct? I think it would be in the best interest of the team if things like this were handled with more professionalism. I can't think of a single reason why you wouldn't have clued him in sooner. We gained absolutely nothing by handling it in that manner, except to alienate our head coach."

Donald's brow furrowed. "Well, in this business you will come to learn you have to strike while the iron is hot. I can't go running to Howard Ivy every time I come up with an idea. But it honestly wasn't my intention to tweak his nose. It just all came together while Howard was meeting with his coaching staff. I didn't have time to talk with him prior to this meeting."

There were a lot of holes in Donald's defense, though her point had been made so she decided to let it slide.

"Anything else?" Donald said.

"I do have one other question," she said. "What do you have against Jack Driftwood?" She tried to sound benign and as neutral as possible, but she wasn't sure she was quite able to pull it off.

Donald reacted swiftly. "I've seen his act for a long, long time and I am sick of it. The man has absolutely no respect for authority. I started with this team during his rookie year, and I've seen him walk around here like he owns the place ever since. He doesn't treat people right, especially anybody with authority. And he has this incredible attitude of entitlement when he is nothing more than a sleazy biker in pads.

"At some point he is going down in flames and I don't want him taking this team or your father with him. He's dirty and I know it. Everything has always been so easy for Mr. Prince Charming. He's one of those golden boys who has had everything handed to him since people realized he could play football. Makes me sick to my stomach!"

She was shocked by the intensity of darkness that so quickly consumed him when speaking of Jack.

"Whoa, calm down, Donald, I was just asking."

"Well, now you have your answer. And I will say this, he had better play his tail off and keep his nose clean now, or Billy Brogan will be our new starter at linebacker and Jack Driftwood will be on the streets where he belongs."

With that he stormed out of the room, leaving Gerry Wainscott baffled. There had to be more to this dispute than what met the eye. She intended to find out before things got completely out of hand.

# Chapter Six

"Damn, white boy," Donny Butters said as he was making his way down the spacious, circular staircase leading into the basement great room of Steven Stark's beautiful new lakefront home. Butters had been the Blizzard's third-string quarterback for the past six years and liked rookies and their big signing bonuses.

"You got you some paper, dog, I'm talkin' Oprah money. This criz is the shiz!"

"It's a little better than the double-wide JK grew up in," Jack said.

He elbowed past Jerry Killings to set up a shot on Stark's brand-new, once-used, nine-foot slate pool table. Stark had just moved into the place and was having a few of the boys over for a little test run of his new party palace.

"Thanks, bro," Stark said with his goofy-ass smile. "I be pretty fly for a white guy."

"Shut the fuck up, and don't ever talk like that again," Jack said.

"He right," Butters said. "You just ain't got it, Stark. Now cool-ass Drifty here can get away with some talk, but you, you is way too damn white."

"Hey, fuck you guys," Stark said, "I got some soul."

"No, Stark, you really don't," Jack said, "but you do have a refrigerator, so be a good little host and fetch the *real* soul brothers some beer."

The first major purchase Stark had made with his 22.5-million-dollar signing bonus was a cottage just south of Mayville, New York, on the western shore of Lake Chautauqua and a couple miles north of the popular, touristy town of Bemus Point.

Cottage is such a humble word. It was woefully inadequate in describing the beautiful cedar and brick, four-thousand-square-foot walk-out manse standing a scant one hundred feet off the western shoreline of the dark, deep lake. The fabulous country-house had six bedrooms, eight and a half bathrooms, a three-stall garage, and a massive recreation room in the walk-out basement. A thirty-foot, custom-made oak bar, a top of the line pool table, a ping-pong table, a foosball table, sofas, and a sixty-inch LCD TV above the fireplace made the place a wonderland for big kids. Stark was generally the frugal sort, but when he went, he went big.

Stark grabbed a few beers from the fridge and dropped them into a bucket of ice which he deliberately set in front of the cue ball on the pool table. Driftwood was running the table in a game of 8-Ball with Killings and didn't appreciate the interruption, but that didn't stop him from grabbing one of the beers. Wordlessly he removed the bucket and was lining up his next shot when his cell phone blew up. The room went silent as they all froze to watch Jack slowly pull the phone from the front pocket of his cargo shorts. Cut-down day in the NAFA was definitely not a good day for a player to hear his phone ring, especially when the call is from the team headquarters.

"Ah, shit," Jack said. "It's the Blizzard office. Feegs is finally gonna run me out of here."

"Bullshit," Stark said.

"Serious," Driftwood replied.

They all gathered around Jack as he answered the call. The hard truth was they would all get that call someday, in some way. It was as sure as death and taxes; nobody plays forever.

"Hello, this is Jack."

"Hey, Jack. Gary Chuckles here."

Jack covered the phone and said with relief, "It's just fuckin' Chuckles." He brought the phone back up to his ear. "Chuckles, you douche, why the hell would you call me from an office phone? You tryin' to give an old man a heart attack? I thought it was Feegs calling to finally cut my ass."

Chuckles chuckled. Jack hit the speaker button on his phone so they could all hear the news.

"Sorry, big guy," Chuckles said, "I never even thought about that. But I do have some juice for you. I just got out of a big personnel meeting and we are bringing in Billy Brogan from Orlando. We traded for him, gave up a conditional fifth rounder in next year's draft."

"No shit. Billy Brogan, huh?"

"Yep. Feegs ambushed ol' Howie at the end of the personnel meeting. He had everyone do their homework on the guy behind Howie's back and then rammed it up his ass. Coach is hot about the way Feegs did it but actually doesn't think it's a bad idea. He told me he has always liked Brogan. The kid's a good player and you can never have enough of those."

"Have you met him?" Jack asked. "What kinda dude is he?"

"No, I've never met him, but he sounds like a real straight-laced soldier. A regular boy scout. An actual human being, much unlike the current crop of knuckle-draggers we have masquerading as linebackers on this team."

"I'll drag my knuckles across your friggin' chin. How's that for a boy scout? Any surprises on the roster?"

Gary started with little bursts of laughter but it soon morphed into a full belly-laugh, having elicited the desired response of fake ire from Driftwood.

"Well, I tried to get them to cut that poser, first-round draft pick named Stark, but nobody would listen to me."

"Cram it, Chuckles!" Stark yelled.

Now Chuckles roared with laughter. He loved his own jokes way more than anybody else ever did and he was on fire.

"Seriously," he continued, "it's all pretty much what we expected. I just thought I would let you know. Tell the rookie not to drown anybody on that speedboat of his."

"Don't worry, I'm lifeguarding," Jack said. He picked the phone back up and punched it off speaker.

"Shit, now I am worried."

"Chuckles got jokes today. Funny fucker. But don't be callin' me from a Blizzard phone again, you douche. Thanks for the heads up, though."

"Got it. No problem, but you didn't hear it from me."

"Never do."

Driftwood hung up and headed over to the computer desk where Jerry Killings was already looking up Billy Brogan online.

Killings let out a low whistle. "Ooh, you are shit out of luck now, Jackie-boy."

They began reading about the great Billy Brogan on the Orlando Rage's NAFA website. Killings had already sent a couple of pages to the printer.

"At least he's a pretty good looking guy," Stark said. "That's a major improvement already."

"Gay," was Jack's only response.

"Says here he led the team in tackles the last three years," Killings added. "He plays Mack linebacker. Hey, didn't you used to play Mack, Jack?"

"I'm amphibious, I can swim at both Mack and Mike. But you guys are very fuckin' funny," Jack said. "What you mouth-breathers forget is I tell you dumbasses where to go damn near every play. What if your new boyfriend, Billy Brogan, ain't so nice or smart? Will his good looks help you then, rookie?

"Hey, here go a big story bout the dude's wife," Beeson said after searching Billy Brogan on his phone. "She was in charge of the Orlando Wives' Club. I heard about this chick. She a lawyer and an agent, represents Brogan and a dozen other guys. Says here ol' girl is ten years older than Brogan. Oh shit, Drifty. This cougar gonna run you right out of town."

"She wouldn't be the first one to try," Jack said.

Killings brought up a photo of Nicole Brogan. She was a beautiful brunette looking very sharp and imposing in a pant suit with a low cut blouse.

"Holy shit," Stark said. "She is locked and loaded! Those have to be fake totties."

"How many times do I have to tell you, son," Driftwood said. "There is no such thing as *fake* totties. They are all real. Deal with it."

"True story," Killings added, nodding sagely.

Stark looked around the room with his big, goofy grin and was met with a unanimous round of nods in agreement. The rookie was going to learn.

"Ha-ha! Jack, check this out," Killings said. "Your boy Budd Kilmer just weighed in with a column about the trade."

"Great," Jack said, "Just what I need, my number one critic to tell me how bad I suck again."

"I sent it to the printer so you can take it home, put it in your scrapbook," Killings teased.

Budd Kilmer had been covering the Blizzard for the Buffalo News for the past forty years; his word was considered gospel by the vast majority of Blizzard fans. Driftwood had a long history of butting heads with Kilmer and wondered how badly the jerk ripped him in this post. It was a weird relationship, as they had developed an odd respect for one another despite basically publicly feuding for the past decade. Even with the constant criticism, Jack grudgingly admired the venerable sage's ability to turn a phrase. Some of Kilmer's shit was so outrageous it was funny.

**Blizzard Trade Up Again For Another Inside Linebacker**
***Brogan Expected To Become a Starter Sooner than Later***
By Budd Kilmer
Buffalo News Sports Editor

(Buffalo, NY) The Buffalo Blizzard executed yet another shrewd move earlier today to shore up their defense before tomorrow's final roster cut down. The team sent a conditional fifth-round pick in next spring's 2016 NAFA draft to Orlando for inside linebacker Billy Brogan. If Brogan starts two games this season, which is a surety, the pick moves up to a third rounder. But even at that, it is still an excellent deal for the Blizzard.

Blizzard General Manager Donald Allen Fegel Jr. was extremely excited about the deal. "This acquisition will not only solidify our depth at the inside linebacker spot, it will provide us with a top of the line starter to play alongside our first round pick, Steven Stark, for many years to come."

Brogan, out of Northwestern, is in his fifth NAFA season and led the Rage in tackles the past three years. He is familiar with the Blizzard's defensive schemes as former Buffalo linebacker coach Don Schwantz is Orlando's defensive coordinator. Schwantz left town for Orlando two years ago, taking Buffalo's defensive playbook with him. Knowing the calls and terminology of the Blizzard's defensive system should help expedite Brogan's inevitable ascent into the Buffalo starting lineup.

This means the washed up lumber that is Jack Driftwood will become a surefire casualty. It's about time. While it was marginally understandable to keep Driftwood afloat to help in bringing Stark along during training camp, it is simply unreasonable to expect washed up wood to do anything more than perhaps adorn the front lawn of the Wigwam as a piece of retro landscaping. If Driftwood ever had any better days, assuredly they have passed him by after a 17-year career marked by astounding mediocrity.

The Blizzard has held on to such middling talents far too long in the past. This fact is arguably the primary reason they have yet to get over the playoff hump in more than a decade and a half. Jettisoning dead wood from the roster is long overdue. This issue has not escaped the attention of Mr. Fegel, who has done an admirable job of late in the monumental task of refurbishing the Buffalo roster.

With continued shrewd moves such as this master stroke, perhaps Buffalo will have a shot at playing into January this season – knock on wood. So long as it isn't Driftwood.

That Kilmer had done it again. Jack and company laughed their asses off with Jack taking all the teasing with good humor, at least for most of the day. But he became a bit more distant as time wore on. Sure, he had a good time zipping around the lake in Stark's new Mastercraft X-10 speedboat, but he couldn't shake a certain sense of foreboding. There was no doubt Fegel was out to get him and using that hack Budd Kilmer was obviously part of the plan. It was just a matter of time before Fegel would prevail and send him packing. Hell, it was a minor miracle it hadn't already happened. But Jack wasn't going anywhere just yet, and even then, not without a fight.

Billy Brogan stepped off the plane and into the Buffalo-Niagara International Airport right on time at 10:05 Monday morning. That was the thing about Billy, he was always on time. He had been on time from the day he was born precisely on his mother's due date, to the day he stepped on campus at Northwestern, to the day he got to the church on time to marry his wife, Nicole.

He had also shown up right on time, moments before Nicole gave birth to each of their two daughters, despite the fact both were born in the middle of football season. Things always seemed to work out right on time for Billy. And it all made perfect sense to him, because Billy, if nothing else, was one timely son of a bitch.

"Hey, you're right on time," an excited Donald Fegel said.

Donald had used his connections at the airport to bypass security and wait for Billy at the gate. It was relatively unheard of that the general manager of a professional sports franchise would pick up a player at the airport, but Donald wanted to make an impression on his new charge. He had cleared his schedule to do just that. This thing was his baby; he had gone through a lot of trouble orchestrating the trade for Billy and wanted the gratification of putting the final touches on the deal. He had big plans for Billy Brogan, primarily to replace Jack Driftwood, and the sooner the better. Showing up at the airport would only help Billy understand the opportunity at hand.

"That's me," Billy said, "right on time."

He extended his hand toward Donald, who eagerly grabbed it and pulled him into a clumsy man-hug that crossed the border of comfort for the new prospect.

"Donald Fegel," he said by way of introduction, oblivious to Brogan's reaction. "I want to personally welcome you into the Blizzard family."

"That was awful nice of you, Mr. Fegel," Brogan said. He unconsciously wiped his arms as if he could brush away Donald's touch.

"Please, call me Donald. We are excited to have you here, Billy. That's why I came down to pick you up myself. I want to establish a rapport with you, you know, make sure the transition goes smoothly for you and your family. I also wanted the chance to talk a little business. When does Nicole arrive?"

"She is tying up a few loose ends, finishing the packing and then she and the girls will fly up the beginning of next week," Brogan replied. "We really appreciate the offer of staying in the townhouse; it should be perfect for us."

Billy's wife Nicole had jumped at Donald's generous offer of the use of an elegantly appointed waterfront, three-bedroom townhouse in downtown Buffalo for the duration of the season, all on the club's dime. Nicole had also shrewdly negotiated a promise from Donald to extend Billy's current contract if he started four games during the coming season.

Donald had taken an immediate liking to Nicole Brogan. Oddly, it had been a bit of a turn-on for him to discuss a football contract with an intelligent, beautiful, and apparently ruthless woman. The whole thing had caught him off guard, but he liked it. He liked it a lot.

"That's great," Donald said. "Be sure to tell her how happy I personally am to have the whole family coming to Buffalo and to call me if she needs anything or has any questions. I want you all to feel right at home here."

"Will do, Mr. Fegel."

After the driver gathered Mr. Brogan's luggage, they climbed into the back of the stretch limo Donald had rented for the occasion. He was pulling out all the stops to impress his new player. He instructed the driver to head straight to the Wigwam and then rolled up the divider for some privacy.

Billy stared out the tinted window studying the foreign landscape of his new home. He had never been to Buffalo before and wondered if it was a bad as a few of his Orlando teammates had said.

"Look, Billy," Donald said, breaking what was becoming an uncomfortable silence. "I need you to fully understand the magnitude of the opportunity you have here in Buffalo. As you know, I traded up to get Steven Stark with our first draft pick last April. The kid is the real deal. He will make the whole defense better. But the other inside linebacker spot is a problem. Now, to shoot you straight, I don't like the guy currently there, never have. He's old and rickety, too slow, and he doesn't like to follow the rules. Some say he is just an old throwback, blah, blah, blah, but that is just an excuse."

"Jack Driftwood?" Billy said. "That guy is a legend."

"In his own mind, maybe," Donald snapped, "but I don't buy into his bullshit. I don't care for him or his type. I only tolerate his presence on this team because Coach Ivy and Coach Faber think it's important to have a veteran around to help Stark with the learning curve. But I'm here to tell you, the legendary Mr. Driftwood's playing days in Buffalo are numbered."

Billy remained silent, letting Mr. Fegel do the talking. Never in his five-year pro career had he heard a GM be so openly conspiratorial or negative regarding another player. He wasn't sure what to think, but he did like the sound of getting on the field right away. He just wanted to play some ball.

"Now, I've checked you out pretty good, Billy. Extensively, in fact. And I think you're one helluva football player whose best days are still ahead of you. You already know our system right down to the terminology and technique. So what I need is for you to show these qualities to the coaches and I need you to show you can help Stark develop, too. You do those two things and I promise you will be in the starting lineup before you know it. I'll see to it myself, one way or another."

"Wow. That all sounds really good, Mr. Fegel, but I don't want anything just given to me. My intentions are to work my tail off and earn this job on the field, and of course, I will gladly help any of my teammates get better."

Donald looked hard at Brogan. It was as if the kid wasn't listening to what he was trying to tell him. He laughed too hard and reached forward across the expanse of the limo and slapped Billy on the foot. Things were going to work out exactly as he had planned. Of that he was sure, if only because this Billy Brogan was too good to be true.

"That's exactly what I am talking about. You do all of that and things will work out just fine. I've put together a good football team here. We're ready to win. And let me tell you, this town is so hungry for a winner they can taste it.

Once we do start winning, you will be amazed at how things will be thrown at you. This town will love you like no other."

"Yes sir, Mr. Fegel," Billy replied.

Donald just laughed and slapped Billy's foot again. "Call me Donald, Billy. Call me Donald." Then he laughed even harder. No doubt Billy Brogan would get the job done. That's what the kid did. And he did it on time.

When they arrived at the Wigwam, Gary Chuckles was waiting for them to take Billy directly to the linebacker meeting. After quick introductions they headed straight to the team meeting rooms on the field level, one floor below them. Billy was immediately impressed with the Blizzard's facilities as Chuckles squired him through the hallways and down the stairs toward the linebacker meeting room.

Billy let out a low whistle. "Dude, this place is awesome."

"You ain't seen nothing yet. Mr. Wainscott and the Seneca's spared no expense in building this place." Chuckles was quite proud of the Blizzard's new home. "We've got the best facilities in the country – college or pro – bar none! I can give you the five-star tour after practice today. During lunch break I'll find you and show you to your locker, get you hooked up with our equipment guy, Danny Steeley, to get you your gear, and introduce you to Coach Ivy and the rest of the staff."

"Thanks, that would be great."

They made their way down a wide, lushly carpeted hallway from the stairwell to the second set of double doors to their right. The walls were painted in the team's red, white, and powder blue colors with the Blizzard logo splashed intermittently in various sizes throughout the passageway. Next to the doors hung a fancy display board entitled "Defensive Goals-2015."

"Well, here we are, the linebacker meeting room," Chuckles said. He rapped on the door and popped his head inside like a groundhog looking for his shadow.

Coach Faber was in the far corner at the front of the room with the collar of his sweatshirt pulled up over his nose. He looked like he was ready to rob a bank, except his eyes were red and watering, almost as if he had been crying. The rest of the players were scrambling over chairs and desks fighting to get to the back of the room. Sitting calmly in the front row amidst the chaos was Ukey Gallop. You could almost see a misty, malevolent cloud hanging in the air around Ukey's thick dreadlocks.

When Chuckles stepped into the room he immediately found himself in a battle for control of his gag reflex. The omnipresent long white hairs sticking out of his nose visibly curled as he staggered sideways in the doorway.

"Do not go in there," he rasped as he went to a knee and quickly pulled his Blizzard sweatshirt up over his mouth and nose.

"Hey, Billy," Lester Faber greeted as he crossed the room. His voice was muffled by his shirt, which was still pulled up covering the bottom half of his face. "Take five, boys," he said to the players in the room. "And Ukey, you go see the trainer, you may be dying."

Ukey sat there with a big smile on his face as the rest of the group piled out into the hallway from another exit at the back of the room. Apparently everybody loves their own brand, especially Ukey Gallop.

"Sorry about the foul greeting," Coach Faber said. He let the shirt fall from his face after making it out into the hallway where he stuck out his hand to greet his new player.

Billy smiled wide. "No problem, Coach Schwantz clears the defensive meeting room on a weekly basis down in Orlando."

Coach Faber laughed and grabbed Brogan's arm and gave it a good squeeze as they shook hands. It was an old habit the coach had of feeling up players and prospects. He was immediately impressed by the bulging bicep of his new keep.

"What kind of shape you in, Billy?"

"Pretty good, Coach, they didn't beat us up too badly in camp, which was a huge disappointment to Coach Schwantz."

They shared another knowing laugh as Jack and the rest of the group of linebackers made their way over.

"Hey, Billy, good to meet you, I'm Jack Driftwood, we're all looking forward to having another set of fresh legs around here to eat up some reps."

"Glad to be of service," Billy said. He shook hands with Jack and then the rest of the linebackers.

"So, has Schwantzy shit on anybody's desk lately?" Jack asked.

"No way! That's a true story?"

They laughed together and Jack told the legendary story of Coach Schwantz who, in his younger, wilder days, defecated on the desk of a college president who had had the temerity to miss a scheduled appointment with him.

With the ice broken they talked easily during the break while the air in their meeting room cleared. At lunch they broke out more old war stories, much to the delight of the wide-eyed, goofy-grinning Steven Stark, who was mesmerized by the tall tales. As much as he tried, Driftwood couldn't hate Billy Brogan. Truth was, he had liked him immediately. What cinched it for him was when Billy had asked him what the hell was up with that Fegel dude. It wasn't Billy Brogan's fault Donald Fegel was such a douchebag. The man handled that quite nicely all by himself, to which they all readily agreed. Billy Brogan was a football player and Jack respected that fact. But to Fegel, Billy was a boot aimed directly at the hindquarters of Jack Driftwood, a pawn in a much larger game.

# Chapter Seven

The Annual Kickoff Luncheon was a time-honored tradition carried on by every NAFA club across the league. Even at five hundred dollars per plate, the extravaganza had sold out a month in advance in Buffalo. The event served as a perk for sponsors, prominent local business persons, well-heeled luxury suite owners, and sometimes even a regular, average fan who somehow managed to get their hands on a ticket. It was also a free meal for the press, which always created a buzz within their ranks. Player attendance at the luncheon, as always, was mandatory on this Tuesday of opening week of the 2015 NAFA season. As much as the attendees enjoyed the occasion, it was considered a royal pain in the ass by most of the players. They considered the event a total waste of time, if not an imposition into their personal lives.

However, Jack Driftwood was no longer among that group; he looked forward to the event. After the team's morning weightlifting session, he had hurried through the shower and donned his personally-owned tuxedo. He was dressed in his Sunday best when he took the elevator up to the third floor of the Wigwam to join the party at 11:30 that morning, half an hour before the proceedings were to start. He was among the first players to arrive, surprising himself with his excitement. Every player was assigned a table where they were to chat up the dozen people seated with them before breaking bread. This was the primary drawing card for the attendees; they got to have lunch, in person, with a real, live Blizzard player.

Driftwood had been to the previous seventeen of these shindigs and marveled at how his attitude towards the event had shifted over the years. Back in his younger days he had despised the very thought of the entire ordeal. He remembered being extremely shy and reticent, sitting at a table of complete strangers wishing he could disappear. He would quietly answer questions directed at him with monosyllabic, mumbled responses, praying for it all to be over as soon as possible.

As the years had progressed, though, a metamorphosis had occurred; he had come out of his shell. It helped that he knew more and more people each year, making him infinitely more comfortable in this formal setting. By now he knew practically everybody in the town's tightly-knit business community, and they all sure as hell knew him.

This time around he was feted with celebrity status as the life of the party, the most honored and esteemed guest and he ate it up. Jack Driftwood was in the house! He started at one end of the room and worked his way to the other, stopping for high-fives, quick jokes, man-hugs, fist-bumps, or Hollywood kisses at nearly every table. He was loud and boisterous in his greetings and slapped more backs than Fegel had washed jocks. It was a show in itself watching the big linebacker work the room with unbridled enthusiasm.

He stood over six feet five inches tall in his snakeskin cowboy boots that somehow matched his tuxedo perfectly. But he seemed even larger – larger than life. A friendly giant, he towered over the adoring crowd that gathered to him like moths to light. His charm meter was dialed all the way up. It was obvious the dude was having one hell of a good time.

After much fanfare, he finally made it through the entire room. In so doing, he had worked up a powerful thirst. He spotted the bar along the inside wall which extended nearly the length of the elegantly furnished room and made a bee-line for it. He wasn't sure where he was supposed to sit, but at that point he didn't care. Man, he needed a beer; unfortunately, the NAFA didn't allow players to imbibe at any official team or league function. A Mountain Dew would have to do the trick. He ordered up a Dew, slugged down a few gulps, and turned to relax, take a breath, and survey the crowd. Maybe he had missed greeting somebody, but he doubted it.

Gerry Wainscott watched in awe and amazement as the old linebacker worked his way across the room. She was never one for these idle gatherings as she found them generally boring, although she knew she needed to meet the city's business leaders. But this gathering was proving to be very interesting because Jack Driftwood was providing her with some unexpected entertainment.

He seemed to know everybody in the place by name and handled them all with such grace and humility as they anxiously awaited his brief but sincere attention. She watched him smile, shake hands and even fist bump the normally staid and uptight business types. Surprisingly, Jack loosened them up to where they acted like little children, giddy and awestruck by the very prospect of meeting this gridiron god. He was easily the most popular and sought after player in the room. Even more impressive was the way he handled the attention and adoration with such poise and natural aplomb.

Most of what she had heard about the man, primarily from Donald and his cronies, not to mention her own personal interactions with him, had left her wondering what anyone could see in him. However, as she continued to watch Jack light up the room she couldn't help but wonder who he truly was.

"Ah. I see you are watching the Jack Driftwood show, too," Senator William F. Blutarsky said, coming up behind her.

The Senator was speaking at the luncheon on behalf of the Buffalo Mega Bowl Wigwam Committee which had been extremely instrumental in winning the bid to bring Mega Bowl 50 to Buffalo. The Senator had been the high-profile politician representing the state's interests in the stadium project. He was charged with making a few comments on behalf of the committee and introducing the NAFA Commissioner, Bob Goldman, who was the keynote speaker.

"Oh, yeah, I guess. Nice to see you, Senator. I must say, he is surprisingly social."

Instinctively Gerry did not care much for the Senator. His predatory looks and prolonged staring totally creeped her out, not to mention the man's politics. Blutarsky assumed way too much in her opinion.

"I'm not sure what Driftwood's politics are – god only knows – but with that kind of charisma it really wouldn't matter. Put a little biscuit such as yourself on his arm and you've got yourself a major power couple." The Senator laughed at the deliciousness of it.

"Really? I highly doubt that, Senator."

"What's the matter? Is he not your type?"

"My type is no concern of yours," Gerry said.

Whether it was her desire to get to know Jack better or to get away from the repugnant politician, she decided it was the perfect time to go check him out for herself. She saw her opening and hit the hole like Earl Johnson on a zone read play, leaving the Senator to eat her dust. She stuck her foot in the ground and went for it – straight ahead, no fair dodging.

Jack was hunched over the bar feeling better than any man had a right to feel. The cold Mountain Dew was going down way too fast, but that didn't dissuade him from signaling the bartender for another round. He turned back to take another gander around the room and there she was, appearing out of nowhere once again. It was Cinderella, standing smack dab in front of him.

"Hey," she said softly and gracefully held out a highly-manicured hand.

Jack took her hand and instinctively wrapped his other arm around her and pulled her into an embrace. He gave her a tight hug and a peck on the cheek before turning the lass loose. Gerry felt the air rush out of her and her fair skin began to glow and gain color. She fit against him perfectly.

"Hey, to you," he said and stepped back to look her over.

She was in an elegant, black cocktail dress that did little to hide her curves. Her eyes were bright and lively and seemed to have a hunger to them, but for what he could only guess.

*Hopefully me,* he thought as he stared into her beautiful, hazel eyes.

"Ms. Wainscott, you are truly a vision of loveliness, a veritable oasis in an otherwise arid landscape, a desert flower in full bloom."

"Wow, you are quite the charmer, Mayor Driftwood. No wonder the masses seem to love you. That was quite a show you put on there. You did everything but kiss babies."

"Jack Driftwood loves the people, ma'am."

"Apparently the people love Jack Driftwood. I believe you could run for office once you retire and win by a landslide."

"Well, you and your daddy have folks pretty excited around here and we haven't even won a game yet. Imagine how crazy it will get once we start rolling."

"Will we, Jack?" she asked. She reached out and touched his arm as she spoke. "Will we win this year?"

Jack examined his glass as if it were some great, mysterious oracle. He loved to hear her say his name. He killed the remaining yellow liquid and set the bottle onto the bar before looking deep into the eyes of his new owner.

"Yes, we will. Big. We're going to win big, Gerry," he said. "I'd bet that sweet, little ass of yours on it."

She released her grip from his arm and looked right back at him, straight in the eyes. "You can't bet what isn't yours, Mr. Driftwood."

"I suppose, but I would if I could, if you know what I mean."

Gerry turned away from his gaze and back to the crowd, but not before Jack caught a slight smile taking form on her face.

Before he could follow up, the clock struck noon, although it felt like midnight to Jack as his Cinderella was about to vanish again. Dodge Brophy, the longtime Blizzard radio play-by-play announcer, tapped on the microphone set up at the head table and cleared his throat.

"If ol' number fifty-seven, Jack Driftwood, is done campaigning we can get this show on the road."

The room erupted with laughter and everyone began to make their way to their assigned tables.

"I'm good, Dodge. Unless you got some babies around here in need of a kiss," Jack called out from the bar to yet more laughter. He turned back to face Gerry. "It sure was a pleasure chatting with you, Ms. Wainscott. And I wasn't kidding, we are going to win. I'm sure of it. I believe I heard you say you wanted it all. Well, I hope you can handle it."

"I think I can but who knows, I may need some help," she said.

"I'm a big helper, you know. I love to help."

"I'm sure you do. Good luck in Atlanta on Sunday, Jack."

"Thanks," he said as she walked away.

He headed off to find his assigned table, but he wasn't sure if his feet were touching the ground. He felt like he could jump a fence. Any fence.

# Chapter Eight

Georgia hadn't moved the ball effectively all day, yet somehow they had managed to eke out 10 points. The Wild Hogs had scored their lone touchdown on defense way back in the first quarter when Buffalo's Ben Brady had been sacked and fumbled the ball after a blindside hit on a corner blitz. Nobody saw the guy coming, especially Brady. He had blitzed off the short-side edge untouched and swiped the ball from the Buffalo QB like an expert pick-pocket. Before anyone knew what had happened the Georgia cornerback scampered 23 yards into the end zone for the touchdown; the ball never even touched the ground.

Georgia had also managed a field goal, the result of yet another Blizzard turnover, this one an interception thrown by Brady. The pick was more a result of bad luck than anything else, as the ball had been tipped at the line of scrimmage before falling directly into the hands of a Wild Hog linebacker. The result was Georgia ball at the Buffalo 20. However, the Blizzard defense stiffened, and after three plays the Hogs had lost 12 yards and were forced to kick a 49-yard field goal.

Buffalo, on the other hand, had moved the ball up and down the field all afternoon. Their problem was scoring touchdowns; they just couldn't seem to punch one into the end zone. Their 12 points had come from four field goals by Bennie Tenudo, the longest of which was only 32 yards. Each score had been preceded by a long Buffalo drive originating in their own territory.

Despite controlling the action, Buffalo only led 12-10 with time becoming a factor as 10:32 remained in the contest. That's precisely when the Georgia offense showed signs of coming alive. They had taken over possession at their own 32-yard line on downs after Brady had fumbled the snap on a 4th and 1 quarterback sneak attempt. He had managed to recover the ball but was still well short of the first down.

The Brady fumble was the same kind of mishap that had marked the previous decade plus of Blizzard football. Frustrated fans had seen this scenario play out far too often over the years. It seemed their team would play it close or be leading for three quarters and then find a new, inventive way to lose the game in the end. It was almost as if they were cursed. Some fans would shut the TV off or change channels. But it was only a bluff. They always put the game back on; they couldn't help themselves, especially when hope was still alive.

The home crowd erupted after the fourth-down stop smelling blood in the water. The momentum had finally swung their way and just in the nick of time. Their team had been thoroughly outplayed all afternoon, yet they had hung around. They sensed it was time for their boys to rise up and snatch victory from the jaws of defeat. After all, they were playing Buffalo, a team notorious for blowing this type of game. What could possibly go wrong?

Driftwood stood arms akimbo in front of the huddle awaiting the signal from Coach Faber on the sidelines. It was situations like these when he truly felt the most alive, as if his life had meaning and value. He fed off of the buzz of the crowd's renewed energy. Coach Faber stood stoically on the sideline, sticking out like a sore thumb in a Day-Glo yellow shirt studying his call sheet, pondering his next move. Things often got hazy and crazy on the field and the bright attire helped the players spot their fearless signal caller.

Coach Faber was old school to the core and preferred to signal the defense in rather than use the sideline to helmet communication system the NAFA had implemented a half-dozen years prior. To keep people from stealing the signals he would use the communications system intermittently throughout the game while continuing to give bogus signals. Thus far nobody had cracked his code.

"I love this shit," Driftwood said, commanding the eyes of every man in the huddle. "It's fuckin' shutdown time. P – O – D! Pissed-off defense! '42 Opie Even Play It.' Watch the play-action pass! Ready…"

"Break!"

The Buffalo defense scrambled to get in formation as the Hogs were already lined up. They were in regular, or 12 personnel, with a tight end and two backs, and had lined up in an I-pro right set. Their quarterback, Mark Neely, a fifth-year sensation, had led Georgia to the playoffs three consecutive years, and along with Ben Brady and a handful of others, carried the mantle for the next generation of NAFA superstar quarterbacks.

He surveyed the defense intently and then quickly stepped under center and took the snap on the first sound. He reversed out and faked the deep handoff to his tailback before dropping into the pocket, setting up a play-action pass. The flanker to Neely's right ran a deep post pattern in an attempt to split the Blizzard's two deep safeties. From the same side the tight end dragged across the field on a shallow crossing route, designed to pull the linebackers out of the intermediate area while the backside split end ran a dig route, 15 yards up the field with a 90-degree cut over the middle.

Driftwood recognized the Post-Dig route combination immediately and got good depth in his zone to take away the dig. The split end saw him and choked down the pattern so he wouldn't cross into Driftwood's path. He was wide-ass open sitting in backside hole begging for the ball.

The opening was created because Stark had bit too hard on the run fake and was late getting to his drop. To compound matters the rookie took the bait and jumped the tight end on the shallow crossing route, leaving a huge hole in the intermediate zone behind him. It was exactly what Neely wanted. He spun a rope into the open zone, right where Stark should have been. The split end caught the ball and whirled back away from Driftwood, who was charging fast.

*Where the hell is Stark? Fuckin' rookie!*

Driftwood caught the receiver from behind along the sideline at the Buffalo 45 with help from the Blizzard's corner, Leroy Clarkson. Clarkson was pissed, too.

"Shit, where the hell you at, Drifty? You gotta drop deep, take the dig, I got the tight end, fucka was coming right to me, ya'll can't be chasin'."

Leroy spoke fast enough as it was, but when he was agitated only the most practiced ear could understand him. Driftwood got most of it.

"My bad, Leroy," Driftwood said. "Won't happen again. We gotta stop 'em here."

"No shit, that's all I'm tryin' to say."

There wasn't any time for chit-chat. Georgia had gone into the hurry-up mode and was already at the line. Neely was holding his arms out wide and moving them up and down to give his receivers their routes.

"Bingo, Bingo, Bingo!" Driftwood yelled. He crossed his arms up over his head to signal the defense to his teammates. The Bingo call told everyone to run the same defense as the play before.

Georgia quickly snapped the ball before Buffalo could get lined up properly, especially Leroy Clarkson, who was way too far off of his receiver. The guy ran a simple eight-yard speed cut to the outside and the ball arrived right on time. He easily hauled it in and tapped both toes before stepping out of bounds. It was a gain of eight, making it 2nd and 2 from the Buffalo 37. The Hogs' offense was in a groove while the Buffalo defense was on its heels. Again, Neely went no huddle, even with the clock stopped because the receiver had gone out of bounds.

Driftwood knew they were trying to dictate the same coverage again with the fast tempo. They wanted Cover 2, meaning only two safeties would be covering deep, one responsible for each half of the field. They had seen the Blizzard run it all afternoon against the hurry-up and hoped to get it again. Georgia quickly shifted to the shotgun and moved the tight end into one slot and the tailback into the other, spreading the field in a balanced, four-wide-receiver look.

"Storm, Storm, Storm!" Driftwood yelled as loud as he could through the din of the crowd while waving one hand over his head to relay the matching signal.

He grabbed strong safety Eric Stillwaters and yelled, "Max four verts," and pushed him away as the ball was snapped. As anticipated, Georgia was trying to steal one by taking a deep shot. They sent all four receivers on deep, vertical routes spreading them evenly across the field, thus stretching the defense vertically and horizontally and overloading the back end.

No such luck this time. Driftwood had checked to a three-deep zone and had also sent his strong safety deep. Everybody was well covered and Neely had to chuck it out of bounds. Count one for Driftwood and the Buffalo defense.

With the incomplete pass the clock had stopped again and this time Georgia huddled up. It was now 3rd and 2 at the Buffalo 37 with 7:53 remaining in the game. The Hogs shuffled their personnel, bringing in a pair of extra receivers along with their third-down back, Traverse Jenkins. They lined up in Trips Open with three receivers to the wide side and one to the short side with Neely under center and Jenkins six yards deep, directly behind him.

Usually Coach Faber would match personnel and bring in the Nickel defense, but when he expected run or short pass he would often stay with his Base personnel. That was why they had drafted Steven Stark in the first place; he could play out in the slot to cover the pass and inside to stuff the run.

Buffalo countered the Wild Hogs' set by bumping to an even, four-man front with Sam Beeson, the outside linebacker, sliding down to play defensive end. That put Driftwood alone in the middle and moved Stark out to cover the weak slot. The other outside linebacker, Ukey Gallop, moved into the slot to the strong side. It was a basic Nickel alignment with Base personnel in the ball game. As Neely went through his signals, Driftwood smelled a rat and yelled for Stark to come back inside. At the last instant, Stark slid back into his normal linebacker alignment, bumping Driftwood over to balance the defensive front into a 4-2 look. The perfect timing of their shift prevented Neely from checking out of the play.

Just as Driftwood had anticipated, Georgia ran a draw play to Jenkins. The back stepped to his right and feigned a pass block while waiting for Neely to carry the ball back to him. The play was contained perfectly, as both Buffalo defensive ends rushed up the field, forcing Jenkins to take it into the middle of the line. Driftwood attacked the guard to his side, not buying into the perfunctory fake by Neely, who held the ball extra high on his drop, trying to sell the pass to the defense. Nobody was buying.

Driftwood instinctively hollered "Draw," although he doubted it did any good. By keeping outside leverage, he forced the ball back into Stark who had also been playing draw. At the last second Stark slipped inside the block of his guard and met Jenkins head on at the line of scrimmage and knocked him sideways with a pretty healthy lick. Driftwood shed the other guard's block and arrived in time to sandwich the Georgia back from the opposite side. Jenkins fought hard but was no match as several more Blizzard defenders jumped on the pile. Once the heap of bodies was untangled the chains were brought in and stretched out. Georgia was barely a half yard shy of the first down. That made it 4th and a short 1 to go. Chalk up another one for Driftwood and the Buffalo D.

Georgia called a timeout with the ball resting just inside the Buffalo 36-yard line. They wanted to talk it over, but there was little doubt they would go for it.

They were looking at a 54-yard field goal attempt, down two, with 6:52 left to play and less than a yard to go for the first down. The deciding factor was they had very little confidence in their kicker beyond 50 yards. They could always punt, but they were right on the edge of the scoring zone. Momentum had swung in their favor so why not take a chance and ride it? It wasn't the end of the world if they didn't make it; they would have to rely on their defense to hold and get them the ball back. There was still plenty of time for that.

Coach Faber called his defense to the sideline while talking on the headset with his defensive backs coach, Archie Beatle, upstairs in the booth. The Blizzard defenders all gathered around Coach Faber awaiting instructions while sucking down water and gasping for air.

"All right," Coach Faber said, "Archie says it looks like they are going with heavy personnel. They like Iso and Toss. I doubt they'll sneak it – Neely's no pile-pusher. Don't fall asleep on the pass. We are going with 60 personnel. Don't be a dumbass and jump offsides, watch the damned ball. That means you, Sellars. Let's go '60 Pinch Lock' and send these bastards to the showers."

"Ooh, good call, Coach!" Driftwood said and gave Coach Faber a good, hard whack on the ass.

"I'm glad you like it," Coach Faber said, trying to rub the sting out of his ass cheek. "Now make a fucking play, for once."

Driftwood, who had started skipping back onto the field, roared with laughter.

Coach Faber shook his head and muttered to no one in particular, "That guy has a fucking screw loose. That's probably why I like him."

Georgia was indeed going for it and they came out in heavy personnel as Archie had projected. They aligned with three tight ends, one on each side with the third as a wingback to their left. The backs were stacked in an I-formation. Neely used a hard count to try to draw the hyped up defensive line off-sides, but the big boys held their water, even Sellars. Neely kicked up his heel, which sent the wingback in motion to his right toward the wide side of the field. Driftwood and Stark were both fairly well protected, as Buffalo had brought in an extra defensive lineman, taking the free safety, Dave Gaston, out of the game. Both Blizzard linebackers bumped over toward the wide side in unison with the motion. On the third hut, the ball was finally snapped to Neely, who wheeled and pitched it to Jenkins on a toss-sweep toward the motion and the wide side. Both Atlanta guards pulled to lead the way. It was one of the oldest plays in the book: the Toss Sweep.

Buffalo's contain held strong as Sam Beeson refused to be hooked by the tight end. There wasn't anybody on the planet who could hook Beeson – so he claimed. Beeson strung the play out laterally as Jenkins tried in vain to get around the edge. Finally, Jenkins realized there was no getting around Sam Beeson and went to plan B, the cut-back. He saw a possible opening in the alley if he could just beat one man. Jenkins brought his feet to balance and made a nifty, inside jump cut, avoiding a lunging Eric Stillwaters, who was filling the alley. Jenkins eyes grew big as he accelerated toward daylight, and for an instant it appeared he could bust loose and go the distance.

But the crease closed as quickly as it had opened as heavy resistance in the form of a two-man wall appeared. Both Stark and Driftwood had skated outside, avoiding the tangle of arms and legs along the line before coming downhill to meet Jenkins at the pass. They drilled him simultaneously just behind the line of scrimmage. There was no forward progress.

The crunch of pads could be heard over the crowd as both of Buffalo's inside linebackers drove through the airborne Jenkins, planting him four yards deep into the Georgia backfield. The hit was of the crowd pleaser variety, one of those rare, pure instances of contact that caught the breath of seventy thousand people and held it. The gasp was followed by a brief silence before a low moan of "ooh" involuntarily escaped from the fans exhaling in unison.

Back in Buffalo people came up off of their couches. Some even ran out into the streets whooping and hollering with their neighbors. Complete strangers hugged each other and jumped up and down in the town's bars and taverns. Gerald Wainscott III nearly fell over as he half jumped out of his seat up in the visiting owner's luxury suite. Donald Fegel, sitting close by, caught him by the arm and kept the old boy upright. It was mayhem.

All nine remaining Buffalo defenders had run to the pile, screaming and dancing and pounding on Stark and Driftwood. Coach Ivy was apoplectic on the sideline, yelling at the defense to get off the field. The last thing he wanted was a 15-yard excessive celebration penalty.

He needn't have worried; the referee took the opportunity to call a media timeout with the change of possession. The officials spotted the ball at the point of impact, a good yard short of the first down. They didn't even bother to measure. Buffalo took over on downs at their own 37 and the Georgia momentum was history.

After the extended break, Buffalo's offense took the field with a renewed confidence. On the first play, Earl "the Pearl" Johnson took the handoff and ripped off 13 yards right up the middle, advancing the ball to midfield. This is where Jerry Sturm, Buffalo's offensive coordinator, made the call of the day. Brady took the snap from the shotgun and perfunctorily faked a handoff to Johnson followed by a pump fake of a quick screen to the right side.

The desperate Georgia defense bit hard, as Buffalo had had success with the quick screen all day. They jumped the great pump-fake by Brady, who then turned and launched a missile down the left sideline to a wide-open Alex Cunningham, also known as AC. The ball was slightly overthrown but AC made an incredible leaping grab and pulled it in, deep in the corner of the end zone. He cradled the ball as he rolled out of the field of play and then bounced to his feet, holding it high in the air for all to see. The back judge nodded and looked at the side judge who nodded back at him and they both threw their hands into the air.

Touchdown Buffalo!

Nobody can overthrow AC, not even Ben Brady. The Brady pass had traveled over 65 yards through the air and had barely gotten more than 20 yards off the ground. The kid had a cannon.

Tenudo tacked on the extra point and Buffalo extended their lead to 19-10 with 4:51 left to play. The Wild Hogs self-destructed after that, turning the ball over to Buffalo on downs again, this time near midfield. Three Earl Johnson runs garnered 12 yards and a Blizzard first down and that was all she wrote. Brady took a knee a couple of times and Buffalo was 1-0, heading back to the Wigwam for their home opener.

# Chapter Nine

Thursday night, the week of the inaugural game at the Wigwam against Pittsburgh, the fish were biting in a new club called the Longhouse, which sat in the shadow of the stadium in the hot, vibrant Casino District in downtown Buffalo. That meant Jack Driftwood and company were out angling to land a big one while trying to catch their limit.

"What'll it be, boys?" the well-endowed cocktail waitress asked.

"Two pickets to Tittsburgh, please," Brady said.

The group roared in drunken laughter; some of them despite the fact, others due to the fact that they had been hearing this same punchline all week long.

Driftwood stood and slung his arm around the fair maiden. "Don't pay attention to him, darlin', he didn't have no home training. What we really want is a fresh tub of Molson Golden and a couple of jugs of Jahouga Juice."

Jahouga Juice was unofficially the official drink of the Buffalo Blizzard. It was a pre-mixed, bottled shot that tasted sublime. A former Blizzard player by the name of T. Graham Brown had invented the sweet yet sour, highly potent elixir. It all started when he mixed large batches of the concoction at Ben Brady's parties to appease the tremendous demand from the crowd. It took off and was now a staple in drinking establishments across the country.

The waitress turned her ample assets directly into Jack and deliberately gave them a little shake.

"That's *two* jugs?" she asked.

Jack stooped to get a closer look at her chest before straightening up to look her in the eye.

"Yes. Yes it is, miss. That's two jugs if I've ever seen 'em."

"Play your cards right and you just may."

They all hooted and hollered and were soon discussing Driftwood's odds of actually eyeballing the young ladies bodacious set of ta-ta's before the night was over. Ah yes, the evening was young and the prospects were looking mighty good!

Jack had picked up Steven Stark to test the waters three nights before the home opener. He figured it was high time his rookie was indoctrinated into the Thursday Night Out routine many of the veteran Blizzard players considered a religion. Stark was ready to be baptized. He was quite excited by the prospect of becoming a new convert. He had been hearing stories about Thursday Night Out since he was back in high school down in Mayville. The stories about the phenomenon were legendary throughout Blizzard Country.

Thursday Night Out wasn't a weekly ritual for Jack, but he tried to make it to the party at least once a month, if only to keep an eye on his boys and up with the social scene in town. But every once in a while it was just the call of the wild that sent him hunting for some strange. Nature has her ways.

The buzz in the club picked up when the DJ announced the Blizzard was in the house. Women were coming out of the woodwork and suddenly none of the players' money was good anymore. Blizzard fans were lining up to buy drinks for their guys. The place was packed, the beer was ice-cold, and the music was good and loud.

It didn't take long before Jack and Stark had the undivided attention of several talented young ladies tangled up on a couch in a semi-private alcove just off the dance floor. Things were starting to get interesting as they were trying to figure out which of them were the best kissers. So far there were no clear-cut losers.

Stark had suggested the kissing contest move to his place when the party was interrupted by the sound of breaking glass and shouting. Jack hated to extricate himself from the voluptuous company on the couch, but he knew Earl Johnson's drunk-assed, high-pitched hollering when he heard it. He flew around the corner onto the dance floor and landed right in the middle of the fray.

A drunk, staggering Johnson was squared off with a pair of big rednecks in flannel shirts with the sleeves ripped off over the top of wife-beater t-shirts, not an entirely uncommon look to the area, although out of place in the Longhouse.

As it always does, the crowded dance floor had opened up, creating a natural ring for the fight. They were in for a treat as this was no pedestrian bar brawl; it was a tag-team title match featuring Earl "the Pearl" Johnson and Old Jack Driftwood against Larry the Cable Guy and his evil twin.

Johnson's eyes were as wide as they were wild when he took a roundhouse swing at one of the big boys. He missed by a mile and the momentum of the errant punch twirled the Pearl completely around. He would have fallen to the floor if he hadn't landed on a table, sending several drinks crashing to the floor. The first redneck pounced on Earl's back and threw a flurry of short rabbit punches at the back of his head. Jack jumped on the guy from behind and put him in a rear-naked choke. Stark had followed Jack into the fray and he and a couple of other Blizzard players held off the redneck's apparent twin while Jack continued to apply pressure to the choke hold on the other. Slowly the big boy went limp under the pressure, never bothering to tap out.

"Quick, get that dumb ass away from here," Jack said to another pair of Blizzard players who had moved close to the action ready to assist.

They grabbed Earl, but not before he took another wobbly swing at the unconscious redneck which harmlessly grazed the limp guy's shoulder. They wrapped up the squirming running back and took him around the corner away from the carnage and dumped him onto the couch where Jack and Stark had been. It was over almost as quickly as it had started. A couple of bouncers appeared to escort the two troublemakers from the premises while Jack went to the restroom to clean off the sweat and stench from his contact with the smelly bastard.

After he had tidied up a bit he went looking for his boy Earl. Of course, the inebriated running back was in Jack's spot, having picked up the kissing contest right where things had left off when all the bullshit started. The lovely ladies had added poor Earl to the game and were fawning all over him.

"Goddammit, Earl," Jack said, "if you wanted to meet these ladies all you had to do was ask. You didn't have to try to kick the shit out of every redneck in the club."

"Fuckin' Drifty, you know I be stuck on stupid." Johnson turned to the girls on the sofa. "Now this one cool-ass white boy, here."

He popped up off the couch and gave Jack a big hug and kissed him on the cheek. Then he plopped back onto the couch into the laps of the lovelies.

"I loves that man, right there," he said.

"What the hell happened, Pearl?" Stark asked.

"That dude say Pittsburgh gonna whip our ass and I was goin' down. So I slaps the Budweiser out his hand. Dude got up n' squared off. Next thing I know, Drifty is chokin' that motherfucka and I gets thrown in here with all these sweet lil' thangs like I had done died n' gone to heaven. Shee-it! This calls for a damn drank. We need some a that Jahouga Juice, y'all."

And so it was. Several jugs of Jahouga Juice magically appeared and the party went on into the wee hours of the morning. By all appearances catastrophe had been averted.

It was rainy, cold, and cloudy the following morning when Jack rolled himself out of the sack. He quickly gobbled up a couple of Motrin 800's and quaffed down a big jug of purple G2 Gatorade. He didn't feel too rung out after the long night but had to take care of himself. The last thing he needed was to be stumbling around the locker room with a vindictive hangover that could take away from his focus. Friday served as the final day of serious on-field preparation for Pittsburgh and he wanted things to go perfectly out on the practice field. This was a big game and he intended to be prepared.

He flipped on the TV to check the weather forecast. It was supposed to be unseasonably cool with temperatures barely reaching the mid-fifties and wet, rainy conditions the rest of the day. However, the good news was this weather was departing the area as Pittsburgh was scheduled to arrive, meaning the roof of the Wigwam should remain open for the game. Jack had mixed feelings about their new stadium. He loved the opulence and the amenities the place afforded and the awesome location on the lake front. He was sure it was going to be loud as hell in there; Buffalo's fans would take care of that.

But what he didn't like was the idea of playing indoors late in the season where the weather conditions in Buffalo most assuredly would necessitate closing the sliding glass roof shrouding the massive structure. Over the years he had seen more than a few warm-climate teams, especially South Florida, come into Buffalo as early as mid-October and peer nervously at the sky as they came out for pregame warm-ups. They were more worried about the cold and the possibility of snow than they were about the football game. Many folded up their tents before even stepping onto the field. Having the roof overhead would take away a longtime, inherent home-field advantage.

Moreover, Jack loved playing in inclement weather; it slowed everyone else down and didn't seem to affect him at all. When conditions were too tough for everyone else, they were just right for Jack Driftwood. Or so he told himself. The bottom line was football was meant to be played outdoors on grass – end of story.

He was broken from his reverie when Earl Johnson's mug appeared on the TV.

*Ah shit! What now?*

The pretty face of Channel Four News Buffalo reporter Jillian Pierce, a special friend of Jack's, began telling the story of the previous night's tragedy. He quickly snagged the remote off the kitchen counter and cranked up the volume.

"...The wee hours earlier this morning. Shortly after the new Casino District nightclub, the Longhouse, closed its doors, two men jumped and battered Blizzard star running back Earl Johnson. Sources say the two men were involved in a brief confrontation with Johnson earlier in the evening inside the club."

Pierce paused to look down at her notes. "Buffalo police say Johnson was later attacked around four a.m. this morning in the Longhouse parking lot. The suspects assaulted Johnson, whacking him multiple times with a tire iron and were seen kicking the Blizzard running back as he lay defenseless on the ground. After the heinous attack the assailants cowardly fled the scene on foot and are still at large. The police currently have no suspects in the case. If anybody saw anything or has any information regarding this odious crime please call the Buffalo Police Department Tip-line at 847-2255 or just go to B-P-D-N-Y dot org and click on the Tip-line tab.

"Two unidentified women with Johnson were unharmed. Johnson was rushed to Buffalo General Hospital where he was admitted and remains. Hospital authorities are not giving out any details concerning the Star-Bowl running back's condition, saying only that he is in serious but stable condition. Earlier this morning the Buffalo Blizzard vice-president of media relations, David Blitzer, had this to say."

The TV station rolled a clip of a stoic Blitzer shot in front of the team offices before the sun had come up because the club's media center was not yet open.

"Right now, we are guardedly optimistic concerning the condition of Earl Johnson. Our thoughts and prayers are with Earl and his family and we greatly appreciate the thoughts and prayers of Blizzard fans on his behalf as he recovers from this monstrous and cowardly attack. Obviously, Earl will not be playing this week against Pittsburgh. It's too early to tell after that. If anyone has any information regarding this incident please contact your local law enforcement offices."

The station then aired B-Roll of a couple of Johnson's runs from the Georgia game the previous Sunday as Pierce continued.

"Buffalo hosts Pittsburgh on Sunday night right here on Channel Four at eight p.m. in the grand opening of the Wigwam, just two days from now. Be sure to tune in for our hour-long special, 'Building a Wigwam,' at seven o'clock Sunday night. Stay tuned to Channel Four for further updates."

Jack grabbed his cell phone from the table and found Pierce's number in the phone's memory. He had dated Jillian off and on the past couple of years but it wasn't anything serious, although it inevitably turned physical in a very hot and heavy fashion when they did hook up.

She answered on the first ring.

"Hi, Jack, you ok?" she asked.

"Yeah, I'm good, I just saw your report, what the fuck happened to Earl?"

"Pretty much what you just heard me say on the tube. I don't know much else. Blitzer said it wasn't life threatening or anything like that. He got whacked on the head and arm and then kicked around a little bit. They think he may have a broken arm and a concussion and some bruises."

"Damn, they got any idea who those bozos are that done it?"

"You should know, word has it you started the whole thing by choking one of them out at the Longhouse."

"What? No. Where the hell did you hear that?"

"I got my sources," she said.

"Don't pull that shit with *me*, Jillian."

"Hey, lighten up, big guy, I'm just playing with you. I miss you."

Jack held his silence knowing it would break her almost instantly.

"OK, ok. One of the bouncers at the club told the cops about it. A friend of mine at the Downtown Police station leaked it to me. They are keeping that part of it quiet for now at the request of Sir Donald Fegel, on behalf of Mr. Wainscott. Nobody has a clue yet as to who those creeps are."

"Great," Jack said, "I'm right in the middle of this shit."

"Aren't you always?"

Jack paused to ponder the question, rhetorical as it was. "I suppose it seems that way, but as you know, there is always more to the story."

Jillian laughed. "Speaking of more to the story, what did happen in the Longhouse last night?"

"I stood up for one of my boys, Jillian. Just like I'll always do."

"I don't doubt that. But you know I'm always here for you, Jack. Call me when you get lonely, you know I love to see you."

"You know I will."

With no such intentions Jack hung up the phone and punched up Gary Chuckles' cell number.

The first words out of Gary's mouth were, "What the hell did you guys do now?"

"Never mind that," Jack replied, "how's Earl?"

Chuckles sighed. "He's gonna be alright, got knocked on the head pretty good and the bastards broke his arm with the crowbar. Probably out six to eight weeks. Doc Verdin put a plate in his arm with a handful of screws and it will be better than ever."

"Those motherfuckers! But I suppose it could have been worse. What about them bastards? Any word on them?"

"You mean other than you choked one of them?"

"Shit, does everybody know about that?"

"Pretty much, you should be getting a call from Feegs shortly. He's been ranting and raving around here all morning trying to blame the whole thing on you."

"Figures," Jack said. "Any other players names being mentioned?"

"Actually, just yours. Why, were more of our guys down there?"

"Oh no, Gary. Not any of our *choirboys*. I'm sure everybody was home in bed all tucked in before fuckin' midnight."

"Sarcasm is ugly, Jack," Chuckles said. "You should get in here and talk to Feegs, head this thing off at the pass."

"Yeah, you're right. I'm on my way in, see you in a little bit."

Jack hung up the phone. He had a couple more calls to make before crawling, hat in hand, to the Wigwam and Donald Fegel's office to face the music. First, he dialed up an old friend who happened to be a detective with the Buffalo Police Department, Vinny Cappolla. Vinny had heard the story but had no further details as of yet. He promised to call back when he heard anything new. Jack felt a little better knowing his friend was looking into it, but only a little.

His next call was in the opposite direction, to his connection into the underworld of Western New York and well beyond. He somewhat reluctantly dialed the digits of Chaz Davenport, a charter member of his fan club, the Driftwoodies. Chaz was an old Vietnam veteran who had been known to run around with a pretty unsavory crowd at times. Put nicely, the man was well connected. Although the two of them were close in an odd, intellectual, fraternal way, Jack tried to keep a safe and reasonable distance between himself and Chaz. The dude could be dangerous.

Chaz was usually holed up in an underground bunker on Hemlock Lake, the westernmost of the Finger Lakes, but could be anywhere on the globe at any given time. He kept a boat docked up in North Tonawanda and stayed on it whenever he was in the Buffalo area.

A nocturnal creature by habit, he often slept during the day and operated at night. Chaz could get his hands on anything one might need regardless of what it was, and, more importantly, he could get whatever needed to be done, done. He also kept things quiet. Really quiet. His methods didn't often follow the letter of the law but they were undeniably effective. Jack knew when trouble knocked Chaz would answer.

However, Chaz wasn't answering. This neither surprised nor disappointed Jack. He preferred leaving a message anyway, because just talking with Chaz could creep him out.

"Yo, Chaz, it's Jack. Need a favor. Can you look into Earl getting jumped last night? Two big country fucks, likely brothers or some kind of kin. They are out there laughing about it right now. Gotta make this right, I'm taking some heat for it. Hit me back."

Between Vinny Cappolla and the Buffalo Police Department and Chaz's underworld wide web, Driftwood was confident it wouldn't be long before some answers would be forthcoming.

Jack walked through the front doors of the Wigwam not exactly sure what to expect. He knew Earl Johnson was going to be fine, at least in the long run, which was good news. His biggest concern was how the loss of the Pearl would affect the team in the short term. The one thing he was sure about was Fegel would try to run his head through the masher and blame him for the entire incident.

He wished he would have stuck around the Longhouse a little longer to make sure everyone got home safely, but what the hell? Was he the big babysitter? Did he have to escort everybody to their cars at night? How could he have known those rednecks would be waiting in the weeds to jump Earl?

Figuring he would do well to take Chuckles' advice and meet the thing head on, he took the elevator to the fifth floor and forced himself to go to the office of Donald Allen Fegel Jr. before he could change his mind. Fegel hadn't called him onto the carpet as of yet, so maybe he could buy some favor by coming in to talk to the GM on his own.

Jack went directly to the desk of Fegel's secretary, Janice Cole.

"Hi, Janice, you sure look nice today."

"Oh, hi, Jack. You're so sweet. You have been quite the popular boy around here this morning."

"Really?"

"Actually, no," she said. "I'll tell Mr. Fegel you are here."

"Didn't think so. Thanks, Janice."

When summoned Jack entered Fegel's office and closed the door behind him. He felt like some cheese-eating, pimple-faced punk being sent down to detention. Fegel was seated behind his desk; Howard Ivy was in one overstuffed leather chair while Gerry Wainscott was in another identical one situated to the right of Fegel's desk, which was perched atop a riser so the man could look down upon all who entered. A smaller chair had been placed out in front of them in the middle of the room. The seat of inquisition, no doubt. Jack took the hot seat and sat down amid a deafening silence. He nodded to both the coach and the owner's daughter and was about to make a smart-assed comment to break the ice but thought better of it.

Fegel let the silence hang in the suddenly hot, stagnant air for what seemed like an eternity. Finally, he spoke.

"So, Mr. Driftwood, what do you have to say for yourself?"

"I'm not sure what you are referring to," Jack said, angry at himself that his voice had cracked a little under the pressure. It felt like he was talking to a police interrogator and he wondered if he should have brought his attorney along.

"I think you know *exactly* what I am referring to, mister!" Fegel said. "But so as not to tax your concussion-addled brain, I'll spell it out for you. We have a report that you started a ruckus at the Longhouse bar last night where you choked some poor guy until he blacked out. Then you conveniently skipped out and Earl Johnson paid the price for it and is now in the hospital. Ring a bell?"

Jack would have laughed if he had not been so pissed off. He took a couple of deep breaths in order to cool off before answering the charges.

"I don't know where you got your information, Mr. Fegel, but I assure you it is erroneous. The truth of the matter is I was sitting in the Longhouse enjoying a quiet conversation when it came to my attention Earl Johnson was in the need of assistance. I saw some big guy punching him in the head so I grabbed the guy to defuse the situation. I used as little force as possible to control what was a highly volatile situation. I got Earl away from the fray and turned those guys over to the bouncers, who then removed them from the premises. My only regret is getting home at a decent hour rather than waiting 'til Earl was ready to go so I could escort him to his car and tuck him into bed."

Despite his attempt to control it, Jack's voice rose until he was almost yelling by the end. Not to be outdone, Fegel took it up another notch.

"Oh, well then, please forgive me. You're really the hero here. Let's see if we can get you a medal!"

"What the hell would you have had me do?"

"Oh, I don't know, maybe stay home and get your rest before the big game? Or maybe, if you are so stupid and selfish that you had to go out, perhaps you could have left the premises at the first sign of trouble. That's what we ask you to do, but no, you're big Jack Driftwood, and you got to jump into trouble and then make yourself out to be some kind of goddamn folk hero! Meanwhile, Earl Johnson is sitting up in the hospital with a concussion and a broken arm."

Jack's first instinct was to tell Fegel to go fuck himself. Nearly half the team was in that club. Besides, the Pearl was the dumb shit who got in a fight, all Jack did was clean it up. But arguing sure as hell wasn't going to get him anywhere. He bit his tongue and took one for the team and remained silent. But Fegel wasn't done.

"Why is it that anytime there is trouble around here you are always smack dab in the middle of it? For just once it'd be nice to have a problem that didn't involve Jack Driftwood. Every time—"

"That's enough, Donald," Coach Ivy said. Then he turned to Jack. "Any idea who those guys were?"

"No, sir"

"Alright, then. I'll see you in the meeting."

Jack could not get out of there fast enough but he did steal a glance at Gerry as he was leaving. The hurt and confused look on her pretty face ripped his guts out as he skulked out of the little man's office.

**Driftwood Lays Lumber In Bar Fight**
***Blizzard Linebacker Sought By Police***
By Budd Kilmer
Buffalo News Sports Editor

(Buffalo, NY) Unless you are living in a cave, undoubtedly somewhere in Jack Driftwood's neighborhood, you have, no doubt, heard about the beating Buffalo Blizzard running back Earl Johnson sustained early this morning in the parking lot of the sizzling new casino-district nightclub, the Longhouse. What you haven't heard is why Johnson was on the business end of a tire iron. In a word, the reason for this atrocity is simple: Driftwood.

As you can tell by the picture accompanying this column, it was Jack Driftwood who initiated the escalation of the confrontation in the early morning hours at the controversial new party spot. Don't stare too long into the eyes of this madman as it may prove hazardous to your sanity.

Assuredly, Driftwood will use the time honored self-defense excuse for the excessively violent show of force he used in the incident. But ask yourself this: How is jumping on a man's back and choking him until he passes out self-defense? Because that is what Driftwood did to kick of a night of drunken debauchery.

The so-called "perps" were so antagonized by Driftwood they, in defense of their very honor, struck back in the still of the night as they rained blow after damaging blow onto the hide of poor Earl Johnson. I'm not here to justify what these men did to Johnson, by any means. But I am honor-bound to point out their acts were an escalation in retaliation to what Jack Driftwood started.

A picture paints a thousand words, but only one word is needed here and it isn't pretty: Murderous. Looking onto the eyes of the man in this picture is akin to looking into the deeply troubled eyes of a full-blown sociopath. Does the man have no conscience? You be the judge.

Whatever Jack Driftwood says about this I already know the ugly truth – I can see it in his eyes.

So who's at fault here? Well, Driftwood is a known ringleader of a weekly outing Blizzard players simply call "Thursday Night Out." The players gather in a pack and bar hop while drinking to excess, ultimately leaving a trail of destruction and mayhem through the popular night spots of our fair city. This is not the first time these excursions have led to trouble. In fact, this barbarism has been going on for as long as yours truly has been covering this football team. It is long past time somebody put an end to this weekly carnage. Are you out there, Mr. Fegel?

It's telling how Driftwood gets into the middle of an argument and then turns it into a full scale riot capped off with a revenge beating. While he is home sleeping it off, the price gets paid. Sleep well, Jack. Sleep like a piece of Driftwood.

## Chapter Ten

As if the Sunday Night matchup between Buffalo and Pittsburgh wasn't big enough, the Earl Johnson story had blown the roof off. Throw in the fact it was the Grand Opening of the Wigwam and you had the makings of one of the biggest games in franchise history. The Longhouse incident was receiving an incredible amount of national attention as rumors were rampant on talk radio, the internet, and in the papers.

Various versions of Jack Driftwood's role in the incident were being reported. One rumor had him busting a pool cue over some guy's head and another report gaining traction had him knocking three guys out with a toilet seat. The police had questioned Jack later that day but did not release any details regarding his statements or the extent of his involvement. The assailants were still at large and Blizzard fans were frothing for justice. A police sketch of the two suspects was ubiquitous in the local media. If those guys were stupid enough to show their faces in Buffalo, they would be toast, more than likely victims of instantaneous vigilante justice.

Opinion was split over whether Driftwood was a hero who had protected a teammate and diffused a highly volatile situation in the Longhouse or a murderous, out-of-control troublemaker who had only escalated the conflict and had no business playing against Pittsburgh while Earl languished in Buffalo General Hospital. As usual, the truth lay somewhere in the middle.

It wasn't just sport's talk shows having a field day with the issue, the discussion had crossed over into the mainstream national media. Former players and pundits across the dial were debating whether Earl Johnson should have had a gun to defend himself and whether Jack had overstepped his bounds. It was exactly the kind of spotlight nobody wanted to be in.

The commentators took to their pulpits and rehashed the long list of previous incidents of off-the-field violence in the recent history of the NAFA. The league had developed a serious problem in this regard and this most recent incident had only served to cause further damage to an already tainted reputation. The league's Commissioner, Bob Goldman, had been tasked with cleaning up the NAFA's image, and he promised a full investigation into the incident.

Meanwhile, in the city of Buffalo the excitement for a game hadn't been this rampant since the first time the town had hosted an EFC Championship game twenty years prior, back in January of 1996. Everybody had an opinion about the game, Jack Driftwood, and the absence of Earl Johnson. It was the perfect storm.

Many agreed with the Buffalo News, which was crying about how the Blizzard season had started so promisingly and now was in major jeopardy given the absence of Johnson and the polarizing distraction the Longhouse episode had caused. Some of the wiser, older fans felt this could be an advantage for the Blizzard; the team would band together and circle the wagons, which had, at least historically, been a trademark of the franchise, especially under Howard Ivy.

The Blizzard had a couple of good options to fill in for Earl Johnson at running back but neither could be considered a sure thing. Jesse Devon, the backup, was more suited to the role of a third-down back. The worry regarding Devon was mostly concern about his ability to take the pounding of a featured back.

The other option was a youngster, a second-year stud-hoss, by the name of Anthony Petrucci. The problem with Petrucci was he was unproven in regular season play. He had yet to have an official carry in the NAFA but had been dominant in the preseason the past two years, albeit against mostly second and third stringers. The hulking Italian was an immense, bruising, 250-pound back whom the Blizzard was extremely high on. He ran hard, using his size to his advantage, but also possessed very quick feet and above average hands. He had played his college ball nearby at Syracuse, thus Western New York football fans were aware of his brutal style of running. They had already dubbed the youngster the "Italian Stallion." The Stallion would be getting his chance to shine sooner than he or anyone else had imagined and it would come under the glare of the national spotlight.

Typically the team had a locker room reporting deadline of two hours prior to kick-off, but most of the players showed up sooner. Jack had liked to cut it close earlier in his career. The older he got, though, the more time it took to get his body battle-ready. At this stage of his career he generally arrived at the stadium three and a half to four hours before kickoff. He was soaking in a hot tub in the training room by 5 p.m. and by 5:15 he was laid out on a training table getting a full body massage. Following that, one of the trainers put him through a half-hour stretching routine.

The result of the hour-long process left Jack thoroughly loose and relaxed, although he still carried an ice ball in the pit of his stomach. It was the same ice ball he first discovered when he began playing the game as a seven-year-old kid back in his Pop Warner days in Maryville, Missouri. The ice ball varied in size depending on myriad factors but would invariably melt slowly, counting down to kickoff, making his stomach tickle and shiver. It didn't totally evaporate until that first hit. He had always maintained if the ice ball quit forming in his stomach it would be time to retire from the game. So far that hadn't been a problem, and it sure as hell wasn't an issue on this evening; the thing was as big as a damn basketball.

The team took the field for pregame warmups in stages beginning with the kickers and other specialists an hour and a half before kickoff. The next group went out fifteen minutes later and consisted of everybody but the lineman and linebackers. Then, an hour before kickoff the entire squad would take the field. This warm up lasted approximately forty minutes before they filed back into the locker room to wait anxiously another fifteen minutes or so before being called back out to the field.

It was during this excruciating waiting period that Leroy Clarkson would make his final rounds. Leroy always worked himself into an emotional frenzy before the games. He would go to every man in the locker room, including trainers, coaches, and equipment men, and give them the hardest high-five he could muster. Driftwood often joked it was no wonder when Leroy dropped an interception, his hands had to be numb from the pounding. Some of the guys would go into hiding when Leroy initiated his lap around the locker room. No one blamed them, not even Leroy, who felt it was his honor-bound duty to make sure every man who was willing felt the wrath and intensity he was going to bring to the party. It was a not-so-subtle challenge for his teammates to match his commitment.

Invariably, their venerable owner, Gerald Wainscott, would show up in the locker room prior to each game to wish his players luck. And as luck would have it, he arrived just as Leroy began making his rounds. Mr. Wainscott was familiar with Leroy's routine and had taken the heavy-handed high-five on several occasions, but he didn't see Leroy coming for this one. The special circumstances surrounding this game had Clarkson amped up and in rare form. As soon as he spotted Mr. Wainscott making his rounds in the locker room, he strode purposely across the room to get himself some. Mr. Wainscott was talking with the Blizzard's center, Nick Loney, when Leroy drew a bead on him. At the last second the owner saw Leroy and managed to raise his hand but didn't have a chance to fully brace himself for the shock and fury.

Leroy's slap made such a loud pop that everyone in the area who wasn't watching flinched. All eyes went to see who had prematurely popped the cork on a bottle of bubbly. Gerald Wainscott's knees buckled from the force of the blow, but miraculously the old boy caught himself and managed to stay on his feet. Nick Loney reached out to steady Mr. Wainscott. The room held its collective breath in mortal fear that Clarkson had just maimed the man.

You had to give Wainscott credit. He couldn't wipe the silly, wide-assed smile off his face despite the obvious pain.

"Atta boy, Leroy. Let's give it to 'em today."

The old bird loved it! Jack was amazed, once again.

A huge cheer went up in the previously tense locker room. Guys started shouting out random encouragements and threats about what was in store for Pittsburgh. Jack was so jacked up he knew he had to calm himself down. He looked over at Stark to see how the rookie was handling things. He must have had a scowl of intensity on his face because Stark started laughing at him.

"Settle down, old man," Stark said, "you don't want to have a heart attack."

"I know," Jack said, shaking his head at himself. "I may have miss-timed my drugs because I am jumping out of my skin waiting for this one. The old man got me fired up. Did you see his fuckin' knees buckle when Leroy hit him?"

"Damn near pissed my pants," Stark said and began to giggle.

"I got to say, Stark, you are a different kind of cat. I have never seen a guy so blasé and calm before a game. Shit, man, don't you ever get fired up?"

"Nah, not really, maybe once in a while after I hit somebody really hard. But my dad always told me to stay relaxed and save my energy and just play like an athlete. This is nothing more than an athletic contest and I'm a superior athlete, so why worry or get all hyped up to where you can't think like most of these morons in here?"

"Yeah, well, you're cheating yourself, sonny boy," Jack said. "There's nothing that gets me higher than the heat of the battle. I know how the Roman Gladiators felt when they were in the bowels of the great Coliseum."

"Well yeah, you were there, weren't you? In the Coliseum?"

Before Driftwood could tell his rookie to fuck off, Coach Ivy entered the locker room and called the team up. Danny Steeley had just delivered the two-minute warning announcement before they were to hit the field. The tradition was for Coach Ivy to select a player to lead the team in the Lord's Prayer. He called upon Shady Solomon and everyone grabbed a hold of somebody else and took a knee as Shady led the prayer. Coach Ivy had his say once they finished.

"Okay, gang, I don't have to pontificate as to the ramifications of this contest," Coach Ivy said. "This is our initial opportunity to go out and establish our new domicile. We are going to play Blizzard football tonight – smart, tough, and hard-nosed. But before we take the field, there is a gentleman with some rather robust sentiments he wishes to share with you."

On cue, Earl Johnson came strolling into the locker room sporting a big cast on his right arm. He had refused to stay in the hospital, demanding to be on the sidelines for the game. The doctors eventually realized Earl was going to the game regardless of what they said and gave in. Many of the players had visited him up at Buffalo General, but no one had expected to see him at the game.

Coach Ivy had masterfully kept him hidden until this exact moment. The boys let out a tremendous cheer for their fallen teammate. When things finally quieted down, Earl, clad in his game jersey, spoke from the heart with tears in his eyes.

"Damn, I'm glad to be in here with y'all! I wish like hell I could strap it on and be playin' in this one. But I can't. So all I'm askin' is for y'all to go out there and get me some! Get me some a that Pittsburgh ass!"

The locker room exploded again and they all collapsed in and around Earl. They raised their fists high into the air together, waiting for the Pearl to break them down.

"The only way we gonna win this one is to come together just like Mr. Wainscott told us back in camp. We gonna come together tonight, y'all. Come together, on three. One, two, three…"

"Come together!"

They charged out the door, through the tunnel, and onto their new home field for the first time. The offense was being introduced so the rest of the team ran to midfield amidst the deafening roar of the crowd and explosions from fireworks set off by the pyrotechnics crew. The huge Teepee in the upper deck of the south end zone lit up like a Christmas tree and began sending out smoke signals. Running onto the field, Driftwood was as light as a feather. He didn't feel his feet hit the ground until about the thirty-yard line. He hadn't been this pumped up before a game since playing in the Mega Bowl his rookie year. He ran over to Stark, jumped into the air and gave the kid a good head butt, which pissed Stark off.

*Good, fucker! Maybe that will get your piss a little hot.*

Driftwood was pumped-up out of his mind, but he still had the wherewithal to stay away from Bo-Bo Karpinski. If Bo-Bo got a hold of you before a big game like this you could easily miss the first quarter recovering from the beating he would put on you.

The offense was introduced and the crowd hit a higher pitch as each new name was called out. Earl Johnson was introduced last and when he danced his way out of the tunnel the Wigwam shook so much it registered as a minor earthquake at the University at Buffalo Seismology Institute. It was so loud Driftwood felt a sense of vertigo and had to catch his balance. The Wigwam was a mad house!

Riding the tremendous wave of early emotion, Buffalo jumped out to an early 7-0 lead. The Brawlers had won the toss and elected to receive the opening kickoff. They went three-and-out as the Buffalo defense was charged up. The crowd hung on every snap and was on the verge of delirium every time Buffalo made any sort of positive play. The Blizzard took advantage of excellent field position on their opening drive after a spectacular 20-yard punt return by Shady Solomon. Solomon had shagged the punt at his own 28 and headed straight up the middle of the field. He made one cut to his right to avoid a defender, which put him on a collision path with yet another. At the last second he sprung into the air and hurdled the would-be tackler. It was an incredible display of athleticism which made the crowd go wild and bought the speedy Shady another 12 yards before he was taken down.

Ben Brady brought the offense out and immediately went into the Blizzard's trademark no-huddle, hurry-up attack. They drove 52 yards in just six plays, putting up the game's first points on an 11-yard Anthony Petrucci run right up the gut. Petrucci carried at least five Pittsburgh defenders the final few yards into the end zone. His effort had the crowd chanting "Stallion-Stallion-Stallion" at the top of their lungs as the Rocky theme blared over the Wigwam's state-of-the-art audio system.

After the initial Buffalo fireworks, the game settled in and the teams exchanged punts during the rest of a fast moving first quarter. Each side was trying to grind it out on the ground and, other than Buffalo's initial drive, had yet to really open up their offenses. The Blizzard had gone back to huddling on offense to eat clock and shorten the game a bit. Things were playing out like a heavyweight championship fight where the early rounds were a feeling out process. It was just a matter of time before somebody would connect with another haymaker.

Buffalo had the ball and was beginning to mount a drive early in the second quarter. Petrucci was playing like a man possessed and on a critical 3rd and 1 he bowled over the entire line, pushing the pile forward for a first down and then some, picking up nine rough and tumble yards. The ball was near midfield, spotted at the Buffalo 48. The running game, featuring the power of the big back, was beginning to wear on the vaunted Brawler defense. Perfect time for a play action pass, or so thought Buffalo offensive coordinator Jerry Sturm.

Brady received the call through the communication device inside his helmet and immediately liked it. He barked out the play in the huddle with supreme confidence and the rest of the Blizzard offense picked up the vibe. Before breaking the huddle, he made a little adjustment of his own. The play called for AC to run a skinny post, but Brady had noticed the Pittsburgh free safety hedging toward the middle of the field, looking for the post route.

"AC, run a Poco on this one. Don't slow down, I'll get the fucker to you. I need a little extra time up front. This is gonna be a big one, boys. Let's go! Ready…"

"Break!"

Brady sauntered to the line waving his arms to quiet the crowd before barking out the signals. On cue, the savvy Blizzard fans ratcheted the noise down a few decibels. Brady began to go through his cadence and pre-snap gyrations. It was all for show; no audible was necessary because the trap was set. The free safety had crept subtly to the post as anticipated. Brady saw the cheat, licked his chops, and called for the snap. He caught the ball and opened to his right, faking a handoff to Petrucci. It was a good fake that momentarily froze the defense. Brady dropped back and looked off to his right where Shady Solomon was running a deep out cut. He pump faked the out with a shoulder shrug, drawing the corner down just as AC made his initial move toward the post. The free safety bit hard for the post cut about the same time AC broke to the corner. They were like two ships passing in the night; AC blew right past him.

Talk about easy money! The protection held to give Brady plenty of time to step into the throw. He spun a high-arcing spiral 40 yards up into the air and 60 yards down the field into the right corner of the Pittsburgh end zone. AC never broke stride and there wasn't a defender within 10 yards of him as he made the easy grab.

Touchdown Buffalo!

Bedlam ensued. Loud explosions reverberated through the stadium and confetti, closely mimicking real snow, cascaded down from the edges of the open roof onto the jubilant fans. A blizzard had hit the Wigwam! This effect had long been planned by the stadium ops personnel and was only to be unleashed after a particularly scintillating play. The dazzling 52-yard scoring bomb from Brady to AC was exactly what they had in mind.

The extra point was good and Buffalo now enjoyed a 14-0 lead early in the second quarter. The only problem was Pittsburgh was not the type of team to politely roll over and die. They weren't the defending World Champions for nothing. On their very next drive they answered with a touchdown of their own. Their quarterback, "Wild" Bill Hitchkok, was one of the best in the business. He responded by scrambling for a couple of crucial first downs to keep the drive alive and finished it off by hitting their gigantic Star-Bowl tight end, Lucas McElroy, down the seam for a 17-yard scoring toss. Just like that, it was 14-7.

On the ensuing kickoff, Buffalo fumbled on their own 17 and the Brawlers recovered the football. Martin Bershear, the Blizzard return man, got hit so hard it was several minutes before he was carted off the field. Bershear suffered a concussion and would not return to the game. This sucked a substantial portion of the air out of the building. When play resumed, the crowd, much like Bershear, had not quite yet recovered.

Pittsburgh took a shot into the end zone on first down but Wild Bill barely missed his open receiver, costing them a touchdown. On the next play the Brawlers went back to McElroy, their bread and butter in the red zone. The play was a pick route as Pittsburgh had two tight ends in the game aligned on opposite sides of the formation. They both ran short crossing routes, creating a scissor effect.

The intent of the play was for one of the Buffalo defenders to get caught up in the traffic, thus losing their man. McElroy had delayed slightly before running his route underneath the other crossing tight end in hopes the weak hook zone had been cleared by the action. It had, as far Pittsburgh's QB Hitchkok could tell. But Buffalo had scouted this play and was prepared for it. Prior to the snap Driftwood had alerted Steven Stark to sit on the double cross.

Stark gained some width as the play developed, intending to keep out of Wild Bill's field of vision baiting him to dump the ball down to McElroy. The rookie linebacker set the trap expertly and arrived at the same time as the ball. The crack of pads when Stark delivered the hit on McElroy sounded as if somebody had set off a small bomb.

The breath was sucked out of the crowd due to the magnitude of the hit. McElroy's helmet flew up into the air along with the football from the force of the collision. Bo-Bo Karpinski reached up and snatched the helmet out of the air and took off running like the dickens. He genuinely thought he had caught the football and wasn't the only one, because he was gang-tackled by a Pittsburgh horde after advancing almost 10 yards.

Meanwhile, Jack Driftwood *did* catch the football. He, too, started running like the dickens. Jack had one Brawler in front of him when he caught wind of Leroy Clarkson racing up from behind on the outside. He lateralled the ball safely back to Leroy just as the Pittsburgh tackler shot for his legs. Driftwood took the hit and rolled over on the turf where he had a perfect, ground-level view of Clarkson taking the ball all the way up the sideline the remaining 50 yards into the end zone.

Touchdown Buffalo?

The crowd was at full throttle again, but the officials were blowing their whistles and waving their arms. A couple of them had blown the play dead right where Bo-Bo had gone down and were attempting to mark the ball at that spot, except Bo-Bo didn't have the ball. Two other officials had signaled touchdown, correctly. Mayhem ensued.

The officials huddled in the middle of the field to keep the sidelines from antagonizing their discussion of the bizarre situation. It was a prescient move as Coach Ivy was all the way out to the numbers screaming profanities at them like a drunken sailor on furlough. He wanted his touchdown and he was giving the line judge an earful. A couple of his assistants tried to settle the old coach down after the official had put his hand on his flag as a final warning. The crowd was beginning to get restless as well, awaiting the referee's decision. There was a smattering of boos, but most of the Blizzard faithful were murmuring amongst themselves, gathering for the potential storm.

The ref, after consulting with his crew, went to the sidelines and put on the headset and began the mundane task of reviewing the play. An overzealous Blizzard fan threw a beer at him and it was a perfect shot. The cup landed on top of the replay apparatus and its contents showered the ref. He instinctively started up into the stands after the beer-tosser but quickly regained a measure of self-control. He was still stomping around the sideline, madder than a hornet, fully soaked in beer as he conversed with security to have the fan removed. The whole incident was caught on camera and replayed on both video boards. The crowd howled with delight.

Coach Faber casually approached Driftwood and Stark on the sidelines to weigh in on the matter. "Normally I would consider that a tragic waste of a perfectly good beer."

The beer-tossing fan was escorted out of the Wigwam by security personnel to a rousing round of raspberries from the rest of the crowd. The referee was still hot but toweled off and got back to business. Finally, he came out from under the hood and strode to the center of the field, clicking on his microphone.

"We have an inadvertent whistle on the play occurring after Buffalo had gained possession but before they crossed the goal line. By rule, it is Buffalo ball, first and ten, at the spot of possession when the whistle occurred, which is the Buffalo 30-yard line. There is no touchdown on the play. Buffalo ball, first and ten. Clock operator please put 5:02 on the game clock."

The full fury of the crowd now rained down onto the field. Tragically hundreds of cups of perfectly good beer were wasted. Most of it showered the Pittsburgh bench. The game was delayed again while the mess was cleaned up and order restored. The referee gave Buffalo a 15-yard unsportsmanlike conduct penalty and announced the next time an object was thrown onto the field Buffalo would be penalized 30 yards. This was met with another chorus of boos but thankfully no more beer was wasted.

Things finally settled down and play resumed with Buffalo still up 14-7. The Blizzard offense took full advantage of the Driftwood interception and marched down the field to claim the touchdown that was rightfully theirs. The drive ate up all but 28 seconds of the remainder of the first half and culminated in another Anthony Petrucci touchdown run, this one from a yard out.

On the following kickoff, Billy Brogan tackled the return man back on the Pittsburgh 11-yard line, where the Brawlers took a knee to end the half. The Buffalo players headed to the locker room with a 21-7 lead amidst the gleeful roar of the ninety-two-thousand-plus fans jammed into the Wigwam. Gerald Wainscott III was on cloud nine up in his owner's luxury suite. He could not have scripted a better or more entertaining opening 30 minutes of football to christen their brand new home.

The second half went equally well for Buffalo. They scored on the opening drive as Brady hit Solomon for a 38-yard score. That put the Blizzard up 28-7, leaving Pittsburgh too dispirited to mount any serious comeback. Buffalo went on to post a 34-17 win to go 2-0 on the young NAFA season.

The Italian Stallion was awarded the game ball in the locker room ceremony immediately following the game. As all smart running backs do, he bestowed it upon his offensive line. The offensive line, led by Nick Loney and Jeremy Patton, gave it, in turn, to their owner Mr. Wainscott who was so happy tears of joy streaked his weathered face. He graciously accepted the honor and then made a declaration that everyone on the team would receive a game ball to commemorate the momentous occasion of their first win in the Wigwam. That was icing on the victory cake.

Petrucci was the statistical star of the game with 23 carries for 152 yards and a pair of touchdowns. Earl Johnson was so happy for him he kissed the befuddled Stallion on the lips during the post-game locker room celebration. Being Italian, the big running back understood the gesture, though he did not encourage Earl to repeat it.

The defense was also stout for the second week in a row. They held Pittsburgh to under 300 total yards – 273 to be exact – and had forced a couple of fumbles to go along with Driftwood's interception. Driftwood couldn't remember seeing Coach Faber so happy. The normally reserved and somewhat stodgy coach lit up a fresh stogie in the locker room rather than just gnaw on it like a hungry rodent. It was the first time Coach Faber had smoked one of those bad boys in nearly five years. He threatened death to anyone who dared tell his wife. Jack wasn't sure if he was kidding or not; he sure seemed deadly serious.

Billy Brogan played a fine game as well, as he took over for Jack for most of the fourth quarter and was all over the field. Jack wasn't bothered by the substitution one bit. He figured it was a smart move to give him a rest with the game out of hand. Hell, they had to see if Brogan could play at some point. It didn't even bother him all that much when Fegel made it a point to give his new acquisition a big hug in the post-game locker room. Jack was so happy he didn't even bother to remind Fegel to pick up and wash Billy's jock, although the thought did cross his mind.

Stark was solid throughout the game but no play was bigger than the hit he had put on the Brawlers' tight end. It was a game changer that had torn the heart out of Pittsburgh – exactly the type of play they had envisioned when drafting the young franchise linebacker.

Because it was the Sunday Night Football game, the entire league had the opportunity to watch the Blizzard dismantle the defending World Champions, without the services of star running back Earl "the Pearl" Johnson, no less. Buffalo would not be sneaking up on anybody after this performance, especially next week's divisional opponent, the New York Rough Riders.

# Chapter Eleven

Gerry Wainscott was settling comfortably into her new role as co-owner of the Buffalo Blizzard. However, it wasn't official yet; she was in an interim, trial period. Her father didn't want to force his football team down his only child's throat. He insisted she be certain it was what she truly wanted; that she understood exactly what she was getting herself into. The length of the trial period was indefinite but Gerry could make it official anytime she felt ready. They would get together for a review and evaluation monthly to see how things were progressing. The paperwork had been filed with the NAFA offices, but she had yet to sign the final documents sealing the deal.

Her father, whose main residence was in Cleveland, had stayed in town after the scintillating victory over Pittsburgh to meet with her that very morning. Gerry was preparing for their meeting by reviewing her notes from the past few weeks when Donald Fegel knocked on her open office door.

"Come in," she said.

"Hey," Donald said.

He popped through the doorway in his energetic way. She could see why her father liked the man. He could be quite charming and he was incredibly committed to his job and to her father. He had boundless energy and enthusiasm for all things relating to the Blizzard. But she had also seen glimpses of his darker side, especially when it came to Jack Driftwood. Someday she planned to find out why the two men could not stand one another.

"Hello, Donald," she said, "you seem awfully chipper today."

"Beating Pittsburgh on national TV will do that for a man," he replied with the warmest smile he could muster.

He wasn't utterly unattractive, Gerry decided, though he was kind of average and unnoticeable physically in a lot of ways. He had been sporting a bit of a gut back at training camp but she noticed he had melted some of that away. He wasn't tall, just five foot eight, but he had an air of importance about him, albeit self-importance. His short black hair was always meticulously combed over and he held his chin high, perhaps to overcome his lack of height in this world of giant men. Otherwise, he had a pretty bland, featureless face except for the eyes. They were dark and intense and would get beady, almost rat-like, when he got angry. Conversely, they carried a notable gleam when he was excited. He also had a tendency to furrow his brow and clamp his lips in an unflattering way when lost in thought. But today the man was nothing but smiles.

"Donald, that was so exciting! I never expected to get that kind of rush from watching a football game," she said. "I have to tell you, I've never seen my father so proud and happy."

Donald clumsily held up his hand for a high-five. He wanted to touch her in any way possible and he figured this was his best chance. She slapped his hand pretty good, though nothing like Leroy Clarkson. Still, he relished the sting.

"Hopefully we will have many more such experiences together. But I just stopped by to see if there was anything I could do for you or answer any questions you may have before you meet with Mr. Wainscott. Personally, I think you are doing a great job learning this business and making everyone feel so comfortable. You really fit in well here, you know." The color rose in his cheeks as he spoke.

Gerry noticed and was touched. "That is so sweet of you to say, Donald," she said and instinctively put her hand on his arm. "Everyone has been so nice and welcoming to me, especially you. I appreciate it very much. As far as meeting with my father, I think I have everything under control right now but thank you for the offer."

"Roger that," he said with a military salute. "Well, enjoy your meeting and I will see you at lunch." He smiled his best smile and turned and left the room.

*That was kind of weird,* she thought, but then found herself smiling as well.

Donald had never come on to her before but she felt like he was on the verge of taking it up a notch just then. He was an interesting little man, for sure. He had been nothing but chivalrous towards her but maybe that was about to change. That would be …interesting.

Gerald Wainscott III was in a euphoric mood. He had just gotten off of the phone with the NAFA Commissioner, Bob Goldman, who had called to congratulate him on the big win over Pittsburgh. The only negative was Goldman's complaints about the incident concerning the cups of beer tossed onto the field during the game. He had scolded Gerald, reminding him the NAFA was bringing their sacred Mega Bowl 50 celebration to Buffalo and could not afford any such hooliganism disrupting the game.

But even that had not dampened his spirits. He simply assured the Commissioner nothing of the sort would happen in the Mega Bowl and chided the young upstart regarding the way the game had been officiated, warning him that with such poor officiating they were all fortunate nothing worse occurred. In the end, Gerald agreed to take any and all necessary measures to ensure nothing of that nature would happen at the Wigwam again.

Still, Gerald could not remember the last time a NAFA Commissioner had called to congratulate him on a big win. He knew he didn't have many seasons left and felt strongly the Lord was blessing him one last time in his old age with such a great start to the season. He was extremely thankful and had strong faith this year was destined to be a special one. It meant the world to him his daughter was there to enjoy it with him. He was even more thankful when she walked into his office.

"There she is," he said, "the proud new owner of the Buffalo Blizzard."

"That would be the undefeated Buffalo Blizzard," she replied and came around the desk to give her old man a kiss on the cheek.

"How about that?" he said, "I was just thinking of how blessed I am."

"You mean how blessed *we* are."

"Yes. So tell me, what do you think at this point? Are you enjoying yourself?"

"Very much so. I really like all of the people here in the office. Everyone has been so nice to me and I love the players, they are a great bunch of guys. However, I must say I'm a little surprised at the complexity of the business side to football – there's a lot more to it than I anticipated."

"I am so gratified to hear you say that, Gerry. But I must remind you it is still very early in this process. You have yet to experience your first loss, dear. I must warn you, one thing I have learned over the years is a loss hurts a hell of a lot more than a win feels good. Does that make any sense?"

"I suppose."

She made herself comfortable sitting in a chair across from her father. She recalled the days when, as a little girl, she would pull her chair up next to him behind his desk and do her homework. She had always figured she would be back in that office one day.

"I know what you are saying but you sound so grave and serious. Can't we just enjoy the winning for now? I'm sure I will experience losing for myself at some point."

"Well, let's hope that doesn't happen too soon."

"Or too often."

"God forbid," he said. "My spies tell me you hardly ever leave this place, young lady, that you are burning the midnight oil. I know how consuming this business can be, believe me. Let me caution you to make sure you take some time for yourself. You need to strike a balance or this place can chew you up and spit you back out. I've seen it too many times where people burned themselves out over the years. You need to go out on the town, meet some people your own age, loosen up and have some fun."

It was true, she had been so completely consumed trying to get up to speed and there was still so much she didn't know. She hadn't taken a single day off since arriving back in August.

"Are you telling me to get a life, Dad?"

Gerald laughed. "I suppose I am, sweetheart."

"I will take some time, I promise. But you know how it is being the greenhorn. I want to catch up as soon as I can."

"Good! That's my girl."

They continued their talk for a while longer discussing some of the specifics of things Gerry was working on. Currently she was spending much of her time shadowing Donald Fegel, learning the day-to-day mechanics of running the team. She was also studying the NAFA's new collective bargaining agreement with the Player's Association. Upon mastering that tedious document, she was to work hand in hand with David Sullenberger. Sully was going to give her a crash-course on the extreme complexity and inner workings of the NAFA salary cap. She felt like she was back in school. Fortunately, Gerry had always liked school and found most of the work interesting, which was a good sign both to her and her father.

She found what she loved most about the business thus far was the games themselves. She was beginning to comprehend her father's passion and pride while the Blizzard was on the playing field going to war each weekend. She saw what the team meant to the city first hand at the game the previous Sunday night as she walked the concourses of the Wigwam and mingled with the masses during the contest. It had affected her deeply. The exhilaration of providing such an outlet of intense passion and object of such fierce pride for the community had struck a deep chord within her very being. In her mind she had compared it to motherhood, although she had yet to experience that particular joy.

At the age of thirty-eight, she knew her biological clock was ticking. It was beginning to become a concern to her. Although many women her age and even older were having kids, she wondered if and when she would have a family of her own. She had been so close to having all of those things a scant two years ago before the tragic death of her fiancé turned her world upside down. Though she had mostly recovered, it still left her wondering if the dreams of having a family had died with him. In her heart she still wanted all of that but felt no urge to do anything drastic just yet. However, one thing was for certain, there was an abundance of good-looking, strong, smart and passionate single men in the world of professional football. Experience told her she couldn't force it, so for now, anyways, she was content to let things play out as they may.

But her dad was right. She did need a night out on the town.

# Chapter Twelve

His cell phone beeped shortly after midnight, barely moments after Jack had turned out the lights to try to catch some ZZZ's. He had popped a couple of Norco, compliments of Blizzard trainer Alvin Kaplan, half an hour earlier and was lying in bed waiting for the wave of relief to wash over him so he could get a decent night's sleep. His body was still sore and beat up from the previous night's game. Thank God he had the next day off, he needed it to heal up enough to be able to function in practice come Wednesday. Jack had snapped the pills in half before ingesting them. He had been told this practice sped up the effects of the magic medicine, though he noticed no perceptible difference himself. Still, it didn't stop him and it had now become a habit.

A flood of good feeling began to hit him, making the pain in his neck and left shoulder melt into the background like a TV left on while sleeping. His mind was alive and awake and he felt energized. He thought about ignoring the beep of the phone but figured what the hell, he was beginning to feel pretty good and there was little sense sleeping through a good buzz. Besides, he was curious as to what thoughtless bastard had the balls to text him at such an hour.

He checked his phone. The text was from Chaz Davenport, a thoughtless bastard if he had ever met one.

**Good game. I hate Tittsburg. Got yer chickens in da coop. Call me ASAP.**

*Shit, this ain't nothing but trouble,* he thought as he hit the callback button.

Chaz answered on the first ring. "Hey, dickwood, I got a little surprise for you. Meet me at the boat. I'll be waiting. Heh-heh-heh."

Chaz hung up before giving Jack a chance to decline, let alone protest. Jack had met Chaz at his first fan club party fifteen years prior. Early in his career Jack was a bit of a free spirit, to put it mildly. He would often attend parties at the house of an old hippie named Larry Blake in the city by the Buffalo Zoo off of Parkside Avenue.

You could score anything you wanted at Larry's place and Driftwood went there to buy his weed and anything else he may have been hankering for back in the day. The regulars who hung out at Larry's house started calling themselves the Driftwoodies in Jack's honor and threw a couple of major blowout parties for him every year.

The thing took on a life of its own and the bashes began to attract a growing number of mainstream Blizzard fans. They organized, put together a website, and the official Jack Driftwood Fan Club, aptly dubbed "The Driftwoodies," was hatched.

Jack had quit smoking weed nine years earlier after he rolled his car while rolling a joint. That was the first time Chaz had gotten him out of a big jam. He called Chaz immediately after flipping his '97 Mercury Cougar into a ditch on a country road somewhere near Gowanda. It happened during the fall when he was hauling a trunk full of freshly harvested, halfway decent homegrown up to Larry's house as a favor. He was pissed he had taken a wrong turn and spun gravel doing a U-turn when the next thing he knew he was upside down, strapped into his car in a ditch layered with concrete slabs. If he hadn't been wearing his seatbelt he may not have survived the accident. One of the concrete slabs had caved in the roof on the driver's side to within an inch of his head.

Chaz had a man at the scene to pick him up five minutes after receiving the call. Shortly after that a tow truck showed up to yank his car out of the ditch and bring it to a local junk yard, minus the contraband. The car was totaled, but Jack escaped unscathed without so much as a scratch or a traffic ticket. He considered it one of the best things to ever happen to him. It woke him up to some harsh realities, and he had been clean ever since. He still hung out at Larry's on occasion and attended several Driftwoodies' events every year but kept his nose clean.

Jack wasn't sure what Chaz was up to this time. He was all but sure it involved Earl Johnson's attackers, though. Chaz wasn't one to call in the middle of the night demanding an appearance for nothing. Of that he was sure. Jack couldn't afford to get dragged into anything that would jeopardize his status with the Blizzard. He was already skating on thin ice with Fegel and this whole Earl the Pearl incident hadn't helped matters. Perhaps calling in reinforcements would be a good idea. After debating with himself while he got dressed, he decided to make the call before heading up to North Tonawanda and Chaz's boat.

He punched up Vinny Cappolla on his cell. He had spoken with Vinny about Earl on Friday morning but had yet to hear back from the Buffalo Detective. Vinny was among the most bitter people Jack had ever met. He was 350 pounds of fat and nasty. Constantly spewing pessimistic venom, punctuated with vulgar oaths in every direction, was how the big man rolled. Despite all of the snarky negativity coming from Vinny, Jack had discovered under all the bitching and blustering lay a heart of gold. Most of the bile from Vinny was satirical commentary on the sick, twisted world with which he dealt on a daily basis on the mean streets of Buffalo. Jack got it and thought it was funny as hell.

Jack figured Vinny would be up and roaming those streets in his Crown Vic; Vinny believed in working while the criminals were working. He also rightly claimed there were infinitely less stupid people around to aggravate him in the middle of the night. But that didn't mean it never happened.

"What the fuck do you want, Driftwood?" Vinny asked upon answering.

"Did you get one of your teammates beat up again?"

"Hey, Vinny, nice to hear from you, too. What donut shop you guarding right now?"

"Very funny, asshole. For your information, I'm a humble public servant trying to protect the town from dangerous dirtbags like you."

"Well, I may actually need your protection. We off the record here?"

"Is a bear Catholic?"

"Listen, are you still working the Earl Johnson case?"

"Yep, and the trail is as cold as my old lady's ass."

"Ouch! Give Beverly my regards. You remember my buddy Chaz Davenport?

"Yeah, isn't he the psycho I like who lives in that bunker out east?" Vinny asked.

"That's the one. I called him about the Earl Johnson thing and he just called me back asking me to meet him at his boat docked at the Smith Boys Marina up in North Tonawanda. He texted me something about the chickens being in the coop. I think the bat-shit bastard caught your boys."

"Excellent! I need some fucking action, been a slow night. Go on up there and see if he has those pathetic pieces of human garbage. If he does, call me back on a secure line. If you can escort those pricks into my jurisdiction I will gladly take care of the rest."

"Will do, chief," Jack said.

"Don't call me chief, I just fucking told you I'm a humble public servant who works for a living. I don't—"

"Whatever," Jack hung up but Vinny continued his tirade for quite some time before realizing his buddy had clicked off.

Jack jumped into his Jeep Rubicon and snaked his way through downtown to the 33 on his way up to North Tonawanda. He figured it would take him just shy of half an hour to reach the marina. He had been on Chaz's boat on two previous occasions; one a pleasant, day-long cruise featuring drinking and fishing out on the Niagara River, the other a short test ride after Chaz had been working on one of the engines.

The boat was a classic 1969 Chris-Craft Cavalier with original twin 327 cubic-inch Corvette engines. The thirty-footer had been totally restored to its original form and was in mint condition. Chaz had named her "NotyerBidness." And he meant it.

Once on the island of North Tonawanda, Jack pulled off of River Road and into the parking lot of Smith Boys Marina. The lights were on in the 'Bidness but the drapes of the cabin were closed. Otherwise the Marina was dark and quiet as you might expect in the middle of the night.

Chaz jumped off the boat and onto the narrow cement slab dock and waddled up to meet his guest. He was a block of a man, seemingly as wide as he was tall. He wore thick, black framed, boxy-looking glasses and his long, reddish-brown hair was pulled back into a ponytail, serving to highlight his receding hairline. He looked like Ben Franklin on steroids. For a man a ways into his sixties, Chaz was in remarkable shape.

He stuck out a beefy mitt to shake Jack's hand and pulled him in for a heartfelt man-hug. The guy reminded Jack of a bear. Ironically, one of the Jack's favorite Chaz stories was from the time he had actually wrestled a bear and pinned it at a Sportsman show some thirty years ago. The 638-pound black bear by the name of Sampson had only been pinned three other times in its ten-year wrestling career. Those other three losses occurred against the same woman who, after a good sniffing session from Sampson, seduced the hairy beast to lie down with her. Oh, the power of such a thing! Fortunately for all, especially Sampson, Chaz had deployed a different strategy in pinning the beast. Noting the irony, Chaz had wrapped Sampson in a bear-hug and pinned him flat on his back. The animal had strangely submitted once prone on its backside and laid docilely while licking Chaz's head with its raspy tongue.

"Hey, Jack," Chaz greeted. "You're looking good, brother. Great game Sunday night! Thanks for the tickets, I was right behind the Tittsburgh bench and doused those pricks with beer."

"Figures you would be in the middle of that," Jack said. "You cost us fifteen fuckin' yards."

"Well, I am sorry about that. But it was great. Hee-hee. But I got something even better for you back there in the 'Bidness," Chaz said, hooking a thumb over his shoulder towards the boat.

"What might that be, Chaz?"

Chaz, as was his habit when he got overly excited, rubbed his hands together in front of him as if to warm them over a fire. He could barely contain himself and unabashedly giggled.

"C'mon, I'll show you."

Jack followed Chaz back to the boat but before stepping onto the craft he stopped cold in his tracks. "Permission to come aboard, sir?"

"Permission granted," Chaz replied.

Now they both giggled. Jack had done this routine with Chaz each time before boarding the 'Bidness and Chaz got a big kick out of it every time. He took it as intended, as a show of respect.

The door to the cabin below was closed and Chaz had to turn slightly sideways to fit down three steps to pop it open. Driftwood followed closely behind and was not surprised in the least to see two men bound, blindfolded, and gagged, stuffed into the sleeping quarters at the bow of the 'Bidness.

Driftwood recognized the men right away and strode to the front of the boat and kicked the one closest to him fairly hard, square in the ass.

"That was for Earl you piece of shit," he snarled. "I ought to put the boots to both you country-ass fuckups."

"Help yourself," Chaz said, "although I already took the liberty of administering some behavior modification techniques. Of course, I didn't leave any marks. That would be crass and unprofessional."

"Right," Jack said.

"So, I got the chickens, you got a plan?"

"As a matter of fact, I do. Fire this bad boy up, I've never seen anyone go over Niagara Falls without a barrel."

Their two captives started trying to holler through their gags and roll around in the bunk. Chaz grabbed a Taser out of his fishing vest and pulled the trigger, striking a life jacket hanging above their detainees.

"You boys had better settle down or Uncle Chaz is gonna singe the hair on your tiny, little balls."

They immediately went silent, making Jack think it wouldn't be the first time Uncle Chaz delivered on such a threat.

Chaz fired up the twin Corvette engines while Driftwood cast off the lines. Jack helped guide them away from the dock with a long tethering pole and at the last minute hopped back aboard the 'Bidness as the bow cleared the end of the dock. The Norco was in full force and Jack was pain free and felt like he could climb a tree for the first time since late Sunday night. They headed out of the marina and into the open waters of the Niagara, south toward the city.

"So, you gonna tell me where and how you caught those bastards?"

"Nah, I don't think that is such a good idea. Perhaps another time," Chaz answered.

"Yeah, that's what I thought you'd say, but it was worth a shot. Regardless, I just want to say thanks, Chaz. This means a shitload to a lot of people."

"Means a shitload to me too, pards. Earl is good people, not to mention he's on my fantasy team. Picked up Petrucci though, so I kicked ass this week."

"Wow, I'm *really* glad to hear that," Jack said.

Chaz laughed it off and dug a satellite phone out of an old army bag. The phone was high tech with a scrambled signal so Jack could make an untraceable, anonymous call to anywhere in the world.

Jack grabbed the phone and dialed up Vinny Cappolla.

"Hey, pork chop," Jack said.

"Speaking."

"I got a package for you. I am going to deliver it by sea."

"Goodie! Where?"

"You know the dock by the old Huron Cement Factory where they used to bring in the sand?"

"Does the Pope shit in the woods?"

"Don't get funny. I will leave the chickens handcuffed to the silo in exactly one hour. I'll call you when the chickens are in the coop."

"Will I see you there?" Vinny asked.

"Nah, no need for that. It's probably not a good idea," Jack replied.

"True that."

"Bring in the fuckin' cavalry if you want, but give me an hour. You're gonna be a goddamn hero, big guy."

"I already am a goddamn hero and don't you forget it, dipshit. How many times—"

"Whatever," Jack said and punched off of the call. A silly smile came to his face as he handed the satellite phone back to Chaz.

"What?" Chaz asked.

"Every conversation I have with that dude ends up with me saying 'whatever,' and hanging up while dumb fuck keeps on bitching. I guarantee he is still going off right now like some Chris Farley character."

"That's a good friend there, pards. Although, I never really cared all that much for the fat fuck myself." They both busted out laughing. "Well, let's us just see if this old girl can still get up and go."

Chaz shut off the 'Bidness' running lights and put the hammer down, sliding both throttles to nearly full power. The bow of the boat came out of the water and it soon planed out very nicely. They were cruising now. It wasn't long and the moonlit Buffalo Skyline came into view. It took forty-five minutes to reach the docks, which Chaz claimed as an all-time best.

While Jack tied off the 'Bidness, Chaz fished into his bag again and pulled out a Glock before heading below decks to retrieve their passengers. They herded the chickens off the boat and walked them up to a pair of silos near the old cement factory.

"Now, I got a fucking gun on you boys and you both know from personal experience that Uncle Chaz don't lie. So don't do anything stupid and keep your mouths shut or I'll pump hot lead into your hindquarters."

Upon reaching the silos, Chaz pulled a pair of leg irons out of his vest while Driftwood kept the Glock trained on their captives. He found an iron loop protruding out of one of the silos and ran the chain through the loop and slapped the cuffs on a leg of each of their captives.

"Fuckers will have to gnaw off a foot to get out of these," he said to Jack before turning his attention back to the chickens chained to the silo. "Here's your story, boys. You never saw me or my partner here. Never heard of neither of us.

You were sneaking through this place when Detective Cappolla, who will be along in just a minute, found you and arrested you. Now Uncle Chaz has ears and eyes everywhere, including on the inside. How do you think I found you pussies in the first place? Think about that for a second. Now if I catch wind of either of you breathing one fucking word other than what I just told you, consider yourself a dead man. Do we have an understanding?"

The two men were still gagged and looked at each other, then back at Chaz, nodding.

"Are we sure?" Chaz asked, pulling out the Taser and pointing it at them. They nodded again, this time with infinitely more vigor.

"There we go, that's more like it. I knew you boys weren't that dumb."

After checking the leg irons again Chaz grunted his satisfaction. He took the Glock back from Jack and they both took off running for the boat, laughing all the while like a pair of mischievous kids who had just pulled off the perfect late-night prank.

They boarded the 'Bidness, shoved off, and headed back down the Niagara, going north with the current on their return trip. Jack called Vinny back to tell him his chickens were in the coop and to relay Chaz's story and make sure he reiterated it to his new captives.

After wrapping up the call, Jack took the helm while Chaz went below deck to dig up some refreshments. He returned shortly with a small cooler stocked with ice-cold beer and some bags of chips. They had a much more leisurely trip back up to North Tonawanda, laughing and telling old war stories the whole way home.

Detective Cappolla called in a couple of black and whites after finding the package chained to the silos just a few minutes after Jack's call. Vinny took no chances and had been parked on Fuhrman Boulevard watching Jack and Chaz bring the scum off the boat through his high-powered night-vision field glasses. He had even pulled the throwaway .22 caliber pistol from his sock holster just in case something went awry. He had kept his official issue Glock model 19 holstered.

After twenty-five years on the force, Vinny was old school to the bone. He had seen too many operations go to shit over the course of his career and never took anything for granted. He was prepared to do whatever it took to get the job done. After all, he was just a humble public servant doing his best to protect and serve.

And Jack was right, Vinny Cappolla *was* a goddamn hero. His picture was plastered all over the internet and in the Buffalo News as the officer who single-handedly collared the two most wanted men in Western New York. Another example of Buffalo's finest, at their finest.

# Chapter Thirteen

The New York Rough Riders shuffled off to Buffalo with a well-deserved 0-2 record and had managed a meager 13 points total in their first two games, combined. Their defense had allowed the second most points in the league, to boot. The wise guys had the Blizzard as 15-point favorites, the largest spread in the young NAFA season thus far. These facts had made Howard Ivy a nervous wreck all week long. He'd seen too many upsets in his day and spent most of the week trying to convince anyone who would listen, and especially those who wouldn't, that New York was not that bad. Nobody seemed to be taking him seriously, which had the old coach frustrated and dumbfounded. That's why he had let his team hear it one more time before they took the field at the Wigwam that Sunday, and still nobody listened.

*This is professional football, why don't people believe you can lose on any given Sunday? Why the hell do they think it's a cliché – because it's true!*

There was another sellout crowd on hand at the Wigwam under unseasonably hot and humid conditions. The September sun was having its last hurrah and blazed through the open roof of the Wigwam. Unfortunately for the Blizzard, the only thing hotter than the weather was the Rough Riders. New York came out firing, playing loose like they had nothing to lose. They took advantage of a couple of early Buffalo turnovers and jumped up to a 10-0 first-quarter lead. Buffalo finally got things going on offense when Brady hit Shady Solomon for a long pass to set up a Petrucci touchdown run early in the second quarter. They trailed 10-7, and the Stallion's touchdown had momentarily gotten the crowd fired up and back into the game.

But the Buffalo defense was still a little flat and seemed one step behind New York. Donovan Billups, the Rough Riders' first-round draft pick from the previous April, was making his first start at quarterback. Billups was as quick as a hiccup and Buffalo's front seven were getting embarrassed trying to keep him contained. It was putting Coach Faber's normally rock solid game-day patience to the ultimate test.

New York was facing a 3rd and 12 at midfield. Rather than sit back in zone and make the fledgling QB check it down underneath so they could make the tackle and force the punt, Coach Faber's frustration led to him be aggressive. He dialed up an all-out blitz with tight man-to-man coverage in the back end. He knew Billups would check to quick passes and would likely be a sitting duck with nowhere to go with the ball. The kid would become just another sad victim of a

Blizzard jailbreak. They needed a spark and Coach Faber was bent on forcing the issue by cranking up the pressure. He did hedge his bet by putting Steven Stark in a spy technique. This put Stark on Billups, and if the QB were to evade the rush and scramble, Stark was charged with cleaning up the mess. It was about as good a match up as Coach Faber could make; but it wasn't good enough.

Billups saw the tight coverage and stepped up into a pocket thick with unfriendly traffic. By all appearances he was trapped, but at the last instant he ducked inside and under the big swinging arm of Bo-Bo Karpinski and squirted past him toward the line of scrimmage. Stark had been tracking Billups from behind the line and stepped up into the hole where Billups was supposed to emerge. But the QB never showed. Somehow he had hopped backwards out of the hole and skipped sideways and shot through the seam behind the pile where Stark had been. Stark had over committed and was now walled off from the slick rookie QB, who slashed past him into the open field. Driftwood was next in line to be humiliated and did not disappoint.

Driftwood came in on an outside-in angle and was taking his best shot. He knew if he tried to break down, come to balance, and then try to close the deal, Billups would just laugh and run away from him. His only chance was a calculated full speed intercept. He closed like a heat-seeking missile. Billups looked Driftwood in the eye briefly, holding his gaze for just a tic and then looked beyond Jack to the next level.

*Shit! Not again.*

It had been Driftwood's experience when a back stopped looking at him in the open field it meant the guy already had him beat. He closed another step and then launched. Initially, he thought he had gotten enough contact on the slippery bastard, but Billups proved to be quicker and stronger than Driftwood had credited him. Billups pulled up, swatted Driftwood on past him, and set off back down the field in search of his next victims. When the smoke all cleared the New York rookie QB had covered the full 50 yards to the end zone, breaking six tackles along the way, one for each point he had just scored.

Coach Faber rarely got angry during the course of a ball game; it was one of the many reasons Driftwood loved to play for the man. Sure, he would ride your ass at times, mostly during the week, but come game day Lester Faber was his biggest supporter, his number one fan. But when Coach Faber did blow up, he blew up big, akin to Mount Vesuvius. The veteran players knew this all too well, having experienced an eruption or two in their day. But the young guys were about to get their first introduction to the rarity of Coach Faber's game-day wrath.

The Blizzard appeared lifeless as they trudged up the tunnel under a shower of resounding boos, trailing the Rough Riders 17-7 at halftime. The usual halftime routine saw the coaches get together to review the first half and strategize for the first few minutes while the players took care of personal issues such as using the restroom, getting re-taped, or changing their undershirts. After that the players would gather in assigned areas with their position coaches for the specific implementation of any halftime adjustments. Then the team gathered by units – offense and defense – as the coordinators would have their say to their respective divisions before the whole team would gather up for Coach Ivy to address them, en masse. However, that was not to be the routine on this day, at least not for the defense.

Coach Faber barged into the locker room like a charging buffalo. "I want all you cocksuckers who are supposedly playing defense to get your goddamn asses into the meeting room, right fucking now!"

Driftwood leaned in close to Stark and Brogan. "Holy shit, nine years and I ain't never seen Lester this hot."

All the defensive players quickly and quietly hustled ass to their meeting room just down the hall from the locker room. They were still getting settled in when Coach Faber bulled his way through the door.

"What the fuck is going on out there! You guys are letting a goddamn rookie quarterback chew you up and spit you out. I've never seen such bullshit tackling. You gotta do your job out there. If you have contain on the son of a bitch, then contain the son of a bitch! If you are spying the cocksucker, then spy the cocksucker. We got no fire out there. You all thought we were playing a shitty team so we can go fuck around. Well, it ain't about *who* you play. It's about you and how *you* fucking play. We play to a goddamn standard and so far I wouldn't piss on the best part of what we did, even if it *was* on fire."

The room was deadly silent as the coach scowled and glared around the room from player to player, almost daring them to say something. Suddenly, a cell phone rang, breaking the silence.

*I feel sorry for the poor bastard who owns that phone,* Driftwood thought, instinctively patting his hips for his own phone.

Coach Faber seemed stunned for an instant like he had been hit by a surprise left. He snapped back to attention and searched wide-eyed around the room for the source of the ring. Quickly, however, he recognized his ringtone and the fact it was emanating from his own jacket pocket. He had forgotten to take the thing out.

He dug the little device out and hurled it as hard as he could against the wall. The phone blew up upon impact with little pieces flying all over the place. The bulk of it landed in a trash can stationed directly below the impact point. Nobody dared to laugh, although later they would roll as it would become an all-time favorite Coach Faber story.

"Goddamn thing," he said. But the spell was broken and the moment lost as the air had been taken out of his rage. "Start playing some fucking football, will you?"

With that he wheeled and shuffled back out of the room totally deflated. It was quiet for another moment as the specter of the tongue-lashing weighed on their hearts and minds. "*Start playing some fucking football.*" Coach Faber sure knew how to cut straight to the heart of the matter.

Driftwood spoke up, breaking the hush. "Coach is right, guys, I don't know what that shit was, but it wasn't fuckin' football. We gotta pick this shit up right now."

"Damn straight, Drifty," Leroy Clarkson said. "Bring your shit up in here!"

Leroy raised his hand up in the air and the rest of the team scrambled to gather around him and reached their hands on high as well.

"That wasn't us, y'all know Coach Faber is right. Yeah, these is the dog-ass Rough Riders we playin'. But we still gotta play! Now let's get our shit straight. All we gotta do is play us some ball. Gimme a 'Yeah, baby' on three. One, two, three…"

"Yeah, baby!"

They emerged from the meeting room with a new hop to their step and by all appearances were finally ready to play Blizzard football. The air begin to fill with encouragements that soon built into a collective intensity. Driftwood felt his temperature go up a few degrees. Even Stark was affected by the emotion in the room as he punched Driftwood in the arm and gave him a nod.

That got Driftwood even more stoked. "We gonna have us some fun this second half!"

The rest of the team felt the surge of energy now palpable from the defense. The infectious nature of the renewed enthusiasm cranked up the locker room buzz.

When Coach Ivy entered the room amidst the yelling and shouting he immediately recognized his football team – the one that had been AWOL – was back in the fold and ready to do work. Any long-winded rah-rah speech would have been redundant at that point. He kept his remarks short and sweet.

"Well, it's nice to see the imposters have departed and the authentic Blizzard has finally appeared. Welcome back, gentlemen, now let's go play some football."

Buffalo was an entirely different football team in the second half. On the first play from scrimmage, Coach Faber, intending to capitalize on their revived intensity, again called for an all-out Zero blitz. The Rough Riders were expecting Buffalo to lay back in zone coverage to help corral the run and thought they could fool them with a play-action pass – not a good idea.

The nascent QB, Billups, failed to recognize the subtle, pre-snap movement of the Buffalo defense as they crept closer and jumped the snap. Driftwood timed it perfectly and shot untouched through the backside A-gap between the guard and center. He had a direct path to Billups and this time the youngster had nowhere to go. Driftwood hit him so hard he watched the kid's eyes roll back up into his skull. Stark, who had looped around behind Driftwood, scooped up the resulting fumble and waltzed into the end zone for a defensive touchdown. The tide had turned.

Leroy Clarkson was first to reach Stark. He kept screaming "Yeah, baby" at the top of his lungs while pounding on Stark's shoulder pads. The rest of the defense arrived and, along with the crowd, were also going nuts. Bo-Bo was late to the party but made quite an entrance. He resembled a perfectly rolled bowling ball hitting the pocket as he barreled into the mass of players. It was a strike as the entire pile – seven men total – blew up like bowling pins clattering to the ground. By the time everybody got back up and laughed their way to the sidelines, Buffalo had drawn a flag for excessive celebration. Coach Ivy didn't even care; he was leading the cheers, overjoyed at seeing his team roar back to life.

Stark wouldn't let go of the football even when he got to the bench. The head equipment man, Danny Steeley, was trying to wrest it from the rookie's grasp to put it in a trunk for safe keeping, but Stark wouldn't let it go.

"Give him the damn ball, you douche," Driftwood said. "He'll lock it away and you can get it later."

"I scored a touchdown," Stark sang completely off tune. He cradled the ball like a newborn baby and kissed it before releasing the pigskin into the custody of Steeley.

"Thanks to me," Driftwood said.

"Whatever, dude," Stark replied. "I'm the beautiful son of a bitch who scored six."

Coach Faber came to the bench where they had settled and was infinitely happier. "Now that's what I am talking about," he said and slapped them both on the head.

"You know," Driftwood said, "in all of my seventeen-plus years, I have never scored a touchdown."

"That's because you ain't as good as me. I got one in only my third game. You must really suck."

That brought about a round of laughter and Buffalo continued laughing the rest of the afternoon as they pounded the Rough Riders by a final count of 37-17. New York didn't cross midfield the entire second half and managed a paltry 56 yards of total offense. Brady threw four touchdown passes and the Stallion ran for another 134 yards. More importantly, the Blizzard stayed unbeaten and ran their record to 3-0.

Even though they weren't even a quarter of the way through the regular season, the town was coming down with Mega Bowl fever. Everybody was well aware the host team had never, in the history of the NAFA, played in a Mega Bowl. Blizzard fans could already taste it, despite the fact they hadn't even been to the playoffs in sixteen years. Man, did it taste good! It was time to get on board because the Buffalo bandwagon was filing up fast.

# Chapter Fourteen

Blackjack was Jack Driftwood's game. He didn't play all that often because he knew the odds would catch up and it would ultimately be tantamount to giving away his hard-earned money. At what point do you just write a check to the Seneca Nation and call it a day? He wasn't any more superstitious than the next guy and didn't really have a system. It was a "feel" thing with him. And when the feeling hit, he would tidy up, slide into one of his designer suits, and call his favorite talisman, Cheese, and together they would head to the casino to do work.

Occasionally Jack would go with a group of guys, but that was a totally different animal. He wouldn't get dressed up or play at the high stake's tables when he was out with the boys. Those impromptu occasions were always of a social nature – have a few drinks, eyeball the ladies, play a bunch of different games and so on.

But when Jack got the "feeling" the shit got serious. And on this particular Wednesday night, the shit was about to get gravely serious. The big dog was ready to eat. Jack figured the stars had aligned, putting him on a bit of a roll. The Blizzard was off to a 3-0 start, he was healthy and playing well, and he had just helped apprehend the scumbags who had beaten up Earl Johnson. Adding it all up, he arrived at the conclusion it was time to hit the tables. When you're hot, you're hot. And maybe after the tables it was time to try his hand with the ladies somewhere. It was shaping up to be a pretty good Wednesday evening.

Plus, he genuinely had the feeling. This was not something he was trying to force; it was legit, deep down in his bones. At least that is what he had allowed himself to believe as he dialed up his close friend Cheese.

He had met Joseppi "Cheese" Barcheezzi some fifteen years ago while waiting to tee off at a local, municipal golf course. The man was in a hot argument with the starter about who was up next on the tee box. The course had a first come, first served policy and didn't take tee times. Cheese had been in line but had to literally run to make one of his frequent emergency bathroom stops. When he returned, the starter had put several other groups in front of him despite the fact his turn had not come up yet. The conflict almost came to blows until Jack, who was up next, stepped in and suggested Cheese and his partner join his twosome. Disaster was averted and a friendship was born.

Cheese was a lifelong resident of Buffalo. He may or may not have had ties to the local mob; Jack was smart enough not to ask too many questions. He wasn't exactly sure what Cheese did for a living and never bothered to ask. One thing he did know, however, was whenever he needed a golf buddy, a high-stakes gambling partner, or anything, for that matter, Cheese was always available. This Wednesday night being no exception.

"Chee-ee-eese," Jack said.

"How you doin', Jackie-boy? I know you got that feeling!"

"Damn straight I do."

"That's exactly what I was thinking! What time you want me to pick you up?"

"Scoop me around eight, we'll go get some dinner at Frankie's before we clean house," Jack said. "I've got to watch a little film first and study these Baltimore pricks' tendencies, you know, put my time in."

"Perfect, I'll see you at eight."

Jack settled comfortably into his home office to do his homework. He couldn't have been happier with his new digs. He had sold his home in Orchard Park six months prior and moved downtown to be close to the Wigwam and back in the city. His loft took up a quarter of the seventh and top floor of a renovated warehouse off of South Park Street, a couple of blocks east of Michigan Avenue. There were great views of Lake Erie and the Wigwam to the south and west. His building was on the outskirts of the new Casino District and he loved the booming vivacity emerging in the area.

The structure inherited original twelve-foot ceilings and had been partitioned into six main rooms. There was an entry way, three bedrooms – each with its own full bathroom – a laundry room with another full bathroom, and his private den. The rest of the floor plan was completely open, containing the kitchen, dining room, and living room. The far end of the living room featured a pool table and bar. All combined his living space was well over twenty-five hundred square feet. It was the quintessential bachelor pad.

Time flew as Jack studied his scouting report on the Baltimore Avengers and watched a cut-up video of their offense culled from their first three games. Buffalo hadn't played the Avengers in a couple of years, thus Jack was not as familiar with their attack as he would have preferred. He was trying to close the information gap with extra study. The Avengers had steamrolled to a 3-0 start themselves and would not be an easy out, particularly at their place.

He was ready to roll when Cheese showed up a little before eight o'clock. Cheese let himself in and let out a low whistle when he saw Jack.

"Nice threads, Pisano," he said.

"Not too, shabby, eh?"

Driftwood shuffled his feet in a little Bo Jangles-like tap dance move. His charcoal jacket and slacks were accented with a black dress shirt and a hot, almost neon pink necktie and handkerchief. Jack was a bit of a clothes horse and when the occasion called for it, he could dress with the best. He bought his suits from a friend in the business in New York City who always had the latest cuts. This little number was custom tailored, fresh off a boat from Italy and had set him back fifteen hundred.

"Where to, *capo*?" Cheese asked.

"Let's hit Frankie's first, strap on the feedbag, then go get our money."

Frankie's was a humble Italian eatery featuring some of the best grub in town. The place wasn't much to look at but the food was divine.

"Just don't overdo it," Jack warned. "I don't want to lose you to the porcelain gods halfway through the night again."

"No shit. Literally!"

Cheese was notorious for having bad pipes, and when he overdid rich food or alcohol it was neither pretty nor pleasant. Jack had seen the poor guy barely make it to the facilities on many occasions and not at all on several others. He had had to look away as Cheese dropped trou and copped a squat in the bushes on multiple occasions, usually on a golf course. Nobody should have to see that.

Cheese valet-parked at the new Buffalo Seneca Casino Hotel, directly across the street from the Wigwam. Jack had yet to get his feet wet at the new casino and was quite excited at the prospect. The high stakes, one-hundred-dollar-minimum tables were located in a separate room on the second floor of the eighteen-story building. The third floor consisted of meeting rooms, while the pool, spa, and offices took up the fourth floor. The rest of the building served as a luxury hotel. Driftwood was struck by the opulence and craftsmanship of the structure. He had heard the place was done in a first-class manner, but the décor and workmanship exceeded his expectations.

The two high-rollers rode the escalator up to the second floor and entered the classy, high stakes parlor. Their usual routine was to take a lap around the room to case the joint out before selecting a table. Generally they preferred to play by themselves, but if they found a fun group they wouldn't hesitate to jump in. The casino wasn't very busy, although that was no surprise considering it was 10:30 on a Wednesday night.

After taking their lap, Cheese and Jack settled in at an open table. They each threw twenty Ben Franklins down and the game was on. Jack played two hands at a time while Cheese preferred to concentrate on just one. An attractive, young cocktail waitress brought Jack a Crown and water on the rocks with a twist of lemon. Cheese no longer imbibed very often, especially after eating such a rich meal, and stayed with a simple bottle of water.

Just as Jack had suspected, his feeling was right on the money. Big money. He was up almost five grand within the first half hour, hitting it big on multiple double downs. Cheese played a little more conservatively but was also getting good cards. He was up almost two grand when the Seneca's brought in a new dealer.

Jack was a little pissed; he liked the older gentleman named Edward who had been flipping their red-hot cards. Edward had a good sense of humor, kept the game moving, and, hey, who doesn't like the dealer when they are winning?

"Wouldn't you know it," Jack said. "They see us win a little money and they bring in the fuckin' cooler."

Jack had been playing two black chips on each of his spots but wisely decided to pull back. He played one spot and one black chip as a taciturn, older woman named Marta took over as their dealer. Sure enough, Marta hit blackjack on the first hand and a five-card twenty-one the second.

"I've seen enough," Jack said, "how 'bout you, Cheese?"

"Let's blow this pop stand."

They colored up their chips and left the table to take a bathroom break. When they returned to the gaming area a wave of excitement was coming from a table on the far side of the room.

"Let's go see what that's all about," Jack suggested.

"No doubt," Cheese said. "Damn! Check out the *bella ragazza* in the little black number, maybe that's why everyone is so excited."

As Jack approached the table he realized the magnitude of his "feeling" was potentially much greater than even he had thought. That little black number just happened to be covering the lovely form of Gerry Wainscott. Jack slipped up behind her unnoticed and slid into the open seat directly to her right.

"Cinder-fucking-rella," he said close to her ear, drawing in a deep, intoxicating whiff of her wonderful scent.

"Jack-fucking-Driftwood!"

She threw her arms around him and surprised him with a big hug. Time froze in the heat of their embrace, until reluctantly he turned her loose. He hadn't expected such a warm welcome from the Ice Princess but wasn't complaining. The lovely lady was either high on winning big or deep into her cups; perhaps both.

"So, the lady is a player," Jack said, motioning to the huge pile of chips stacked in front of Gerry.

"Blackjack is my game, and tonight is my night."

"You got that right, you mind if my boy Cheese and I join in the fun?"

"By all means."

Cheese had sat down next to Jack and reached across the table to take Gerry's hand.

"Pleasure to meet you, Gerry," he said. "Jack told me how beautiful you were but I didn't believe him. Shame on me."

"Uh-oh, another charmer. Did Jack just say your name is Cheese?"

"Joseppi Barcheezzi, at your service, ma'am. But yes, please, call me Cheese."

Gerry burst out laughing. "Cheese – what a great name. Well good luck, Cheese, let's get this table hopping."

There were several others standing around the table watching, drawn to the action by Gerry's excitement over her streak of good fortune. Her luck was about to get even better. She bet five hundred on the first hand and hit a blackjack. She was bouncing up and down and grabbed Jack's leg in excitement. She wasn't the only one getting excited as Jack nudged closer to her.

Both he and Cheese won their bets as well, as the dealer busted on a four. Now they were all hopping up and down. This went on for nearly another half hour. Jack and Gerry were laughing, high-fiving, and touching through the entire run, getting a little friendlier with each winning hand. The drinks were on the house so Jack ordered a round of shots of top-shelf tequila and even Cheese got caught up in the moment and slurped one down. They were having a great time and Jack was amazed at how funny and loose Gerry turned out to be. He had figured she may have a bit of a wild side and knew how to have fun, but not to this extent. The girl was a hoot!

Taking stock, Jack figured he was up close to ten grand, and, by the looks of the pile of chips in front of Gerry, she had nearly twice that. Cheese wasn't doing too bad himself. But Jack knew from experience all good things must come to an end, especially when it came to gambling.

The key to winning was pretty simple: just get the hell out of there while you were still ahead and you would never lose. Easy to say, almost impossible to do. He was also feeling a little amorous and wouldn't mind finding a more intimate setting to see where things might go with the lovely Ms. Wainscott.

His mind was at work kicking around plausible exit strategies when things took care of themselves. Marta, the cooler, arrived at their table, stern and reticent, to relieve their dealer.

"Aw shit, here comes the goddamn cooler again," Jack said.

"The cooler? What's the cooler?" Gerry asked. It sounded like koo-luh.

"The *cooler,*" Jack said, "is the new dealer who comes in to fuck up your mojo and take back everything you just won and more. And Marta is as cool as a cooler can be."

"That's not very nice, Jack. I'm sure Marta will do us just fine. Won't you, sweetie?"

Marta just looked at Gerry with a blank expression, causing Jack to break out into laughter.

"I'll tell you what, let's make a little side bet. This black chip here says Miss Marta hits a blackjack on the first hand."

Jack slid a black chip toward Gerry.

"No way. You are on, mister."

She slid her own black chip next to Jack's.

Cheese shook his head. "I wouldn't do it."

Marta dealt herself an Ace and after everybody declined insurance she flipped over a ten of hearts. Blackjack. Gerry couldn't believe it.

"Now she is going to pull a twenty or a twenty-one," Jack said.

"I still don't believe you. Double or nothing," Gerry said.

"It's your money, darlin'."

Marta smirked, breaking character for the first time all night. She dealt the cards and had a six showing. Nobody took a card so Marta flipped her hole card. It was a jack. Sitting at sixteen she had to take a hit. She flipped over a four for a total of twenty. Gerry slugged Jack in the arm as he reached out and slid her two black chips to his pile.

"Come on," he said. "Let's cash in and get the hell out of here before Marta takes it all back."

Nobody argued the point. Jack tipped Marta the two black chips he had just won from Gerry plus a couple more and thanked her kindly. It was the first time he could recall being happy about the arrival of a cooler. The pit boss escorted them to the cashier where they cashed in their chips. They each walked away with a considerable amount of cash.

"So did Cinderella take her own golden carriage here tonight?" Jack asked, fishing for a clue as to what she might be thinking.

"Not really," Gerry answered coyly. "I didn't need one."

Jack gave her a quizzical, confused glance.

"This is my castle. I'm staying up in the penthouse for now until I can find a place."

Jack's mind did the math and he couldn't help the smile that smacked him in the kisser.

*So that's what's up.*

"It's not safe, you walking around with that kind of cash," Jack said to Gerry. "You need a bodyguard and I am just the man for the job."

"I'm sure you want to do more to my body than just guard it," she said. She was a little tipsy on her feet as the fun was obviously catching up to her.

"Yeah, I guess I didn't do a very good job of keeping that a secret."

"Must be that youthful protuberance of yours," she said, giggling.

Right on cue, Cheese had begun experiencing gastronomical issues, interrupting things. He was slightly bent over holding his stomach and moaning.

"It was great to meet you, Gerry, but I don't think that tequila is sitting too well," Cheese said.

Jack broke into a loud laugh and Gerry looked confused.

"My boy Cheese needs his ass fixiated," he said.

"Asphyxiated? Can you breathe? Are you going to be okay, Cheese?" she asked.

"Yes, but I have to excuse myself." Cheese gave Gerry a peck on the cheek and quickly waddled towards the nearest men's room.

"Poor bastard," Jack said. "I am going to have to get him home shortly or they will never let us back in here, but I will gladly guard your body safely up to your room."

"Aw, how very sweet of you, Jack," she said, taking his arm in hers.

They got onto an empty elevator and no sooner had the door closed and they were all over each other. She wrapped one of her legs around his as they embraced and kissed with a startling hunger. They were getting lost in each other, but the dinging of the elevator announcing their arrival at the eighteenth floor broke the spell. They pulled away from one another and straightened up their clothes as if nothing had happened. This set them both into a fit of laughter as they made their way out of the car. Jack walked her down the hall to her room and she waived her key in front of the door unlocking it.

"How long do these Cheese episodes usually last?" she inquired.

"Shit, I've seen 'em go on for a week at a time."

Gerry stared hard into Jack's eyes with a look that could only be described as predatory. "Well, that should be enough time."

"I don't know about that, Ms. Wainscott," Jack said, openly ogling her up and down. "From what I can see it's gonna take me a lot longer than that."

She clumsily grabbed Jack's tie and pulled him slowly to her. He kissed her deeply and lifted her slight frame easily off the ground.

"Well then, you better get started," she said.

*Dammit, she's all fucked up. It shouldn't go down like this, it's no good.*

He carried her into the room and reluctantly set her down on the sofa.

"I'd love to stay, Gerry, I really would. But I think we've had maybe a bit too much to drink and I really don't want it to go —"

"Excuse me?"

"This just ain't a great idea, right now. If things are meant to be we'll have our chance."

He bent and kissed her again, this time lightly on the forehead. A look of bewilderment came over her face.

"Who would have thought Prince Charming was such a pussy."

Jack didn't respond. Instead, he did one of the hardest things he had ever done in his entire life; he walked out of the room without looking back and hurried to the elevator before he changed his mind.

# Chapter Fifteen

"All rookies, don't forget the chicken!" Eric "Big E" Sellars yelled the message in singsong immediately after Coach Ivy released the team from their Saturday morning walk-thru. Big E loved fried chicken more than life itself, and more than any man Jack Driftwood had ever known. Reminding the rookies to bring chicken for Blizzard away trips was a righteous crusade to the big man.

"All rookies, don't forget the chicken!" He sang it over and over.

Driftwood punched his rookie Stark in the kidneys as he ran past him toward the locker room and repeated the reminder.

"Big E is preachin' the truth, son. All rookies, don't forget the chicken. That means you, Stark."

"Fuck you. I ain't getting you no chicken," Stark replied.

Driftwood just laughed and kept running toward the locker room.

"You illiterate douche, that's a double negative. You just agreed to bring me my chicken. All rookies, don't forget the chicken!"

Jack sang the catchy phrase while skipping his way to the locker room. The dude wasn't quite right in the head and Stark was beginning to get suspicious. Jack had been in a great mood the past couple of days. Regardless of what Stark did to needle or to get a rise out of him, nothing worked. Usually it was easy pickings; he could get Jack hopping mad at least a couple of times a day. That was what made their relationship so much fun – their constant back and forth ball-busting.

Stark was getting annoyed. Finally, he put the pieces together. He confronted Jack when he arrived at his locker, which was right next to Jack's.

"You got laid didn't you?"

"I don't know, touchdown boy, did I?"

"Who was it, do I know her? You gotta tell me, it's Man-law," Stark said.

"Man-law? Naw, Man-law is you get me some chicken. I'll tell you what, I'm not sayin' I got laid, but you bring me a bucket of chicken and Uncle Jack will tell you one of the best Puss Stories you've ever heard in your short, perverted life."

"I already told you I ain't getting no fucking chicken."

"Well, then I ain't telling you no fuckin' Puss Story."

Playing hardball with the rookie, Jack turned and headed for the door. He knew the kid would crumble.

"All right, all right," Stark said. "I'll get your chicken but it had better be worth it."

Jack stopped in his tracks. He could almost taste the chicken. He knew the lad couldn't resist what he referred to as a Puss Story. They were one of young Steven's favorite things. The kid was some kind of amateur sexual anthropologist. Whenever anybody talked about having sex Stark was in the front row hanging on every word. He would probe for details and ask endless questions whenever somebody was willing to open up with the gory details of their sex life. The sexual exploits of others was Stark's favorite subject, fascinating him to no end.

"I promise you this will be one of the best, if not the best, Puss Story your twisted, non-virgin ears have ever heard."

"I knew it! You've been walking around here all week like you got a good pussy whipping," Stark said.

"All rookies, don't forget the chicken!" Jack sang as his only response and strolled out of the locker room.

Gerry arrived early at the Prior Aviation Terminal on the north side of the Buffalo-Niagara International Airport, well before the team charter was scheduled to depart to Baltimore. She had developed a habit of arriving at the airport with plenty of time to spare. With just about every terminal now equipped with Wi-Fi, she could settle in to work and not worry about missing a flight. No sense in being late for a plane just because she was trying to get some extra work done. It also gave her the opportunity to do some people-watching, which she greatly enjoyed.

However, today was different. She didn't have any significant work to catch up on and the flight was chartered. Gerry had considered taking a commercial flight to Baltimore later that night but decided against it. Being new to her ownership role, she figured it important to establish her presence and traveling with the team was a big part of that.

The real reason for her early arrival was her hope to see Jack Driftwood. She hadn't talked to him, let alone seen him, since he walked away from her hotel suite Wednesday night. A part of her wanted to avoid him like the plague, but she couldn't ignore the feelings he aroused deep within her. She was a bit of a hot mess when it came to the broad-shouldered linebacker.

*How could I have been so stupid? I'm pretty sure that's not what Dad had in mind when he told me to "let loose."*

"Hey, Gerry, is everything ok?"

She looked up and saw Donald Fegel staring at her, obviously concerned.

"What? Oh, no, everything is fine, I was just caught up in a day dream. How are you?"

"I'm fine, thank you. But it looked like more of a nightmare."

Gerry laughed it off and stood. There was no way she would let Donald pry into her private thoughts and quickly changed the subject. She noticed Ed Stinson was behind Donald upon standing.

"Oh, hi, Ed…my goodness, I'm so sorry. I completely forgot I was supposed to be your shadow on this excursion. But I have to run to the ladies' room for a minute. I'll meet you right back here."

"No problem, ma'am. I'll be right here waiting," Ed replied.

Stinson was the head of security for the organization and Gerry was going to tail him on the trip as part of her continuing on-the-job training.

Gerry left the two men standing there and made her way across the lobby towards the ladies' room. She had been so caught up in thinking about Jack she had totally forgotten about shadowing Stinson. She hadn't been able to stop thinking about him since their chance meeting at the casino Wednesday night. She knew it was not good practice to get involved with employees but things weren't that simple. They never were.

It was all wrong, she knew, but something inside of her was telling her to let go of her reservations, to give Jack a chance. She hadn't been with anyone since her fiancé had passed away and two years was a long time, no matter how you sliced it. There had been on a few dates but nothing came of them. There was something more to Jack, though, something behind the macho bravado. She wanted desperately to delve deeper, to get to know him properly, but didn't know how to begin.

Fate, as it often does, intervened. As she rounded the corner, she saw Jack Driftwood through the window approaching the terminal entrance. She stopped and leaned against the wall to watch him. There was a small group of players ahead of him laughing and chatting as they breezed past one of the flight attendants struggling trying to carry her small suitcase and an overstuffed grocery bag. Jack noticed and immediately threw his carry-on bag over his shoulder and took the grocery bag from the harried woman's arms.

*Whoever said chivalry is dead apparently hasn't met Jack Driftwood.*

The genuine smile on his face totally disarmed Gerry as she watched him carry the bag to the door and open it for the woman before following her inside. The mere sight of him made her stomach flutter as if it were full of butterflies. It seemed like every time she encountered him he surprised her in a positive way. This gigantic, muscular, beast of a man acted tough and looked a bit dangerous, but in reality he was nothing more than an overgrown boy scout with the heart of a teddy bear.

She was still watching him, lost in her thoughts, when he turned and looked directly at her, catching her eyes. Feeling like she had been busted spying on him, she quickly turned away and headed toward the restroom but his voice stopped her cold.

"Hey, Gerry," he called from across the lobby, "hang on a sec."

Her initial instinct was to run right to the bathroom, but she suppressed it. She turned back to face him and leaned back against the wall, watching his smile widen as he approached. Realizing she was also smiling like a big fool, she covered her mouth and attempted a neutral expression.

Before she could say anything, he beat her to the punch. "Listen, Gerry, I want to apologize for the other night. I know it probably ain't right for us to be doing that and I should have never even made it up to your room. I hope I didn't offend you in any way."

Gerry was momentarily taken aback.

*He's apologizing to me? I'm the one who acted like a slut and called him a pussy. I should be apologizing to him!*

"No, not at all," she said. "I'm the one who should be apologizing to you, Jack. Obviously, I'd had a few too many drinks and I put you in a tough situation. However, I must say I've never had a man just get up and walk away from me like that. The truth is, it kind of pissed me off."

Jack Laughed. "I know, right? I should have my damn-fool head examined. Honestly, I can't recall a time where I ever walked away from a situation like that, either. Especially from someone as lovely as you."

"Always the charmer, huh?" She said, trying to hide a smile. "Looking back, though, you did what I should have done. You saved me from myself. I know I am new to this business, but I'm pretty sure it's not a good idea for me to get involved with a player. But…but it, I don't know. It's…it's just too complicated."

"I hear you. This is uncharted territory for me, too. I'm not sure what the rules of engagement are."

"Well, let's try to figure that out. I'd love to have that conversation with you, privately." She paused and looked around but nobody could see them as they were around the corner from the lobby. "Perhaps we can get together and have a nice, long conversation about our, um, situation. Can we do that, Jack?"

"You bet your sweet, little ass we can."

"Really?" Gerry said, this time not bothering to hide her smile. "You can't bet what isn't yours, Mr. Driftwood. Not yet, anyways."

She looked around again, and after seeing the coast was clear, she stepped up close to him and rose to her tip toes. Jack bent slightly, meeting her at the pass. Their lips met as she gave him a tender, teasingly quick kiss before she turned and hurried into the ladies' room laughing.

Jack boarded the plane a short while later. He had spent a brief cooling off period in the men's room inside the terminal. It wouldn't have been advisable to attempt boarding the plane looking like he was smuggling a cucumber in his suit pants. He made his way to the back of the plane where Stark was already sitting back in the last row, waiting for him. Stark had a bucket of Colonel Sanders' best sitting on his lap. Jack busted out laughing at the sight. He snapped a picture with his phone to post at Driftwoodies.com.

For the eighteenth consecutive year Jack sat in the last row of the Blizzard's chartered jet on away trips. The habit had started when, as a rookie, he randomly took the spot because it was open, undoubtedly because it was considered among the least desirable seats on the plane.

However, Jack preferred it. For starters, it put him as far away as possible from the front office staff, coaches, and, most importantly, Donald Fegel, who all sat up in the front. It also put him close to the restroom and the back kitchen area where the flight attendants hung out. He had seen multiple changings of the guard of flight attendants over the years, but most of the current crew had been with the team for five years now. They had become a part of the Blizzard extended family.

The lead flight attendant was a cougar by the name of Sandy Thompson. Jack had engaged in a torrid romance with Sandy when she joined the crew five years ago that had carried on for several seasons. Sandy had gotten married prior to the previous season, but they remained good friends. A new girl was added to the crew this year by the name of Maryanne Comelia. She was a comely, young lass and Jack and Sandy had been at work trying to set her up with Steven Stark. They were both young, virile, and single, so why not? The results were more or less inevitable.

Jack greeted Sandy and Maryanne with hugs before sitting down in the aisle seat next to his anxiously awaiting understudy.

"Here's your chicken, old man," Stark said.

"All rookies, don't forget the chicken," Jack sang and opened the lid. Half of the bird was already gone. Jack raised his eyebrows at Stark.

"I got hungry," the rookie said, flashing his big, goofy grin.

Jack pawed through the remains of the bucket. "No shit. Did you leave me any thighs?"

"Maybe."

"Ah, here's one," Jack said and sunk his teeth into the still warm bird.

Eric Sellars clamored down the aisle, on the prowl for fowl. "Who got that barnyard pimp? Give it up, y'all. Big E want some big bird. Drifty? How bout ya? I know my main man Drifty got some a that pimp. Give it up, boy. Big E hungry."

Jack snagged a leg to go along with the thigh clenched between his teeth and handed the bucket to Sellars.

"Here you go, Big E," he said through a mouthful of bird, "compliments of my rookie, Stark, here."

"Oh yeah!" Big E hollered. "Stark know about that barnyard pimp. You my boy, Stark!"

Big E cradled the bucket in his massive right arm and made his way back to his seat toward the front of the plane, singing and extolling the virtues of the barnyard pimp the entire way. The team was loose and loud as they prepared for takeoff. Jack considered it a good sign.

Jack was reading from a pocket-sized bible, as was his habit whenever he flew. It made the time go by and he figured if the plane ever crashed at least he would be in the "Word" when it went down. That had to count for something. Jack was quite impressed by the patience Steven Stark was displaying. The kid hadn't badgered him for his Puss Story yet, which was uncharacteristic, if not amazing. No sooner had Jack made that mental note and Stark began to stir.

"Let's have it, homey," Stark said. He had pulled out his earphones and leaned in closer to Jack.

For certain, Jack planned to keep this thing quiet, at least until he had a chance to sit down with Gerry to figure things out, but he was dying to tell somebody. It might as well be Stark. Jack trusted him to keep quiet, and clearly nobody would enjoy the escapade more than the amateur sex anthropologist, Steven Stark.

Jack tucked the miniature bible into the front pocket of his dress shirt and took an exaggerated deep breath.

"All right," he said, "but you have to swear on everything you hold sacred you won't repeat a word of this to anyone."

"Whatever," Stark said.

"Goddammit, I'm serious."

"All right, all right, I swear."

Jack paused for effect and looked hard at the rookie, an overt attempt to determine his sincerity level. He looked around one last time to make sure no one was eavesdropping and then leaned over the empty seat between them and quietly began to spill the beans.

"Okay," he finally said. "You know how I told you I went and got my money from the Seneca's on Wednesday night, right?"

"Yeah, you slayed the bastards."

"Right, well, what I didn't tell you was after our first run, me and Cheese took a break and when we came back we spotted this unbelievably hot babe in a short, black, cocktail dress whooping it up at a table. The girl was fine, bro. Fine as hell! She was killing it too, had a big ol' stack of chips in front of her. So we jumped in and went on this unbelievable run. We were winning practically every hand, hollerin', laughin', and drinking shots, having a grand old time. Next thing I know, we start celebrating by getting all touchy-feely under the table. I was rubbing that ass all up and down and she kept brushing her hand against my junk. I think ol' girl was trying to see what I was packing."

"Must have disappointed her, huh."

"Hey, fuck-stick, you wanna hear the story or not?"

"Yeah, yeah. I'm sorry. I couldn't help it."

Stark was battling his big, goofy grin, trying to wipe it from his face. They were briefly interrupted as Sandy stopped to see if they needed anything.

"Ooh, this looks like a pretty serious conversation," she observed.

"I'm just telling the kid a little Puss Story," Jack said.

"It had better not be about *me*," she said.

"Don't worry," Stark said, "he already told me all of those."

"Jack!"

"No I didn't," Jack said, "those are for next week."

"You better not!" She playfully punched him on the arm and passed them each a bottle of water and worked her way up to the next row.

"Proceed," Stark said, eager to get back to the story.

"All right. So anyway, this goes on for about a half an hour and we were all over each other. I'm trying to figure out how to get her out of there and Bam! They bring in the cooler."

"I hate it when they do that."

"I know, right? But this time it worked out perfectly. We lost two hands in a row and decided to cash in our chips. Right on cue, my boy Cheese goes into his bad stomach routine. I'm not saying he was faking, but either way the guy is a genius; he is the ultimate cock-enabler and the single best wingman in the known free world. Ol' Cheese headed to the bathroom, leaving us just standing there and she tells me she is staying up in the penthouse."

"No she didn't," Stark said.

"Oh, yes she did."

"Damn. She must be some kind of high-roller. That's so hot!"

"You ain't never lied. So, I offer to be her bodyguard and escort her up to the room with all the loot, which she thinks is a great idea. We get on the elevator and no sooner does the door close and we are all over each other mashing to beat the band. We made out all the way up to the eighteenth floor and my hands were all over that poor girl like white on rice. She's got a rack that just won't quit. We make it to her door and she grabs me by the tie and pulls me into the room."

"This is fucking awesome, bro. You were right," Stark said. "So then what? You beat that thing up all night long, stud?"

"Well, not quite," Jack said. "You see, there are some complications to the whole thing."

"Complications? We talking whiskey dick? Jesus, old man, they got pills for that shit now, you know. You need to get your shit checked because I got half a stiffy just hearing the story."

"No, dickweed, that ain't never been a problem."

"Well, what the hell was?"

"It's not the 'what' that's a problem. It's more like the 'who.'"

"Who? Who?"

"What are you, some kinda fuckin' owl now? Hoo-hoo!"

Jack laughed, knowing Stark was about to lose his patience, if not his mind.

"Quit fucking around. Who was it?"

Jack took another quick look around to make sure nobody was listening before leaning in close to drop the bomb on Stark.

"I'll tell you who, *mejo*. You would know her as Cinder-fucking-rella."

It took a second to register, but when it did, Stark's eyes got as big as saucers.

"No. No way! Holy shit! That's the coolest thing I have ever heard. You really are my hero now, dude." Stark was pounding the armrests and bouncing in his seat.

"Shh! Keep it down, man. I don't need the hassle," Jack said.

"You got it, bro. But that is so awesome. I see why you made me promise to keep my mouth shut. This shit is radioactive." Stark couldn't get over it. His day had been made. "Wait a minute…what happened then…did she shut you down or did you go gently into the night?"

"I don't know," Jack said slowly. "She was for sure good to go, but she was pretty damn drunk, you know. I didn't want it to be a hit it and quit it deal, like, one and done. Who knows, I might really like this girl, so I took the long view on this one."

Stark pounded his fist onto the armrest and convulsed into a fit of laughter, making a bit of a scene. Several guys turned around to see what was going on, but Jack just shrugged and smiled at them, hoping they would turn back around and mind their own goddamn business.

"I knew I shouldn't have told your dumb ass."

"No, it's okay, man. It's all good. My lips are sealed. I promise."

Jack grunted and got up to use the bathroom. The whole thing finally seemed real to him after sharing it with Stark. Real as real could get.

# Chapter Sixteen

Chesapeake Bank Stadium sat at the south end of Camden Yards, adjacent to Oriole Park. It was one of the most modern, technologically-advanced stadiums in all of the NAFA. The Avenger Club seats came with wireless tablets that provided up to the minute stats and video replays on demand from myriad camera angles. The suites were equally interactive and luxurious. The massive video boards in each corner of the stadium were among the biggest and most advanced in the world. In short, it was a great place to go to watch a game.

However, Driftwood didn't care much for it; to be blunt, he fucking *hated* it. This was another nugget for the mental list he was compiling: The Avengers, the city of Baltimore, the seventy-one thousand or so people in the stands, and now their stadium were a sampling from his growing Hate List.

The Hate List was an old Jedi mind-trick his father, Big Ed Driftwood, had taught Jack back when he was embarking on his high school football career. Big Ed had played center for the Kansas Jayhawks back in the Big Seven Conference days of the early 1950's when guts and toughness, rather than size and strength, were at a premium. Jack had been elevated to the varsity squad as a freshman at Maryville High School and Big Ed figured his only son would need some sort of an edge to consistently compete with the older Spoofhounds.

Big Ed knew first-hand the greatest edge in football was intensity, which was a product of mental toughness. He had taught young Jack how to work himself up into a frenzy that could be downright intimidating, if not altogether frightening. The elder Driftwood believed strongly it was the only way to play the game.

He had told his son, "I know you've got a bunch of pent up anger and rage inside of you, Jack. Most people do. What you need to learn is how to nurture your fury, make it work *for* you, not against you. Sometimes life is hard. That's why the good Lord gave us football, so we could vent in a positive way and not get locked up. In order to get your mind right and channel this aggression, you need to think of all those things that really piss you off. The more you dwell on that shit, the angrier you will get. Then use it to fuel your intensity on the field."

"You mean like make a Hate List, Dad?" Jack had asked.

"I suppose. I never thought of it in quite those terms, but yeah, if that's what you want to call it, son, then Hate List it is."

This tactic had come in handy for Jack many times over the course of his career – and life, for that matter. He didn't resort to it too often because it invariably put him in a piss-poor mood and sucked the joy from life. Furthermore, nobody liked a bitter bastard and it had been his experience the most miserable people were always the ones who went on and on about how they got screwed at every turn. That wasn't him; but he had enough of it in him to make the tactic effective. Very effective.

The Hate List served to bring to boil a stewpot of righteous indignation, unfettered anger, and an extreme desire for vengeance. All the shitters in the world had it in for him and were out to get him and he knew it. And the doubters? Too many to count. But not to worry because he would show them, too. He'd show them all. They could collectively kiss his white ass. And so it went…

Jack knew any edge he'd had was totally blown out of the water by his midweek dalliance with Gerry Wainscott. The whole thing had become a huge distraction and he was consumed with it and her. He'd been walking around the past several days with his head in the clouds like some love-sick puppy. He sure as hell wasn't ready to play football. Here it was, the night before a big-ass game, and he'd yet to feel the tickle of the ice ball that would normally be already forming in his stomach.

"Good loving can be a fun ride but it don't pay the freight," as Big Ed used to say.

Unfortunately, Jack's type of intensity was not of the "flip-the-switch" variety. Some players could do that. The lights came up and they would transform from slap-happy jag-offs to cold-blooded assassins; from playing grab-ass to kicking major ass. Driftwood, on the other hand, was geared more towards a steady "escalation until eruption" type of process; build up so you can blow up. He had to ratchet up the pressure in his tank before releasing his venom in a violent torrent.

The plain and simple truth was Jack was not ready to play a NAFA game. He had done his homework and knew the game plan, but his mind wasn't right. He had been too loosey-goosey the past several days. He was flatter than an eight-year-old girl and he knew it. He began to formulate his Hate List.

Big Ed's lesson from so long ago, as always, proved effective. In virtually no time, Jack had driven himself into one piss-poor, foul-ass mood. It wasn't long before he was hating on everything.

It had helped immensely that he encountered Donald Fegel at the team's pregame meal in their hotel. Driftwood was slouched over his plate shoveling scrambled eggs and bacon down his gullet when Fegel sat down right across from him between his two pretty little pets, Stark and Brogan.

"How are the NAFA's top two linebacker's this fine morning?" A chipper Fegel inquired.

Both Brogan and Stark mumbled they were fine.

"I woke with a strong premonition this morning that the two of you are going to play one hell of a game today. It's going to be the first of many, many more to come. There is no doubt in my mind you two will become the most dynamic linebacker duo in the entire league. But then, that's why I brought you both here and put you together, now isn't it? As soon as we can get some of the, ahem, dead wood out of the way, you boys will get your chance to really shine."

Fegel laughed and slapped himself on the thigh.

"Fuckin' asshole," Driftwood muttered, barely audible, and he threw his fork on the table before storming out of the room, mid meal.

As he stomped out the door he heard Fegel say "What's up his ass?" and laugh too hard again. Driftwood wanted nothing more than to go back and pummel the little fucker, but he pumped his brakes and stopped himself. Big Ed's number one rule for the Hate List was keep it on the field. Jack reigned himself in, saving it, instead, for Baltimore.

Driftwood had worked himself into such a state before kickoff he didn't even have the usual ice ball in his gut. Replacing it was a coldness in his heart. He was clearly ready to play some football now and had already tried to start a fight in pregame warmups – with his own team. He punched Nick Loney in the facemask on the first play of the team drill and had to be separated from the Tank, who had intervened on Nick's behalf. Even Stark, who delighted in getting under Driftwood's skin, sensed what time it was and didn't mess with him after breaking things up.

Driftwood paced the sidelines and was wisely given a wide berth by his teammates. They had seen Jack in this mode previously, dark and brooding, but never to this extreme. There was no reasoning with him when he got into this kind of funk, so they left him alone. Meanwhile, Driftwood was praying they would lose the coin toss and play defense first; if he didn't get to hit somebody soon he was going to lose his fucking mind.

"Oooh-wheee! Yeah, baby! Drifty got his pee hot today, y'all," Leroy Clarkson hollered from a safe distance.

Driftwood stomped past him with no response. And then his prayers were answered; Baltimore won the toss and elected to receive.

Points would not come easy on this mild yet windy and rainy afternoon on the Chesapeake Bay. The Avengers didn't possess a potent offense, though they were an opportunistic bunch. They traditionally relied on a stifling defense, good special teams, and protecting the football; this season was no different. They were good at what they did, too, as their 3-0 record testified.

Bennie Tenudo, with wind howling at his back, kicked the ball through the uprights and almost into the stands for a touchback, thus the Avengers took possession at their own 20-yard line to start the drive. The first play from scrimmage was a simple zone read play; a run directed at the bubble in front of Jack Driftwood in Buffalo's 3-4 front.

*People just don't fuckin' listen…*

Driftwood had already decided he didn't give a shit what the Avengers ran on the first play; he was going after their right guard, Ben Needham, with everything he had to set the tone and vent some venom. He usually didn't talk much smack during games, but he yelled at Needham as the hulking giant of a man came out of the huddle to the line.

"I'm gonna run you right the fuck over, fat ass!"

Needham cocked his head sideways and smiled at him. "No shit."

Driftwood howled at the moon and then backed his alignment up to four and a half yards to get himself a good running start. He was counting on the snap being on one and timed his get-off to the cadence. If he was wrong, tough titties. He was still going to knock Needham on his fat ass whether it cost his team five yards or not.

With an early jump and malicious intent he destroyed the Avengers' guard with the just the tip of the fury he had been nurturing for the past sixteen hours. Needham had barely gotten out of his stance when Driftwood hit him so hard he went flying backwards like he was being tossed out of a saloon. Needham took out his own running back in the process, tripping him up for a loss of a couple of yards. Driftwood made sure of it by jumping on the ball carrier, who was trying to scramble to his feet.

"All day, motherfuckers! I'm gonna be here all day!"

The running back, Willie James, was a former teammate of Driftwood's, having played in Buffalo a few years previous. It wasn't the happy reunion he had hoped for.

"Damn, Drifty, what's wrong with you?"

"Not today, Willie," Driftwood screamed at him, getting right up in his former teammate's face. "Don't even fuckin' talk to me today, Willie. I ain't havin' it."

Willie shook his head and trotted back to the huddle. Well, Jack Driftwood was still a crazy-ass white-boy. That much was for sure.

Even the Buffalo defense was shocked at the level of Driftwood's intensity. Usually he had a humor to him amidst his fury. He had fun. Not today; he was all business.

"You good, Drifty?" Big E asked when they huddled up.

"Never better, now make a fuckin' play."

"Yeah, baby," Leroy Clarkson hollered. Leroy loved it. "Pee hot! Drifty got his Pee hot today. Let's get this ass, y'all!"

On second down Baltimore attempted a screen pass. Driftwood saw it develop and attacked it with the perfect inside-out angle. The Avenger offensive tackle saw him coming, but late. He went low, trying to salvage his block by cutting Driftwood down at the knees.

*Cheap-shot cocksucker! You're better than that, man.*

Driftwood hurdled the diving tackle cleanly without breaking stride. Willie James caught the pass but didn't anticipate anybody being upon him so quickly. He was a deer in Driftwood's headlights. Willie ducked his head at the last second as Driftwood hit him at full speed, bringing a full load of the wood.

It took better than five minutes to scrape poor Willie up off the field. Driftwood was sure he had heard something pop in Willie's neck upon contact. Bad shit happened in football when people dropped their heads, everybody knew that.

Driftwood did not feel the slightest bit of regret or remorse. Football was violent. They all took the same chances. Lord knows, he had suffered his share of injuries over the years. There was nothing he could do about it now.

*Fuck it.*

Baltimore lined back up facing a 3rd and 14 from their own 16-yard line. They tried to get off a pass in the face of a Buffalo blitz. Driftwood came free, using big Bo-Bo to create a natural pick, and sacked the quarterback for a six-yard loss with another punishing hit. Just like that, the Avengers went three-and-out, losing 10 yards in the process. Driftwood had made all three tackles – all for a loss – including his sack. Some guys would have considered that a career. He had also knocked out Baltimore's starting running back. It reminded Driftwood of his Pop Warner days when he used to make kids on the other team cry. No doubt, it was a decent start, but his bloodlust was far from sated, plus nobody on the Baltimore Avenger sidline was crying yet. Making a few plays did little to curb his appetite for more.

His teammates tried to celebrate with him but he roughly pushed them away. He smacked Bo-Bo Karpinski upside the head so hard the mammoth man wobbled and saw stars. Seeing Bo-Bo get whacked served as an effective deterrent to the rest of his teammates who gave him an even wider berth. When they came off the field Driftwood sat alone on the cold, wet, metal bench rocking back and forth, keeping his mind right until the next series.

Buffalo took advantage of the outstanding field position and managed to garner three points off of a 42-yard Tenudo field goal. Tenudo bombed the ensuing kickoff out of the back of the end zone again and the Avengers started another drive from their own 20. Driftwood sprinted from the sidelines to get in front of the huddle which didn't arrive until a few seconds later. He was literally out of his mind.

Baltimore tried a toss sweep on first down and Driftwood shot the gap from the backside, creaming their new running back for a three-yard loss. He got up from the tackle raging and screaming at the Baltimore bench.

"Toss? You fuckin' kidding me? No one runs toss on me, motherfuckers!"

His teammates left him alone this time. No one else wanted to get hit, especially Bo-Bo, who was still a trifle wobbly.

On 2nd and 13, Baltimore threw a quick screen to the receiver wide to their right side in front of their bench. In anticipation of the play, Driftwood had loosened his alignment and diagnosed it quickly. Leroy Clarkson beat his blocker on the edge, containing the play and forcing the receiver back inside, right into the path of an oncoming Mack truck. Driftwood hit him so hard he thought he had decapitated him.

Fortunately, the guy was close to his own sideline, so they didn't have far to help him off the field. After the play, Driftwood picked another fight, this time with the entire Baltimore bench. The officials quickly broke things up and called off-setting unsportsmanlike conduct penalties and issued warnings to both benches. Despite the wind and rain, the heat ratcheted up another notch.

The play gained three yards, setting up a 3rd and 10. Buffalo went to Nickel personnel, which meant Driftwood was supposed to come out of the game. He alternated series with Stark as the Nickel linebacker and it was Stark's turn to stay in. Driftwood glared menacingly at the rookie.

"You take it," Stark said and ran off the field.

When he got to the sideline Coach Faber lifted his arms, palms up, in a classic "what the fuck" gesture.

"What are you doing, Stark, it's *your* series!"

"You take him out! The crazy bastard looked at me like he wanted to kill me and he's made every goddamn tackle so far."

Coach Faber nodded and smiled his sickest smile.

On the field, Baltimore lined up in a double slot formation and ran a crossing route with the two inside receivers. Eric Sellars, fueled by the barnyard pimp, got around the edge on a speed rush and hit the quarterback just as he let the ball go. It fluttered, hanging in the air over the middle for what seemed like an eternity. Driftwood saw the ball floating toward him as if in slow motion and knew he had a chance. He launched himself into the air at the same time as the Avengers' tight end, but got to the football an instant before the hellacious collision. Both players bounced backward on impact and landed hard on the ground. The Baltimore tight end laid motionless on the ground. Driftwood couldn't breathe, but somehow, through the sheer force of his will, he popped up and flip the ball to the umpire.

Interception! Blizzard ball.

The crowd booed mercilessly as the Avengers tight end was now writhing on the ground. Driftwood trotted to the sideline, his breath coming back slowly but surely. He was especially thankful none of his teammates jumped on him to celebrate. Call them quick learners. Instead, they celebrated amongst themselves. Big E was getting the bulk of the love for forcing the play. From the outside looking in, it was almost as if Driftwood was pitching a perfect game and nobody wanted to jinx him as he sat alone on the bench once more.

So far, it *was* a perfect game. In six plays, he had made five tackles, three of them for losses, a sack, and he had knocked a running back, a wide receiver, and now the tight end out of the game. He had delivered thundering hits on each of his tackles and on the sixth play he intercepted a pass.

The Buffalo offense once again capitalized on the excellent field position. This time Ben Brady hit his own tight end, Delvin Simpson, up the seam for a 22-yard touchdown strike and the Blizzard took a 10-0 lead.

The weather worsened and both teams struggled to move the ball with any consistency the remainder of the game. Buffalo added another touchdown late in the third quarter after a Baltimore fumble deep in their own territory. Petrucci plowed into the end zone and the lead went to 17-0. Driftwood's tackle streak had ended after the second series, but he maintained his intensity all the way through to the start of the fourth quarter when Coach Faber lifted him from the game for Billy Brogan.

Driftwood had never before protested when Coach Faber took him out of a game but was pissed this time around.

"What the fuck are you doing, Lester?"

"Hey, fuck you," Coach Faber said. "I coach this defense and I'll play who I want whenever the hell I want."

"That's bullshit. All you fuckers are trying to take my job and shove it up Brogan's ass. It's a bunch of bullshit!"

At that point he had taken a wild, round-house swing at Coach Faber right there on the sideline. Chuckles and a couple of players were already holding Driftwood back and the punch had no chance of landing. It was more symbolic than anything.

But not to Lester Faber. A couple of guys had to hold him back as the old coach had some fight in him, too. He was ready to do any dance Driftwood knew and maybe a few he didn't. This mayhem was all caught by the television cameras and the game announcers were having a field day with it. Driftwood already had 23 tackles in the game and had been killing guys all over the field, playing like a madman for the past two and a half hours. Now the guy was trying to hit his coach as well. This dude was nuts. It was all quite entertaining.

After things settled down, Jack sat on the bench and began a slow, steady crash. He hadn't lost his mind to that extreme in years and he had very little recollection of the game. Steadily he came out of his rage, and by the end of the game he had almost settled down to his normal, jovial self. But a hollow, empty feeling lingered in his chest.

Walking to the locker room after the 17-0 victory, Stark lagged behind to check on his partner. "Dude, what the hell got into you today?"

"Hate List," Jack said. "It's something my dad taught me a long time ago. I played this game for him and my mom and against every cocksucker in the universe – real or imagined."

Jack pictured the last time he had seen Big Ed and Erma in his mind the same way he always did when thinking of them: They were sitting in the front seat of Big Ed's Caddy, which was packed to the gills, fixing to drive all the way back home to Missouri. They both had tears in their eyes, which was something of a Driftwood family tradition during good-byes. Those tears began to rise in the eyes of their battle-worn son.

"God, I miss them," he choked.

Jack was an emotional mess from building and then unleashing his hatred with unmatched intensity over the past twenty-four hours. Now his heart felt like a cold stone in an otherwise empty box as he thought about his mom and dad. Were they proud of him? He started to sob and the last surge of emotion came gushing out of him at once like a flashflood.

The outburst was over as quickly as it started as Jack pulled himself together. Jack leaned into Stark and threw his arm around him. Together they walked through the wind and rain, across the soaked field toward the celebration going on in their victorious locker room. The way the rain was coming down you couldn't tell who was crying.

# Chapter Seventeen

**Driftwood Spoils Great Game with Wild Punch**
***How Long until Blizzard Linebacker Goes Completely Off the Rails?***
By Budd Kilmer
Buffalo News Sports Editor

(Baltimore, MD) Jack Driftwood played like a man possessed in leading the Buffalo Blizzard defense to their first shutout in more than three years in yesterday's 17-0 win over the Baltimore Avengers. Possessed by what, however, is anybody's guess, although evil would have to be included in the description. Perhaps it was the same spirit that overtook him in The Longhouse not two weeks ago when he choked a Pittsburgh Brawler fan into unconscious submission, which led to the brutal revenge beating of Blizzard running back Earl Johnson. If you don't remember the incident just go ask Earl and his busted arm.

Driftwood started the game in a similar rage which saw him choke the life out of the Avenger offense, especially in the first two series when he tallied five tackles, three for loss, a sack, an interception, and three cart-offs of Baltimore players. The carnage continued for three full quarters, in which Driftwood amassed an amazing 23 tackles, until Buffalo defensive coordinator Lester Faber decided to call off the dog. But even Coach Faber couldn't control this rabid fleabag.

Upon being informed he was done for the day, Driftwood felt the need for one more hit. But the target was no longer wearing an Avenger uniform. Driftwood was still spitting fire on the Buffalo bench and went after one of his own. After a heated verbal exchange, the unstable Buffalo Linebacker took a wild, roundhouse swing at Lester Faber, his own coach.

Faber is no small man nor an easy mark. I personally watched him play an aggressive brand of linebacker in the NAFA, albeit some 28 years or so ago. And yet, I would have hated to see the resulting damage to the venerable old coach had Driftwood connected. Who knows, perhaps Driftwood would have put Faber on the shelf, too. Right next to Earl Johnson and that Pittsburgh fan.

While Driftwood's on field dominance was incredible and easily the best defensive performance this reporter has seen in his 40-

plus year's covering the NAFA brand of football, his sideline sucker-punch attempt was the most egregious performance witnessed over that same span. One has to wonder if anybody is going to address this issue and actually do something about it.

Or is this a reprisal of the exciting but disconcertingly undisciplined brand of football we observed during Head Coach Howard Ivy's first tenure in Buffalo? Is Jack Driftwood's heinous and disgusting behavior a symptom of deep-seated respect and discipline issues beneath the glass roof of the Wigwam? Do you recall the "Bickering Blizzard" days of yore when Ivy's teams seemed to teeter on the edge of chaos? Ultimately, was it their lack of discipline and harmony within the ranks that cost Buffalo multiple Mega Bowl titles?

There is an old proverb that says the first time a dog bites it's the dog's fault; the second time it's the master who is to blame. How many times must Jack Driftwood bite before he is put down? I guess only Donald Fegel has that answer. Let's hope Mr. Fegel figures it out before Driftwood turns truly rabid and bites again. Bad Dog!

Officially Jack Driftwood had 23 tackles, six tackles for loss, a sack, an interception, two passes broken up, and 10 big hits in the Baltimore game. When the NAFA weekly awards were announced the following day there was no doubt who would be the Defensive Player of the Week. ESPN had spliced together the first six defensive plays from the game and had made the resulting montage their number one play of the day.

Unfortunately, they had tagged Jack's swing at Coach Faber on the end as the final image. Once again, Jack Driftwood was portrayed in the media as an out of control madman. Nobody could remember a more dominating performance by a defender in the history of the league. However, the focus of most of the conversation was on Jack's fateful punch and the rage that fueled it. The man clearly had anger issues.

In the locker room after the game, Coach Ivy had given him the game ball. In return, Jack had given it to Coach Faber and made a tearful apology for his outburst and for taking a poke at his coach. Coach Faber accepted the apology but refused to take the football. He told Jack in front of the team that it was the best damn game he had ever seen a linebacker play and if anyone ever deserved a game ball it was Jack Driftwood. They embraced and the whole team had gone crazy cheering.

And that was the end of it. Only it wasn't. It was just the beginning.

The trouble started when Donald Fegel got hit with several emails from a few of his friendly fellow NAFA General Managers busting his balls about his obvious lack of control over the team and how Driftwood could kick his ass. Donald was not amused. That was bad enough, but the Budd Kilmer article had sent him through the roof.

Imagine: A star player takes a swing at your defensive coordinator on national TV, this after the player had played the game of his life and the team had won in a shutout to remain undefeated! It didn't make sense. Donald, in his whole life, had never seen anything like it. To him it was cut and dried. You win, you are happy; you lose, you are miserable. The intensity and emotional swings of playing the game were like a foreign language to him; he didn't comprehend it. Moreover, it was much simpler and infinitely more convenient to blame Jack Driftwood for the whole ugly mess.

Donald must have watched the replay of the incident a hundred times before deciding he was humiliated and embarrassed that such a thing had occurred on his sidelines during a game. He tried to tell himself it really didn't even matter that it was Jack Driftwood who was responsible. This type of behavior was unacceptable, regardless of who had done it.

But it *was* Jack Driftwood who did it; Driftwood, again. He kept pushing the envelope, hanging ten over the abyss. A part of Donald almost respected that. But it was an infinitesimally small part.

He intended to test the waters at the full staff meeting to see if anyone else was as appalled as he was and also thought some action need be taken. He wanted Driftwood fined and put on a zero tolerance probation. So much as a sideways glance from the outlaw and he would be cut – no questions asked. He would even be in favor of a suspension but knew there was little to no chance of that happening. Everybody was all agog because the son of a bitch had played his tail off. It was the only thing currently saving his skin, at least in Donald's mind.

He decided against talking privately with Howard about the matter prior to the meeting. Howard had a soft, if not blind, spot for Driftwood. The Golden Boy could do no wrong in the old man's eyes. But Donald knew from personal experience that shit flowed downhill, and if he poured enough of it in Driftwood's direction the guy was bound to get some on him. That would surely ratchet up the pressure on Driftwood. The way the guy was going he was bound to self-destruct before too long as it was. Perhaps a subtle push was all that was needed.

The meeting went smoothly and was a rather jovial occasion, such was the case when the taste of defeat has yet to touch one's lips. Donald had breezed through his agenda, and after hitting each item on his list he broached the Driftwood issue.

"There is one other bit of business I wanted to discuss before we get out of here," Donald said. "As you are all aware, during the game yesterday we had an altercation between one of our players and his coach on the sidelines that was graphically documented by the national television broadcast. A clip of the incident is being played all over the media to the point where it is ubiquitous. We are becoming the laughingstock of the NAFA. I have reviewed the footage of the incident multiple times and personally find it very distasteful, demeaning, and humiliating. It undermines the authority of our coaching staff and, by extension, management, myself and Mr. Wainscott. I am concerned to the point of contemplating fining the player involved and perhaps even suspending him. I also want him on probation – one more incident and he is gone, no questions asked. Opinions?"

"Donald," Gerry said, "are you for real? You can't be serious. I —"

"Excuse me, Miss Wainscott," Howard Ivy cut in before she could finish, "please allow me to handle this. After all, team discipline of this nature falls directly under the realm of my jurisdiction."

Gerry leaned back, raising her hands in deference. "It's all yours, Howard."

Coach Ivy nodded at her in appreciation before wading in. "Donald, though I appreciate your concern in this matter, if there is dysfunction on my staff in regards to the discipline of a player, I will personally address said dysfunction. Furthermore, this is not the appropriate setting in which to discuss this type of matter. In the future, if you have concerns pertaining to the discipline of *my* football team, I would appreciate it if you would approach me in private so we can properly address it, together. In private.

"I would also caution you to not let your personal vendettas or feelings cloud your judgment regarding such issues. Football is a very emotional game and conflict is an inherent aspect of it. It is very easy to sit up here in your ivory tower and pass judgment on such things. As far as I am concerned this matter was closed after the player, whose name is Jack Driftwood, by the way, apologized in the locker room after the game. Now, if there is nothing else you wish to discuss, I have *serious* work to do."

With that Coach Ivy got up and left the meeting without awaiting a response. Donald went from speechless to furious.

"This meeting is adjourned," he snapped as Howard exited the room.

Everyone else quickly left as well, except for Gerry. Somebody needed to try to patch things up before they blew out of proportion. Diffusing volatile situations was something she had always excelled at. Regardless of how antagonistic things became, she possessed a gift where she would somehow find a way to build a consensus and keep relationships positive and productive. This ability and empathy had been the cornerstone of her success in London and she could already see this becoming an important part of her role within the Blizzard organization. Lord knows, they had enough conflict around the place.

After fuming until they were completely alone, Donald was ready to speak.

"Well, what do *you* think?"

"I think Howard is right on this one," Gerry said. "I was there in the locker room right next to you when Jack apologized. It's over. It ended right there. And I don't think there will be any detrimental effect on the team. I was just as shocked as you were by Jack's behavior, but it's time to move on – nobody got hit or hurt and people can laugh all they want, we are undefeated. Besides, the guy played one of the best games in the history of the league, cut him some slack. You would think you would be fighting to keep him on the field so we keep winning."

She had him there. Donald cared about winning above all else. He grunted and was beginning to let it go. He just hated that Driftwood could get away with going after a coach just because he played a decent ball game. The guy always got preferential treatment while the real people had to work their butt off to get anywhere while paying the full price for their mistakes.

"You also need to approach Howard and clear the air with him, he was quite upset by this and you owe the man an apology. This kind of thing is really something you should have gone directly to him about rather than throwing it out in a full-staff, non-football meeting like that. You know better than that. The rumors flying around this place right now will be on the news by dinnertime."

Donald lowered his head slowly until his forehead rested on the table and then lightly he pounded it on the table a few times.

"I was just trying to make sure everything keeps going well around here. Run a tight ship."

Gerry put a hand on his shoulder. "Donald, after tailing you and observing for a while now, I have figured out a large part of your job consists of solving everybody else's biggest problems. Every issue that arises that somebody can't handle on their own gets thrown onto your plate. And that's how you thrive; it's what you're good at. But when things are going well and there are no problems, you start looking for them when they aren't there. You *do* know things go good once in a while, don't you? And right now, things are pretty darn good around here."

She rubbed his shoulder and her softly spoken but firm words had a soothing effect on him. Donald softened under her gentle touch. She was right. She was right about everything; things were pretty darn good, especially with the way she was touching him. He reached over and took her hand from his shoulder into both of his.

"You are right, I will go talk to Howard right away. Thank you, Gerry. Your dad would be so proud of you."

He softly kissed the palm of her hand before he turned and left the room.

Howard Ivy was livid. He stormed into his office and slammed himself into his chair. Gary Chuckles was hot on his heels, eager to calm his coach down.

"Gary, what the hell just happened in there? Was I out of line? Because I don't believe so. This episode with Lester and Jack was nothing. Why does Donald have to make such a big deal out of it? I'll tell you why, because he has deeply entrenched personal issues with Jack. Well, guess what? That's just *too* damn bad. Grow up and get over it."

Gary Chuckles was a great listener. It was one of the many reasons he had survived and thrived for so long in the Blizzard organization. He knew when to shut up and he knew when to talk. Occasionally, he provided sage advice under duress.

"I wouldn't get too upset. Feegs is just doing what he does. He's always got to have a problem and when he doesn't, he manufactures one. And his favorite problem is Jack Driftwood."

Before Howard could even begin to respond, Donald Fegel popped into the doorway, startling them both. Gary started to get up to leave.

"You're okay, Gary. Please, stay," Donald said. "Coach, I have to apologize. You were right about everything you said back there. I should have come to you right off the bat if I had a problem. Sometimes I don't handle it very well when things are going so good. I tend to go from crisis to crisis, but you and your coaches are doing such a bang-up job there is nothing for me to fix right now. I am truly sorry for not coming to you with my concerns."

This was the most contrite Howard had ever seen Donald Fegel. He was almost at a loss for words.

"I greatly appreciate that, Donald. I certainly understand, and, frankly, it is a remarkable insight on your part. I'm impressed. You are wholly forgiven."

Donald smiled and shook Howard's hand. He even shook Gary's hand before jauntily ambling from the room.

After Donald's exit, Howard looked Gary Chuckles dead in the eye. "Who the hell was that and what has he done with Donald Fegel?"

When he got back to his office Donald sat in his chair and thought about Gerry Wainscott and how she made him a better man. He was becoming awfully attracted to the lovely Ms. Wainscott. He could see it in his mind, if things continued to move forward, who knows what could happen between the two of them down the line. Perhaps they would get serious. Very serious. Then no one could hold him back. The whole shooting match would be his.

He clicked on the TV in his office feeling much better about things. He looked up at the TV and there was Jack Driftwood's face covering the entire surface of the fifty-seven-inch flat-screen monitor hanging on the office wall. Apparently people could not get enough of this circus sideshow freak.

All of his anger and rage came roaring back in that instant. He shut the thing off, but it was too late. His mood was already ruined again. Because they were all wrong; he did have a big problem that just wouldn't go away. That problem was the man on the TV screen and he knew he would never be completely happy with Jack Driftwood still around.

*No matter what, it'll never work with that bastard. He's got to go, one way or the other. And the sooner the better!*

# Chapter Eighteen

The Buffalo Seneca Casino was packed, racked, and stacked for action on a Monday evening in late September. The Nation was doing extremely well financially with their new downtown operation and was smartly running a Monday Night Football promotion. A sure-fire way to drum up interest for any event in Buffalo was as simple as slapping the NAFA logo on it. Regardless of the product or promotion, tie it to the Blizzard and odds were pretty good it'd come out a winner.

Jack was duly impressed with the transformation of the waterfront; the casino, the Wigwam, and the ancillary businesses the project had spawned were a major hit in downtown Buffalo. The Chippewa Street bars were still going strong and it seemed most of the commerce in the Casino District was new. The town was enjoying a rare economic uptick.

A revitalized downtown pleased Jack, as Buffalo had become his home. He was planning to stay and live in town after his playing days were finally over, which would undoubtedly occur in a few, short months. He wasn't sure what he would do to make a buck and fill his time once he hung up the cleats. He had originally contemplated a career in coaching but knew it was a thankless, all-consuming vocation. One intriguing possibility was getting into the television business as a football game analyst. By all appearances those guys had life by the balls. He would often talk shop with the current announcers when they were in town to call a Blizzard game.

The consensus was the job was akin to playing, only nobody beat the hell out of you every Sunday afternoon, at least physically. You still got to speak the language, hang out with coaches and players, and watch film; not to mention the travel and notoriety. From what Jack could gather the money was pretty good, especially at the upper levels of the industry. Many former players and coaches had successfully made the transition from the field to the television booth. Why the hell not him as well?

Jack was thinking about all those things as he pulled his Jeep into the valet parking lane. He was dressed casually in jeans and a T-shirt underneath the Maryville Spoofhounds pullover his Uncle Jack had sent him. His former high school was the only one in the country with the nickname Spoofhounds, a source of fierce pride.

Jack tried to remain as anonymous as possible as he entered the vast lobby of the luxury hotel. It wasn't like it was a big deal, he just didn't care for people all up in his business. He pulled down the hoodie, effectively shrouding his face, and quickly made his way through the crowded lobby to the escalator that would take him to the second floor and the Bull's Horn, the restaurant where he had agreed to meet Gerry Wainscott.

He had wasted no time wrangling an opportunity to spend a little quality time with the lovely Ms. Wainscott after their encounter at Prior Aviation. He knew from experience if a relationship was to have even half a chance at becoming meaningful and long lasting, there had to be a "Talk." It was imperative to lay out the parameters of a budding romance, especially one facing such impossible circumstances. Jack was a little nervous; for all he knew she might tell him to piss off. The preposterous thought made him smile. It certainly was a possibility but highly unlikely. He knew the girl liked him, she liked him a lot and had already demonstrated as much.

However, he couldn't think of a bigger conflict of interest than an owner dating a player. There had to be rules or policies strictly forbidding such an unlikely liaison. Or was it so far-fetched that nobody had even thought to outlaw it? Jack supposed he would find out soon enough.

Despite the myriad complications and impossible hurdles, they were still contemplating an attempt at a relationship. Jack shook his head, overwhelmed at the thought of it all. It was too much to think about; all he knew was he liked the way she made him feel. He liked thinking about her and hearing her say his name. This was about more than just getting into her bloomers, though the thought *had* definitely crossed his mind.

"So there must be *something* wrong with the perfect Mr. Jack Driftwood," Gerry said, although if there was she had yet to find it.

The guy was starting to seem too good to be true. He had met her for a few drinks at the bar inside the Bull's Horn to talk about their relationship. So far they had discussed everything but. That was about to change, though.

Jack attempted a thoughtful pause before replying. "Well, I am humble to a fault, but the rest is a secret."

"I don't know about humble, but the secret part is a good idea, Jack." Gerry looked into his eyes and saw a flicker of pain as her message registered. "I hate that it has to be that way, but for now I think it best to keep things under wraps. We don't need the attention or the potential distraction it could bring. Imagine the field day Budd Kilmer and his cronies in the media would have."

"Yeah, but we ain't doing nothing wrong, you know. We're both single, consenting adults. But I figured that would have to be the case, for now, anyways. I don't want to cause trouble for you with the team or especially with your father."

"I know. Honestly, I am not sure what he would think, but he has enough to worry about as it is. We can just start out seeing each other on the sly. It's actually kind of a turn-on. A trifle naughty."

She spoke in a husky, conspiratorial tone and leaned in close enough to Jack that she could smell him. A subtle mixt of musk and sandalwood. He even smelled perfect.

"I think you are gonna end up wearing my ass out," he said.

"I doubt that."

She laughed and felt a flush of heat radiate through her body at the thought of it. She wasn't sure how this was going to go but she had a feeling it was going to be a lot of fun finding out.

"So what's it like sitting with the future NAFA Defensive Player of the Week," Jack asked, perking up in his chair like a peacock.

Things were pretty much settled and they were going to see one another secretly for a time to see if their mutual attraction was more than just pheromones and overactive glands. Fair enough. Now Jack was eager to move on to talking about other things.

"Oh my goodness! You were an animal, Jack! I'm no expert on football – yet – but you made every tackle. If you aren't the NAFA Defensive Player of the Week then I don't know what it would take."

"Aw shucks," Jack said, "it was nothing. Aren't you the lucky girl, sitting here with a big football star and all?"

"It was like you lost your mind out there, though," she said with clear concern, utterly ignoring his false modesty and pretension. "Seriously Jack, you really scared me. To see you in a rage like that…it was awful. How do you get like that when just the day before I saw you go out of your way to help that poor flight attendant carry her bag?"

"I don't know," Jack said. "It isn't as easy as it looks, at least not for me. I gotta work at it, you know. I have to have a whole different mindset when I go out on that field."

"I *know* that. I mean, how do you turn on your darker side? What makes you so angry?"

Jack could see she was truly interested in what made him tick. The only problem with that was he wasn't completely sure himself, but he *was* warming up to the idea of discussing it with her.

"Sometimes, I use an old Jedi mind-trick my dad taught me when I was younger. I focus on all the shit I hate leading up to the game and work myself into a bit of a frenzy. I kinda like put together a Hate List. That's what I did in

Baltimore, anyway. Of course, it didn't hurt when Feegs got me all pissed off at the pregame meal."

"Why? What did Donald do?"

"I was sitting there across from Brogan and Stark, minding my own business, quietly eating when he swaggers up to our table like some bigshot dickhead. Then he pulls his usual shit where he absolutely ignores me and tells Steven and Billy how great they are and how they are going to be the best ever once he gets me out of the way. I was already worked up because of the Hate List and all, so I throw my fork onto the table and kinda mutter something about a 'fuckin' asshole' and storm out. I was pretty much done eating anyway. So as I'm walking out I hear him say, 'What's up his ass?' and then laugh all loud like he is some kind of comedian. I wanted to turn around and go punch him in the face, but I'm glad I didn't. Ironically, I probably ought to thank the fucker for putting me over the edge."

"Do you make a Hate List every week?" she asked.

"Nah, I only do that when I need to. No offense, but in the spirit of full disclosure, I felt like I had lost my edge because I was so damn giddy about seeing you last Wednesday night. I was walking around with my head up my ass up after that. I'm not one of those guys who *plays* football, Gerry; I go to war. I have to each and every Sunday, because I'm physically overmatched going up against some of these young studs. I need some kind of edge because knowledge only takes you so far. So I made myself as miserable as possible and took it out on Baltimore."

"Jesus, Jack, you were killing those poor guys! You were like a schoolyard bully out there. Please remind me to never piss you off."

"I don't think that would be possible," he said.

"I don't know, I can be a serious bitch." Gerry tried to be serious but burst out laughing.

"I don't doubt that."

"Hey," she protested and playfully punched him in the arm. "You know, Donald wanted to fine you today for taking that swing at Coach Faber."

"What?" Jack said louder than he intended, snapping upright in his chair.

She instantly regretted bringing it up. "Don't worry, Jack. Coach Ivy wouldn't hear of it. He told Donald he was way out of line and the matter was settled. I spoke to him after everybody left the meeting and told him he needed to go apologize. And he did. He went right to Howard's office and made nice."

Jack settled back down into the chair and assumed his usual slouch.

"You know, I don't even give a shit. That guy has hated me pretty much since I got here, so nothing surprises me when it comes to him. The prick."

"What's the deal with that?" she asked. "Why do you two hate each other so much?"

Jack sighed and shook his head. It was a long, sad story spanning nearly two decades, and he didn't plan on wasting his time with her talking about that jackass Fegel. But she needed to know what kind of bastard the man really was, if only for her own good.

"I guess, for my part, it's because I know what a scumbag, low-life crook he is. He's nothing more than a common thief. Back when I was a rookie a bunch of money and jewelry disappeared from the locker room. I know it was him. He never got caught, but I know, Gerry. He did it, alright. And I've seen him stab people in the back countless times over the years. He loves to talk behind people's backs. I truly believe he would sell out his own mother if he thought it would give him an edge. He's just a bad egg. And the reason he hates me is because I know it. I know it and he knows I know it, and that's why he hates me."

"Then why does my dad think so much of him?" she asked.

"Good question," Jack said with a tinge of bitterness.

"Seriously."

"Look, your dad is as loyal a person as I have ever met. He's the only reason I'm still here. He's been better to me than anyone I have ever known other than my parents. And I have to give it to Fegel, he has worked his ass off for your dad. He may even care for him, as much as he is capable, anyways. I'm not denying Feegs has worked hard to get where he's at, and your dad has rewarded him handsomely for that. *Very handsomely*. But Feegs is a goddamn weasel. He has shit on a ton of people over the years but never your father, and rarely in front of him. He's a compulsive criminal and I guarantee you he is stealing from somewhere. That's what thieves do. And that's what worries me. He has access to everything and I'm afraid before it's all over he is gonna take one big, final dump on all of us – your father, this organization, me, you – all of us. A mega-dump, and it's gonna rain shit down everywhere. Unless I can stop his ass first."

"What do you mean?"

"I don't know exactly what it will be, but I know Feegs, and the fucker is a defective human being. He's missing some inner parts. The guy is a sociopath and with people like that it's just a matter of time…"

"I don't know about all of that," she said skeptically. "He isn't perfect, but I don't think he is evil. And I hope you are wrong about him hurting my father and the team. That would be just awful."

"I hope I am wrong, too. I really do. But I doubt it. Once a shitter always a shitter, I say."

Gerry smiled to herself when the elevator car arrived and was empty. She wasn't sure if Jack was going for a repeat performance of their previous ascent to the eighteenth floor, but she was ready, able, and willing. The more time she spent with the tall, handsome man, the more she liked him. Not to mention he was one exceptional kisser, at least as far as she could remember. She had been fairly drunk the previous Wednesday. Though if memory served her, and it usually did, the guy knew his way around a woman's mouth. She was musing about their previous experience when the elevator door closed and Jack grabbed her and pulled her into his arms.

He kissed her with an incredible hunger and she pushed right back against his hard, rippling body. He reached around and cupped her bottom with both hands and a pleasurable moan escaped her as she gasped for breath. Reciprocating, she wrapped her arms around his waist and massaged his large bubble butt with her petite hands. He lifted her off the ground so her face was even with his. Instinctively she wrapped her legs around him and he pushed her against the wall, grinding away at her with his hips. She squeezed him with her legs as tightly as she could and drove her tongue deep into his mouth. It was on!

The spell was broken when the elevator dinged, announcing they had arrived at the eighteenth floor. Before the door could open Jack set her back down and they both straightened themselves up. She caught his eye and they burst into laughter. It was a good thing the building wasn't any taller, she wasn't sure what would have happened if they had spent more time in that elevator.

By the time they reached her room she had simmered down a bit. Though she was sorely tempted to invite him in, there would be a time for that. After their previous episode she needed to reestablish her self-control as much as he needed to see her do so.

"Thank you for a wonderful time, but –"

"Whoa, whoa, whoa," Jack interrupted. "Wait a second here. Are you shutting me down? After calling me a pussy last week? Oh my God! You are. *You* are shutting *me* down? That is hilarious."

"I can't have you thinking I'm some easy piece of ass, now, can I?"

"No, that wouldn't be right. But I won't think that, I promise."

"Now you are begging. Very unbecoming, especially for a man of your stature." She laughed at him as he feigned great pain.

"Guilt now, too? Man, you are good. Alright then, missy. But just so you know, I'm going to be watching you very closely from afar. And your day is coming, sweetlips. Your day is coming."

"I guess we will have to see about that," she said as she slipped into her room. "Goodbye, Jack."

She closed the door behind her and collapsed against it, hugging herself. That was a close call, but she managed to keep her dignity intact this time. A long cold shower and she would be just fine.

# Chapter Nineteen

Every team, from Pop Warner leagues to the big leagues, has an arch rival. Some of these rivalries are geographical; some are built around a repeated history of close, high-stakes games; others originated with personality conflicts. On occasion, a rivalry will stem from getting your ass kicked for an entire decade. Such was the case in the intense rivalry between Buffalo and the South Florida Riptide. Back in the '70s South Florida beat the Blizzard twenty consecutive times; an entire decade of ass-whippings.

South Florida had started the season with a 3-1 record, so this particular edition of the rivalry had the added excitement of being an early season battle for the top of the Seaboard Division. Kickoff had been moved back to 4:25 p.m. to accommodate the television folks who had made it the featured late afternoon game.

Buffalo, with their 4-0 start, was beginning to garner a modicum of respect from around the league. However, there were still plenty of skeptics. People had seen this act play out in Buffalo before. The Blizzard were notorious for starting fast before fading into the sunset come crunch time, as evidenced by their epic collapse the previous season. The "wait and see" crowd had a valid point.

One of the main attractions in this game was South Florida's Star-Bowl running back, Weston "Scoop" Brackett. Brackett had led the NAFA in rushing the past three seasons and was tearing it up again. Brackett had acquired the nickname Scoop as a child. He was a chubby, roly-poly little guy who would do anything for a scoop of ice cream. His mother began calling her little man Scoop and still does to this day. So does everybody else.

Scoop was averaging 172 yards rushing per game and nobody had yet been able to slow him down. There was no argument; Scoop was the best back the NAFA had seen in a long time, perhaps ever. This played right into South Florida's style of play – they relied on the running game to speed up the clock and played opportunistic defense with stout special teams. The success of the ground game also produced one of the best play-action passing attacks in the league, creating big chunk plays for the Riptide offense.

It was a typical late-September day in Miami: Sunny with highs in the upper eighties and a chance for a passing shower late in the afternoon. South Florida won the toss and took the football. They wasted no time driving down the field using a heavy dose of Scoop Brackett. Scoop was a unique combination of size, speed, quickness and power. He stood six foot two and weighed 245 pounds and ran a sub 4.4 forty. The first time Driftwood tackled him it felt like running into a damn oak tree.

The Riptide had pounded the ball inside the Buffalo 10-yard line and had it 1st and goal to go at the seven. They came out in 22 personnel, a power running set deploying two backs, two tight ends, and one wide receiver. In an obvious attempt to establish their physical brand of ball, they ran a basic power play right into the teeth of the Buffalo defense. The strategy was simple enough – mass big bodies at the point of attack. They pulled the backside guard around to kick out the contain man and also led with the fullback into the hole. It was straight ahead power football as the Riptide quarterback, Bill Harris, pivoted and handed the ball to Scoop deep in the backfield.

Stark was the play-side linebacker and attacked the fullback with his inside shoulder, effectively executing his responsibility of turning the play back inside. On the backside, Driftwood scraped over the top but was intercepted by the block of the center. The center had a perfect cut-off angle because Bo-Bo had let the guy off the line clean.

*Goddammit, Bo-Bo! Do your job!*

Driftwood had to give ground to clear the center and was late and a little bit off balance by the time he filled the hole. His chest was open from his late escape, and Scoop hit him in the sternum with a lowered shoulder, picking him up off the ground. Scoop transported Driftwood all the way into the end zone where he dumped him onto the ground. To rub it in, Scoop put his hand on Driftwood's facemask to leverage himself up off the ground.

Once up, Scoop stood over Driftwood screaming and yelling at him while pounding on his chest with one arm and holding the football high over his head with the other.

"You just got Scooped, old man!"

Driftwood scrambled to get up and go after him, but he was too late. Stark heard the exchange and pushed Scoop hard from behind. The big back stumbled over the still supine Driftwood before landing on top of him. The two battle-clad gladiators began rolling around on the ground engaging in close-quarter, hand-to-hand combat. Driftwood grabbed a handful of Scoop's exposed skin at his waist and twisted, squeezed, and pinched as hard as he could as they continued to grapple. Scoop let out a shrilly howl, sounding like a little girl. Flags flew all over the place as players and officials arrived at the fray to break it up.

When they got everyone untangled Scoop was still pissed. An official had him wrapped up with both arms around his waist to prevent him from going back after Driftwood.

"That chicken-shit motherfucka pinched me like a little bitch!"

Scoop stepped back out of the refs grasp and lifted up his jersey to show him an ugly welt on his right hip that was reddening before their eyes.

"Gosh," Driftwood said, "that looks pretty nasty, Mr. Scoop-dog. You ought to be more careful."

"Fuck you, Drifty."

He renewed his attempt to engage and got close enough to try to poke Driftwood in the eyes through his facemask. In doing so, he hit the official with his arm, which knocked off his hat. More flags flew as Scoop's teammates finally pulled him away from the fracas and back toward their sideline. Due to Scoop's last outburst South Florida was penalized 15 yards on the ensuing kickoff.

After huddling, the officiating crew determined the contact with the ref was unintended and incidental and they decided to let Brackett stay in the game despite the rule for contacting an official that called for immediate expulsion. They also took the preventative measure of warning both benches. It was a good thing; this game was already getting out of hand and it had just begun.

Buffalo took full advantage of the Riptide penalty when Martin Bershear caught the ensuing kickoff at his own 24-yard line and busted it straight up the middle untouched for a 76-yard touchdown return. The extra point was good and just like that it was 7-7 with 9:03 left in the first quarter.

The Buffalo defense had to go right back onto the field with little rest. South Florida kept to their plan of grinding it out on the ground. It was obvious they intended to wear the Blizzard defense down to a nub. Scoop was running like a man possessed, but he was also taking a serious pounding in the process as both teams were playing pissed off now. The Riptide moved steadily into Buffalo territory, reaching the 42 after seven consecutive running plays. They had forced the Blizzard to commit eight men up in the box to stop the run, and even that wasn't entirely effective.

On the next down, the Riptide went to the play-action pass and caught the Blizzard secondary flat-footed, cheating up for the run. Harris faked it to Scoop and then hit James Sifton, his top wide receiver, on a deep square in for a gain of 23 down to the Buffalo 19. The Blizzard defenders were exhausted. The late afternoon heat was taking its toll on the cold-weather-conditioned northerners. Driftwood looked around at his teammates and knew another score was inevitable unless his boys had a chance to catch a blow. He signaled to the umpire burning a timeout.

He and Stark came to the sideline while the rest of the troops watered up and took a knee on the closely-cropped carpet of natural Bermuda grass. Bo-Bo started puking on the football due to the heat and his exhaustion and could have kissed Driftwood when he called the timeout. Driftwood would have politely declined.

Coach Faber stood stoically on the sidelines with his arms crossed awaiting his linebackers as they made their way over to him. Driftwood and Stark were huffing and puffing as they came and stood beside their coach. That was one thing Driftwood loved about Coach Faber. The man had played the game; he knew what it was like to be in the heat of the battle and would take input from his charges seriously. Coach Faber knew there was more than one way to skin a cat. He could draw up all kinds of brilliant schemes, but if his players didn't get it or buy in, it wouldn't amount to shit.

"Well, what do you think?"

"We need to blitz the fuckers," Driftwood gasped. "We need a big play, break their rhythm and get 'em behind the chains so they have to throw it."

Coach Faber nodded. "Let's go with 'Blitz the Set.' Archie says they are heavy running to the strength on early downs. Keep them guys going out there!"

Blitz the Set was a special defense Buffalo had installed for this game. The premise was to determine their blitz on the fly, based on South Florida's formation, which would confuse their blocking assignments and create unblocked "free-runners," as Coach Faber called them. Things would vary as far as who was blitzing, but the pressure would automatically come from the side of the strength of the formation at the snap. It was risky because a blown assignment could give up an easy score. If executed properly, though, it was a hell of a scheme, at least on paper. Turns out it wasn't too bad on the field, either.

The new scheme totally confused the Riptide's offensive line. The pressure from the initial free-runners, Driftwood and strong safety Eric Stillwaters, stopped the play before it could get started. Stillwaters arrived first and shot low, grabbing Scoop Brackett by the ankles three yards deep in the South Florida backfield. Stillwaters hung on to Scoop with both hands and started to roll like a crocodile, spinning Scoop around with him. The twisting action made Scoop a sitting duck when Driftwood came flying in high to finish things off. He hit Scoop with everything he had and the force of the blow knocked Brackett's helmet clean off, sending it rolling down the field.

Driftwood jumped up off the ground and bent over Scoop. "You just got Jacked, young man!"

Scoop looked up at Driftwood a bit shocked at first. Then he tossed his head back and started laughing. Driftwood laughed with him.

"That's a good one, there," Scoop said. "I gotta give you that one. But that pinching shit, man…"

"Sorry about that, Scoop, I lost my head for a minute there."

For the first time in his career, Jack Driftwood reached down and helped an opponent up off the ground. He couldn't help himself. He had never done so because he considered it aiding and abetting the enemy and had read a study stating such an act could cut aggressiveness up to thirty percent. He couldn't afford losing such a margin. He and Scoop shared a quick hug and a pat on the backside and then both headed back to their respective huddles. It was quite a spectacle, two fearless warriors displaying tremendous respect on the field of battle. But you could bet your boots they were both going to bring it on the next play.

South Florida was now behind the chains facing a 2nd and 13. They tried a screen pass but it was batted down by Bo-Bo. The big man had gotten his wind back after losing his lunch. On 3rd and long the Riptide threw another incomplete pass and had to settle for a 40-yard field goal. They took the lead, 10-7, but the Blizzard defense had stemmed the tide.

The score stayed that way until the final play of the first half when Bennie Tenudo knotted it up at 10-10 with a booming 52-yard field goal. The Buffalo offense had been dreadful throughout the first half. They couldn't get the running game going and Brady had very little time to throw the ball. On the other hand, the defense had settled in and was playing pretty well after their initial problems in stopping Scoop Brackett. The switch to using pressure on running downs had been effective, although Scoop still had 103 yards rushing in the half.

The Blizzard received the second-half kickoff and Martin Bershear almost broke another one. He smashed through the first wave of tacklers and scooted outside up the sideline. He was finally run out of bounds all the way down at the South Florida 35-yard line. That's where the Blizzard offense took over. The call in the huddle was a run, but Brady saw press coverage on Shady Solomon on the outside as the free safety was creeping up to blitz. He gave Shady a quick look and they both knew what time it was.

Brady checked to max protection at the line and took the snap. He took a five-step drop and let it fly down the sideline to Solomon, who beat the press coverage by cornerback by a couple steps. The ball was perfectly thrown and Shady gathered it in, coasting into the end zone for the touchdown. Buffalo took the lead. Tenudo shanked the extra point off the left upright, though, making the score 16-10.

The game continued to be a hard-fought, back-and-forth battle. South Florida finally got back on the board early in the fourth quarter on a long run by Brackett. The big back ran a simple off-tackle play and broke a couple of tackles and 45 yards later he was dancing in the end zone. The extra point was good and the Riptide had taken a slim lead, 17-16.

Because of the heat and the total number of plays on defense, Coach Faber was substituting liberally. Brogan was rotating with Driftwood and Stark on every other series. With 3:09 left in the game it paid off for the Blizzard. Eric Sellars tipped a pass at the line of scrimmage and Brogan intercepted it and brought it all the way back to the Riptide 27-yard line. The offense stalled out, but Tenudo made a 39-yard field goal and Buffalo regained the lead, 19-17.

Time was running out when South Florida got the ball back and began a desperation drive in an attempt to pull out the victory. They moved the ball to midfield with just 17 seconds left to play. The Riptide had one timeout remaining and needed to gain 15 to 20 yards to get into makeable field goal range. Harris was operating out of the shotgun and he sent all four of his receivers on vertical routes straight up the field. The inside slot receiver to his right was the tall and lanky James Sifton, the man Harris tended to look for in desperate situations.

Buffalo's free safety, Dave Gaston, had the coverage on Sifton and was in perfect position as Harris let the pass fly on a rope, 20 yards down the field through the middle of the Buffalo secondary. Just as the ball was arriving, Gaston planted to go up and knock it away. He was in perfect position to make the play but somehow the earth moved under his feet and he slipped, leaving Sifton wide open. Sifton easily caught the pass and went down immediately. Buffalo had no timeouts left and South Florida let the clock run down to three seconds remaining before using their final timeout.

The Riptide lined up for a 47-yard, game-winning field goal attempt. Buffalo came after it with everything they had, but the kick was a beauty and split the uprights perfectly with leg to spare. The Riptide won the game on the final play, 20-19.

Those missed extra points always seem to come back to bite you in the ass.

It was deathly quiet in the Buffalo locker room after the game. Dave Gaston was inconsolable. Many of the Blizzard players stopped at his locker to tell him it wasn't his fault and to keep his head up, others just patted him on the back in a show of support as they filed by. Driftwood pulled up a stool and sat down next to Dave, who had his head buried in his hands and was slumped over on the stool in front of his locker. He whispered into the young, second-year player's ear.

"Dave, you got to let it go right now and man up. You didn't lose this goddamn game, *we did.* Quit being selfish and share the blame. We win as one and lose as one, so take it like a man. Lift your head up, take a shower, and let's get the fuck out of here. Let's go."

To Gaston's credit, he did just that.

There is a long standing rule in all professional sports known as the "twenty-four-hour rule." Simply stated, win or lose, after twenty-four hours you move on to the next game. You couldn't get caught up in the emotions, you had to let it go. Otherwise, you wouldn't be ready to start mentally preparing for the next opponent. The old saying was "you can't let the same team beat you twice." It was all about maintaining an even keel; get too high after a win and you get complacent, get to low after a loss and you can't pull yourself out of that hole. Everybody, from the owner down to the last man on the bench, knew and abided by the rule. To do otherwise would drive you crazy.

However, this was not the case regarding Donald Allen Fegel Jr. He knew the twenty-four hour rule and personally considered it bullshit. Hanging onto losses was the best and only true motivation Donald had ever known. He didn't understand how people could just shrug off an agonizing defeat and come back to work smiling like nothing happened.

Donald was in his office at 6 a.m. the morning following the South Florida loss. He loved being in the office early in the morning with nobody else around. It made him feel like the whole place was his, the king of this mighty castle. His first order of business was to read the Buffalo News to see how badly they had hammered him and his team. But the hometown press had taken it relatively easy on the Blizzard, calling the hard-fought loss "disappointing but actual proof the Blizzard could go on the road and play with the NAFA's elite."

After reading the paper Donald punched up a copy of the team's roster and began to go through it name by name, feverishly comparing each player to his ready list of available prospects at each respective position. He was trying to determine if the Blizzard would be better served by jettisoning some old, stale meat and picking some that was both new and fresh, straight off the hoof.

*Something's got to be done to get these players' attention!*

After going through his entire list, he was satisfied the team currently had its personnel issues under control. He would bring a handful of possible new players in for a workout that Tuesday, as he did every week, but there was nobody on the list who really made him overly excited or was an immediate, certain upgrade.

The loss from the previous day still ate at his insides. He decided to bring in a pair of kickers for a gong-show competition against Tenudo. Putting a little extra pressure on Bennie could only help him regain his focus, and it would send a little message to the rest of them. Failure to execute in a critical situation may just cost you your job; as well it should.

This was a "what have you done for me lately" business, and getting too cozy or comfortable could derail even the most talented outfits. Besides, if that goddamn Tenudo had made the extra point, they may well be 5-0 right now. But the guy blew it so why shouldn't he have to sweat it out?

*Kickers. You never notice them until they screw it all up.*

He made a mental note to consult Howard about the plan; he didn't need him crying again.

Donald was entering his fourth year as the Blizzard General Manager after serving as the assistant GM for five years prior to that. He was driven to make a name for himself in the game and become wealthy in the process. He had already made his mark by putting together the deal with the Seneca Nation and the State of New York to build the Wigwam. It had been his pet project and personal obsession over the previous five years. He had not only overseen every detail of the deal with the Seneca Nation, but he also handled the contracting for the construction of the Wigwam and adjacent casino and hotel project. By cutting some corners in the material used in construction, as well as arranging some lucrative kickbacks with select contractors, he had managed to acquire a significant seven-figure personal windfall. The beauty of it was nobody was the wiser, nor would they be.

Mr. Wainscott had put his full trust in Donald to handle the project, and pressured him to not only to get it done on time, but also bring it in under budget. And that is exactly what Donald had done. It only reinforced the owner's nearly blind trust in him. So what if he made himself a millionaire in the process; Donald felt he deserved every single dime he had skimmed from the project, and more. After all, he was the one who had worked his ass off, logging hundred-hour weeks year-round handling every stinking detail of the immense undertaking.

He had had to dance with the devil himself to pull it off. But he did it. He had found and paid off the right people in the Seneca Nation to keep things quiet. He had dealt very carefully with the esteemed Senator from Western New York, William F. Blutarsky, to get his hands on over four hundred million tax-payer dollars to help fund the project. Of course, Senator Blutarsky was also handsomely rewarded for his part. Donald had greased the wheels of the almighty machine to fast track the entire deal. Hell, everybody had been so happy and excited about the project they would have turned a blind eye to even the most egregious bending of the law and building codes.

One of the benefits of the process was the creation of a network of people who could get things done and keep quiet about it. Donald had quite a list of unsavory characters he could count on to do whatever it took to do his bidding. He often contemplated how he and his faithful assistant, Colin Meade, might deploy this collection of talent to help his team win football games, but he had yet to figure that part of it out. Sending someone out to break the legs of the opposing quarterback, as good as the idea sounded, just could not be done – go ask Tonya Harding. Even so, just knowing he had that kind of muscle out on the streets made Donald feel invincible.

Colin Meade had also turned into an excellent find. He had met Meade many years ago in a luxury suite at a Sabre's hockey game and took an immediately liking to the odd, little fellow. They shared the same misanthropic ideals and mutual vigor to exact vengeance on a world that had delivered them both more than their fair share of hard knocks. Plus, Meade was the one who had the underground contacts on the mean streets of the world. It was ironic how a skinny, frail man like Meade knew how to manipulate people and get things done, one way or another. It helped that the man didn't have a moral bone in his body. Theirs was a match made in heaven, if one believed in such a place. However, neither of them did.

Donald's ultimate goal was to own the whole shebang: the stadium, the football franchise, the town. He had ingratiated himself to Mr. Wainscott early on, knowing it would be the key to his rise through the ranks. The old bird was loyal to a fault and he had fully exploited that weakness. He had been in excellent position to make a play for the team once Wainscott finally passed away. Then a curve ball came out of left field when Wainscott brought his daughter Gerry into the picture. Donald wasn't sure how that would alter the landscape, thus he had been playing things slow and easy, watching closely and calculating what his next move might be.

And now he was falling for her – how about that for your twisted ending! The more he thought about it, the more he realized she just may be his golden ticket. His path to owning the team could be as simple as a stroll down the aisle. How ironic would that be after all the work and maneuvering he had done to get to his current position. His pass to paradise could end up being the custom known as matrimony. Life was a funny thing.

The more time he spent around Gerry, the more he liked her. She could become the top trophy in his case. She was smart, beautiful, and caring. He hoped she would see the wisdom of such an alliance with him. And if she didn't, she would be no match for his drive, resources, and guile. Not in the long run. The team was going to be his.

A complete nobody who had never met his father and whose mother was nothing more than a superstitious crack-whore would lift himself up by his bootstraps, rise through the rank and file, and become the owner of a NAFA franchise. Even Hollywood couldn't come up with something like that, but to be sure, they would do a full-length motion picture telling his story. Donald sometimes fantasized about which famous movie star would play him in the movie. Brad Pitt seemed to work, right nice.

In the end, he would control, nay, own some of the strongest, most violent men on the planet. He would walk with kings and beautiful women would throw themselves at him. No longer would be he the scrawny kid wearing rags that all the bullies harassed and laughed at. He'd be the guy telling them what to do and writing their checks.

*Who's laughing now, bitches!*

# Chapter Twenty

The month of October was good to the Blizzard. They recovered nicely from the loss to South Florida despite the concerns of Donald Fegel and the usual cadre of their most self-loathing fans. They whipped Cleveland at home, 34-12, as the defense held the Greyhounds to just four field goals. Driftwood had a pretty average game in his mind, although it was quite productive on the stat sheet. He snagged a pair of interceptions and had a dozen tackles. But he was upset with himself over a couple of mental errors that could have been costly against a better opponent. He silently and solemnly vowed to clean things up.

He was awarded the game ball afterwards in the locker room, but he didn't feel his performance was worthy of the honor, so he passed it on to Gerald Wainscott III to proudly display in his Cleveland office. The owner graciously accepted the football. The win meant a lot to Wainscott personally, and it would certainly make his life much easier in Cleveland. It gave him bragging rights for at least another year and meant he wouldn't have to take any baloney from friends and business associates around town. Danny Steeley would have the ball neatly painted up with the date and score and it would be prominently displayed in the front window of his downtown Cleveland office. There it would serve as a reminder to all who came to call and a deterrent to any of the potential baloney-talkers.

The next week they travelled to Toronto and squeaked by the Gladiators, 24-21. Ben Brady tossed three TD passes, all to AC, and Bennie Tenudo redeemed himself for the missed extra point versus South Florida by hitting a game-winning, 42-yard field goal into a stiff wind with just 27 seconds left to play. That win ran their season record to a stout 6-1.

A visit from Montreal was up next. The Mayhem were struggling, having won only one game on the year and were no match for a hot Buffalo team. The Blizzard rolled big in this one, blowing out Montreal 37-7. The highlight of the game came in the third quarter when Driftwood intercepted his NAFA-leading fifth pass of the year.

The pick came when he stepped in front of a curl route by the outside receiver. Montreal had hit that route twice earlier in the game to convert first downs. On each occasion Coach Faber hadn't said a word. He just gave Driftwood a disparaging look and a sad shake of his head. The disappointment on Coach Faber's face had hurt Driftwood more than if his coach had yelled and chucked his cell phone at him.

Jack knew the play was coming the third time and baited the overconfident quarterback into making the throw. At the last instant, he dove in front of the receiver and snatched the ball out of the air, popped up, and was off and running. He had a nice return going, too, as he had maneuvered 20 yards down the field before running into traffic.

As he was being tackled he flipped the ball backwards, option style, to Steven Stark, who had followed him down the field screaming for the ball. Jack's lateral had been perfect and looked like a triple-option play from his high school days when he played quarterback in the Veer offense for the Spoofhounds. Stark scooted the remaining 30 yards to pay dirt, notching the second touchdown of his budding career.

Naturally, he came back to the Buffalo bench skipping and singing. "I scored another touchdown, I scored another touchdown!"

Jack wanted to kill him. He tried to claim half of the touchdown for himself but there were no "halfsies" when it came to touchdowns, and Stark was not much for sharing. The rookie was dancing, singing, and waiving a copy of the official stats tauntingly in Jack's face in the locker room after the game.

"Who scored another touchdown? Stark did. *Stark* did."

Jack tried to filch the stat sheet from Stark but the prick was too quick. Jack chased him around the locker room but couldn't catch the singing Steven. The whole team got a kick out of that.

Buffalo was 7-1 at the halfway point of the season, which translated into party time all over town. The excitement was palpable and nobody wanted to leave the Wigwam after they had put the boots to Montreal. The South Florida vs. Boston game was going on and Mr. Wainscott had it beamed live onto the stadium's video boards and paid the vendors to stick around to continue selling beer and food. Nearly half the crowd stayed to watch the game and they were rewarded with a Boston victory, putting Buffalo all alone atop the Seaboard Division.

Ben Brady arrived at the obvious conclusion it was time to host a major blow-out. Somebody must have dropped a hat. Brady didn't mess around when it came to such matters. He invited the entire Blizzard organization to his house in Clarence after the win over Montreal for the impromptu celebration. Being of the generous sort, the Blizzard signal caller wanted to spread the wealth.

He had already flown the Bacardi 151 Bikini Babes into town as weekend guests. This particular flock consisted of twelve young tanned and toned beauties from Tampa Bay, which added to the excitement and dramatically increased the morale of the team. There was a short-lived movement among the married players to all leave their wives at home after seeing the Bacardi Babes calendar Brady had posted in the locker room after the game, but it quickly died; nobody was that stupid.

Brady appointed his younger brother, Jimmy, to handle the details, telling the lad to spare no expense. This was young Jimmy's area of expertise, though he was barely legal to buy the booze himself. He immediately went to work and by eight o'clock that night things were rolling along quite nicely. Frankie's was catering the event on short notice and prepared appetizers for two hundred people. The Bacardi folks pitched in enough rum for a fleet of pirate ships and Jimmy had a half-dozen kegs of beer on ice. They weren't messing around.

Jack called Cheese who was more than happy to pick him up and escort him to Brady's Buffalo Blizzard Bacardi Bikini Babes Blowout Bash, as the event had been alliteratively branded. He texted Chaz to inform him about the little shindig, but Chaz hit him back informing Jack he was already planning on being there. You couldn't keep a secret from Chaz, particularly when it came to a party. Jack also called Vinny Cappolla to have him stop by and bring the wife, Beverly. But once Vinny caught wind the Bacardi Babes would be on hand, he claimed Bev was, unfortunately, too busy to join him. The big boy even offered to tip off the Clarence police to pre-empt any potential problems. It was the first time Jack could recall the detective enthusiastically offering unsolicited help. Say what you want about those damn Bacardi Babes, but they were proving to be quality motivators and brought the best out of some of the boys.

Jack had a few beers and popped a couple of the Norco tablets he had acquired from head trainer Alvin Kaplan following the game while he waited on Cheese. The soreness from the day's battle was beginning to settle in and he was finding it took him a little longer each week to recover from the games. It was tough to get proper sleep on Sunday and Monday nights without the benefit of Kappy's magic beans. There was no doubt this would be his final season; his battered body couldn't take the pounding anymore. He just hoped he could hang on to the end.

It was a mild but dark and overcast night, perfect cover for a party. When Cheese and Jack arrived at the Brady residence things were already going hot and heavy. The road had turned into a parking lot so they had to park Cheese's Escalade over on the next block. Brady's house was spectacular and had been featured on the new NAFA Network TV show "Football Cribs" during the off season.

The palatial edifice was set on five wooded acres, including two hundred feet of frontage on a small but significantly deep lake behind the estate. The lake had been a five-hundred-foot deep, open-pit slate mine some thirty years prior when overnight it had filled with water. All the mining equipment, including a couple of trucks, still rested at the bottom.

The home itself was a sixty-five-hundred-square-foot, three-story walk-out mansion. The basement was best described as a night club, complete with a dance floor, several bars, pool tables, six huge flat-panel TVs, and a state-of-the-art sound system. There were gender specific bathrooms with multiple stalls for the gals and urinals for the guys. Several pairs of French doors walked out to a vast treated-concrete deck which surrounded a built-in swimming pool featuring two attached Jacuzzi's on the near end, giving the pool an unintended – though often noted – phallic appearance. Behind the pool was a lighted asphalt path meandering thirty yards or so through the wooded lot to the waterfront where a huge fire pit was already roaring on the beach.

Upon arrival, Jack and Cheese went around the house and straight to a mini-bar set up poolside. Jack got a Crown and water with a twist; Cheese stuck to bottled water.

Two buxom, bikini-clad Bacardi Babes came running by and jumped into the heated pool. Another pair were making out in one of the hot tubs being cheered on through the rising steam by some of Jack's teammates.

"Hold on to your hat tonight, partner," Cheese said.

"I would say it's gonna get stupid," Jack said, "but it already is."

"I know, isn't God good?"

"That He is, Cheese. That He is."

"Let's go inside and see what's happening."

Jack nodded and followed Cheese to the house. The music was blaring and the Sunday Night Football matchup between the Houston Space Invaders and the Kansas City Demolition was airing on three of the big screens, while a replay of the Blizzard game from earlier that afternoon was showing on the other three. There was a pretty good crowd already on hand and Jack knew most of them. They passed by a pool table where Big E had removed his shirt and was sweating like the devil playing pool with a beautiful girl Jack had never seen before.

"Drifty in the house!" Big E yelled. He saluted Jack and Cheese and went right back to his pool game with his typical intensity.

Jack saluted right back. "Whatever Big E is on, I need me some of that. On second thought, it might fuckin' kill me."

Cheese nodded sagely in agreement; he'd been down that dark road.

Jack saw Stark sitting with Billy Brogan and his wife Nicole on a couch directly in front of one of the big screens showing the replay of the Blizzard game. He headed over to the bar, grabbed a jug of Jahouga Juice, and plopped down on the sofa next to his rookie. Stark was already piss drunk and punched Jack way too hard in the ribs. Jack was feeling very little pain but felt the punch. He set the jug on the floor and started couch-wrestling with Stark.

They were giggling like little brothers wrestling in the backyard. And as they usually do, things quickly escalated. When Stark pulled Jack over top of him they rolled across the sofa right into Billy Brogan's lap. Billy was slow to react, but when he did finally join the fray he put Jack into a headlock, and in the process accidently knocked his wife's drink out of her hand and all down the front of her lovely and very expensive dress. Oblivious, Billy had joined the giggling and the wrestling match until Nicole's shriek stopped him cold.

"You assholes!"

The horseplay halted immediately and all three linebackers peered up into Nicole's glare like naughty, little boys caught in the middle of another mischievous atrocity. Stark snickered and then laughed uncontrollably. The laughter proved to be contagious, as both Jack and Billy couldn't help themselves and begin roaring along with him.

Nicole did not see the humor; she was plain pissed. Her dress didn't require any under garments and the drink had been spilled across her ample bosom. If there would have been a wet t-shirt contest that night, Nicole Brogan would have won, hands down, although a few of the Bacardi Babes may have given her a run for the money.

Gerry Wainscott had just entered the room and saw the whole thing happen. She hurried over and gave Nicole her sweater to cover up and shot the naughty boys on the sofa a stern look.

"Men are total assholes," she confirmed to Nicole.

She escorted Nicole upstairs where the poor thing could clean up and regather her poise. The boys on the couch kept laughing and passing the bottle of Jahouga Juice back and forth. After a while Billy came to his senses and headed upstairs to try to make amends with his wife. He knew he would pay for it but at this point he was having too good of a time to worry much about Nicole and her chronic bitching. He could handle it.

Stark's attention turned back to the replay of the game.

"Oh shit! Jack, look." He started jumping up and down on the sofa singing his touchdown song.

The entire room had stopped to watch the replay with the bouncing rookie. When Stark crossed the goal line the place erupted into a tremendous cheer. Stark jumped as high as he could on the sofa and nearly hit his head on the twelve-foot ceiling. He pulled his knees into his chest at the zenith of his jump and seemingly paused in midair like Michael Jordan flying to the rack. It was an impressive athletic move.

Before he came down, Jack yanked the cushion off the couch. Stark came down hard, straightening his legs out late and his feet tore right through the canvas and springs, crashing through to the floor. He was stuck in the sofa like he had on cement shoes. The whole place was up for grabs with laughter. Stark was shocked at first but slowly that big, stupid, silly grin spread across his reddening face.

Ben Brady came out from behind the bar and looked the rookie up and down. Finally, Brady busted out laughing and held up his hand for a high-five.

"You owe me a new fucking sofa, bro." Then he motioned to one of the more blessed Bacardi Babes. "Brandi, can you help this man-child get out of there and make sure he doesn't get into any more trouble for me?"

"He's kinda cute. I'll take good care of him, Ben."

She gave Brady a deep French kiss and then helped poor Stark get untangled from the sofa. Shortly after that, the two of them discreetly disappeared. Jack did not see his rookie again that night, but he considered that a good thing, especially since the lad owed him a good Puss Story.

The party kept blazing and sifted itself out. On the main floor, the older, quieter crowd, which included most of the Blizzard management and players' parents, including Brady's, were enjoying casual conversation. The younger, rowdier, heavy-drinking group of players and their wives, friends, and girlfriends were in the basement and out around the pool, drinking hard, dancing, and looking to hook up. The hardcore partiers and druggies had hit the beach and assembled around the bonfire passing joints like it was 4:20. There was always something for everybody at a Ben Brady bash.

Jack headed upstairs to see what was going on amongst the civilized folks and also to see if he could track down the lovely Ms. Wainscott. He made his way into the kitchen where he ran into Henny Brady, Ben's dad. The Bradys hailed from Eau Clare, Wisconsin, and made it to Buffalo for nearly every home game and would often stay over at Ben's place during home stands. Henny was gripping a Leinenkugal Red when he greeted Jack with a big, one-armed hug.

"Looky who is here, Gertie," Henny said, "my favorite linebacker in the whole world, Jack Driftwood."

Gertie squealed and jumped up from the table and wrapped Jack up in a full bear-hug. The Bradys loved them some Jack Driftwood! He had been especially kind and helpful to their son Ben when he first came to Buffalo as a rookie. Jack had set him up with a banker, realtor, and several other business connections. Henny and Gertie were forever grateful.

"Nice game today, Jack," Henny said. "I got to say, whatever Mr. Fegel over there is paying you, it ain't enough. You are playing better than any other linebacker in the whole darn league right now, son. You should be headed to the Star Bowl this year!"

Jack briefly eyeballed Donald Fegel, who was sitting quietly at the kitchen table in front of a piece of Gertie's famous Wisconsin apple pie.

"Well, maybe you can sit down right here at the kitchen table and negotiate me a new deal with Mr. Fegel, right now," Jack said.

The Bradys cackled at the thought. Momentarily tongue-tied, Fegel sat there until finally breaking into a loud, disingenuous laugh himself. The Bradys sat back down at the table, rejoining Donald and their other guests. Gertie reached out and patted Donald's hand.

"Donald here is a fair man, Jack," she said. "I am sure he will take care of you."

"Yeah, Donald's been trying to take care of me for years, all right. Maybe y'all can talk him in to keeping me around for the rest of the season. It was great to see you both. Have a nice evening."

The Bradys laughed again and thanked him for coming. Jack had to get the hell out of there and away from Fegel.

*Talk about a buzz kill.*

He finally found Gerry hanging out with Cheese at the bar by the pool. They decided to take a walk down to the lake. There they ran into Chaz regaling a group of people by the bonfire. Chaz was telling a story Jack had heard on several occasions about the time Chaz was leading a small group of U.S. Marines in Vietnam behind enemy lines. They were booby trapping tunnels when they got ambushed. Chaz claimed he didn't know exactly what happened then, or how it had all gone down, but the next thing he knew he was looking down at six dead Viet Cong soldiers with a bloody knife in his hand. Dude could tell some stories.

The night was right and Jack was feeling pretty good but he had to get out of there. He wanted to get little Ms. Wainscott somewhere alone and…naked?

*Yeah, naked.*

He hadn't seen her since they had talked things out in the bar at the Bull's Horn and was looking forward to perhaps joining her for a sleepover. He motioned to Gerry and she followed him up the path leading back to the house.

"What do you say we get the hell out of here?"

"I thought you'd never ask."

Jack went back to say his good byes when he ran into Robert "Tree Spirit" Hansen, an acquaintance of his who was a member of the Seneca Nation Tribal Council. The guy was a talker and claimed he had an extremely sensitive issue to discuss. He seemed nervous and kept looking over his shoulder. Jack didn't have the time to deal with Tree Spirit and his wildly-spun conspiracy theories, he had a date. But he knew somebody who had nothing but time. He figured Tree Spirit would be an excellent match for Chaz and introduced the two. They hit it off immediately and Jack was off the hook.

Or so he thought.

Donald Fegel had consumed a half a dozen or so Leinie's while sitting with the Bradys and figured that was probably his limit. It had been a pleasant evening and he reveled in all of the compliments being showered upon him regarding the Blizzard. He was pretty puffed up and feeling good about himself as he walked out the front door after saying his farewells. He had a little bit of a buzz on but was in control and figured driving home would not be an issue. After hitting the cold night air, though, pissing his pants might be.

Under an overcast, moonless sky, Donald stopped to relieve himself. He wobbled slightly as he stepped into an opening between a line of Douglas firs. Giggling, he fished into his pants, unleashed the dragon, and began to take a leak in the shadows of Ben Brady's front lawn. He knew it was stupid – peeing in his star quarterback's front yard during a party – but there was nobody around and his back teeth were floating. Donald had yet to bust the seal and his first piss of the evening was a good, long, glorious one.

As he was shaking it off he heard muffled conversation from down the street. Curious, he poked his head around one of the trees and saw a large man getting into a small car. He thought nothing of it but then something registered deep in his brain. He darted back around the tree, still fumbling with his zipper, as the car pulled away from the curb.

He could have sworn it was Jack Driftwood, halfway down the block, who had just hopped into Gerry Wainscott's pretty little Jaguar and sped off down the street. He rubbed his eyes and tried to replay the sequence over in his head. He didn't get a look at the guy's face, it was too far away but the build and the way the guy moved…

"Hey, dude," a man's voice said from behind him, "there are like twenty bathrooms in the house."

The woman who was with the guy giggled as Donald finished closing his barn door. He ducked his head and hastily walked to his car.

*That was Jack Driftwood! It had to be. What the hell is going on? Is Driftwood moving into my territory? How could Gerry be so stupid as to get mixed up with that ass-clown?*

Donald started up his car still not one hundred percent sure what he had just seen, or, for that matter, what to do about it. But he was going to figure it out, that much was for damn sure.

He finally had a task for his underworld minions.

# Chapter Twenty-One

Colin Meade was summoned by Donald Fegel bright and early the Monday morning following Brady's party. Usually the boss liked to be alone in the early morning hours, thus Colin was on his toes when he walked into Donald's office.

"Colin, something potentially very disturbing came to my attention last night and I need your assistance," Mr. Fegel said. "I need some surveillance work done."

"I'm listening." Colin was getting excited simply because Mr. Fegel seemed so ominous and serious. And he wasn't yelling.

*Finally, maybe something good again!*

Colin had not fallen out of favor with the boss, but he wasn't directly involved with the on-field product. That wasn't his business. Unfortunately, his business had been pushed to the back burner as the football heated up and the Wigwam construction project came to a close. He was getting a little anxious about things and wondered if it wasn't yet time to fly the coop, which, in his mind, was an inevitability. Now that he had himself a considerable stake, compliments of the Wigwam scam, he was ready to expand his horizons. It was merely a matter of when…

"I want you to put a tail on Jack Driftwood until further notice. I want to know who he sees, where he goes, and what he does when he gets there – are you listening? Put your best man on it. Obviously, I don't want him to know he is being watched."

"No problem, sir…may I inquire as to what specifically you are looking for? You know, to help my source. That is, if there is anything specific?"

"I prefer to keep that to myself, at least for now," Mr. Fegel said. "I only want to confirm a suspicion. It's probably nothing."

Colin was disappointed. He and Mr. Fegel had very few, if any, secrets; at least that he was aware of. They were in deep water together and their common survival depended on full disclosure and trust. Their mutual destruction was assured if things leaked or blew up. Colin tried to cover it up, but Mr. Fegel must have noticed the look of disenchantment on his face.

"I'm sorry, Colin," he said, "but this is a personal matter. I need you to give your man the number to my B-phone and have him report directly to me on this. Have him call me at nine p.m. sharp every night until further notice. If my suspicions are correct I will bring you in on this thing and we will address it together, but at this point there is no reason to bother you with the details."

"No problem, Mr. Fegel. I will get right on it."

Colin was the real brains behind the operation. He knew his way around a spreadsheet and was very good at hiding things, often in plain sight. Without him they had nothing. He was the one who set up a shell corporation in the Cayman Islands to hide the money skimmed from the construction project. The stadium and casino was a 1.2-billion-dollar mega-deal, meaning there was a lot of meat on the bone. Meade had carved it up with the deft touch of a transplant surgeon, making himself and Mr. Fegel very wealthy.

They had tried the tactic of tailing Driftwood at the end of the previous season when Mr. Fegel went on a witch-hunt for scapegoats during their losing streak, but the guy had come up as clean as a freshly-wiped baby's bottom. Colin wondered what had changed to make Mr. Fegel think that had changed. More than likely it was just his passionate hatred for the man run amok. Personally, Colin didn't care about Jack Driftwood one way or the other, but the boss sure hated the guy, which was good enough for him.

A quick phone call was all it took for him to make the surveillance arrangements regarding Driftwood. However, he told his operative to report to him *before* calling Mr. Fegel, and to make sure the boss didn't know. It was worth the extra hundred dollars per day just to satisfy Colin's curiosity. After all, where is honor amongst thieves?

Donald went to see Gerry Wainscott to do some snooping around. He was awaiting confirmation before he confronted her regarding her secret liaison with Driftwood. He found her alone in her office, sipping from a cup of coffee, gazing out the window at a calm Lake Erie.

"Hi, Gerry," he said. "I hope I am not interrupting anything important."

"Oh, no, Donald, I was just engaged in a little daydreaming, again. What can I do for you?"

"Huh, oh, nothing really. I was just checking in to see how things are going. I missed you at the end of the party last night."

Donald scoured her face for any shred of guilt.

"Oh, yeah, I was *really* tired from such a long and exciting day, so I left pretty early."

"Yes, it was an exciting day and another exciting victory – by the way, Gerry, Nicole Brogan called me this morning and she was quite upset about an incident that occurred at the party. Apparently Jack Driftwood dumped a drink on her and ruined a very expensive dress. That guy just doesn't have any sense or couth. Nicole asked me to take a couple thousand dollars out of Driftwood's check to pay for the dress."

"Are you kidding me?" Gerry asked.

"Actually, I am quite serious."

"Well, you can't just do that."

"No, I can't. But I wish I could. It might teach him some manners."

"I saw what happened," she said. "If anybody dumped that drink on her it was her own husband, Billy. But the whole thing was a complete accident. Jack was wrestling around with Steven Stark on a sofa and Stark pulled him onto Billy Brogan's lap, who joined the wrestling match and that's what spilled her drink. I can't believe she asked you to deduct money from Jack's check, that's a bit ridiculous."

"Not if you look at it from Nicole's point of view. She's out one very expensive garment. Besides, why do you always come to Driftwood's defense?"

"Jesus, Donald, I'm not defending anybody. I'm just telling you what happened."

Donald knew she was getting upset and defensive, so he backed off. But what he really wanted to do was grab her and shake some sense into her, make her confess and then forsake Jack Driftwood and fall into his loving arms to beg forgiveness.

*What can she possibly see in that Neanderthal? What does anyone see?*

"Relax, Gerry," he said. "It's no big deal. I'm just keeping you up to speed. I have to go, but I will see you at lunch, right?"

"Yeah, sure."

Donald left the room knowing in his heart she was seeing Driftwood. It was the way she said his name. She said it with a certain yet undefinable intimacy: she could not help herself. He recognized this because it was the same way he heard himself speak her name. He would await confirmation from Meade before doing anything but something was rotten. His mind was already at work, figuring out how he would use and manipulate this new information to his advantage. Of this much he was sure; Jack Driftwood's days in a Blizzard uniform were numbered.

Bernie Radowski sat in his non-descript car in a half-full parking lot across from the renovated warehouse. He was listening to the Monday Night Football game on WJR to pass the time while keeping one eye on the parking garage entrance across the street. Tailing Driftwood was nothing new to him; he still couldn't believe how boring the guy was. If he were a bigshot, NAFA star linebacker he sure wouldn't be a do-nothing homebody like this Driftwood putz.

Bernie had been a Buffalo detective for twenty years before taking early retirement. He had decided he no longer cared for being told what to do. It was really that simple. He divorced his wife, left his job, and moved into a dumpy, two-bedroom apartment in South Buffalo. It was heaven. He had started his own private investigator business and became his own boss. Now, he called the shots. He took only the assignments he wanted and only *when* he wanted. And nobody bitched at him. What else could a man ask for?

Colin Meade was sitting at the small desk in the guest-room-turned-office in his humble Snyder home when he received a call a little before 9 p.m. He was idly surfing through his usual internet porn sites on his desktop computer when his phone beeped.

"This is Meade."

"Yeah, it's Ber – er, Buffalo Bill," Bernie said. "The subject just arrived at the Buffalo Seneca Casino Hotel. He valet parked his vehicle and took the elevator directly to the eighteenth floor. Please advise."

It came together instantly in Meade's head. Gerry Wainscott was living in the Penthouse over there until she could find more suitable, long-term lodging.

*That bastard Driftwood is tagging the owner's daughter! No wonder Mr. Fegel wants to keep things quiet.*

"Go ahead and call your contact," Colin said. "I would like to know when the subject departs and I imagine he will, too. You might as well get comfortable."

Jack knocked on the door and readied himself. Like clockwork, Gerry pulled it open and flung herself into his arms. The girl sure knew how to make a guy feel welcome. Quickly, and with blatant expertise, she unbuttoned Jack's red flannel shirt with a series of flicks of her left hand while doing the same to her own cotton blouse with her right. Jack hoisted her onto one of his hips and was fumbling around to grapple her out of her jeans.

They didn't quite make it the bedroom. Instead, he dumped her on the leather couch where he could get some leverage and maybe some extra traction; he sensed he would need to dig in just to keep up.

It was on. It stayed on for quite some time before he even had the chance to say a simple "hello."

Donald took the call on his B-phone, a second, private cell phone which was both secure and unlisted. It was the phone he used for his more sensitive activities.

"Fegel," he said.

"This is Buffalo Bill," came the reply.

By design, Donald had no idea of the true identity of Buffalo Bill. He had insulated himself from Colin Meade's underworld contacts from the onset. It made him feel safer and far superior to the despicable rat-man and his dirty business. It also provided him with what he considered plausible deniability were trouble to arise.

"I'm listening," Donald said.

"I picked up the subject at six twenty this evening as he was leaving the Wigwam. Subject went directly to his residence." Buffalo Bill spoke in a monotone voice, as if reading from a script. "The Subject remained at his residence until exactly eight thirty-five this evening. At that time he entered his vehicle and drove straight to the Buffalo Seneca Casino Hotel. The subject then valet parked his car and took the elevator all the way up to the top floor."

"What the hell is doing up there?" Donald asked.

Buffalo Bill went off-script with his reply. "My best guess is this is your classic gash-stash, sir. He has some stray piece of ass stashed away up there and he is headed to P-Town, I've seen it a million times. I have the place staked out and will keep track of his, uh, *comings* and goings. Heh-heh."

Donald was stunned into silence when it hit him. Gerry was staying in the Penthouse on the top floor of the casino hotel.

*What the hell is Jack Driftwood doing there?*

He knew the answer to that stupid question; he knew damn well what Driftwood was doing there, and who, for that matter. He had still harbored a wisp of hope in the deepest regions of his heart that he had been wrong about the whole thing and Gerry was yet unsullied. That hope was shattered. His heart quickly hardened. A callous began to form over the soft spot reserved for Gerry Wainscott.

"Uh-hum," Buffalo Bill said into the lengthy silence on the other end of the connection.

Donald snapped back. "Very well then, stick with the plan. I want to know when the son of a bitch leaves."

"Yes, sir. Will do."

After they had had a bit of a go, Jack flipped on the Monday Night Football game and ordered a snack from room service. Gerry went for a dessert and they settled in under a blanket on the couch to watch the ballgame and wait for their food. The only negative thing about room service was you had to be dressed when they delivered it to your door.

Jack was elucidating some of the finer points of the game to Gerry while bitching about the announcers who often missed those finer points. She thought it was hilarious.

"You should be in the booth, Mr. Know-it-all."

"You're damn right I should," he said. "I'd be better than these posers. I have thought about it, you know. I'm gonna be needing a new job after this season."

"What?"

"This is definitely my last go around, girl. I'm hanging them up. My old ass can't take the pounding anymore. Besides, I doubt the Blizzard would have me back for another year."

"But Jack," she said, "you're playing so well. You're having a Star-Bowl season – at least that's what everyone's saying."

"Maybe, maybe not. But even if I am, it just means I get to go out on top. But I don't give a shit about no Star Bowl, it's a fuckin' beauty contest. I want to go to the Mega Bowl again. And win it this time."

"Wouldn't that be awesome? To win it all, right here in Buffalo. That would be unbelievable!"

"Let's not jinx it or get ahead of ourselves. There is a lot of football left to be played."

"True…" Gerry said, "but I get so excited just thinking about it and what it would mean to my dad."

"He deserves it, that's for sure."

"So you are saying you want to go out on top, huh?"

Gerry laid on her back on the bed and struck a suggestive pose.

Jack didn't have to be told twice. He jumped right on top of her.

"No, I want to *come* out on top."

# Chapter Twenty-Two

The Arizona Roadrunners came to town the last weekend of October. They were the top team in the NAFA's Western Conference, sporting an identical mark to Buffalo at 7-1. All of the experts were calling it a possible Mega Bowl preview, considering it was being played in the Wigwam between the top team from each conference and all. The game was another complete sellout and the city of Buffalo was at fever pitch. This was shaping up as the most exciting season in a generation. Each game seemed bigger than the last.

Adding to the excitement was the return of Earl Johnson to the Buffalo lineup. Earl had healed up quite nicely from the tire-iron beating he had taken the second week of the season. He had been gradually integrated into practice and was raring and ready for game action. Even though he had to wear protective padding over his left forearm where several screws and a metal plate had been surgically inserted, Earl, by all appearances, was back to being the Pearl. He had publicly claimed the arm was now bionic and better and stronger than ever. There was no cause to doubt him.

Winter was beginning to stretch its muscles – a warm up for the coming months – on the northernmost shores of Lake Erie. The air had recently acquired a bite. There was frost on the pumpkin early that morning and the high temperatures for the day was forecast into the mid-thirties. It was what most people in the area referred to as football weather.

A bitter debate had been waged all week with regards to the roof of the Wigwam, and whether to close it or leave it open. For as long as Buffalo had been a NAFA franchise, they had sustained an inherent home-field advantage over warm weather teams later in the season. Those thin-blooded southern boys arrived in town to battle not only the Blizzard but also the elements of Western New York – which occasionally included a blizzard.

It was a tough call, really. Some fans preferred warmth and comfort provided by the new protective glass roof system, while the diehard traditionalists wanted it to be as cold, nasty, and uncomfortable as possible for the southern softies.

In a last-minute executive decision, Mr. Wainscott had determined the roof would remain open. This *was* Buffalo, after all. There was no precipitation in the forecast, so water damage was not a concern, and they would keep the heat on in the building. It wouldn't be the usual sixty-eight degrees, but it wouldn't be freezing either. In short, it would be football weather. It proved to be a very popular decision – unless, of course, you hailed from Arizona. The crowd was revved up and ready and there was a huge roar of approval when the public address announcer declared the roof would remain open for the duration of the afternoon. He also announced it was currently ninety-two degrees and sunny in Phoenix, which was roundly booed.

The game started particularly well for the Blizzard. They took the ball and drove down the field with a dizzying array of short passes and Earl Johnson runs from the hurry-up, no-huddle attack. The drive culminated in a 13-yard Johnson touchdown scamper and the home team took a 7-0 lead. The Pearl took a bow to a standing ovation upon scooting into the end zone. It was good to have him back.

Arizona had one of the top offenses in the league that hung on a strong-armed veteran quarterback and a cadre of some of the most talented wide receivers in all of the NAFA. They also mixed in a fairly effective running game. But perhaps the biggest threat they posed was they were so damned unpredictable. Driftwood had studied the video of all eight of their previous games, yet he still had not drawn a complete bead on their play-calling. It pissed him off to have to give them credit; but he did, albeit grudgingly.

Buffalo would have to rely more on an old-fashioned read-and-react style of defense in this one, because there were few, if any, reliable statistical tendencies to hang a hat on. With some of their opponents, after watching a few games Driftwood could tell you what play they were going to run next with uncanny accuracy. He knew what they were going to run before they did. Such was not the case with these masters of deception; they were liable to take a deep shot from anywhere on the field, at any given time. The Roadrunners had no conscience. They lived – and lived well – off the big play.

Coach Faber and his defensive staff had every intention of taking the deep ball away. The plan was to force the Roadrunners to prove they could consistently drive the length of the field. Coach Faber didn't believe they could. Defensive backs coach Archie Beatle wholeheartedly agreed. They both were betting Arizona's quarterback, Bob Dreisen, would remain true to form, get greedy, and try to force the ball downtown, where they would be waiting. To theoretically give his guys a better chance at playing the deep ball, Archie also planned to deploy his secondary a couple of yards deeper than normal. Buffalo intended to incorporate multiple zone coverages with a sprinkling of zone blitzes and very little man-to-man.

On paper, the plan made perfect sense. But as Coach Faber reminded them, people wipe their ass with paper every day. However, the first series saw the plan work to perfection. After picking up a couple of first downs with several short, easy passes, Dreisen probed downfield with a couple deep shots to no avail. On 3rd and 9 Arizona was called for a false start, backing them up another five yards. Dreisen took one more shot down the seam and Stark made a last-ditch, diving deflection to knock the ball away. It was an extremely athletic play but he landed awkwardly on the Wigwam turf. The crowd went crazy only to realize Stark was not getting up. A hush fell over the entire stadium as the medical personnel hurried out to tend to the fallen star.

Driftwood stood over his rookie who was sitting on the ground cussing a blue-streak. "Get the fuck up, you're lying on sacred ground making a damned fool of yourself."

"I know, but my foot is fucked up, I heard it pop."

"Get the hell out of the way, Driftwood."

Alvin Kaplan elbowed past Driftwood to get to Stark.

"Blow me, Kappy. The kid's all right, let's just get his ass off the field."

"Yeah," Stark said, "I'm okay, just get me off the field."

"Fuck you both," Kaplan said. "I don't tell you pussies how to tackle, so don't you tell me how to do my job. I heard the thing pop all the way on the goddamn sidelines."

Kaplan carefully stabilized Stark's foot and began to take it through a series of basic range of motion tests while gauging the pain level from Stark's reaction. Clarence Verdin, the team's orthopedic surgeon, was bent over next to Kaplan watching closely as well. It was so tender and swollen they dared not remove his shoe until they got into the locker room. Driftwood knew from personal experience that was not a good sign.

"Let's put the leg in an air cast and get him off the field. We need the cart. I don't want him putting so much as an ounce of pressure on it," Doc Verdin said.

Stark started to protest. "Not the fucking cart! I can walk."

"No. I'm sorry, Steven, not this time," Doc Verdin said. "I don't want you to put any weight on it at all. None, whatsoever. At least not until we get some x-rays and determine the damage. Do no harm is the best course."

Kaplan signaled for the cart, which came barreling onto the field. Together they lifted Stark up onto the platform on the back.

"Keep your chin up, dog," Driftwood said to Stark, slapping him on the shoulder pads. Then to Kaplan, "Tape a fuckin' aspirin to it, rub some dirt on it, and get his ass ready for the second half."

"We'll see," Kaplan said, "but this ain't like the old days, Jack."

"I know, but shit, the kid is old school and we need his ass."

Driftwood felt utterly helpless standing there in the middle of the field watching Stark being whisked away on the cart. Stark was only twenty-one years old – Driftwood could have easily been his father – but there was no time for a pity-party. Coach Faber was yelling at him to get his dumb ass off the field. Driftwood realized the punt return team was already lining up and hustled to the sideline. It was still game time, he needed to snap back his focus.

The crowd gave Stark a hearty cheer as he rode up the tunnel. His image lit up every video board in the stadium showing his ride into the bowels of the Wigwam. He was waving at the camera flashing his goofy grin like he was in some kind of parade.

Driftwood was shaking his head as he made it over to the Coach Faber. "Did you see that kid? He thinks he's in a fuckin' beauty pageant, smiling and waving."

"Ignorance knows no boundaries, Jack. You of all people know that. Get with Billy and get him up to speed. It's up to you two, now...Stark will be all right."

Driftwood gave one last look toward the tunnel through which Stark had disappeared. "Thanks, Coach. I hope so."

The rest of the first half went quickly with both teams adding touchdowns to the tally. Ben Brady hit Shady Solomon for a 20-yard score to put the Blizzard up 14-0 early in the second quarter. Arizona got on the board on their next drive as Dreisen connected with Larry Harris, the NAFA's leading receiver, on a 72-yard bomb.

Archie Beatle was spitting mad. Inexcusably, Buffalo's field-side cornerback, Viceroy Jenkins, got beat deep on the play. Coach Faber had to calm Archie down. Both teams struggled to mount another offensive threat the remainder of the half, thus after 30 minutes Buffalo was on top, 14-7.

Jack went straight to the training room at halftime. Stark had not reappeared since leaving the field in the first quarter. There was little doubt he was done for the day. He found Steven sitting on one of the taping tables in the trainer's room with his left foot in a clumsy contraption known as an orthopedic walking boot. There was a pair of crutches leaning against the table. Steven had already showered and was in his street clothes.

"What's the good news?" Jack asked.

"They took an x-ray and nothing is broken," Stark said.

"What's the bad news?"

"They think I might have torn the plantar fascia off the bone. I'm out from four to six weeks and it will be a pain in my ass the rest of the season, if not the rest of my life." Stark's reply was matter of fact, but his face was stuck in that grin.

"You seem to be taking it well. Kappy give you some candy?"

"The good shit. He's been holding out on you, old man," Stark said and began laughing, though at what Jack hadn't a clue.

"Well shit, what happened?"

"I don't know, man," Stark said, "I dove to knock down the ball and I landed funny and my foot just popped."

"What the hell, man. You must be some kind of fuckin' china doll."

"Fuck you."

Jack laughed and headed for the defensive meeting room. He was nearly out the door when Stark hollered back at him.

"Hey, grandpa. Go out there and win this one – for me."

Jack stopped and turned to look back at Stark. The kid's big, goofy grin had transformed into a shit-eating one.

"You're a dick. You do know that, right?"

Buffalo came out and stopped the Roadrunners cold in the third quarter while the offense managed to pile up another 10 points. The Blizzard took a solid 24-7 lead into the final stanza, but Arizona wasn't done. They were a confident bunch and well aware they had a quick-strike offense. They were also one of those teams with the pride and veteran leadership to play hard the entire game, regardless of the score. They hadn't been to two of the past five Mega Bowls by laying down late in a game.

Arizona took possession at their own 20-yard line and started moving the ball down the field one chunk at a time. Dreisen and the offense settled in and started patiently taking what the Buffalo defense was giving them. They had moved the ball to the Buffalo 13 when the drive appeared to stall with the Roadrunners facing a critical 4th and 1.

Conventional wisdom called for a field goal attempt since they were down by 17, but Arizona was anything but conventional; they decided to go for it. The Blizzard crowd was in full throat as the Roadrunners broke the huddle. If the roof hadn't been open it might have blown right off. Needing just a yard, they ran an Isolation play, sending their burly fullback, Timmy Askew, straight into the hole with the tailback on his heels. His assignment was to block the linebacker, which happened to be Driftwood.

Both Driftwood and Brogan knew the play was coming. Loading up for the challenge, they backed up to a depth of nearly five yards in their pre-snap alignment. It always helped to have a running head start in anticipation of a big collision. The impact between Driftwood and Askew mimicked one of those wildlife TV shows where two stud rams ran at each other with the full force of their being to smack racks, and it sucked the breath from the entire crowd.

Brogan came flying over the top the pile Driftwood had created and stopped the Arizona tailback in his tracks before flinging him backwards away from the line. The officials measured to be sure, but everybody in the stadium had already known the outcome. Arizona was short by almost a yard. The Blizzard defense had held! The crowd collectively exhaled before going berserk; hardly anybody noticed Driftwood had knocked his left shoulder down in the process.

The pain was immediate and fiery hot, though not unfamiliar. Driftwood had separated that same shoulder on two previous occasions and knew immediately he had done it again. Holding his left arm against his body, he got up from the pile and ran directly to the sidelines where Kaplan was waiting for him.

"What the hell is going on with my linebackers today? How bad is it?" the concerned trainer asked.

"Probably a grade two. I'm gonna need a shot and some oral meds, Kappy."

"Let's go," a grim Kaplan replied, grabbing Jack by the arm and marching him toward the tunnel.

Doc Verdin joined them as they passed Coach Faber, who gave Driftwood a bewildered look.

"Don't worry, Coach, I'll be right back."

Faber shook his head. First Stark and now Driftwood, what the hell had he done to deserve this?

Jack looked away and bit into a towel as Doc Verdin stabbed the needle deep into the AC joint of his left shoulder. Jack couldn't determine which was worse, the injury or the remedy. Doc moved the needle around, making sure the numbing medicine and the steroidal anti-inflammatory permeated the affected area entirely. It was simply torture; Jack was ready to confess.

However, the pain was short-lived as almost immediately the shoulder began to numb up. The intense, searing pain was gone, replaced by a deep, dull, almost far-away ache. The shoulder felt like it was becoming almost invisible, like an apparition. He tried to loosen it up by lifting and swinging his arm and after a moment he had gotten back most of his range of motion and much of the strength in his left hand. He grabbed his helmet, thanked the Doc, and headed back to the field on the hop.

While Driftwood had been in the locker room getting his treatment, the Roadrunners had administered a painful treatment of their own with a quick touchdown on a fumble return. Earl Johnson got hit directly on his padded arm and the football popped out. An Arizona defender snatched it out of the air and scooted in for the score. Earl was on the sideline cursing the arm pad and waving around a pair of scissors he had grabbed from the trainer's kit. He was in a full-throated argument with Kaplan about cutting the damn thing off, an argument Earl was sure to lose. It was now 24-14 Buffalo with 8:54 left in the game.

The Blizzard offense had the ball and managed to churn out a couple of first downs before punting it away with 5:32 left in the game. Driftwood and the Blizzard defense took the field. Arizona began to move the ball again, using the short passing game and mixing in the run. Driftwood made a couple of tackles of the one-armed variety. He was instinctively protecting his left shoulder, though it hadn't affected his effectiveness.

The Buffalo crowd was already out of control, urging their defense on, but somehow reached another level when a rogue snow squall came in off of Lake Erie and light, fluffy flakes began to fall inside the open stadium. It was a light snow that evaporated immediately and would bring no accumulation or affect the game. Nonetheless, it was snow! More snow than Phoenix, Arizona, had seen in the last ten years combined. The Buffalo faithful took it as a sign from above and the roar was deafening. For certain, football gods were obviously smiling on the Blizzard!

Arizona was facing a 1st and 10 on the Buffalo 42 when there was an official timeout to get an injured Roadrunner player off the field. Driftwood went to the sideline to discuss the situation with Coach Faber.

"Goddammit, Lester, quit playing pussy-ass zones and giving them easy completions. The game is on the line, let's go get his ass. Man up and go after Dreisen, he's been sitting back there all day picking us apart. Tell Archie to drop a set!"

Driftwood was sick of playing the soft defense and so were the rest of the guys. They had been bitching about it in the huddle all game long.

Coach Faber looked at him like he had sprouted another head and didn't say a word. Then he slid the microphone from his headset down over his mouth to consult with Archie up in the booth.

"Coach Driftwood down here thinks we ought to heat Mr. Dreisen up. And he pretty much challenged our manhood."

Archie had been the driving force behind the plan to play back and force Arizona to throw the short stuff. He had also occasionally butted heads with Driftwood over the schemes they deployed on defense. It was a bit of a running feud, though nothing serious; mostly it was two dogs marking out their territory. And yet, Archie always took it personally when there was the slightest hint of a challenge to his authority. Having never played the game professionally, he harbored some legitimate insecurities.

"You tell Driftwood to go fuck himself!" he hollered. "We're not going to play man coverage on the best goddamn receivers in the league and give up an easy touchdown, that's crazy!"

Coach Faber, who, in spite of himself, was enjoying the exchange, calmly relayed a slightly tamer version of Archie's response. "Archie doesn't really like your idea."

"Tell him tough titty," Driftwood said. "Our guys are sick of sitting back and taking it in the ass. Come on, Lester, we are better when we are aggressive and you know it. It's time for you two to trust us."

Coach Faber pondered the situation. He knew what it was like in the heat of the battle. His own blood had been spilled on the sacred turf of many a NAFA playing field over the years. He had always prided himself in that if he were ever to go down, at least he'd be swinging.

"All right, goddammit, go after his ass. 'House Cover Zero,' but you better get home."

"Sir, yes, sir!" Jack shouted and ran back onto the field with an obvious new found sense of purpose and excitement.

Up in the coaches' booth Archie went ape shit. He tore up his call sheet, threw his headset onto the table, and punched the wall, cursing incoherently.

Driftwood got back to the huddle and growled. "Listen up, homeboys. We ain't playin' no more soft shit. We're getting after this cocksucker with everything we got!"

A buzz of energy hit the huddle like a pulse wave and they cheered in unison.

"About fuckin' time," Leroy Clarkson said, "We been lettin' these little bitches make us look a damn fool all day. My man been catchin' passes all over the damn place and *that* shit don't happen."

"Not anymore," Driftwood said. "Bo-Bo, pin the center away from the slide and Brogan will come free. 'House, Cover Press Zero.' Ready…"

"Break!"

For the first time all day the Buffalo corners came up and pressed the Arizona receivers at the line. Immediately Dreisen began checking the play, animatedly calling an audible. He signaled to each side and then cupped his hands around his mouth hoping his line could hear him scream the protection over the roar of the crowd. Arizona had been waiting and hoping for this all day. It was time for Larry Harris, the best deep threat on the planet, to head downtown to get his money.

A fraction before the snap Brogan took off, getting an excellent jump on his blitz path that had him circling around the nose guard. Bo-Bo grabbed the center and held him, keeping him from sliding into his gap where Brogan was attacking. On the same side Driftwood hit the B-Gap, pulling the guard outside with him. It was offensive defense when you thought about it, because the result was a cavernous hole in the Arizona line that opened up like the Red Sea at the hand of Moses.

Dreisen had not been rattled or hit hard all day. He was due. His plan was to take a quick drop and launch a fade up along the sideline for Harris to run under. Dreisen figured he was going to have to pay for it, and he was correct. Because of the pressure he had to hurry the throw and didn't quite get it off before Brogan burst into the Arizona backfield. Billy whacked the QB hard in the chest before driving him to the ground. The force and timing of the blow grossly affected the flight of the ball; it fluttered high in the air toward Harris and the sideline.

Leroy Clarkson had press coverage on Harris and managed a fairly decent jam at the line, forcing an outside release. He settled behind Harris's inside hip in a trail technique and focused on the man's hips. Just when he thought the play wasn't coming his way, Leroy saw Harris's eyes get big and heard someone yelling "Ball!"

Leroy flipped his eyes back to the QB and picked up the fluttering football floating toward him amongst the falling flakes. Everything seemed to slow down to the point where, later, Leroy would claim he could read the commissioner's name on the spinning ball while it was in the air. He slowed to gather and then leapt, hanging in the atmosphere for a Jordan-esque eternity of frozen time before reaching up and lightly gathering it in.

In real time, Leroy jumped up and snagged the ball away from Larry Harris, who had unsuccessfully tried to come over his back.

Interception! Yeah, baby!

Buffalo ate up the rest of the clock and beat Arizona 24-14, but in the process took a beating of their own. Stark and Driftwood were both injured and they also lost their right guard, Manny Tuisopo, to a season-ending knee injury. They had run their record to an improbable NAFA-best 8-1 and had beaten the Western Conference's top team, but they were beat up and bleeding heading into the stretch run. Donald Fegel was about to earn his money; there were some holes in the juggernaut that needed patching and some parts to replace in order to keep the machine running smoothly.

# Chapter Twenty-Three

The following morning Jack woke up to throbbing pain in his left shoulder and both frontal lobes. The shoulder hurt from the separation suffered in the game, his head from all the booze he had consumed afterwards in an effort to kill the shoulder pain. It was a vicious cycle.

Jack popped a couple of the pain pills Doc Verdin had given him after the game. Then he took another one, figuring if two was good, then three had to be better. It was simple math. His shoulder was singing when he climbed into his custom shower featuring three separate massage-action heads coming out of each adjacent wall. He plopped down on the seat in the middle and let the multiple jets of hot water run on him until the meds kicked in. He was thinking the way his shoulder felt, he might well miss the next two games before their upcoming bye-week.

He finally pulled himself out of the shower and called Gerry Wainscott. "I am going to need some serious, tender, loving care tonight."

"Please hold for a moment," she said and then told her executive assistant, Cindy Chuckles, Gary's wife, "I really have to take this call, why don't we take a break?"

"Sure, no problem," Cindy said. She closed the door on her way out.

"Jack, shouldn't you be in the hospital resting? Are you going to be all right?"

"Relax, Gerry. I don't need no stinking hospital. It's just a little shoulder separation, I've had 'em before. I'm going to be fine but it hurts like hell right now. You are going to have to take it easy on me tonight. No jumping me at the door."

"Well, I'll try to remember, but I can't promise you anything. I should be getting out of here a little early, what time are you coming by?"

"Probably around nine. Hey, don't forget about the Driftwoodies' Halloween Party on Wednesday night. Make sure your costume is appropriately inappropriate and a good disguise. Maybe we can act like we actually know each other in public."

"Oh, I've got that covered – it will be right up your alley."

"Jack likes that. Jack likes that a lot."

"I knew Jack would because Jack is a big horn-dog."

"Look who's talking."

"I'll see you tonight, then."

"Remember, no jumping Jack," he said.

"Jumping Jack," she repeated.

Donald Allen Fegel Jr. had instructed Colin Meade to remove the tail from Driftwood and slap it on Gerry Wainscott earlier in the week. He wanted to see how much of a whore she really was. For all he knew she could be banging half of Buffalo like a screen door. So far it was only that damn Driftwood on the hit-list, but Buffalo Bill had been on the case for just a couple of days. Donald had finally confided in Meade regarding the reason for the surveillance. Meade had acted appropriately surprised and equally appalled Gerry would even consider such atrocious, risky behavior. They had discussed how to use the information to their advantage but had yet to arrive at any conclusions.

That whole business was moved to the backburner in Donald's mind. He had more urgent business to attend, because even though his team had won the game the previous day, they had taken a physical beating. Lost for the season was Manny Tuisopo with a torn ACL in his right knee. Steven Stark was out for at least a month with a sprained foot and Driftwood was nursing a separated shoulder. They were a walking MASH unit.

Donald had spent most of the morning scouring the waiver wire and going through all available personnel channels looking to find an offensive lineman and a linebacker or two. He put the Gerry Wainscott situation out of his mind as much out of necessity as due to the fact he wasn't quite yet sure how to handle it.

Even though his initial reaction to her secret affair with Driftwood was to close the door and write her off, he couldn't stop thinking about her. And the more he thought about her, the more he realized he still had a thing for her. But what really drove him was he couldn't stand losing her to Driftwood. If it had been anybody else, he most likely could have let it go.

The Driftwoodies had organized their Seventh Annual Hallow-Weenie Bash for that Wednesday night. They were holding the shindig on Coach Quinni's farm in Wheatfield, half an hour or so north of the city. The host, Melvin Quinni, was a loyal and original member of Jack's fan club and a good friend of Jack's. He had been an area high-school football coach for as long as anyone could remember. They had met the summer after Jack's rookie season. Jack was Coach Quinni's guest at the banquet preceding the area High School All-Star Football Game and had spoken at the banquet every year since.

The farm was on an eighty-acre plot currently consisting of pretty much just hay fields, although Darlene Quinni, the coach's wife, cultivated a large vegetable garden. The big barn was massive and recently renovated. It was a side business for the Quinnis as they regularly rented out the place for parties, banquets, and the like. They had installed a modern kitchen and bathroom facilities to turn the old barn into party central. The old coach and his wife boarded a handful of horses on the property that were kept in the smaller, original barn, directly behind their old farmhouse. Coach Quinni used his finely groomed beasts to pull the wagons for the popular hayrides offered at the parties. To be sure, the farm was the ideal setup for a Driftwoodies Halloween Party.

Jack had come dressed up as the Lone Ranger and Cheese was a pretty convincing Tonto. As soon as they arrived, the costumed lawman and his sidekick headed straight for the old farmhouse to say hello to Darlene, who was sitting on the back porch in a wicked witch costume, chain-smoking Marlboro Greens.

"Howdy, ma'am," Jack said, ambling up the porch steps.

"Jack-fucking-Driftwood, as I live and breathe," Darlene rasped. "What kind of stupid ass costume is that?"

Jack leaned down and gave her a smooch on the cheek. "Nice to see you, too, Darlene."

"Is that fucking Cheese? Goddammit, now that is a good costume. You look like a regular thieving injun and I bet you're already piss drunk."

"Not quite yet," a stone-cold sober Cheese said. "Where's your costume, Darlene?"

"Very fucking funny, Cheese, I wish I was a witch, I'd turn your dumb ass into a toad. Coach Quinni is getting the wagon ready – he insists on taking you boys on a hayride, although I can't imagine why. I don't want to hear of any of that gay, queer shit going on, either. You keep your hands to yourself, Jack."

"Yes, ma'am. You can count on that," he said.

"There is an old Seneca asshole I need you to talk to tonight, Jack. Tree Spirit Hansen – I think you know him – has been telling me stories that are just crazy enough to believe. I was hoping you could take a minute from your shitty, shallow existence and hear the crazy bastard out. Do you think you could manage that without stepping all over your dick?"

"It would be my pleasure to do that for you. I saw him at Brady's party last weekend and he said he had a story to tell."

"Good. Now you boys keep your peckers in your pants tonight. Last thing I need is a slew of fornicators on my farm. If something pops up you just bring it right over here to Darlene."

"Yes, ma'am," Cheese said.

Jack and Cheese headed over to the big barn to grab a drink and check out the party. They were especially anxious to scope out the sexy costumes the ladies always wore to Halloween parties. It seemed to get better or worse every year, depending on one's point of view.

They laughed and joked about Darlene. What a character! She talked like she had been in a locker room her whole life, which she pretty much had. She had been a loyal, long-time assistant coach for her husband until up to just a few years prior when she finally retired. She smoked like a chimney, cussed like a sailor, and drank like a fish but was as healthy as a horse. Darlene Quinni was one of Jack's favorite people.

As they were walking out of the barn, drinks in hand, a late-model black Towne Car pulled onto the farm. The driver pulled up to the front doors of the party barn and scrambled out to open the back door. A beautiful maiden in a long, flowing, white gown emerged from the chariot. It was Cinderella.

The beautiful princess adjusted her snuggly fitting bustier that lifted her ample bosom almost into her throat and made sure the mask covering most of her face was properly fastened before stepping from backseat of the Towne Car.

Cheese whistled. "That's her, isn't it?"

"If it ain't, it is now."

Jack made his way over to greet the fair maiden whose identity, but not beauty, was obscured by her costume.

"Well, if it isn't Cinder-fucking-rella herself."

Gerry looked around briefly before her eyes settled on the Lone Ranger and his Indian friend.

"I expected Prince Charming, not some ass-clown cowboy," she said.

"Don't talk to the long arm of the law in that tone, missy, or I will have to tie you up and have my way with you."

"Ooh, do you promise?"

Jack put his arm around her and gave her a quick kiss and they headed for the barn to get a drink.

"Hi, Cheese," she said. "How are you doing?"

"*Bene, grazie*, I keep waiting for Jack to get that feeling again so we can play some more blackjack."

"We don't need the cowboy to play cards. Let me know when you're ready – I would love to play," she said.

They joined the party for a while before Coach Quinni declared the wagon ready. Jack rounded up Chaz and Vinny Cappolla and his wife Beverly to join them. They had just gotten comfortable on the hay wagon when a 1999 Cadillac with bull horns fastened onto the hood came racing into the yard.

"Fucking Boss Hogg is here," Vinny said.

Beverly elbowed him in the ribs.

"Why does it have to be 'effing' Boss Hogg?" she asked. "Can you not even say one sentence without using that word?"

"How the *fuck* should I know?"

All the boys busted out laughing. Gerry just looked at the large, foul man, unsure what to make of him.

"Hold on there, Coach," Chaz said, "I believe that's Tree Spirit Hansen in the Boss Hogg mobile. He said he wanted to talk – sounded desperate. Let's see if he wants to take a little hayride."

"When *doesn't* that guy sound desperate," Jack said to no one in particular.

A tall, gaunt man got out of the car and checked his perimeter, then ducked his head like he was exiting a helicopter and ran gracefully with long strides to the hay wagon and hopped aboard.

"What the hell, Tree Spirit," Jack said, "you playing Cowboys and Indians, again? As I recall, that didn't turn out so well for you guys the first go around."

"Hi, Jack, I see you and Cheese are playing the same game," Tree Spirit said.

"Have a seat, Mr. Spirit," Chaz said. "We are about to embark on the sacred, rural tradition of the Great American Hayride."

Tree Spirit settled into the middle of the wagon and gladly received the jug of Jahouga Juice that landed in his lap. He took a long pull off the bottle but still seemed nervous. Either somebody really was trying to get him, or he was one whacked-out, paranoid freak. Only time would tell.

"Hiya!" Coach Quinni urged the horses to get a move on and the wagon began wending its way down the road; the hayride was underway.

It was a chilly night, but Coach Quinni had supplied a stack of blankets for the riders to keep themselves warm during the roughly forty-five-minute trek through the back roads of the local countryside. Jack had snuggled in next to Gerry under a hand-made quilt and kept trying to feel her up under the blanket. She discreetly fought off his advances, but not too hard.

They were all gathered around Tree Spirit, who looked much more settled and comfortable.

"Well, Cochise," Chaz said, "we're all friends here, what's on your mind?"

Tree Spirit looked around anxiously at the dimly lit pale faces – except for Cheese – surrounding him under the waning moon and took a deep breath.

"About a month ago, I was looking over some of the paperwork on the casino and stadium deals. As a member of the Tribal Council most of these documents were readily at my disposal. I noticed there were a few small irregularities with some of the numbers. You know, some things just didn't seem to add up. They didn't *feel* right. I also had serious reservations about what I had witnessed during the construction.

"So I pulled every document I could about the entire project, A to Z. I had the paper on the materials, construction, contractors, accounts payable, receivables – the whole story. I began to run the numbers for myself. I have a history in construction management, twenty-seven years in the business, and I know how to run the books, and I also know when something stinks and this thing smelled of rotting fish. I took it to the tribe's Security Chief, Neil Dadoska. He confiscated the paperwork I showed him and said he would open a case and take a poke at it, but then he said if I knew what was good for me, I would keep quiet and mind my own business."

Gerry was instantly alarmed. "What are you trying to say? Is there a problem with the Stadium and the Blizzard?"

Tree Spirit looked at her with mild suspicion; he had no idea who she was behind her mask.

"It's okay, Mr. Spirit," Chaz said. "Everyone here is cool. We're all on the same team."

Tree Spirit looked around at the faces on the wagon again, and then gazed past them into the darkness beyond, obviously burdened and in need of help. His hope was he had come to the right place.

"Well, there are major problems. I don't have the specifics, but if I were to venture a guess, I would say as much as one hundred million dollars may have been skimmed from both the casino and the stadium projects. I don't know by whom just yet, but I have my suspicions.

"Security Chief Dadoska is part of it, for sure. He has cut me off from all of the paperwork and changed the passwords to the Nation's computer system so I can no longer access the books. Some very unsavory people have threatened me and I am being followed. To be completely honest, I fear for my life. Many years ago, a member of our Tribal Council stumbled onto some information about some shady dealings by others within the council. Shortly thereafter, that man disappeared without a trace. I am worried I will meet that same fate…whatever it was."

Nobody knew quite what to say. Gerry was astonished there could be some liability on the part of the Blizzard regarding the stadium dealings. She knew Donald Fegel had handled the entire thing. He had dealt with Senator Blutarsky to line up the state money and with the Seneca's to get theirs. He had managed the entire building project. Donald was a lot of things, but she could not believe he was a crook, too.

"Who are these unsavory fuckers?" Vinny asked, breaking the silence. "I can take care of that shit right now with one phone call. I'll have those bastards picked up and put in the slammer before Cheese can fart the alphabet!"

"Vincenzo!" Beverly said, but Vinny held up a hand in a manner that quickly quieted his wife.

Well," Chaz said, "I do believe you have come to the right people to help you get to the bottom of this mess and, more importantly, keep your red ass alive in the process."

"Thank you, Chaz, I have not had a good night's sleep in two weeks – my house has been broken into and ransacked twice already. I need some help or I fear I won't make it much longer."

"Ol' Chaz is on the case, Tree Spirit," Cheese said. "Forget about it, we're all on the case."

Gerry looked at Chaz. He was an unassuming man, but everyone else on the hayride seemed to defer to him.

"So what *is* the plan, Chaz?" She asked.

"Let me work on that, but for now, everyone here has to keep their mouths shut about this whole thing. Assume your phones are tapped and your homes are bugged. They are probably even tailing some of us. You mustn't speak of this amongst yourselves unless you are one hundred percent sure you are in a secure situation. Even then, proceed with extreme caution. How much of that paper did you manage to save, Cochise?"

"I stashed away some of the original stuff I gathered. But they got a lot of it the first time they flipped my house," Tree Spirit said.

"Well, at least there is something. Tonight, you will disappear for a while, Mr. Spirit. I have the perfect safe-house for you to stay at while I snoop around and see what's going on. I'll bet our friend, Senator Blutarsky, got himself a piece of this pie on the state side of things, huh, Vinny?"

"I was just thinking the same thing," Vinny said. "I will tiptoe around and see what I can scare up on that end."

"You, tiptoe?" Jack said. "Lord help us all."

The mental image of the massive Vinny Cappolla tiptoeing around anything was too much and eased the tension a notch. Everyone burst into laughter, none more animated than Vinny himself. Even Gerry smiled, though she was quite disturbed by the discussion. Even more disturbing was the unsettling news there could be illegal activities on the part of the Blizzard involving the Wigwam. She felt horrible for her father and a growing anger at Donald Fegel. She looked at Jack, who mouthed the words "mega-dump."

Chaz climbed to the front of the wagon and leaned in and had a quick conversation with Coach Quinni. The coach nodded vigorously and shortly thereafter guided the horses up a driveway and into the open barn of one of his neighbors. Chaz had Tree Spirit jump off the wagon and hide out in the barn until he could come by later to pick him up. Tree Spirit was officially on the lam.

# Chapter Twenty-Four

The offices of the Seneca Nation were situated on the fourth floor of the new Buffalo Seneca Casino. The corner office, with a view of the Wigwam to the west and Lake Erie to the south, was occupied by the Seneca Nation Security Chief, Neil Dadoska. Neil did not have a single drop of Seneca blood running through his veins but had married into the tribe twenty-seven years ago. His wife passed a year later, but by then he was family. He had worked his way into a position of power by being a shrewd businessman and a solemn keeper of secrets. It didn't hurt that he was also ruthlessly violent and a borderline sociopath. He did whatever it took to get the job done, never giving it a second thought.

Despite having no tribal blood, he was consistently mistaken as a Native American. Dadoska was big and burly with absolutely no neck. He had long, stringy hair which he kept pulled back into a ponytail, but he was mostly bald on top. He had a dark complexion and a broad nose on his flat-featured face. A long, thin scar marked that rugged face beginning under his left eye and running all the way to his left ear. Few could argue he did not look the part of an Indian security chief. A chronic scowl only added to his presence that proved to be downright intimidating to Colin Meade, who sat across the desk from the Chief.

"Thanks for coming to see me on such short notice," Dadoska said in his rich baritone.

"Not a problem," Colin squeaked in stark contrast. "It's actually very convenient being as my office is just across the street."

Dadoska grunted and picked up an old, wood-handled hunting knife from the desk and began to clean his fingernails. Colin was thoroughly disgusted and considered Dadoska to be a savage of a man. He only dealt with this beast out of necessity. The man's silence also bothered him. He considered himself to be a man of certain importance; it was well beneath his pedigree to watch this brutish cretin catch up on his personal hygiene.

"So what is so urgent that I had to rush right over here, Mr. D?" Colin asked.

Dadoska fixed a stare at him and slowly put the knife back onto his highly polished oak desk.

"We have a potential problem, Mr. Meade," he said as dramatically as possible. "There is a member of our Tribal Council by the name of Robert 'Tree Spirit' Hansen who came to me with a stack of paper and a bunch of questions regarding both the casino deal and the stadium financing. I sternly warned him not to pursue the matter and have been following him. We turned his house upside down a couple of times, scared him pretty good, I believe. He really doesn't have anything except a lot of questions and suspicions.

"I was having him followed, but now he's disappeared. My scouts tailed him to a farm up in Wheatfield where one of your players, Jack Driftwood, was throwing a wild party two nights ago. He got on a hayride with Driftwood and a small group of people, including a Buffalo cop named Vinny Cappolla. We haven't seen Mr. Hansen since. A friend of mine from the downtown precinct told me Cappolla is sniffing around concerning Senator Blutarsky and his involvement with the Stadium funding. Now I am certain the Seneca end of the deal is properly covered, but my question is, Mr. Meade, how well are your tracks covered?"

"Jack Driftwood?" Colin asked, a bit overwhelmed at what he was hearing. "What the hell does he have to do with this?"

"I thought you might be able to answer that," Dadoska replied.

"I have to think this is totally a coincidence. As far as our tracks being covered, I would not be concerned about that. I did all the paperwork myself, and I assure you there is nothing out of order on our end."

"Well, I just wanted you to be aware of the situation. However, I am not one to believe in coincidence. I suggest you take this seriously. We are going to find the meddling Tree Spirit and make sure he keeps quiet. If you need help doing the same with Jack Driftwood, the cop, or anyone else, you just let me know. Public servants and pro athletes have been known to have unfortunate accidents, just like anyone else."

Colin was shocked at the thought of everything coming unraveled and was momentarily at a loss for words. Was it all coincidence? He had to take some time to think about it.

*Didn't Buffalo Bill tell me Gerry Wainscott went to that party and took a hayride with Driftwood? What does she know?*

Maybe the boss was right about Jack Driftwood. This shit was getting too crazy. Colin in no way looked forward to relaying the results of this consult to the boss; it wasn't going to be pretty, of that he was sure.

"I will let you know, Mr. D., but for right now I think we should wait before doing anything rash. I will talk to Mr. Fegel immediately regarding this situation and get back to you, post haste. Let me know if anything changes."

"You can bet your ass on that," Dadoska said. "Post fucking haste."

It sounded like a threat.

Donald had just wrapped up an emergency personnel meeting with Coach Ivy, Chuckles, Bob Johnson, Gerry, Alvin Kaplan, and Meade. They had come to a consensus the Blizzard would pull the trigger on a trade with the Las Vegas

Gamblers for an offensive lineman by the name of Steve Watson. The Gamblers had been jerking them around since Monday and Donald was ready to walk when they came to their senses. It now looked like the deal was imminent. The cost to Buffalo would be a conditional late-round pick, which they were more than willing to part with for the services of Watson. They were waiting on the Gamblers' final decision, but with the trade deadline less than forty-eight hours away, time was running short.

The medical report from Kaplan on Driftwood was at least somewhat positive. The MRI had shown the shoulder wasn't as badly separated as initially thought. Kaplan said he could construct a protective pad that would help Driftwood get through the next couple of games with a significantly reduced risk of sustaining any further damage. Then he would have a good chance of healing up entirely during their bye week. Also, Driftwood would, no doubt, take another injection in the shoulder if needed.

Billy Brogan would start in Stark's spot while he nursed his foot back to full strength, which would take a month at least. In the interim, the Blizzard's depth at inside linebacker would have to come from Jerry Killings. They also had a young player, Jimmy Williams, on the practice squad who was a promising prospect they would activate. He could take Brogan's spot on special teams and fill in at linebacker in a pinch.

Meade waited patiently while Donald fielded the call from the Gamblers. The trade was a go as Donald shot him a thumbs up while on the phone with the Gamblers' GM. Donald finally gave him his full attention. Meade recounted his entire conversation with Security Chief Dadoska to the boss without interruption.

Initially Donald sat silently, looking at him with his mouth agape, disbelief marking his features. Then he became furious.

"Jack Driftwood?" he nearly shouted. "Are you shitting me? What the hell does *he* have to do with this? Gerry was there too? And a Buffalo cop? What in the fuck is going on, Colin?"

"I think it is just a coincidence, there is no other rational way to explain it."

"Well, we are going to find out! I want the both of them followed again and we need to tap their phones. That would tell us right away just exactly what they know and what we are dealing with. I may have to ratchet up some pressure on Ms. Wainscott, too. Threaten to tell her precious daddy she is banging one of his players. See if the bastard Driftwood can weather that storm."

"Yes, sir," Meade said. "I will take care of their phones. What about their homes? I can probably bug them as well."

Donald thought about it briefly. "No, just do the phones for now. And keep me posted."

He was not ready to hear Gerry making love to that Neanderthal. He still harbored the fantasy of him and Gerry together once this whole thing went away.

Driftwood was going to be a goner soon and he would swoop in and pick up the pieces. But he did not need his mind tormented with the sounds of her infidelity, especially with the cowboy.

"Yes, sir," Meade said.

He got up to leave before Donald's voice froze him in his tracks.

"One more thing, we are properly insulated, are we not?"

"Totally. I know what I'm doing, Donald. I've been around the proverbial block a few times. Short of one of us making a confession, there is nothing to worry about."

"Good, then I won't worry."

The look on Donald Fegel's face said otherwise, something he hoped Meade didn't pick up on.

Jack Driftwood was torn. He was going to play; that was not the issue. His mind was made up; he would strap it on and play against Boston that very afternoon. The dilemma under contemplation was whether or not to take a pain-numbing shot from Doc Verdin's over-sized, deep-probing hypodermic needle.

Jack knew if he took the shot of juice from Dr. Feel-Good the shoulder would hardly feel a thing for the next six hours or so. After that, however, it would feel like mincemeat at best. The real issue was he hated that goddamn needle. The injection hurt as much or more than anything else he would have to endure.

If he played without the shot he knew he would instinctively protect his shoulder. This meant playing like a pussy, but at least he would know if and when he did more damage to the damn thing. Jack sat in the bowels of the Wigwam agonizing over the decision with the kickoff looming.

"Goddammit, Kappy," he said, "I just don't know what to do with this thing. If it felt just a little bit better I wouldn't even need a shot – a couple of those little pills of Doc's would do the trick."

"I don't know what to tell you," Kaplan said. "You're a big boy, you know the deal."

"Yeah, I know, but if—"

"Don't be such a pussy."

Jack turned around to see Stark hopping in on crutches. "Ha! Look who is talking. I saw his foot yesterday, he's milking it so bad there's a nipple growing on it."

"Bullshit, this here is a real injury, not some half-assed sore shoulder."

"Both of you ain't worth a shit," Kaplan said. "Let's go, Jack. Doc is ready for you."

Jack paused, looking back and forth from the goofy smile on Stark's mug to the grim determination on Kaplan's.

"You fuckers. You knew I was gonna take the shot all along, didn't you, Kappy?"

"Let's just say I've seen your act for long time now, Jackie-boy. Let's just get it over with."

Driftwood took the shot but it didn't much matter. For whatever reason, he and his Buffalo Blizzard were not ready to play football that Sunday afternoon. No matter what they tried, it wasn't happening; it was one of those days. Boston got every break in handing Buffalo its first ever loss at the Wigwam. The final score ended up with the Revolution on top 30-25, but Buffalo had scored a last second touchdown to make the game appear closer than it had ever been throughout the afternoon. The Blizzard's record dropped to 8-2 on the season.

The only good news as far as Driftwood was concerned was he made it through the day without seriously re-injuring the shoulder. It was still sore as hell, to the extent he couldn't raise his arm above his head after the game. Danny Steeley had to cut his jersey off of him.

After a long, hot shower he packed the shoulder in ice, got a handful of pain meds from Doc Verdin, and began the slow trek out to the parking lot. He was in no mood to party on this night. He had neither the energy nor the heart for it. The plan was to go home and spend some quality time feeling sorry for himself. Such is the lot of losers.

When he arrived at his warehouse flat, Chaz was sitting at the kitchen table with a bucket of steaming-hot barbecued chicken wings and a pepperoni pizza spread out in front of him.

"I figured you'd be hungry after an ass-whipping like that, Cochise," he said.

"Thanks," Jack said, "and go ahead, just let yourself in."

"Man, I forgot what a grumpy little bitch you are when we lose. Take a couple of those pills of yours and mellow out."

Jack gently massaged his throbbing left shoulder. "Already did, those bad boys should be kicking in any minute now. And what's this 'we' shit?"

"Good for you. Wasn't much of a game, huh? I could tell early on you guys didn't seem to have your normal energy. Weird how that works."

"I know, right. You'd think we could get up for every game, what with only twenty or so of them in a season. But it's been my experience that you really only hit a collective fever pitch maybe half the time. And that's if you're lucky. That's why coaching and talent matter, they can get you over the hump when you ain't feeling it."

Chaz nodded thoughtfully in agreement. Emotion was one of life's great mysteries.

"What's the latest with Tree Spirit?" Jack asked.

Chaz chuckled. "I gotta tell you, bro, I thought *I* was one fucked-up hombre, but this guy takes the cake. He does this transcendental meditation shit where puts himself into a trance and will sit Indian-style humming for hours. Then, after he snaps out of it, he has this unbelievable, frenetic energy. The dude bounces off the walls all night while normal people sleep. Speaking of which, he hardly sleeps at all, but he sure as hell can cook. He has already been worth his keep. He can whip me up a meal anytime, hoss."

"What about the deal with the Wigwam and Feegs? Does he have something there?"

"He sure as hell *thinks* he does," Chaz said. "He believes Fegel and Meade cooked the books and skimmed around one hundred mil off the deal – split it up with Blutarsky and that Tribal Council Security Chief prick. He says they worked out kickback deals with a bunch of the subcontractors, inflated material prices, and also used some sub-standard materials in the construction, pocketing the difference. You know, the old trick where the paperwork says they ordered top of the line shit but then they use off-brand crap snuck in from China. Probably slapped bogus name-brand stickers on shit to hide it all. He is absolutely positive they used inferior heating elements on the snow-melt system built into the glass roof. Claims to have seen that first hand when he was sniffing around during the construction."

"No shit. You believe him?"

"Why else would they be fucking with him? I honestly believe his life is in danger if he shows his face around here again. I went over to his place and it was tossed by some pros – serious fucking customers. I was thinking about sending him down to stay at my place in Mexico for a few weeks. You know, let things cool off while I sniff around to see if I can come up with anything. You guys have a bye week coming up, don't you?"

"Yeah, we play the dog-ass Rough Riders in New York next Sunday and then we are off the whole next week. Why?"

"I was just thinking you and your secret squeeze ought to take a little hiatus down to Mexico. Stay at my place and get the scoop from Tree Spirit, first hand. Maybe have the princess look at the paper he has, see what she thinks. Tree Spirit could whip up some romantic meals and you and old girl can hold hands and enjoy the beach for a few days. All I ask is that you replace the sheets when you are done."

Jack stared at Chaz, a chicken wing dangling from his mouth. The man was a genius. "Replace your own sheets…but that may be the best goddamn idea you have ever come up with!"

Suddenly, Jack was in an infinitely better mood. Perhaps it was because the pills had kicked in, or maybe it was simply the thought of an interlude in paradise with Gerry Wainscott; more likely it was the combination. Regardless, his malaise had magically lifted. Jack was genuinely excited.

"Obviously," Chaz said, "I don't have to tell you to keep things quiet, but be careful about chatting on your phones. I gotta believe Tree Spirit was followed to your Halloween party, they were closing in on him. Whoever they are, they know he went missing after that hayride with us."

"Yeah, I hear you."

"You haven't noticed anyone following you, have you?" Chaz asked.

"Funny you should mention that," Jack said. "I haven't actually seen anyone, but I have been getting this weird feeling like I am being watched."

"That probably means you are, the human mind is an amazing thing. Your subconscious has been picking up the signals. Just be careful, I had a few run-ins with these Seneca's over the years and they can be a nasty bunch."

Jack flipped his middle finger at Chaz. "Is your subconscious picking up this signal?"

"I'm serious," Chaz said.

"I know you are, that's what makes you such a treasure of an asshole."

"Laugh it up, dickwood, but I can tell you when you are surviving by just your wits in the middle of the jungle with enemies all around you, you learn to rely on that shit. Or die."

"Easy, Jackknife Johnny. We aren't on the Ho Chi Minh Trail, here. I know what you are saying, though. I get it on the field sometimes. I get so tuned in that everything slows way down and I just know what is going to happen next – I see it in my mind before it happens. Back in college I used to call it tapping into the Over-soul after reading some Emerson and Thoreau in an American Lit class."

"Ah, the New England Transcendentalist bullshit of the 1840's. I gotta tell you, Ralph Waldo and Henry David were a couple of pathetic slackers. Neither of them boys ever did an honest day's work in their entire wretched lives. Nor did they believe in the God who owns and controls this universe. But to be fair, I suppose they did provide a little fodder for discussion."

"You are full of surprises, Chaz. I thought for sure you would be a fan of the Thoreau-lifestyle, you know, living in a homemade hut, communing with nature out on Walden Pond."

"Oh, I can dig the lifestyle, just not the philosophy."

Jack laughed out loud and shook his head. He seemed to have the most existential conversations with Chaz. The more time he spent with the old boy, the more he enjoyed his company. Now *that* was scary.

## Chapter Twenty-Five

Jack leaned back in the big leather chair in the First Class section of the Delta Airbus flying south at thirty-eight thousand feet somewhere over Georgia. The pills and alcohol had combined to mask most of the pain in his aching body. The game with the dog-ass Rough Riders had been a brutal battle. No matter how pathetic New York's record was, they always got up to play a tough, physical game with the boys from Buffalo. This one was no exception.

Buffalo had won 27-13 earlier that afternoon to run their Eastern-Conference-leading record to 9-2 heading into their bye week. It had been a close game, tied 13 all, until two fourth-quarter Blizzard touchdowns had sealed the deal. Billy Brogan had played well again in place of the injured Steven Stark. He had forced and recovered a fumble that had led to the go-ahead score midway through the final stanza. Surprisingly, Jack enjoyed playing alongside Brogan. The guy was a smart player who had a certain toughness to him. They didn't talk much away from the field, but once they were on it, they were in sync. Jack figured Brogan's bitch of a wife, Nicole, would forever keep them from becoming real friends. But as long as everything worked out on the field it didn't matter. Jack had plenty of friends but damn few, if any, could play linebacker in the NAFA.

Jack was content to sit back and replay the game over in his mind. He was always wound up after games; his mind would not rest until he had fully digested every play. This process had begun back when he played for the Spoofhounds on Wednesday nights in middle school. He couldn't fall asleep after those contests even way back then and spent the long nights tossing and turning. Then he would drag around the next morning due to the lack of sleep. Sometimes his mother would let him stay in bed on those mornings, but only when his father was out of the house. Big Ed didn't believe in shirking any duties and missing school was nonsense not to be tolerated.

Jack always reviewed his mistakes first, going over in his head what he had seen and why he had messed up. After justifying the errors in his mind and vowing not to repeat them, he would move on to the good plays he had made. He would use the same process, playing them over in his mind from every angle, reinforcing the positives of what he had done. He felt this was as important as any part of his quest to be the best. He used the fresh memories to sear in the positive and weed out the negative.

There were always a few plays where he wasn't sure what had happened. Those were the ones that drove him crazy until he could review the game film.

The video filled in the blanks of what he couldn't recall and reinforced what he could. Watching game tape was the best learning tool in the box, and he had mastered the use of it.

He had procured a DVD of the television broadcast of the Rough Riders' game from a friend on the TV crew who had covered the contest. He decided he would wait until he was settled in at Chaz's beach house before performing the post mortem on DVD. He was satisfied with his memories at that point; after all, they had won and he had played pretty well.

However, he was eager to review one play in particular. Driftwood had anticipated the tight end running a crossing route and dove to knock the ball away at the last second. After the tip he had tucked into a full somersault, landing on the upper middle of his back. He used his momentum to spring himself up to his feet and forward where he rolled into a cartwheel. He finished the dazzling display with a front round-off, nailing the landing. The opposing crowd couldn't help but appreciate his display of athleticism, giving him a rousing ovation. Never shy about basking in the glory, Jack took a bow.

He giggled to himself at the thought of it.

*I'm such an asshole!*

He signaled the sturdy battle-axe of a flight attendant to fetch a refill on his glass of Crown and water with a twist. For now he was content to sit in the glow of another Blizzard win and the happy haze of the alcohol and Norco buzz and daydream about the next few days of relaxation on a pristine Mexican beach.

Tree Spirit was as high as a kite when he rolled into the Cancun airport to pick up Jack. After one look Jack told him to slide over into the passenger seat. Tree Spirit quickly complied and then regaled him with stories of the wild women and local tequila he had discovered in the past week. He smoked from a blunt about the size of Jack's arm and drank Jahouga Juice from a leather flask the entire thirty-five-minute ride to the beachfront bungalow.

Jack swore he caught a contact buzz from the hazy blue smoke filling the Jeep Wrangler. He politely declined the offer of direct smoke, but he enthusiastically helped his friend polish off the flask.

They were hooting and hollering by the time they pulled into the garage and parked the Jeep. Jack was starving and Tree Spirit went to work in the kitchen whipping up some eggs with red beans and rice.

"I am so glad you are here, my friend," Tree Spirit said. "I was beginning to get lonely."

"I'm pretty damn happy to be here myself," Jack said. "And I'll be a lot happier when the little woman shows up tomorrow morning."

Jack was still amazed at how easy it had been to convince Gerry to join him on the jaunt down to Mexico. At his core, he was a hopeless romantic. This had led him to stop at a downtown florist and pick up a dozen pink roses before heading up to her penthouse last Thursday. He had on one of his favorite corny, brightly-colored tropical shirts along with Bermuda shorts and flip-flops. He knew he looked like a damn fool and would be far from inconspicuous heading into the Buffalo Seneca Casino lobby in his Caribbean get-up, but he didn't care.

He had knocked on the door to Gerry's penthouse brandishing the flowers out in front of him, hoping to ward her off in case she forgot about his injured shoulder again and jumped him upon opening the door.

Sure enough, Gerry whipped the door open and was ready to spring into his arms when she was stopped cold by a dozen pink roses.

"Oh, Jack! They're beautiful! How did you know I love pink roses?"

"Hey, I pay attention. I'm not just some meathead jock you can use and abuse for his body and sexual prowess."

After responding with a dubious expression, she put the roses on the table and walked over and stood directly in front of him, as close as she could get without touching. She looked up into his eyes.

"What's up with the getup?"

"I thought you would never ask," he said. "Basically I am trying to get into the spirit of things."

"What things?"

Jack began to move his hands over her body without touching her. He got as close as he could, even cupping her breasts and giving her ass the courtesy of a reach around, but he never broke her force-field.

"I got a plan. After we whip the dog-ass Rough Riders on Sunday, yours truly is going to board a plane at LaGuardia headed for Cancun, Mexico. I intend to take a five-day tropical vacation. My only problem is I don't have a hot owner's daughter to go with me – you know where I can find one?"

Gerry eyes widened and she jumped into the air, throwing her arms and legs around Jack squeezing as hard as she could. It never hurt so good when he snatched her up and wrapped both arms around her, squeezing her right back.

*I'll take that as a yes!*

Tree Spirit let out a soft wolf-whistle and then looked to the heavens, taking off his sombrero and bowing deeply to give his respects to the Great Spirit in the sky.

"You are one lucky man, *Señor* Jack," he said and then hurried to grab Gerry's over-sized suitcase.

"Indeed I am."

Gerry was standing on the curb in a state of mild distress wearing a bright yellow sundress and oversized shades under a wide-brimmed straw hat. Her dark, shiny hair lit up with the bright Mexican sun and highlighted her beautiful skin. When she finally saw Jack she dropped her handbag and ran to him, jumping into his arms. Jack grabbed her with his right arm and twirled her around as if she were a small child.

He gave her a full kiss before setting her back onto the ground. It was like a scene out of a cheap romance novel or a network movie of the week. As they embraced again she felt him poking through his shorts.

"You got a mouse in your pocket, or are you just glad to see me?"

Jack grinded his hips into hers. "Mice don't get that big."

"I hope it is a short ride to Chaz's place," Gerry said.

She pressed back into Jack again and didn't want to let him go. It amazed her how natural it felt to touch him and be with him in a public setting. Jack spun her around and she finally noticed Tree Spirit. The smiling Seneca threw his arms wide and leaned over so she could give him a hug and peck on the cheek.

"*Hola, Señorita,*" Tree Spirit said. "You look gorgeous, Ms. Gerry. The football life must suit you well."

"Why, thank you, Mr. Spirit. Aren't you sweet! I am just so glad to be away from it all. This is going to be a wonderful break."

"Yes, ma'am," Tree Spirit said, "it surely is."

Jack slid into the passenger seat and pulled Gerry up onto his lap while Tree Spirit hopped in behind the wheel. They belted up and took off for the bungalow.

Jack gave Gerry a quick tour of the three-bedroom hacienda that was to be their home for the next five days. Tree Spirit was heading to the grocery store and said he would be back in an hour or so. Whether the guy knew what the deal was or he really had to go to the store didn't matter to Jack; he was just thankful for some alone time with his number-one squeeze. As Tree Spirit pulled out of the driveway, Gerry pulled herself out of her clothes and Jack pulled her into the bedroom where he pulled out his bag of tricks.

The bright Mexican sun was relentless. Jack and Gerry had spent the better part of the day basking in it on the private beach in front of Chaz's bungalow. The surf was up so he had been teaching Gerry the fine art of body surfing. Worn out from all the activity, they were enjoying a bottle of fine wine while relaxing in the early evening shade out on the veranda. Tree Spirit refilled their goblets and joined them at the table.

"Would now be an appropriate time to discuss the Wigwam issue?" he asked.

"Way to go, A-hole," Jack said, "why don't you just ruin the most perfect day of my life."

"Jack, don't be so rude to Tree Spirit. He has been the perfect host."

"*Has been* – key phrase, right there."

Gerry mock-glared at Jack and then turned to Tree Spirit. "Of course it would, Mr. Tree Spirit. This is a *perfect* time."

Tree Spirit needed no further encouragement and launched into his story. "It all began a little over a year ago when I was visiting the construction site one evening, just to see how things were going. There was a crew there unloading the glass panels for the roof of the Wigwam. One of the most significant engineering issues was the snow-melt system for the roof. The last thing anyone wanted was a heavy snowstorm to come along and collapse the whole thing. That would not be good."

"No shit, Sherlock," Jack said.

"Jack!"

"Sorry."

"Thank you, Ms. Gerry. I was particularly interested in the roof and in how it would function – it is quite a modern marvel of engineering, you know. I had grabbed a spec sheet from our temporary offices and as I began to inspect the glass panels I noticed an alarming discrepancy in the heating coils built into the glass. Most of the coils were only one-quarter of the size of what the spec sheet called for.

"I asked the supervisor on site about it and he said to take it up with the Project Manager, so I went to him and he said as far as he knew those were the right panels. Next thing I know, the Tribal Security Chief, Neil Dadoska, is telling me to stay away from the construction site and to mind my own business."

"So those substandard panels are on the roof right now?" Gerry asked.

"I'm afraid so. It will be interesting to see what happens when we get a big snowstorm. I suspect they will be okay, unless, of course, we get a wicked blizzard or a heavy ice storm."

"Oh yeah, that'll *never* happen in Buffalo," Jack said.

"I did some pricing on the glass panels, and by using the inferior product they skimmed nearly five million dollars off the cost of the roof alone."

This made both Jack and Gerry sit up a little bit.

"I snuck back onto the work site later and began to look at some of the other materials they used and found other discrepancies. I also know some of the subcontractors on this project, and they are a notorious group of criminals who commonly engage in kickback schemes to secure their bids. My conservative estimation is somebody, most likely Mr. Donald Fegel, milked the stadium project for over fifty million dollars. I would think they got nearly that much from the casino project also."

"That's a pretty good chunk of change there, Tree Spirit," Jack said. "Not to mention a serious allegation. Can you prove any of it?"

"I can prove the roof is substandard, but you would have to get it inspected by a private, third party. That is where Senator Blutarsky comes into the deal. His muscle was instrumental in getting the inspection pushed through – which does not come cheap. There has to be another set of books. Typically, with this large of a sum, the criminals will set up an off-shore bank account to hide the money until they intend to collect it."

Gerry was now more angry than skeptical. "So what can we do about it?"

"That's a good question. I can go through again and maybe find a red herring or two and get an investigation going, but I think we will need more help."

Jack patted his groin. "I got your red herring right here."

"You're such a dick." Gerry punched him in his left shoulder.

"Exactly," Jack said with a smile obviously intended to hide his pain. "But seriously, what do you think about scaring Feegs into a bad move – maybe you tell him you know what he did, Gerry. Then he gets all nervous and does something stupid to try and hide his tracks better."

"I don't know," Tree Spirit said, "I would not want to put Gerry in any danger. The people on the Seneca side of this thing are of a very nasty ilk. When I pressed them about all of this they ransacked my house and threatened to kill me, Jack. And they were serious, I'm not here because I like tacos."

"I'm not scared," Gerry said, "I'm pissed."

"That's my girl," Jack said. "You better watch out, Tree Spirit, this little woman is a hell-cat."

"She does scare the hell out of me."

"You are both a couple of assholes."

"Make that hungry assholes," Jack said. "What smells so good coming out of that kitchen?"

"Oh, you will love this dish," Tree Spirit said, "it is one of my specialties. Chicken pot pie with a golden homemade crust and freshly cut vegetables."

"Mmm, that does sound good," Gerry said. "Perhaps we can think better about what to do on a full stomach."

"Now you are finally making some sense," Jack said. He looked back to Tree Spirit. "I told you she was a hellcat, didn't I?"

"Yes, sir, you did and I believe she truly is," Tree Spirit said as he headed for the kitchen to fetch up their grub.

It was a perfect evening as Jack and Gerry walked the white, pristine sands shortly before sunset. They were leaving the Mexican paradise the next morning and wanted to milk every last drop of their time together on this romantic getaway. They were making their way back to Chaz's cottage when the hair on Jack's neck stood up from a sudden chill. He first thought was it was just his sunburn morphing into a golden tan, but something felt wrong, despite the fact things had never felt so right. He had a foreboding sense of alarm.

He stopped abruptly and shaded his eyes from the glare cast by the setting sun and carefully scanned the horizon towards the bungalow about fifty yards down the beach. He could have sworn he saw movement in one of the bushes next to the front of the Chaz's place.

"What is it?" Gerry asked.

"Shhh."

Jack grabbed her arm and quickly marshalled her into the undergrowth away from the gulf. There were no other buildings between them and Chaz's place, just sparse, low-cut jungle that grew thicker further from the water and plenty of beach. That was one of the great things about Chaz's place, the utter isolation. His cottage was tucked back a quarter-mile off the main road and his property abutted a nature preserve to the south. To the north the nearest building was another bungalow a quarter-mile up the beach.

Jack and Gerry squatted behind a small grove of palm trees with their eyes trained on the cottage. Jack was about to laugh it off when a man wearing what looked like a black ninja outfit came out of the bushes towards the front of the house. His face was partially covered by a bandana.

"What is going on?" Gerry said.

"I don't know, but there are at least two of them creeping around the place, I wish I had a damn gun."

"Tree Spirit is in there all alone, Jack. What are we going to do?"

"*We* ain't doin' nothing. You are staying here. Keep out of sight and keep an eye on the house. I'm going to sneak up there and see what's going on."

"Are you sure, what if they have guns?"

Jack flexed and kissed his right bicep. "I got my twenty-inch guns."

"This shit isn't funny," she said.

"I know, you don't have to tell me," he said, still not sure what to do.

Whenever in tense situations he always made a joke to calm his nerves and hopefully everybody else's. Sometimes it worked; other times, not so much.

Tree Spirit had been sitting on the veranda reading a book when they had left for their walk some forty-five minutes earlier. Now he was nowhere in sight. Suddenly a shot rang out. There was a brief pause of silence and then another smattering of gun fire and yelling came from the front of the bungalow.

"Holy shit! Stay here," Jack said and took off running toward the house, staying as close to the scrub-line as possible.

He snatched up a couple of rocks, both of them nearly the size of a lemon, as he slowed down when he neared bungalow.

"Drop your guns and come out with your hands up. We have you surrounded!" he yelled at the top of his lungs.

The two men in black ran around from the front of the house looking to see where the voice had come from. Jack had taken cover, hiding in the undergrowth near the driveway and the banditos stopped only five yards away from him. Another shot rang out from the edge of the jungle on the opposite side of the house. One of the gunmen ducked and then took off running down the driveway like the bang of the gun was the starting pistol for the 100-meter dash. The other muttered something and followed with much less enthusiasm.

As they hurried away, Jack jumped out onto the driveway, pivoted, and whipped his entire body around as he slung the rock sidearm; it was his trademark throw over to first base from his misspent youth playing the hot corner. And what a beauty she was! The rock whistled through the air like a laser-guided missile. It beaned one of the thugs flush in the back of his head and he went down like a sack of potatoes.

*Holy shit! I hit the fucker!*

Giggling and beside himself, Jack dove back into the undergrowth as the one gunman still standing turned and fired off a couple of rounds in his general direction. The bullets whizzed above and one of them thudded into a palm tree behind him as he laid flat on the ground. He still couldn't believe he had hit the guy with the rock. It was a Dead-Eye-Dick shot if he'd ever seen one. And from thirty yards! He wasn't sure what the hell he was thinking throwing rocks at dudes with guns, but he couldn't just sit there and let them get away without doing something.

Jack peered through the bushes trying to plot his next move in case the gunmen decided to come back after him. Why would he be throwing rocks if he had a gun? Fortunately, the two ruffians didn't think of that until they were well down the road. The driveway followed a slight bend to the right, a hundred yards or so from the house, and the jungle blocked the view around the bend. Jack heard a car motor rattle to life and the spray of gravel on the face of the jungle as they fled the scene of the crime.

He scrambled off the ground and ran toward the house to check for Tree Spirit, but he didn't really expect to find him. He was pretty sure Tree Spirit had fired the gunshot from the edge of the jungle on the other side of the place and then most likely fled through the underbrush.

"Tree! Robert Tree Spirit Hansen! You can come out now. It's me, Jack. They are gone!"

He waited briefly on the steps for a reply and then quickly ducked into the abode. In the middle of the kitchen a very small puddle of blood was obvious. Jack's eyes followed a trail of droplets that led to the back door and stopped. He went back outside and checked the area around the porch, but the trail had ended at the back door. Jack went to call for Gerry and nearly ran into her as she came around the corner out of breath.

"I heard more gunshots. Are you okay?" She asked.

"Yeah, I'm fine…just pumped up on adrenaline. Plus I'm worried about Tree Spirit. I can't find him anywhere."

He embraced her and then held her shoulders and eased her away to look into her eyes. "There is blood in the kitchen – not a lot – just drops that lead to the back door and stop. There is nothing on the porch or sidewalks."

"Oh, Jack!"

"I know, I know, baby. It's gonna be all right. I got you."

"I should kick your dumb ass, too," she said. "Did I actually, with my own two eyes, see you throw a rock at them? Are you trying to get killed? What in the world were you thinking?"

Driftwood was momentarily speechless, a rarity in itself. Then it just tickled him. He broke into a fit of laughter. It was a much needed release from the tension of the moment and Gerry joined in with him. They laughed until their faces hurt and tears streamed down their faces. When Jack could finally speak again he couldn't help but brag.

"I don't know, but I nailed his ass, best shot ever! I bet that fucker has a good-sized knot on his noggin."

"You hit him?"

"Best throw of my life. I dinged right off the back of ol' boy's head."

They laughed again but it ended with a sobering reality.

"We gotta go," Jack said. "We need to get the fuck outta here before they come back with bigger guns or more guys. We don't have a gun, although I could gather up some rocks…"

"My bag is already packed, I'll go grab it."

Jack snatched his computer off of the table and threw it into his bag. He quickly locked all the doors while Gerry wheeled her suitcase out to the Jeep. Jack left a note on the kitchen table in case Tree Spirit came back.

> **TS,**
> **We are safe and hope you are, too. We saw the blood – take care of yourself! Getting out of here, too hot. Hit my cell when you get this. Stay Alive!**
> **JD**
> **PS. See you at the moon?**

Jack threw his bag into the Jeep and they were rolling, headed north towards Cancun and the airport. Chaz had given Jack the name and address of a friend who ran a little mom and pop restaurant near the airport. He had told Jack the guy could help him if any trouble arose.

*If this ain't trouble I don't know what is.*

# Chapter Twenty-Six

Neil Dadoska told his secretary he would take the call in his office. He didn't need the nosy bitch prying into his business. A few days prior he had heard the esteemed Seneca Tribal Councilman, Tree Spirit Hansen, was in Mexico. This news came from a little birdie by the name of Colin Meade. Apparently Meade had a man track Gerry Wainscott from Buffalo to Miami to Cancun. The meathead Driftwood was there as well, obviously involved with the sweet, little ass of the owner's daughter. That was a rich one there. Dadoska couldn't wait to spread that wildfire.

The call was from his man, the one he had sent down to Mexico to take care of the meddling Mr. Hansen. Dadoska had offered Meade a three-for-one special, hoping to take all the trouble makers out of the equation with one fell swoop. It was the perfect setup with all the drug killings down in Mexico.

*Whack, whack, whack, throw some drugs around the place and the trail would be as cold as a witch's titty. Just another shocking tragedy in today's fucked-up world.*

But Meade had wanted no part of it. He made it clear, in no uncertain terms, neither the meathead nor Gerry Wainscott were to be touched.

*So be it, pussy.*

Dadoska was pretty sure their day would be coming sometime real soon, anyway. He sat behind his desk and tapped the blinking button on his four-line phone.

"Dadoska."

"Um, yes, sir, Johnny Quest reporting, sir."

Dadoska was a big fan of old cartoons and gave his henchmen code names from them. Johnny Quest was one of his favorites.

"Yes, Mr. Quest, I assume you and Race completed the little task I had for you."

There was a pause on the other end before a wavering voice answered. "Well, actually, sir, I cannot confirm that at this point."

"What the fuck does that mean?"

"Well, we took the shot and we hit him, but then we had some outside interference."

"What interference? What the hell happened, Mr. Quest?"

"We scoped the place out and the subject was alone. We snuck around to the front and both got off shots, but it was almost like the guy was waiting for us. We were about to go in after him when someone yelled, 'Drop your weapons, we have you surrounded.' We ran around to the back of the place and then another shot was fired at us.

"We were sitting ducks so we got the hell out of there. Then somebody hit Bannon in the back of the head with a rock as we were running down the driveway. We went back a little bit later to see if we could finish the job but they were gone."

"Jesus Christ, did you just say Bannon got hit in the head with a rock?"

"Yes, sir, a big one. Cut up his skull and almost knocked him out cold. We did find a note though when we went back."

"What'd it say?"

"I'll read it to you. 'TS, we are safe and hope you are, too. We saw the blood – take care of yourself! Getting out of here, too hot. Hit my cell when you get this. Stay Alive! JD. PS. See you at the moon?' So we did hit him and he's at large – probably in the jungle bleeding to death. We just don't know for sure."

Dadoska knew JD wasn't John-fucking-Doe. The meathead was smarter than he had thought and apparently could chuck a rock with the best of them.

"I can't tell you how disappointed I am, Johnny, you are supposed to be my number one guy and you can't even take care of a crazy-old half-breed and a guy who throws rocks in a goddamn gunfight!"

"Yes, sir."

"I want you to stake the place out tonight in case any of them come back. If they do, I don't care who it is, take care of them. Do you understand what I am saying?"

"Yes, sir."

"All right, if no one shows up then get on the first plane back here tomorrow and I want you to come see me personally when you land, got it?"

"Yes, sir," Johnny Quest said.

"And for Chrissakes, tell Race to duck next time!"

"Yes, si—"

Neil Dadoska hung up the phone. He figured they were too smart to go back to the house but just in case, he had it covered. He was pissed about the whole botched deal but he still managed to find some humor in the situation.

*Ha-ha! A fucking rock. Ain't that some shit.*

This Jack Driftwood was either a total dipshit or some kind of rough customer; Dadoska couldn't decide which.

The Moon Over Cancun was a well-kempt cantina featuring a full kitchen which served mostly local clientele. Occasionally, a tourist or two would wander in and feel like they had found heaven's Mexican kitchen. The food was authentic and the portions were huge. The chatter in the kitchen and behind the bar was loud and non-stop. The place was alive with energy.

Jack and Gerry loved it from the moment they stepped through the door. The first order of business was to knock back a couple of shots of top-shelf tequila. The food and drink would help ease the inevitable crash once most of the adrenaline from their adventure had evaporated. Jack had asked their waitress, a beautiful, young, fair-skinned *señorita*, if he might have an audience with the proprietor, Juan Chavez.

Juan had played Arena Football and in Europe after spending three years in the NAFA bouncing around on various practice squads. After he retired he moved down back home to Mexico with his wife and kids and opened up a restaurant. It was his lifelong dream come true.

Driftwood was chomping his way through a half dozen mini tacos when a huge grizzly of a man came from the kitchen and approached their table.

"*Hola, amigos,* I am Juan Chavez. My daughter said you would like an audience with me, no?"

Jack stood to greet his host. "Hey, Juan, Chaz told us we should stop by. I'm Jack Driftwood and this is Gerry Wainscott."

Juan Chavez did a double take. "No shit! Hello, Jack Driftwood. This is fantastic. It's a pleasure to meet you both."

He began to shake and was quickly consumed with a belly laugh. Juan lit up like a pinball machine on tilt. He took Gerry's hand and kissed it and then gave Jack a big hug, lifting him off the ground like a small child. He was talking so fast and in a mixture of English and Spanish that Jack could hardly keep up with him. The big man then called his wife, Winona, out from the kitchen along with his three lovely daughters who were working as waitresses and made the introductions.

He quickly snapped his fingers towards the bar and let out a string of commands that sounded like automatic weapons firing. On the hop, the bartender brought over a bottle of the best tequila in the house along with a jug of Jahouga Juice. Juan turned a chair around and sat on it backwards, leaning forward on the chair back, set up for the long haul.

"Please, call me Big Juan, all my friends do. They say it is because I have such a big one."

"Oh, boy," Gerry said, "he's just as naughty as you, Jack. We're in big trouble!"

Juan smiled so wide you could count his teeth. "It is so great to meet you both. I am the number one fan of Jack Driftwood. That cartwheel you did last week in the Rough Riders game made me jump up off the couch and do cartwheels in the living room. Winona was not happy." He shook his head back and forth and then threw it back with a deep laugh.

"*Actually*, it was a tipped pass, forward tuck somersault, to a cartwheel, to a front round-off," Jack said.

"Yes, yes, yes! It was!" Big Juan said, grabbing Jack's arm and pumping it in his excitement. Thankfully it was his right arm. The man clearly did not know his own considerable strength.

"Don't be such a big, fat braggart," Gerry said.

Jack shrugged. "Just sayin'. It was what it was."

Big Juan offered a toast and the tequila never tasted better. Jack and Gerry settled in and told their story. Juan nearly fell off of his chair backwards laughing about Jack zinging one of the gunmen with a rock. His boisterous laugh constantly filled the cantina.

"You are like young David who slayed Goliath with his slingshot."

"It was definitely divine intervention, that's for sure. I'm just lucky I didn't get myself shot."

Big Juan was gravely worried about Tree Spirit and said he would make some calls to his friends in the area in the morning. Somebody had to know something. The Seneca had wandered into the Moon Over Cancun during the week prior to Jack and Gerry's arrival and had made fast friends with the Chavez family. The giant of a man promised to keep them informed and agreed to take Chaz's Jeep back to the bungalow after dropping them off at the airport the following morning.

There was a clean, vacant apartment above the cantina and Juan and Winona insisted Jack and Gerry stay there. After all of the tequila and Jahouga Juice they had drank while telling stories, they were in no condition to argue or drive around looking for a hotel. Jack graciously accepted their offer and he and Gerry were giggling drunk when they stumbled up the stairs to the one-bedroom apartment. The gunfight and the disappearance of Tree Spirit seemed like a dream that had happened a long time ago.

All the lights were off except the bright incandescence of the clip-on lamp attached to Colin Meade's desk. He was at the office late, burning the midnight oil, as they say. He most likely was the only one left in the entire Wigwam except for the security staff and the cleaning people. Just about everyone else had taken days off during the Blizzard's bye week. Not him. Colin was nervously going over the books of the stadium construction project, *again.* He knew he had done everything to perfection. He had gone over these numbers what felt like over a hundred times.

Despite the fact he had them memorized, he still checked every last one. The stakes were getting higher now; they were getting deadly. He had spoken with

Neil Dadoska earlier in the day and the news had not been good. The only positive was this Tree Spirit character was apparently off the grid; Colin hoped it would stay that way.

He had decided not to tell Donald Fegel about the goon squad Mr. Dadoska had sent after Tree Spirit and the fact they had mixed it up Driftwood and Gerry. The boss didn't need to be encumbered with the sordid details. Mr. Fegel was a busy man who had to keep his focus on the big picture.

But Colin wondered how Gerry was going to react when she returned to the Wigwam. She really didn't have a leg to stand on as far as accusing Mr. Fegel of anything at this point. Who would believe her wildly concocted stories from an illicit, romantic trip to Mexico; that is, if she *dared* even tell them? He doubted she would make as much as a peep. She would have to explain to her father why she was shacking up with one of his players halfway across the continent when she was supposed to be in Miami. There goes her credibility right out the window.

He was certain his numbers would hold up under any scrutiny. However, he hoped it would never come to that; and if it ever got close, he wouldn't be around for the party. Maybe getting rid of Driftwood *was* good idea at this point. That crazy bastard was stupid enough to cause real problems. He had just proven that down in Mexico.

Perhaps they should just cut him once Stark got healthy and let the boss work his charm on Gerry Wainscott. But they needed Driftwood to be dirty, or Coach Ivy and Gerald Wainscott would never sign off on releasing him.

Colin had already worked out a scheme to send Driftwood packing. The best thing about it was nobody had to die. He was still going through the scenario in his mind, working through the details. He had decided to sleep on it, review it in the morning, and if he still liked it, he would let Mr. Fegel in on his plan and hopefully get permission to pull the trigger. Jack Driftwood had become a thorn in his side now, too. The guy kept showing up like a bad penny. Colin was beginning to understand Mr. Fegel's overwhelming hatred for the man.

# Chapter Twenty-Seven

It seemed like ages since the Blizzard had taken the field. At least that was how Jack Driftwood felt. They had gone through their bye week and then had to endure another full week of practice plus an extra day because they played on Monday night. The weather in Buffalo finally dictated the closing of the roof of the Wigwam for this November clash with the Toronto Gladiators on Monday Night Football.

A light snow was falling and the heating coils in the glass roof of the stadium were working like a charm. It was an awesome view looking up into the world's biggest skylight watching the light flakes of snow descend out of the darkness and then quickly melt on the glass roof.

The place was packed an hour before kickoff and the buzz was noticeably louder with the roof sealed. It totally changed the feel and sound of the experience, which Jack Driftwood didn't care for. The place had a hollow ring to it and the faux atmosphere did not jibe with his football soul. Jack held to the old-fashioned belief the game of football should be played out of doors on natural grass - no questions asked. But there was no sense crying about it; he'd get used to it, he always did.

No one had yet heard a word from the Seneca Tribal Councilman since his disappearance into the Mexican jungle. Chaz had flown down to help Big Juan search for him but so far there was not a trace. Jack had to put that out of his mind, though. It was time to play some football. He had always possessed the ability to shut out everything going on in his personal life upon entering the sanctity of the gridiron. This situation would be no different.

The truth was, he couldn't wait. His shoulder was finally feeling mostly normal and he hadn't vented his rage since bouncing a rock off some guys head over ten days ago. He was about to get his chance in front of a national television audience.

Buffalo won the toss and opted to receive the opening kickoff. Driftwood hated that. He would often stand behind Coach Ivy during the coin toss and plead with him to defer their choice to the second half if they won the toss. It had become a running joke between them. When Buffalo took the ball, Driftwood let out a loud moan from behind his coach.

Coach Ivy turned and said, "Don't worry, you'll get to hit someone soon enough."

"I sure as hell hope so," Driftwood said.

He was hopping up and down to burn off nervous energy fueled by the familiar ice ball in the pit of his stomach.

During games, when he wasn't on the field, Driftwood could often be found patrolling the sidelines right behind Coach Ivy. He was a student of the game and considered himself a tactical in-game genius. When any kind of game management decision was to be made, he invariably weighed in. He really didn't give a shit; he would follow Coach Ivy around yelling his opinion on what the team should do in each given situation.

Coach Ivy had told him to shut the hell up on more than a few occasions. But Driftwood couldn't help himself and eventually the coach found he was in agreement with just about every suggestion Jack made. Over time the linebacker's kibitzing no longer bothered Coach Ivy; he looked forward to the input.

Coach Ivy mostly got things right, though he was mistaken in his assessment regarding Driftwood being able to hit somebody soon. The Buffalo offense opened the contest with a time-consuming 82-yard drive culminating in a Ben Brady QB sneak to open the scoring. The drive ate up over nine minutes from the game clock.

Toronto had the audacity to fumble the ball on the ensuing kickoff. Buffalo recovered and chewed up another three minutes before settling for a Bennie Tenudo field goal from 21 yards out. There was only 2:25 left to play in the first quarter and the Buffalo defense had yet to take the field.

Driftwood was furious. "Goddammit, Howie, you said I would get a chance to hit somebody!"

"What the hell do you want me to do?" he said. "Quit being irrational and go stand next to Bo-Bo, I'm sure he will hit you."

Coach Ivy pointed down the bench to where Bo-Bo was having his own issues dealing with the delay. Driftwood considered it until he looked over at Karpinski. Bo-Bo had just smashed one of the water coolers with a forearm as he stomped along the bench area.

"Nah, I'm good, Coach, I can wait," he said.

Eventually the Blizzard defense got their chance. They were jumping around going berserk in the huddle before the first play. They were too amped, if that was possible, and were flagged for three penalties in the first four plays. Two of the penalties were for unsportsmanlike conduct, the other was an offsides call on the very first play when Bo-Bo knocked the Gladiators' center on his back on the first sound the QB had uttered.

Benefiting from the charity, the Toronto offense moved the ball down the field on an easy touchdown drive. Driftwood didn't hit anyone the entire drive, blowing his only chance when he missed a tackle. He was steaming mad and pressing way too hard. They all were.

After the extra point attempt, Coach Faber called the entire defense over to the bench. Driftwood thought for sure this would be one of the rare occasions he ripped their asses on game day. They deserved it after that series, nobody played well. But Coach Faber was completely calm.

"Listen up, men. Okay, we got that shit out of our system. Hell, we had to sit on this sideline for an entire quarter, cooling our heels, so I'll take that one. But now it's on you, now it's time to play. Settle down and just do your job. We are going to be all right."

Coach Faber's talk had a calming, confidence-building effect on the defense in general and on Driftwood in particular. He finally relaxed and felt ready to play. Coach Faber was a master at amateur psychology. They shut down the Gladiator offense the rest of the half, forcing a handful of three-and-outs. The Blizzard offense did their part, too. Brady hit Shady Solomon for two touchdowns and Buffalo took a 24-7 lead into the locker room at the half.

And Driftwood finally got to hit somebody. Midway through the second quarter Toronto attempted to run a Crack Toss Sweep, where a wide receiver was supposed to come inside and block the linebacker. The whole premise was based on a sneak attack. The linebacker supposedly would not see the smaller receiver coming from the outside aiming for the unsuspecting bigger man's earhole.

Driftwood sensed the play coming and stuck his facemask right between the eight and the five on the front of receiver's jersey and exploded upwards, rolling his hips through the impact, thus multiplying the force of the blow. The resulting collision left poor number eighty-five unconscious and bleeding profusely from a severe gash under his chin. The Blizzard crowd gave Driftwood a standing ovation after the replay of the hit played over and over on the video boards. He could have died and gone to heaven.

The second half was much the same and the Blizzard poured it on to pound the Gladiators 42-13 and raise their record to 10-2 with four games left to go in the regular season. After sixteen consecutive years of missing the playoffs, the town of Buffalo could now smell, nay, taste a return trip to the post season. The town partied well into the night as revelers danced through the streets, confident their team was going places.

Before even showering after the game, Jack headed straight to the office of the team's equipment manager, Danny Steeley. Steeley's office was a cluttered, rectangular room located directly across the hallway from the training room and served as a sanctuary for certain veteran players. They would come in to use

Steeley's phone at lunch, play cards at a small table in the back during downtime, or just escape the often chaotic atmosphere of the locker room. Team rules stated nobody was allowed in Steeley's office unless specifically invited to enter by Danny Steeley himself. This helped keep the team's equipment from growing legs and walking out.

Steeley had been with the team for twenty-two years and had a gruff exterior that aptly camouflaged his heart of gold. He had to act tough around all of these highly-paid, over-sized men or he'd get pushed around, if not eaten alive. The truth was he would do anything for his players, but he didn't want them knowing that.

His favorite of the bunch was Jack Driftwood. Jack had been extremely generous to Steeley over the years and always treated him like an equal. He demanded the other players do the same. That was rare in these days, as most modern athletes had an attitude of entitlement and expected people to defer to them and wait on them hand and foot.

Jack had given Steeley a hundred bucks for his standing order of a couple of coolers of beer to be iced down and ready and waiting for after the game. This had become a ritual for night home games over the years, as the late start cut seriously into their post-game drinking time. Jack usually couldn't sleep after games anyway and figured the best way to get his rest was to pass out and then come to later the next morning – or afternoon, in some cases. This was a plan that seldom seemed to fail.

When he entered Steeley's abode Steven Stark was waiting for him, sitting alone atop a cooler in the back of the room, two beers in.

"Hey, rookie, you ain't supposed to start without me," Jack said.

"About fucking time you showed up, I thought I was going to have to drink all this cold beer my damn self."

"Get your ass up and give me one of those frosties before I tell Steeley you are in here. You know he hates you rookies."

"You're goddamn right I do," Steeley said, popping into the room and plopping down at his desk. "You better grab two, boy, or I'll throw your ass out of here right now."

Stark hopped up on his good foot and grabbed three beers from the cooler. Jack smiled to himself at how Stark still walked on eggshells around Steeley. He obviously hadn't broken all the way through the rough exterior protecting Steeley's heart yet. But he was making headway; he was the first rookie who had been allowed in the equipment man's office in the past six years, and that was only because of Jack.

"Hey, you are moving pretty good there, *mejo*," Jack said. "What'd Doc say today?"

"I can start running and if things go well I might be back the week after next,"

Stark said. "I can't wait, I'm getting sick of this watching and sitting around bullshit. I want to play some ball instead of *with* my balls."

"You'd still be playing with your balls, Stark. Don't be in too big a hurry," Steeley said. "We need you for the playoffs. I need that bonus money."

"You get playoff money?" Stark asked.

"We did back in the day, but it's been so long now, who knows?" Steeley said. "Truth is, the team votes on if we get full shares or half or whatever."

"Then you're screwed," Jack said. "None of these guys would vote for a crotchety, old bastard like you to get one dime. But I'll take care of you. What size T-shirt do you wear?"

"Fuck you, jackass, the way I take care of you I should get your whole share."

Abruptly, Stark scrambled up to his feet and turned white as a ghost. His eyes grew big and he looked like he wanted to hide. Then he dropped his beer on the floor.

"What the hell you doing, kid?" Steeley said.

He grabbed a towel from his desk to mop up Stark's spilled beer.

"Just what are you doing, Steven? That's no way to treat a beer," Coach Ivy said from the doorway.

Steely set his beer on the desk and quickly stood up. "Hey, Coach, what can I do for you?"

Howard Ivy had just entered the sanctity of the equipment man's office for the first time all season and had closed the door behind him.

"Well, Danny, I was looking for a cold beer or two – that is, if Steven is done dumping them out."

"You came to the right place," Jack said.

He motioned to Stark. Stark quickly opened the cooler and snagged another round from the ice-filled chest.

"Have a seat, Coach," Steeley said.

"Thank you, Danny. I could use a moment to take a load off. It's been an exceedingly long evening."

Coach Ivy sat down and took the beer from Steven, popped its top, and took a long swill.

"Ahhh! There is nothing like cold beer to quench the parched throat of a weary, thirsty, old man."

He took another long pull and nearly finished it. Stark was still frozen like a deer in the headlights. Steeley looked nervously around the room, not sure what to do. Jack had had a couple of beers with Coach Ivy in the past and was relishing Stark's and Steeley's discomfort. He had been around too long to really give a shit, plus he enjoyed the company of his old coach.

"That was a *great* call to take the ball after winning the coin toss, Coach," Jack said.

"Really? I thought you were going to hit me in the first quarter the way you were stalking about."

"You know I always got your back. But that was crazy, I've never seen anything like it in all my years," Jack said. "The first quarter was damn near over and the defense hadn't even been on the field yet. I *hate* that shit."

"That was remarkable," Coach Ivy said. "I remember a time when I was coaching at Hillsdale College back in 1957 where our offense didn't take the field until early in the second quarter. We gave up a long drive to start the game and then fumbled the kick return, and then our defense scored a touchdown on a long interception return. We kicked off again and they went on another long drive. You never know what will transpire in this game."

Stark noticed the coach's beer was running low. "D-Do you want another one, C-C-Coach Ivy?"

"Actually I'd like to procure some travelers, if that is acceptable."

"Sure, no problem, Coach," Steeley said.

He quickly grabbed a clear plastic bag and packed some ice and five beers into it. He found a brown grocery bag in the mess under his desk, and just like that he had whipped up a nice little care package.

"Well, thank you kindly for the pops," Coach Ivy said. "Nice game tonight, Jack. Let's keep this thing going."

"Thanks, Coach, you too. This is a good group, we'll be all right."

Coach Ivy had no sooner left the room and all three of them burst into laughter.

"Holy shit," Steeley said. "I just crapped my pants. I thought for sure I was fired."

"You, how about me?" Stark said. "I'm just a rookie!"

Jack just laughed. "You should have seen the looks on your faces. Stark looked like he had seen a goddamn ghost."

"I've seen everything now," Steeley said. He held out his hand. "Look at me, I'm still shaking."

"Y-y-you w-w-want another one, c-c-coach?" Jack said, mocking Stark.

"Fuck you. Not everybody has been here the last fifty years."

"Give me another beer, Stark. I need to settle my nerves," Steeley said, slumping back into his chair.

"Get me another one, too," Jack said. "Let's chug one in honor of the best coach in the NAFA."

They raised their cans of beer on high and toasted their new drinking buddy, Howard Ivy.

# Chapter Twenty-Eight

Nicole Brogan was stepping out of the shower when her cell phone rang. She leaned over the counter and saw it was the private cell phone of Donald Fegel. She had been waiting for this one. The call, no doubt, was in regards to her husband Billy's contract extension.

"Hello, Donald. Please come rescue me from this awful, cold place and take me to a tropical island where it's so warm people don't have to wear clothes."

"You know I would if I could, Nicole," Donald said.

He laughed at the urgency in her voice, thinking she just may be serious.

"I'm not wearing anything but a towel right now so just come get me!"

"Don't move, I'm on the way."

It was Nicole's turn to laugh. "Seriously, how do you tolerate this cold and snow? I can't take it. I need a drink, and a stiff one."

"Well which is it? A drink or a stiff one?"

"Donald!"

He laughed again at her false umbrage. She had a way about her that cut through all of the usual mundane small talk he so hated engaging in.

"I would love to buy you a drink, Nicole. How about a late lunch at the Longhouse this afternoon? Maybe I can try to raise your spirits a little and we can discuss Billy's contract extension."

"Actually that sounds like a grand idea. How does two o'clock work?"

"Perfect! It's a date. I'll see you there at two."

"Ciao."

Donald stared at the phone for a moment after hanging up. There was something about this girl that did things to him he could not explain. He only knew he liked it. Sure, she was married, even had a couple of rug rats, but she sure didn't act like it around him. Their dialogue seemed to point at two specific outcomes: Billy's contract extended and a certain consummation of the deal between Nicole and himself. Donald liked the idea of both.

Donald felt his heart go up in his throat when he saw her posing, hand on hip, surveying the place as if she was looking at a garbage heap that had swallowed up one of her expensive diamonds. Donald was that diamond. He quickly stood up and waved at Nicole and then hurried over to escort her to their table. Nicole saw him, shifted her weight to the other hip, and pouted as best she could, waiting for him to squire her to their table.

All eyes were riveted on the power couple as they shared a Hollywood kiss, a light peck to each cheek, scarcely touching. She took his arm and they swanked their way to their table. The Longhouse had been collectively holding its breath since her entrance but now exhaled and conversation began to once again fill the room.

"Good god, Nicole, you look absolutely stunning," he said as they sat at their table.

"Thank you, Donald. Now, where is that stiff one you promised me?"

Not that she really needed another drink; she had been nipping back at old Jack Frost since swallowing her mouthwash earlier that morning. It was the only way to fight off this horribly cold environment.

They ordered drinks and then lunch from the Longhouse menu. The Longhouse was proving to be the "it" place in Buffalo's vibrant, new Downtown Casino District. It was the hot spot where the area's prominent people came to see and be seen. The manager had sent his best waiter to their table and relieved him of all other duties. They were going to make sure this couple had everything they desired even before they could ask. Years of experience had demonstrated if you kept the heavy hitters happy even the bottom of the order would see some good pitches.

The drinks flowed right along with the conversation as Donald and Nicole genuinely enjoyed one another's company. They talked about the team, the business of football in general, and finally a little about Billy's contract extension. Donald was anxious to get the deal done as soon as possible, in part because it would give him more leverage in his eternal quest to oust Jack Driftwood. But mainly it would secure the inside linebacker position for the Blizzard for years to come.

"I can't tell you how happy I am with the way Billy has come in here and gotten the job done, Nicole. He has done everything right."

"That's my Billy," she said, "Mr. Perfect. He always does everything right, and on time."

Donald picked up on the tinge of bitterness in her voice. "Is that a problem?"

"No, no, no." she said quickly. "It's just that I'm not like that. Do you know how hard it is to constantly have to live up to an impossible standard? I have a bit of a wild side."

"Really, I hadn't noticed."

"Don't be a prick. Seriously, I feel a tremendous pressure to be Mrs. Perfect. And sometimes I need to let some of that pressure off."

She reached with her foot underneath the table and began to sensually rub it on the back of his calf as she spoke. Donald was at full attention.

"I know exactly what you are saying, Nicole. I have the same kind of pressures, not to mention the constant scrutiny from the media, the fans, and Mr. Wainscott. I think what we need to do is find a place and a time where we can relieve some of that pressure together, before it gets to be too much and we implode on ourselves."

"Implode on ourselves, together?" she asked coyly.

Donald began to stumble over his words. "Well, yes. I think so, I think that is exactly what I am probably suggesting."

She threw her head back and laughed loudly at the flustered man. "That sounds like a truly wonderful solution to our mutual problem. I will have to check my calendar to see if something can come together."

"You know where to find me. I'm pretty much at the Wigwam twenty-four seven. I will make it a priority to have myself available and ready whenever it is convenient for you."

"I don't doubt that, Donald." She covered her mouth to stifle another laugh. "I can hardly wait. I will let you know and we can get these deals done."

"That would be an excellent solution," Donald said.

Donald picked up the check and walked Nicole out to her waiting car. As he was holding the door open for her, a man jumped out of another car and quickly snapped a picture of them and hopped back in the vehicle and sped off.

"What was that all about?" Donald asked, slightly taken aback and not sure what to do. He felt vaguely violated.

"That is what you call paparazzi," the doorman answered as he opened the car door for Nicole.

"In Buffalo?" Donald was amazed and more than a little pleased.

"That just made this day even more special," she said. "But what do you expect? After all, we are the beautiful people."

He smiled at the thought of it. "I suppose we are. Check that calendar, my dear. I look forward to our next meeting."

"Likewise," Nicole said.

She slid into the heated leather seat of her luxury automobile. She revved the engine hard, squawked the tires on the dry pavement, and sped away.

"That girl is one of a kind," Donald said to the doorman.

"I can't argue with that, sir," he replied. "By the way, can I have an autograph, Mr. Fegel? I am a huge fan of the Blizzard. My dad has had season tickets since the old Gravel Pit days."

"It'd be my pleasure," Donald replied.

He was on top of the world, a true Master of the Universe.

## Billy Brogan Extension in the Works?

***Driftwood Era all but over***

By Budd Kilmer
Buffalo News Sports Editor

(Buffalo, NY) Things looked pretty bleak for the Buffalo Blizzard on defense several weeks ago, even after Buffalo had knocked off the Western Conference kings, the Arizona Roadrunners. It appeared the boys in powder blue had won the war, but they lost many to the battle, suffering multiple casualties at inside linebacker during the big win.

Steven Stark, a viable NAFA Defensive Rookie of the Year candidate, and his tired, old mentor, Jack Driftwood, both succumbed to injuries in the game, which will long be remembered as the only one ever played with it snowing inside the Wigwam. Stark is still a week or so away from returning to the field and Driftwood, though seeing a marked drop in production, has continued to play with a sore shoulder.

So what has held the Blizzard Defense together in the interim? In a word: Brogan. You want two words? Billy Brogan.

This reporter was right on the mark lauding Buffalo GM Donald Fegel for trading for the hard-charging, spit-fire of a ballplayer before the season opener. Billy Brogan has made a lot of people look smart during his short tenure with the Blizzard. The only negative is that conditional pick Buffalo used to make the trade is now a third rather than a fifth-round pick because of Brogan's extensive playing time. The Blizzard still got the better end of the deal, though.

Happily, it appears that tenure will grow significantly as Mr. Fegel was spotted earlier this afternoon having a power lunch with Nicole Brogan, Billy's wife and agent, at Buffalo's "beautiful-people" gathering spot, the Longhouse.

No doubt, this informal meeting indicates Fegel is working hard to keep the defensive stalwart in the fold for long after Brogan's contract expires at the close of this season. Fegel continues to make the shrewd decisions needed to build a consistent winner. That's why, when young Steven Stark returns to the lineup, Jack Driftwood will be collecting splinters of wood on the end of the Blizzard bench.

It won't be cheap for Buffalo to hang on to the fifth-year budding star out of Northwestern, but you get what you pay for, and in Brogan's case, that's a lot. Since starting in Stark's stead, he is Buffalo's second-leading tackler and has shown a penchant for making timely, game-saving plays. To wit, his forced fumble and subsequent recovery thereof in the Rough Rider game a few weeks ago single-handedly sparked the Blizzard to victory.

Imagine when Steven Stark returns how stout the Buffalo defense will be with Brogan and his rookie sidekick manning the middle! This inevitability lends strong hope for the Blizzard's playoff chances, not only for this season, but in the years to come.

It's become obvious to this reporter, as well as to other respected opinion-makers across the league, that Jack Driftwood has hit the wall after a surprisingly adequate start to the season.

But don't worry about Driftwood's drastic decline. Billy Brogan's inevitable contract extension and Steven Stark's imminent return will save not only the day, but perhaps the entire season, and many more to follow.

Thus Driftwood and his monumental baggage can hop on the next train out of town. Nobody will likely even notice, because there is a new sheriff in town, and his name is Billy Brogan. And it looks like he is here to stay.

The paparazzi's photo made the front page of USA TODAY and was captioned with a brief description:

> Buffalo Blizzard GM Donald Fegel broke bread with Nicole Brogan, agent and wife of Blizzard linebacker Billy Brogan. The pair power-lunched at the Longhouse, Buffalo's newest hotspot, where the likely topic of discussion was Brogan's expiring contract.

Donald Fegel carefully clipped the picture from the paper and slipped it into his wallet for future reference.

# Chapter Twenty-Nine

The team was fully assembled around the dining room table in Jack Driftwood's warehouse flat. One chair was left empty almost symbolically due to the absence of Robert "Tree Spirit" Hansen; the others were occupied by Chaz, Cheese, Gerry, and Vinny along with their host, Jack. Tree Spirit was still at large and nobody had heard from him in the two weeks since he had been shot along the Gulf of Mexico. The hope was he was fine and had simply been playing dead to protect his friends from further attacks.

They sat at Jack's table willing to do anything to avenge their friend and expose the nefarious parties responsible for the Wigwam heist.

"I'd like to call this meeting to order," Chaz said. "I have an outline for a plan of attack to expose these criminals, and, more importantly, keep us all alive in the process."

"I really like that last part," Jack said.

"Yeah, that's some good fucking thinking there, Mr. President," Vinny said.

"Quit screwing around," Chaz said. "This shit is serious."

"I agree," Gerry said. "Jack and I found that out first hand. Unfortunately, so did Tree Spirit, who for all we know is still laying in the jungle bleeding from that gunshot wound."

"Nah, he'd be dead by now," Jack said.

Gerry shot Jack a look that not only silenced him but also pre-empted all other potential jokesters at the table.

Chaz continued. "I got a couple of ideas to turn up the heat on these pricks. Plus, we need to approach this like law officers so we can ultimately get a conviction." He nodded at Vinny in deference. "First, Gerry, I need copies of any and all documents pertaining to the Wigwam construction project, especially anything you can get from Fegel's or Meade's computers or files. I don't know if you can access that stuff but I would like to have a copy of all the paper on the deal without them knowing anything. I've got the stuff from Tree Spirit but it's pretty sketchy, plus I'd like to have something to compare it with."

"I have access to all of that information – I can get copies for you," Gerry said. "I don't know about getting on their computers because they have their own private passwords, but I can look into it."

"Good. Vinny, I need you to run a background check on the tribe's Security Chief, Neil Dadoska. Tree Spirit said Dadoska was the one making threats and calling the shots and I want to see what kind of baggage this creep is carrying. We also need to figure out who, if anybody, is giving him orders, or if he is top dog. Now that I think about it, run the entire Tribal Council, just to see what we are dealing with."

"I can handle that shit, no problem," Vinny said. "Hey, I checked into the Senator and he was definitely involved with the inspection process of the stadium. He hand-picked the guy who headed that whole charade. That Blutarsky bastard had his hand in the pie and is as dirty as the rest of them fuckers."

As usual, Vinny got himself all worked up as he went on and slammed his beefy fist on the table to punctuate his final accusation.

"Down, big boy," Jack said. "You're going to break my shit, again."

"Sorry, I get a little emotional when I talk about criminals."

"I don't blame you," Chaz said. "But bending a few stupid laws is a lot different than full blown corruption."

"Shit, that's right. I forgot you were a criminal, too, Chaz. Sorry, no offense intended," Vinny said.

Chaz just smiled. "None taken, big man. That brings me to you, Cheese. Word on the street is you have a few connections in the construction business in these parts. I was hoping you could nose around and see if you can find anything on these contractors who worked the project. I'm not looking to take any of them down – not yet anyways – but I was hoping maybe somebody might be willing to cooperate, you know, provide us with some information."

"Consider it done, *capo*," Cheese said. "Personally, I don't know anything, but somebody does, and I'll find them. But there aren't many guys around these days who would throw themselves on a sword, if you know what I mean."

"What about me, Chaz?" Jack asked. "What do you need me to do?" He sounded all excited, like a little kid.

"We need you to play football and get to the Mega Bowl. You need to be at your best so Feegs can't send your ass packing just yet."

"That's bullshit, I can do more than that. This whole plan is bullshit. It's not even really a plan. We have to go after these fuckers. Take a hostage or something. You gotta meet fire with fire."

"Easy, Jack," Chaz said. "Right now we are in a position of ignorance and weakness. No more throwing rocks at the guys with guns. We need to be patient, gather intelligence, and let things play out for now. The time will come when we will make our move, and you know me, I will come out guns-a-blazing."

"I know. I just hate sitting around and just letting things happen. I like to make them happen."

"Make them happen on the field," Chaz said.

Jack still seethed, riding the high of righteous indignation. He wanted a piece of those bastards who had taken a shot at him and Tree Spirit. He also wanted to bring down Donald Fegel and Colin Meade for stealing from Gerald Wainscott and dishonoring the Blizzard franchise. He would have his justice; he had already promised himself as much. One way or another, a day of reckoning would be had.

"The time to make our play will come," Chaz said. "But for now, we need to get some ducks in a row. Jack, you got that speakerphone? It's time to give Big Juan a jingle."

Jack got up, still pissed, but brought the phone to the table and Chaz dialed the number.

"*Hola, amigos*! This is your favorite Mexican chef," boomed the deep voice over the speakerphone, followed by a rich, hearty laugh.

"Big Juan, my friend, it's your boy, Chaz. I have Jack Driftwood, Gerry Wainscott, Vinny Cappolla, and Cheese all here with me."

They all chimed in to say hello.

"You all sound like a bunch of ugly bastards, except for the beautiful voice of Miss Gerry."

"Aww! Thank you, Juan," Gerry said. "You are so sweet and such a handsome, dear man."

"I'm going to be fucking sick," Vinny said.

"You?" Jack said. "How do you think I feel?"

"Enough chitchat," Chaz said. "What can you tell us, *amigo*?"

"Well, my friends, I may have exciting news. I went down to your place yesterday, Chaz, and somebody had been there. They had eaten some of the food I had left previously and there was a bloody bandage in the trash. Your first aid kit has also gone missing. I believe Tree Spirit is alive but taking no chances. I left a note for him to come by the Moon once he feels safe."

"Oh my God! He's alive!" Gerry said.

"That's great news," Chaz said. "But let's not assume too much. Keep checking for him every few days and keep me posted. If Jack and his rag-tag outfit can win a few more games, we will see you up here for the playoffs."

"I'll be ready and waiting," Juan said. "Love to you all but I must go, Winona is calling."

Chaz hung up the phone. "I love that guy."

"He's a beauty, that's for sure," Jack said.

"I say we meet again, soon, maybe in a week, to see where things are and what kind of ammunition we dug up and take it from there. In the meantime, I am going to do some work behind the scenes. As of right now I am under the radar – they don't know who I am or what I do."

"Hell, what's the difference, we don't know who the fuck you are or what you do," Vinny said.

That elicited a good laugh, as the absurdity of the truth often does.

They hung out at Jack's for a while, but before long, the meeting broke up. Jack had asked Chaz to hang around for a minute after everyone else had departed. When he and Chaz were alone Jack wanted some answers. He also wanted to make plans in case things went south, which they often tended to do.

"So, Cochise, what's on your mind?" Chaz asked.

"A couple things. First off, I want to know what you are up to and when, so I can cover *your* back. Secondly, I am worried about Feegs. I think the fucker has something planned for me. He and Meade have been coming down to practice this week, which is rare. Plus, you saw that fucking Kilmer article. They have been watching me, whispering and laughing like a couple of little bitches. Maybe I'm just paranoid, but it's almost like they want me to know they got something cooking. Those pricks are going to ambush me somehow, I know it, so I wanted to give you a heads-up."

"Hmm, I wouldn't doubt they got something up their sleeves. But you have the coaches, Gerry, and the old man in your corner, so they really can't touch you, right?"

"I suppose," Jack said. "As long as I don't shit the bed on the field. But they know that, so they've likely conjured up a way around that. We're talking about a couple of world-class weasels, here."

"True. You do know if you hit that number I will be there in a heartbeat, with the cavalry, if needed."

"Yeah, I know. Been there and done that. And I really do appreciate it, I just hope it won't be too late."

Chaz grunted in response, but Jack could see he wasn't overly concerned, which calmed him down and gave him a shot of confidence.

"As far as my plans go," Chaz said, "I'm thinking about working on Colin Meade. To me, he's the weakest link."

"I like that," Jack said. "That egghead will crack hard and fast."

"I will tell you, the one that worries me is this Neil Dadoska. This guy plays hardball and is a major leaguer. I know he put the hit out on Tree Spirit. Fegel and Meade don't have the balls for that kind of operation, at least not to this point. They aren't desperate enough, yet."

"You're probably right, but I wouldn't put anything past them. And I'm worried about Gerry, too. I don't want her getting hurt or dragged through a bunch of bullshit. I have even considered breaking off our relationship for a while, just to protect her."

"No way. Don't do that. It ain't necessary, man. Besides, you two are meant to be together. Why do you think you are playing so well this season? You finally got the balance in your life that'd been missing. Your focus is better than it has ever been. She is the best thing that ever happened to you. You'd be a damned fool to mess with that."

Jack smiled and nodded. Chaz was right, he hadn't felt this complete and at peace since losing his folks so many years ago. It was like the hole in his heart had, at long last, begun to heal over. Getting whole again was primarily a by-product of his growing intimacy with Gerry Wainscott and he never wanted to lose that feeling. Ever.

"Well, keep me up to speed then, Chaz," he said. "I want to know when and what you are up to so if I have to bail your ass out for once, I can be there to do it."

"I'll let you know, but we keep it between us. You know, I wasn't kidding about you just focusing on football. You guys have the chance of a lifetime and I want to be there in the front row for the entire trip. I mean, let's think about Uncle Chaz for a minute here. Let's try not fuck to this up."

# Chapter Thirty

Every Monday morning during the season there would be a list of eight names posted on the bulletin board in the training room in the Blizzard locker room. It was commonly known as the "Piss List." Each player on the list was expected to report to a sixth-floor lavatory in the Wigwam where they would be required to produce a urine sample for the league-appointed sample collector. This "Pissman," as he was affectionately known, observed while the players pulled their drawers down past their knees to pee into a cup. We're talking full-frontal nudity: humiliating for all, mortifying for some, and comfortable for none.

This procedure was instituted to keep players from concocting imaginative ways to cheat the system. Jack Driftwood remembered the early days of the NAFA's testing procedure when players were allowed to go into the privacy of a bathroom stall to handle their business. The wool over the Pissman's eyes was well worn from all of the pulling back in the day. After one player's sample had produced a positive on a pregnancy test, the NAFA decided they needed a more stringent method of collection. Those good old days were long gone. It was nearly impossible to cheat the new system short of injecting someone else's urine into your bladder. Not many had the gumption to try that.

On this fine Monday morning Jack Driftwood found his name printed at the very top of the Piss List. He didn't consider it a bad thing because he had to piss like a racehorse. He had some time to kill before his linebacker meeting, so he walked gingerly towards the elevators to handle his business.

He was still pretty sore from the previous afternoon's 31-10 victory over Montreal, running the Blizzard's conference-leading record to 11-2. He had been cleated in the shin and the resulting gash had required a few stitches at halftime. He had ripped the damn thing wide open again late in the fourth quarter and needed another set of stitches after the game.

Jack had played a solid ballgame, but Billy Brogan stole the show on defense. He was all over the field wreaking mayhem upon the Mayhem. He had 15 tackles and scored a touchdown on a fumble return, taking the game ball home for his efforts. The more Jack played alongside Billy the more he liked the guy. They were almost becoming friends, but Billy still held back a little. Jack understood. As long as the kid was balling, he didn't really give two shits.

Jack was looking forward to getting Stark back on the field, though. He wasn't sure how much more pounding his old-ass could take, and they needed another body to take some of the practice reps.

He limped into the restroom where Walter Keating, the Blizzard's official sample collector, was waiting for him. A cooler filled with bottled water sat on the lavatory counter for the players to drink in the event they couldn't readily produce a sample. The record for waiting was five hours and thirty-two minutes, held by Bo-Bo Karpinski. The big man had a raging case of stage fright and consumed a dozen bottles of water before nature came calling. Once Bo-Bo got a flow going there was no stopping it; he kept on going and going, overflowing several plastic sample cups and making a mess all over the place.

Walter was a registered nurse but had lost his job due to down-sizing and reorganization on the heels of the National Health Care Reform Act, becoming one of the new law's many victims. He lived in Rochester, New York, and made the trek down the New York State Thruway to Buffalo two days a week during the season to collect samples from the Blizzard. The NAFA paid him a pittance to watch grown men piss into a cup. Walter only did it because he couldn't find any other work. Apparently there wasn't a great demand for sixty-two-year-old male nurses.

Walter found himself plunging below the poverty line with most of his life savings eaten up just to survive. The battle to keep his head above water was beginning to sour his previously happy disposition. Though he maintained his sense of humor, Walter was beginning to break bad.

"Hey, Mr. Pissman," Jack said. "What it bees like?"

"Other than I can't pay the rent because the fucking money's already spent?"

"That bad, huh?"

"Nah, just sick of the same old shit…or piss, as the case may be, I guess."

"I hear you," Jack said. "Life can be a bitch and if you ain't careful you could end up marryin' one."

"You ain't never lied," Walter said. "I played that game once. We was happy for a few years, or so I thought. Then I caught her screwing my best friend. Of course, she took half my crap in the divorce. So yeah, she qualifies."

Jack twisted the top off a water bottle and flicked it into the trash. He held the bottle up as if making a toast.

"I'll drink to that," he said before slugging down half the contents.

Jack's bladder was on burst-alert so he got down to business. He grabbed one of the plastic specimen cups, dropped his sweatpants and briefs down to his ankles, and stood in front of the urinal. Walter came around to his side and watched as Driftwood began to relieve himself.

"You ever get sick of all the dick-watching?" Jack asked.

"I suppose," Walter said. "I've heard all the jokes over the years, but dicks are pretty much just dicks. Seen one, you seen 'em all, near as I can tell. It bothered me for a while when I first started, to be honest with you. I even had dreams about 'em – dicks everywhere. But I don't even think about it anymore. I suppose you can get used to just about anything after a while."

"I guess peter-peeking is just like anything else then, huh?" Jack said.

"A man's gotta make a living."

"I must say though, Walter, you have a gift. I normally don't care for another man sneaking a gander at my salamander, but you are very clinical about it. It don't bother me at all to have you gonad-gazing."

Jack carried the plastic sample cup over to the counter and set it down. Walter reached into his lab coat pocket and produced a test-strip to dip into the warm, yellowish liquid. The test-strip determined whether the sample had both the proper PH level and fell in the correct temperature range at the time of collection.

Walter struggled getting the test-strip into the cup because his hands were shaking. He finally managed to complete the process after spilling some of the foul liquid onto his rubber gloves, much to Jack's amusement. He scribbled a couple of numbers on the accompanying form and poured some of Jack's urine into a test tube over the sink, spilling again. After repeating the same messy process for the B sample, he had Jack initial the labels and sign the form.

"Oh shit. Sorry, Jack, but that was the wrong form," Walter said.

He pointed to another one sitting on the counter along with new labels and picked up the first batch Jack had signed and slid it into his pocket. The forms looked identical to Jack, but he signed them and initialed both labels just to keep Walter happy. The dude was clearly struggling.

"You all right there, Walter?"

"Yeah, just been a long weekend." The Pissman had a slight quiver to his voice. "Not to mention I got to drive all the way over to Syracuse tonight to drop these samples off before backtracking home to Rochester. Plus, I didn't get much sleep last night. Partied too hard after the game."

He took the new labels Jack had initialed and stuck one on each of the urine-filled test tubes. He secured them both in the protective, Styrofoam packaging before sliding it into the box. He sealed the package and affixed the label with the corresponding numbers to the box. The last step of the process required Jack to initial the box confirming it was indeed his urine inside and he had satisfactorily observed Walter seal the contents.

When Walter handed the box to Jack he almost dropped it on the floor; his hands were still shaking like a belly-dancer's hips.

Jack was a little concerned; he had never seen the Pissman in this bad of shape. The guy had turned a lighter shade of pale and broken into a cold sweat.

"You don't look so hot, Walter. You need to sit down before you fall down, man."

"Um, okay. But only for a minute," he said.

He sat on a small stool in front of the sink and took several deep breaths. He seemed to be calming down. Jack opened him a bottle of water. Walter wet his parched whistle.

"You look a little better, you feeling any better?" Jack inquired.

"Yes, I am. Thank you, Jack. Hey, I almost forgot, could you sign one more thing for me? I got one of your football cards from a neighbor of mine. His kid ain't got a pot to piss in and it would mean the world to him. He's a big fan of yours. His name is Elijah – Eli."

"Sure. Anything for the Pissman."

Walter's hands were still trembling as he dug a Jack Driftwood football card of his back pocket. Jack had never known Walter to have issues like this; the Pissman must have really partied his ass off to be this hungover.

"Thanks, Jack. The kid will love it."

Walter Keating stopped by the office of Colin Meade on his way out of the building later that evening. Colin's office was meticulous, if not sterile. The odd little fellow's desk was bare and spotless, as was everything else in the tidy space. He liked to keep things in order. It really made life easier and was the only way to avoid careless mistakes.

Walter handed a thin envelope to Colin and received one thick with one-hundred-dollar bills in return, one hundred of them to be exact. Colin opened his envelope and took out the contents to examine them. He smiled and nodded at Keating.

"Thank you, Mr. Keating. This is exactly what I need," he said.

"You sure you don't need anything else?" Walter asked. "I could use a few more of these here envelopes, if you know what I mean."

Colin took a closer look at the man. Keating's clothes were ill-fitting and wrinkled, his appearance was grossly disheveled, his hair a mess. He was sweating profusely and his color was not good. And no wonder, the man handled people's urine all day, for god sakes! He was probably covered in it. Colin just wanted the grubby slob out of his office before he touched anything. Unconsciously he reached for the ever-present bottle of hand sanitizer in the top drawer of his desk.

"Are you sure you're up for that? If I may say so, you look like hell, Walter."

"No. I mean, I know. It's just the adrenaline and nerves. I'll be fine. I don't usually do this kind of thing, but I'm good at it. And seriously, anything else you need, keep me in mind."

Walter held up the envelope of cash and slapped into his other hand for added emphasis.

Colin rubbed his chin and thought about it. Perhaps another situation would arise where he would need a medical man.

"I think we are good for now, Walter. But should anything come up, I'll be sure to let you know."

Donald Fegel had called off the dogs. He was no longer interested in having Gerry Wainscott or Jack Driftwood followed. The frequency of their secret get-togethers was increasing and Donald preferred not to be reminded of it daily. Things had settled down quite nicely after the disappearance of that Seneca Tribal Councilmen.

By all appearances, the storm that had been brewing had fortuitously washed out to sea. He was still deeply bothered by Gerry's lurid affair with Driftwood, but he would deal with her when the appropriate time arose. She was still the centerpiece of his long range plans whether she knew it or not. As for Driftwood, he was a dead man walking; the cowboy just didn't know it yet. But he would soon enough, that much was for sure.

Besides, Donald was currently consumed with his new pet-project, the renegotiation of Billy Brogan's contract. He reverently removed the grainy newsprint photo from his wallet and he inspected it for about the twentieth time already that day.

First, he examined himself. His head was tilted up in an aristocratic manner, making him look like royalty. He wore a look of cool confidence he found remarkable, if not a bit surprising. Nicole brought that out in him. Her beauty and instinctively self-assured demeanor rubbed off on him. When he was with her he was at his best, and he knew it; he was the man he always knew he could become, a cut above it all.

Then he would study Nicole's face in the picture. The transcendent beauty of a high-fashion model stared back at him. She had the perfect amount of color in her cheeks from the cold. Her brown eyes were alive and enraptured him, piercing his very soul with their radiant sexuality. Just looking at the crude newsprint photo of her did things to him no other woman ever had.

It was so weird. He had never been so hot for any other chick in his entire life. He got the same vibe back from her. When he was with her everything slowed down, as if, when together, they transcended time. This phenomenon put him a step ahead of his usually lame, tired game. He was so attuned to her on a basic, raw, carnal level he instinctively did and said just the right thing. Without fail, she rewarded him with her total acceptance of who he was as a man. They just clicked.

It didn't matter to him Nicole was married to one of his players with two young children. He never really thought about it, because this wasn't about that.

He knew she would never leave Billy Brogan to be with him. This was a deep, cosmic attraction; an impending collision of two worlds that would both be rocked as never before. He held no illusions of a happily ever after, it was all about an unavoidable moment. A moment sure to come. And soon.

# Chapter Thirty-One

Steven Stark was bent over at the waist breathing heavily from exhaustion. Running gassers back and forth across the field turf surface inside the Wigwam was significantly more taxing than the intervals he had been doing on the glider in the Blizzard weight room.

"Stand up straight, rookie," Jack said, wheezing with his hands interlocked behind his neck. "It will help you breathe better."

"Fuck that."

"One more, you pussies!" Coach Kyaat shouted.

Coach Kyaat, or "Bobby K," as they called him, was the Blizzard's strength and conditioning coach. He was responsible for making sure the players were at their optimum conditioning level throughout the season. Each player had his own specified conditioning routine individually negotiated with Bobby K. At the very least, this eliminated the common protest of "This bullshit ain't in my contract" at conditioning time. At this late juncture in the season, they only ran together as a team one day a week, Wednesdays. Once was more than enough, as any of the players would quickly affirm.

Bobby K hollered a warning to the group. "Ten seconds!"

He was counting down the rest period between the gassers. A true gasser consisted of running back and forth across the width of the football field twice. It was a simple enough proposition until you added the element of time. Linebackers were required to finish the 213-yard, one-foot trek in under thirty-eight seconds, with a one-minute rest in between repetitions. Earlier in the season the players were required to run five of those puppies with only thirty seconds of rest in between. However, three with a minute break was sufficient for this particular session. There was nothing to be gained overtraining at this late juncture in the season.

The entire linebacker group finished their final gasser under their prescribed time limit, although Stark had to put on an extra burst at the end to make it. They were all walking slowly towards the locker room, still recovering their breath, when Coach Faber reappeared out of the tunnel. He didn't look particularly happy.

"Hey, Jack, I need to talk to you a second."

"Ooh, you're in trouble now," Stark said. "Coach looks pissed."

"This ain't high school, douchebag," Jack said. "And I'm too old and wise to get into trouble."

"Tell that to Coach, because your ass is definitely in trouble," Stark insisted.

"We'll see, then, won't we?"

Jack left the straggling group and jogged over to Coach Faber.

"What's up, Lester? You look like your damn dog died."

"He ain't dead but he *is* dying. You know, we're *all* dying, Jack, some of us faster than others."

"There's a comforting thought."

A grim look marked Coach Faber's face. "Listen, there ain't no good way to say this, so I'll just say it. With Stark coming back this week, things get a little crowded. Based on the grades over the past three games, Brogan has edged you out, so he is going to get the start this week. The plan is to have all three of you play, a lot – Stark is going to start no matter what happens, for obvious reasons. So going forward, whoever grades out higher between you and Brogan will get the start the following week."

Driftwood was stunned. This was the last thing he would have thought Coach Faber wanted to talk about. Brogan was good, but no way in hell was he as effective as Jack. He could see Coach Faber wasn't exactly enthralled by the dilemma, either.

"Goddammit, Lester, you know this is bullshit. I make more plays than Brogan and run the defense way better. Doesn't that count for anything? This is a royal-fucking-rim-job and you know it."

Coach Faber hung his head and kicked at the turf. He couldn't argue with a word Jack had said.

"Look, this came down from on high, above my pay grade. They are about to sign Brogan to a contract extension and feel like they got their inside linebacker duo set for years to come. They want to get them on the field together now to start building a rapport. It doesn't mean you aren't going to play. You will get your reps – I'll make damned sure of it. And if you grade out higher than Brogan this week, you start the next week."

"What did Coach Ivy say about this?" Jack asked.

He was still hot but calming down. He appreciated Coach Faber leveling with him rather than giving him the usual coach-speak bullshit but knew arguing was useless; their decision had been made.

"You know Howie, he picks his battles, but he fought for you just like I did. Fegel wanted you benched entirely."

"What? Am I supposed to say thanks, now?"

"No, you're supposed to go out there and kick ass on Sunday and let me worry about taking the names," Coach Faber said.

In spite of himself, Jack smiled. "All right, but when I tell you to put me in the fucking game, you had damn well better do it."

"Fair enough. You know, Jack, this is a great game, but a shitty business."

"Who you telling?"

Jack needed a little time before going back to the locker room, so he walked back out onto the field. He looked around the empty, cavernous coliseum until his eyes rested upon the Owner's box, where Fegel watched the games.

*Damn you, Feegs, I can't wait 'til we nail your sorry ass!*

The evening drive home was a relaxing one for Colin Meade. The weather was nice and there wasn't much traffic on Main Street. He took his time, totally lost in thought, as he made the twenty minute drive from the Wigwam. It had been a quality, productive day. They had benched Jack Driftwood, which had made Mr. Fegel a very happy man. So happy that he hadn't bitched at Colin, nor bothered him the entire day. It was days like this that made Colin love his job.

As he pulled into his garage, a strange sense of Deja vu came over him. But it wasn't really Deja vu, it was more of a sense of something ethereal, something in the air that he couldn't quite put a finger on. He was contemplating how strange this was when he walked into the house and came face to face with some startling refrigerator art.

*TREE SPIRIT LIVES!!!*

Colin freaked out. His first instinct was to run. And he did; he had made it all the way back into the garage before he stopped. Then he summoned up every scrap of courage he possessed and headed back into the house. Initially, he had thought the writing on the refrigerator was done in blood. Upon closer examination, though, he realized it was only red paint. If it *had* been blood he knew he would have never been able to sleep in the house again. That would have been too much to handle.

He turned on every light in the place as he went room to room assessing the damage. The place was a mess; somebody had tossed the place pretty good. Colin wasn't one hundred percent sure his violators had left the premises, but he was at ninety-nine. When he got to his bedroom his first instinct was to pick up and re-hide his pornography collection that tended toward the illegal, but he decided he should leave the place exactly as he found it. At least until he figured out his next step.

He went through the entire place and then made his way back into the kitchen. There was a clutter of dishes in the sink, a mess he would have never left to fester all day. Upon closer inspection he noticed the remains of a partially eaten omelet in the sink.

*What the fuck? They cooked breakfast?*

The sight of the half-eaten omelet totally unnerved him again. His heart was beating out of his chest and he felt completely violated and terrified. He hadn't bargained for this shit. Who the hell had done this to him? He had been told this Tree Spirit character had been shot and likely killed down in Mexico. And even if the guy was alive, why would he come after him? He had never even met the man. Colin had absolutely nothing to do with the guy. The hit on Tree Spirit was totally Neil Dadoska's doing. Colin was just a pawn in this whole thing; Mr. Fegel and Mr. Dadoska called the shots.

*Why fuck with me?*

Colin grabbed his cell phone and punched up Donald's private, emergency cell phone number. Neil and Donald had gotten him on the hook, now they could get him off.

"This had better be good," Mr. Fegel said.

"Those bastards hit my house!" Just talking about the violation of the sanctity of his home brought his fear to the next level.

"Calm down, Colin. What are you talking about? Who hit your house?"

"Tree Spirit, or Driftwood, I don't know! But they ransacked my house, stole the hard drive from my computer, and painted graffiti on my fridge. One of them even cooked a fucking omelet in my kitchen!"

"An omelet?"

"Yes, a veggie omelet! And they wrote on my fridge with red spray-paint. It says 'Tree Spirit Lives.'"

"Who are these people?" Mr. Fegel asked.

"That's what I want to know!" Colin was beginning to hyperventilate. "They shredded all my clothes, tossed my files all over the place, and smashed up my computer."

"They didn't get any, ah, you know, evidence or anything, did they?"

"I get my house torn to pieces and all you care about is evidence?"

"No, but it wouldn't be good for any of us if somebody found something, now would it?"

"No, I suppose it wouldn't," Colin said.

He was getting his breathing under control. He felt a little safer, a little less scared, talking to Mr. Fegel. He would know what to do.

"Well, did they?"

"No, there isn't anything here to find. I'm not *that* stupid."

"Good, don't touch anything. I'm going to call Dadoska and we'll be over there within the hour."

"Hurry up, I'm kind of freaked out."

"Don't worry, Colin. We'll figure this thing out. Everything will be okay. We'll be there before you know it."

Talking to the boss had a calming effect on Colin, especially with the way Mr.

Fegel had been so supportive. He relaxed, took a couple more deep breaths and then went back into his bedroom and looked underneath the bed. The safe was gone!

*Shit! Shit! Shit!*

He decided he would keep his mouth shut about that, at least for now.

Neil Dadoska was not a happy camper. He had already knocked back a couple of Manhattan's and was enjoying the glow in quiet solitude. He was sitting in his underwear, in his favorite chair, playing at a five-dollar Texas Hold 'em table on his laptop when he got the call from Donald Fegel.

But when Fegel told him about the break-in at Meade's and, more specifically, what was painted on Colin's fridge, he sobered up in a hurry. He was still mildly irritated by the interruption to his quiet evening, though he was more curious than mad.

He had hoped he had heard the last of Tree Spirit, and maybe he had. But either way, somebody was playing games. Neil liked games. Agreeing to meet Fegel at Meade's house, he took down the address, struggled back into his pants, and was on his way.

Donald Fegel arrived at Meade's humble abode twenty-five minutes after he had received the frantic phone call. Like Meade, the first thing Donald saw upon entering the house was the spray-painted message on the refrigerator.

"I can see why you freaked out," he said to Meade. "Looks like blood."

"I haven't touched a thing and the bastards didn't get anything on us," Meade said.

The way he blurted it out made Donald raise an eyebrow, but after further examination of the man, he put off any suspicion. Meade looked like utter hell. His virtually translucent skin had taken on a pale, milky hue. His eyes were red and swollen and filled their hollowed sockets more than usual.

They were still in the kitchen when another vehicle pulled into the driveway. Neil Dadoska hopped out and came inside to join the party.

"Hello, gentlemen, you got anything to drink in this place?"

"I had a bottle of some good Scotch in the cupboard, unless those bastards drank it with their breakfast," Meade said.

"That'll do." Dadoska looked around at the mess in the kitchen while Meade retrieved the bottle and three glasses. "So you say they cooked up an omelet, huh? Old Tree Spirit is known for his cooking; I bet it was pretty tasty."

"Do you think it was Tree Spirit?" Meade asked.

"I don't know," Dadoska said, "I kinda doubt it. This ain't his style. He's more of a timid bastard, doesn't like to dirty his hands like this."

"Who the hell did, then?" Meade asked, beginning to whine again.

"That, I don't know. At least not yet, anyways."

Donald wasn't sure what to think. Why would they, whoever *they* were, bother with Meade? It didn't make any sense. But he had an idea about who might be behind it. That bastard Driftwood had been seen with Tree Spirit before he disappeared.

Dadoska didn't appear to be concerned in the least, though, as he held his glass up for a toast.

"Here's to a war, boys," he said. "This shit just got escalated. We got us some cowboys out there who want to play games, but they picked the wrong fucking Indian."

They clinked their glasses together and each took a drink. Meade took them on a quick tour of the rest of the place. Dadoska took a particular interest in Meade's porn collection and grabbed one of the magazines and rolled it up and stuffed it into his back pocket. After the quick walk-thru, they sat down with the bottle of Scotch in the living room. It was time to make some battle plans.

"I don't believe involving the police will benefit us any," Donald said. "That will just lead to questions about Tree Spirit, and we don't need that."

"I agree, totally," Dadoska said. "Speaking of that squirrelly bastard, I will send a couple of my guys out to his place just to make sure he isn't stupid enough to have returned."

Donald nodded as Meade sat quietly rocking on the couch, clutching his glass of scotch.

*God, has he always been such a spineless, little pussy?*

"As far as who we are dealing with," Donald said, "it obviously has to be somebody aware of the Tree Spirit situation. That means Jack Driftwood and his crew are involved. They are the only people who know anything about any of this, as far as I know. I don't know what kind of people he pals around with, but I can only imagine what a sorry collection of humanity they must be. But we can find out easily enough. Can you get a list together, Colin?"

"Yes," Meade said, "I can ask my contacts who both Driftwood and Gerry Wainscott have been associating with recently."

"Good," Dadoska said. "Now, as far as I know, Tree Spirit doesn't have many friends and he don't really hang out with any of the other Tribal Council folks. He's too fucking weird, even for them jag-offs. Get me a list of names and I can track these people down and keep an eye on them. If I hear of anything suspicious I will arrange for a little talk with them and get to the bottom of this shit in a hurry."

"Excellent," Donald said. "Of course, it is very important we keep this whole operation quiet and off the radar. The last thing we need is any attention drawn to any of us or this business."

"Agreed," Dadoska said. "What about our friend, the Senator? Do we need to let him know any of this is going on?"

Donald considered it for a moment. Senator Blutarsky was a powerful man and a close ally, but did he really need to be bothered with any of this stuff at this point? He didn't think so.

"I don't think it's necessary to say anything at this juncture. However, if things heat up and there is a chance of some publicity, I wouldn't want him to get blindsided by it."

"Good," Dadoska said before draining the remains of his glass. "What about the little princess? Could she be behind this whole thing?"

"Gerry?"

"Why not? She's got the resources and she was down there in Mexico. Maybe she is sending you a message," Dadoska said.

Donald shook his head. The possibility of Gerry Wainscott being behind any of this had never even entered his mind.

"I highly doubt that, no, this is way beyond anything she would do. It's totally not her style."

"Never say never," Dadoska said. "Well, I hate to break up the party, but I think that about covers it. Get me some names, boys, and I will get to work. We will quell this little uprising as sure as shit on a shingle."

With that, the big man rose from his chair, patted his back pocket to make sure his newly claimed prize was intact, and left the house without so much as a goodbye.

"That is one strange hombre," Donald said.

"I'm just glad he's on our side, he scares the shit out of me," Meade replied, and then he hiccupped.

Donald took a hard gander at his partner in crime. The poor bastard had been put through the wringer on this deal and now he was half drunk. That was probably a good thing, especially if he was hoping to get any sleep that night.

"Are you going to be all right staying here tonight, Colin?"

"I think so, boss, I'm real tired all the sudden. It's prolly from the booze an all the 'citement." Meade rarely drank and it hadn't taken much for him to overdo the scotch.

"All right then, if you are okay I'm going to head home. Take as much time as you need tomorrow to get this place cleaned up, and keep track of what you spend. I'll take care of it. You sure we are good? There was nothing here that could have caused us any trouble?"

"I'm sure, boss. Sure as shittin' out a shingle."

# Chapter Thirty-Two

Driftwood had put on a good face during the week of preparation, but he was devastated and embarrassed by the benching. He vacillated back and forth between rage and despair. He was playing the best football of his career: apparently it still wasn't good enough to start. It was insane but part of the business of pro football. Fegel had blindsided him with political bullshit and sent him to the bench. The sad part was he had been able to ram the edict right past both Faber and Ivy. Why couldn't it just be about the game? It cut his heart out.

Many of his teammates had come to him in private, complaining it was bullshit. Notably, however, Steven Stark hadn't said anything. But he had gone to Billy Brogan's home for dinner and sat with Billy during lunch the entire week. He had even sat by Billy near the front of the plane on their flight to St. Louis. The two of them had become like peas and carrots.

Initially, Jack felt like he did back in junior high school when sweet Allie Dempster had broken his heart for the first time. One day she was his girlfriend and wham! The next day she was going with his best friend, Benny Wilson. It wasn't that he was dating Steven, but nevertheless the rejection stung all the same. Stark still talked to him as if nothing had changed but things were different. Jack didn't really blame the kid, though it still kind of hurt.

The thing that really galled him was Brogan's grade was just one percentage point higher than his; ninety-three to ninety-two. The grading system was based on assignment and technique execution but didn't really gauge game impact or production. Jack had been considerably more productive than Brogan. He recorded more tackles, interceptions, and tackles for loss than Brogan over the previous four-game stretch by a significant margin. Yet *he* was the one riding the pine. He would have laughed at the irony had it not hurt so damn much.

But he had to give Billy Brogan credit. Billy had pulled him aside and told him he appreciated everything Jack had done for him in helping him become a better player, and especially the way Jack had treated him since he had arrived. Billy claimed he was only interested in the Blizzard winning and was willing to do whatever that took. They shook on it.

It had been a rough few days for Jack and he was glad to put it behind him and get on the field and make somebody pay. Getting ready to play this game was not a problem. If anything, he was wired a tad too tight before the game and was making a conscious effort to calm himself and maintain his focus. Tapping into his reservoir of rage would not be an issue; that vat was overflowing.

The St. Louis Nighthawks were having a remarkable season themselves. They had won seven in a row and were tied with Arizona for the top record in the Western Conference at 10-3. Buffalo came into town with the best record in all of the NAFA at 11-2.

The sell-out home crowd was delirious when the Nighthawks got the ball to start the game and began to advance sharply down the field. The drive stalled out inside the Buffalo 10, and St. Louis settled for a field goal to take a 3-0 lead. It killed Driftwood to be sitting on the sideline watching the action. Ironically, Brogan was standing right there next to him, as Buffalo was using their Dime defense to counteract the Run-n-Shoot style of the Nighthawk's offense, deploying six defensive backs and only one linebacker for most of the series.

Stark's foot was not quite one hundred percent and he wasn't exploding out of his breaks in Buffalo's zone pass defense. St. Louis took advantage of this a couple of times on the first drive, hitting open receivers in his area of responsibility. This made Driftwood even more incensed. Were they fucking blind? To have Stark out there limping around with two perfectly healthy linebackers on the bench was the height of stupidity. It was a wonder Driftwood's head didn't explode.

A big part of the Buffalo offensive game plan was to establish the running game, which they hoped would keep the explosive St. Louis offense on the sidelines. With both Petrucci and Johnson healthy it seemed like a great game plan. It didn't quite work out that way on the first series, though, as the Blizzard ran the ball three straight times for a total of seven yards and were forced to punt.

St. Louis went right back to work with their wide-open passing game. Brogan played the Dime-backer position on this series and he, along with the rest of the defense, fared no better. The Nighthawks were hitting on all cylinders as they scored again on a touchdown pass to the running back. Brogan was locked in man-to-man coverage on the back and attempted to jam him at the line. He whiffed. The guy was left wide-open and St. Louis jumped up 10-0.

Driftwood was getting antsy watching his teammates suffer serious embarrassment out there on the field. He hated the Dime defense; he always had. It might have been different if St. Louis was running guys deep down the field challenging the long-speed of the Buffalo defense. But this was not the case. They were finding open holes in the short zones where receivers would sit down and the quarterback, John Tillison, hit them quickly, allowing space and time for the run after the catch. Tillison was playing like a machine and promptly found the open receiver every time. It didn't help matters Buffalo was besieged by sloppy and shoddy tackling.

Driftwood felt they should be playing their regular Base personnel. He reasoned having linebackers take pass drops from short to deep would give them a better chance to get into throwing lanes than defensive backs who, by alignment, had to play things downhill – from deep to short.

The key to defending any style of offense was delivering punishment – the very essence of the game. Pound the shit out of the St. Louis receivers, get them tiptoeing a little bit and wary of going over the middle. Who knows? You might even knock one loose and fall on it. It happened every week.

Linebackers, given their size advantage, made harder tackles and bigger hits; it was basic physics. Also, having linebackers in the game would better stop the draws and screens, with which the Nighthawks had already burned the Blizzard multiple times. Linebackers were trained to recognize then coop and contain those types of plays much more than defensive backs.

Not to mention linebackers were much more adept at stopping the running game than defensive backs and were bigger threats rushing the passer on the blitz. Speaking of the blitz, the presence of linebackers sugaring the blitz by jumping in and around various gaps better served to confuse the pass protection. The advantages went on and on.

The only reason anyone played Dime was because everyone else was doing it. Driftwood conceded there were times when playing Dime was the best call. But these occasions were special situations, not the main thrust of a game plan. That was absurd. Yet that was the unanimous, common approach across the NAFA when defending pass-happy offenses. It blew his mind.

Driftwood had argued this with both Coach Faber and Archie Beatle all week, but they never listened. What was most disturbing to Driftwood was they both dismissed it as his thinly veiled attempt for more playing time. Admittedly, he would benefit on that regard, but it was an unintended consequence. He firmly believed using Base personnel was a far better option than Dime versus the Nighthawks in nearly every situation. Why the hell did they even call it "Base" if they wouldn't even attempt to use it? What kind of a base was that? Thus far, the Dime had given them anything but a base.

The Blizzard offense came to the rescue and put together a drive that ate up the remainder of the first quarter. Earl Johnson and the big boys up front cranked up the running game and the Blizzard put six on the board via a five-yard Johnson jaunt to get back into the game, at least momentarily. Unfortunately, they had to kick it back to a St. Louis offense which they had yet to slow down, let alone stop.

As the defense took the field, Coach Faber gave Driftwood the nod. "Get your ass in there. Let's see if you can stop 'em."

No such luck. Driftwood did make a couple of nice plays; he stopped a draw for no gain and swatted away another pass. But the Nighthawks still moved the ball down the field and put up another touchdown. They were shredding the

Blizzard secondary and Tillison was on fire. When Buffalo tried to blitz him he would quickly get rid of the ball with a precision pass. When they played zone he sat back until he found a dead spot and fired a bullet into it. When a guy gets that hot there isn't much anyone can do about it other than try to survive the onslaught until he cooled off. The Nighthawks' lead jumped to 17-7.

The Buffalo offense stalled after picking up a few first downs and had to punt it away. Stark took the next series as the Blizzard stayed with Dime personnel. With nothing changed, St. Louis marched right down the field again. They scored another touchdown, this one on a screen pass to their multi-threat running back, Javon Steamer, from 14 yards out. Stark missed the tackle on the play and looked silly in doing so. The score was now 24-7; the Buffalo defense was getting run right off the field.

Ben Brady did what he could to keep them in the game, as the offense, on a hurry-up, no-huddle drive, scored a quick-strike touchdown to AC on a 32-yard pass play. They had to scrap the plan of running the ball and eating up clock; they were falling too far behind and had yet to figure out how to stop Tillison and company. Their only shot now was to try to score as fast and often as possible, turning the game into a track meet. It was exactly what the Nighthawks had hoped for.

Billy Brogan took the next series but the results were the same. Taking possession with 2:23 left in the first half, St. Louis executed their two-minute offense to perfection, scoring another touchdown with only 12 seconds left in the half. They rolled into their locker room at halftime with a 31-14 lead. The Buffalo defense hadn't given up 31 points in a game all season, let alone the first half. Something had to change or Tillison and the Nighthawks would continue to have a field day.

Driftwood got into Coach Faber's ear as they headed into the locker room. "Coach, we need to give Base a shot. Dime's getting us killed. Our blitzes are too late, our underneath coverage isn't getting there from over the top, and we aren't getting into the throwing lanes. Dime can't stop the screen or the draw, plus we ain't hitting nobody after they make the catch. We got no balls out there. The linebackers are the balls of this team and you got us sitting next to you dicks. We need to play Base."

Coach Faber started to get defensive but stopped himself. The truth was their Dime was getting shredded. Maybe a different tact was in order here.

"Well, maybe we should give it a try. I'll talk to Archie about it."

"Fuck Archie, he's just going to make excuses for his guys, bitch about the pass rush, and say we can't match up in Base."

Coach Faber started laughing. "That is exactly what he will say. But I am still going to talk to him about it. You get with the linebackers and go over the Base adjustments to those spread formations so we don't screw it up. We'll give Dime one more series to stop them and if we can't do it, we'll give Base a shot. Shit, at that point we won't have anything to lose."

Driftwood gathered the linebackers in front of the grease board in the locker room and began to go through all of their Base adjustments. Archie came into the room and saw him on the board.

"Hey, Driftwood! You ain't a fucking coach. You ain't even a starter anymore. And we *ain't* playing Base defense. I've been telling you all week, for chrissakes! We can't match up. Now, if we could just get some pass rush from the fat-asses up front, we wouldn't be behind by a hundred points!"

"Hey, fuck you, Beatle," Big E said. "Who you calling fat-asses, asshole?"

"Who do you think you are calling asshole? I'm a coach and you had better respect that!"

Bo-Bo joined in on the side of the fat-asses. "Fuck you, Beatle, you're an asshole!"

The big man wasn't much for arguing, vastly preferring action. He moved to get up into Archie's face, but Driftwood hurriedly stepped between them, which was a good thing. Bo-Bo would have squashed Beatle like a bug.

"Easy, boys, we're all on the same side here and fighting amongst ourselves ain't gonna help shit," Driftwood said. "Look, Archie, Coach Faber asked me to go over the adjustments in Base in case he decides to give it a try in the second half. Why don't you just go talk to him?"

"You're goddamn right I'm going to talk to him! And we ain't playing fucking Base!"

With that, the angry Archie stomped out of the locker room. The players started snickering and laughing at the poor bastard.

"Goddamn, Bo-Bo," Leroy Clarkson said, "I thought you was gonna kill my coach."

"If he wasn't, I sure as hell was," Big E said. "Man called me a fat-ass."

"Look behind you, Big E," Leroy said. "You is a fat-ass."

Everybody laughed as Big E looked around at his own ass, which was notoriously the biggest backside on the team and the butt of many jokes.

"She a beauty, though, ain't she?" Big E said.

"Quit looking at your sweet, fat ass and let's get ready to play some defense this second half," Driftwood said. "That shit we just did was pathetic. It don't matter what defense is out there, we still gotta tackle people. That shit was pathetic. That ain't us."

The attitude in the locker room picked up immediately, going from near mutiny to complete unity. There would likely be ramifications from the outburst with

Archie later on, but nobody was worried about it. At that point it was practically forgotten. They were all trying to figure out how to make a game of it in the second half.

As the team was readying to head back out on to the field, Archie skulked out of the coach's locker room, red-faced and still mad as a mud wasp. He didn't say a word to anyone as he headed back up to the coaches' box for the second half.

"Looks like Coach Faber told him we will be playing regular personnel the second half," Brogan said.

"Indeed," Driftwood said, "fucking Base it is." He was unable to hide his smile as he tracked Beatle's exit.

Archie glanced over at him on his way out the door and flipped Driftwood the bird.

"Real mature, Archie," Driftwood yelled. "Real mature."

Buffalo received to start the second half and marched down the field for another touchdown, swiftly cutting the Nighthawks lead to 31-21. The emotion and confidence engendered by the quick strike was a tide that lifted all boats. Not only did the players, coaches, and the rest of the small Buffalo contingent benefit, but the fans back home in New York watching on TV got a huge bump. They were back from the dead! Their Blizzard was going to come back and pull this one out of the fire! This was not the team of yore they had seen curl up and die when facing daunting odds. The losers who made an art form of squandering late leads were officially history. Their team was now a confident, proven winner; a gritty bunch of street fighters who would go down swinging, if at all.

However, the Buffalo defense, as planned, came out in Dime to start the second half with Brogan getting the call the first series. It really didn't matter who was playing Dime-backer because Tillison kept throwing darts. St. Louis marched down the field and effortlessly punched in another score, taking their lead back to 17 points at 38-21.

Buffalo got the ball back on the kickoff, but this time the offense stalled and they punted it back to the Nighthawks for their seventh possession of the game. On the previous six possessions they had rung up a field goal followed by five consecutive touchdowns. There was an old saying: the definition of insanity is doing the same thing over and over again while expecting a different result. On the next series, the insanity finally came to a halt. Coach Faber pulled the plug on the Dime and went with Base personnel.

A cheer rose up from the Blizzard bench when they realized the Base defense was taking the field. A new energy and focus hit the field with them. For the first time all night, St. Louis went three-and-out and was forced to roust their punter. Even though Driftwood had sat out the series, he was pumped up along with the rest of his teammates. The offense took advantage of the field position and had a nice drive going. But they stalled inside the St. Louis 20 and Tenudo booted a 32-yard field goal. Now they were only down by two scores late in the third quarter, 38-24.

Driftwood got the nod from Coach Faber and went in on the next defensive series. The Nighthawks managed to string together a couple of first downs and moved the ball to midfield. They went back to the quick slant route that had been effective in the first half. Driftwood sensed it was coming and he gave Big E a "Mirror" call. This told his six-foot-seven-inch defensive end not to rush the passer but rather stay on the line and get some width into the throwing lane – all the while reading the QB's eyes – intent on batting the pass down.

It worked out better than Driftwood could have hoped. Big E timed his jump perfectly and got his pinky and ring finger on the ball enough to disrupt its flight, sending it directly at Driftwood. On the run, Driftwood seized it out of the air and kept trucking another 30 yards to the Nighthawk 27 before he was knocked out of bounds. The offense went to work and rang up another touchdown with three minutes gone in the fourth quarter. The Blizzard had made it a one-possession game, trailing 38-31, with plenty of time left to play.

The defense held again, led by a Brogan sack and Stark making a shoestring tackle on a screen play, forcing another St. Louis punt. The Buffalo offense could feel the momentum now and drove diligently down the field, eating up yardage on the ground and time off the clock. With just 2:04 left to play Buffalo tied the game on a quarterback draw. Ben Brady called his own number and dove into the end zone, much to the dismay of the home crowd. Tenudo rammed the kick right down Main Street and they were right back to where they had started. It was all knotted up, 38-38.

St. Louis went into their two-minute offense and inexplicably Buffalo brought their Dime defense back onto the field. Archie had been blistering Coach Faber's ears, lobbying on the headsets for the Dime because of the time considerations and the certainty of the pass. Coach Faber caved to his request and Driftwood was incensed.

"What the fuck are you doing, Lester?"

Coach Faber just looked at him like a deer in the headlights.

"Come on Coach, we've been stopping them," Driftwood said.

He was pleading now but Coach Faber just stood there with a blank look on his face.

*What the fuck was wrong with him!*

"Stark's Dime-backer. Get Base personnel ready and stand by me. Brogan and Driftwood are up," Coach Faber finally said.

Stark took the field with the Dime group, and Jack stood directly behind Coach Faber. He wasn't going to give up the battle until the man pulled his head out of his ass. Coach Faber would come around and he'd be right there and ready when he did.

With the Dime defense on the field the Nighthawks quickly completed a series of underneath passes and picked up a first down. Then Tillison broke contain and threw a laser across his body, hitting a sliding receiver at the Buffalo 42-yard line. The receiver was tackled in bounds, keeping the clock running with 1:27 left in the game and counting.

Driftwood hated to do it, but he couldn't take it any longer and stomped down the sideline to Coach Ivy.

"Call a goddamn timeout, Coach."

"Why?" Coach Ivy asked, particularly calm, especially considering the circumstances.

"Because something's wrong with Lester. We should be in Base on defense and he knows it. Everybody but Archie knows it. Lester's got his head halfway up his ass listening to him. Archie is all butt-hurt because he wants to play Dime, but Dime hasn't worked all fucking day."

Coach Ivy, who was not oblivious to the halftime locker room incident or what was happening on the field, stepped onto the field and signaled for a timeout to the side judge with 1:18 remaining. Driftwood escorted his head coach down to where Coach Faber stood amongst the Base personnel subs.

"Lester, what do you think about going with Base personnel here?" Coach Ivy asked.

Coach Faber looked at Driftwood and blinked his eyes. Driftwood had never seen him so out of sorts on the sideline during a game. Something was wrong with him. He noticed his lips were turning a little bluish and his skin was clammy and pale. A light sheen of sweat coated his face and neck and his eyes flickered up into his head before they came back to rest on Driftwood.

"Coach, can you hear me?"

Coach Faber just stared at him and nodded very slowly. "My goddamn left arm is killing me."

"I think he is having a heart attack," Driftwood said. "Doc! Doc!"

The team's medical staff set on Coach Faber like a dog on a bone. Driftwood knelt next to his fallen coach and grasped his hand.

"You're gonna be alright, Coach. Everything is gonna be just fine. You just go with these guys to the hospital and kick some ass and let me worry about taking names."

He began to leave when Coach Faber squeezed his hand and pulled him back. "You were right, Jack, we should be in Base. Should've been the whole goddamn game."

They quickly lifted Coach Faber up onto a cart, pulling him from Driftwood's grasp. They had him off the field and loaded into an ambulance in a matter of moments, thus holding up play only briefly.

One of the biggest challenges of any competition is the ability to stay in the moment, thinking exclusively about the immediate task at hand. Win the down and move on to the next. Perhaps the biggest challenge to this approach is to immediately forget the fallen and focus on the task. It certainly was never easy, especially when dealing with loved ones. Driftwood said a quick prayer, but then it was time to kill them all and let the good Lord sort them out.

Donny Jones, the Blizzard's defensive line coach, took over calling the defenses in Coach Faber's stead and got on the headset with Archie upstairs, who still wanted to play Dime. Coach Ivy stepped in and said no and sent the Base personnel onto the field. He told Archie over the headsets, in no uncertain terms, to calm down and get on board and start looking for ways they could exploit St. Louis from their Base package.

Despite the chaos, things went pretty smoothly. Driftwood and Brogan entered the game as part of the Base group with St. Louis set up 1st and 10 at the Buffalo 42. Tillison's first pass was incomplete as he underthrew a sideline route. He had to short-arm the throw due to pressure from Bo-Bo and Big E. On second down the Nighthawks ran a draw. Driftwood and Brogan combined for the tackle after a gain of five yards, bringing up a 3rd and 5 from the Buffalo 37.

The Nighthawks let the clock run as they huddled up. Buffalo still had two timeouts remaining and Driftwood looked to the sidelines for Coach Ivy. He was about to call the timeout himself when he finally spotted Coach Ivy frantically making the timeout signal. The confusion had cost them five precious seconds as Buffalo got the clock stopped with 1:07 left in the game.

Driftwood came over to the sidelines with Billy Brogan to discuss the situation with Coach Jones. Coach Ivy came over to monitor the discussion.

"Alright," Coach Jones said, "Coach Beatle says he wants Cover 2."

"No fucking way, that would be giving them a first down," Driftwood said. "We have to go after them and press the corners. Make them make a play. A zone will just give Tillison an easy throw for the first down, just like he has been doing all fucking day. Then they turn the lights out and we all go home."

Coach Jones relayed what Driftwood had said upstairs to Archie.

Archie Beatle went crazy in the coaches' box. He was cussing a blue streak about Driftwood trying to change his call. Coach Ivy was listening in and had heard enough.

"Archie, I warned you. Now hand the headset to Chuckles."

"But Coach—"

"Archie!"

"Yes, sir."

Archie meekly handed the headset over to Chuckles, who somehow had materialized in the coaches' box. Archie pretty much gave up at that point. He hunched in his chair and intently watched the action without making another sound.

"You call it, Jack," Coach Ivy said. "Get after his ass."

"Damn straight!" Driftwood shouted.

He and Brogan ran back out to the huddle all fired up. Their teammates urgently gathered tightly around them.

"It's my call. We are getting after their ass with an all-out blitz. Are you with me?" Driftwood asked.

A huge shout of affirmation came from the huddle. They all wanted to go down swinging, too, if at all.

"Come up and press across the board, even you, Stillwaters. Inside leverage, mono-e-fucking-mono, baby! We're going with '70 House Press Zero.' Let's get this fucker down. Ready…"

"Break!"

The huddle broke with an audible clap in perfect unison that cut through the roar of the crowd like the crack of a whip. This group knew each other well and was battle-tested. Together, they had been down many a dark alley from which they emerged with a certain swagger, one they had earned with the price of blood; it was obvious in the way they lined up for the play.

Driftwood had called for a seven-man blitz with man-to-man coverage across the board, with no help for anybody. It was risky, but it put immediate pressure on the Nighthawks to execute perfectly in a short span of time.

Tillison went to the line quickly and took the snap on the first sound. He tried to quick-snap the Blizzard defense to no avail. The D-line was ready and charged off the ball. Tillison took his drop, but the pressure got on top of him before he could set up to throw. Just as he was going down he somehow managed to fling the ball to the outside over the top of the coverage in a perfect arc before getting whacked by another Blizzard blitzer.

The ball came spinning toward the sidelines and seemed to hang in the air for an eternity as it slowly spiraled. Camera flashes lit up the building, capturing the image of the ball headed straight for its target. However, just as the ball landed in the receiver's hands, Leroy Clarkson swooped in late and knocked it to the ground.

The roar from the people in Western New York could be heard from Lockport all the way down into the Southtowns. Both Driftwood and Brogan had come free on the blitz and they pounded Tillison into the turf – hard. Driftwood jumped up off the ground and hugged Brogan as they jumped up and down in an embrace. The incompletion had stopped the clock and made it 4th and 5 for St. Louis with 59 seconds left to play.

The Nighthawks came out with their field goal unit and lined up for a 54-yard try. Their kicker, Bovo Oblouf, calmly split the uprights with a good 10 yards to spare. St. Louis took a 41-38 lead with 53 ticks left to tock, plenty of time for anything to happen.

Oblouf boomed the ensuing kickoff out of the end zone for a touchback, putting the Blizzard at their own 20 with one timeout remaining, needing a field goal to tie and a touchdown to win. It was amazing they were still in the game, let alone holding a golden opportunity to win it.

Ben Brady was the picture of supreme confidence as he broke the huddle and came to the line. He licked his fingers, flicking his tongue out like an agitated snake. He took the shotgun snap and stared down the safety before pivoting right and firing off a pass on the edge toward Shady Solomon, who had run a quick out. The Nighthawks' outside linebacker showed up in the throwing lane and jumped high. He tipped the ball straight up into the air and it came down right to him as he was crunched by Jeremy Patton. He hung on to the ball.

Interception, St. Louis! Checkmate.

The Nighthawks knelt on the ball to run out the clock and escaped with a hard fought 41-38 victory. What a game! Yet to Blizzard Nation it was nothing but another stone-cold heartbreaker in their long, tortured history of falling just short.

# Chapter Thirty-Three

Howard Ivy met with Donald Fegel first thing Monday morning. Both men were dog-tired and worn to a frazzle after their charter flight didn't land until nearly two o'clock earlier that morning. It didn't help matters they were also embittered by the circumstances of the close loss to St. Louis. Yet they were grinding away at the Wigwam at seven o'clock that morning. Such was life at the top in the NAFA.

They both were nursing large cups of coffee as Howard slid into one of the chairs in the GM's office.

"Good morning, Coach."

"Donald. How are you?"

"I've been better, that was a tough loss."

Howard sighed. "I've never had one that wasn't, but I know what you mean. I truly thought we would prevail in the end."

"We had our chances, that's for sure. So what are your thoughts regarding a fill-in for Lester? It looks like he will be gone for as much as a month."

"I consider Gary Chuckles an outstanding alternative for coaching the linebackers," Howard said. "He's been with Coach Faber for years and is well-versed in the nuance of the position. Archie Beatle had an extremely difficult night but is the most evident alternative for defensive coordinator. We may have to rehabilitate his authority after last night's near-mutiny at halftime. Of course, the individual who knows our scheme the best is Jack Driftwood."

"Are you *fucking* kidding me?"

Howard Ivy was fatigued and had simply been ruminating, speaking freely, as he would with his coaches. He had momentarily let his guard down, forgetting where he was and to whom he was speaking. He was, in no way, trying to goad Donald Fegel into an argument, at least not on a conscious level. Thus he was taken aback by the venom in Donald's voice.

"Of course, I am not suggesting Jack as a viable candidate," he said. He was too weary to hash over the same tired arguments. "I know that's not even so much as a remote possibility, I was merely thinking out loud. I'm still a little bleary this morning and have no intention of engaging in another exhaustive argument."

Donald paused, collecting himself before talking again.

"I think your first two suggestions are spot on, Gary will do a fine job and won't try to take over the kingdom. Archie, I'm afraid, will need to be watched like a hawk."

Howard nodded. He was relieved Donald had moved on and was once again impressed by the GM's understanding; the man had a solid grasp on their personnel – both players and coaches.

"Yes, and I intend to oversee him directly. I spoke with him after the game and he was very contrite regarding his outbursts and loss of control. He requested an opportunity to address the defense first thing to apologize and restate his commitment to the team. Hopefully, it will carry weight with the players."

Howard almost mentioned he was going to confer with Driftwood about getting behind Archie to steer the team in that direction but caught himself. Donald needn't be privy to that particular detail, and Howard knew the mere mention of Jack's name could set the man off again.

"I think he should address the entire team, the offense was in that locker room, too," Donald said.

"Excellent point," Howard said. "That will be the first order of business in the team meeting on Thursday."

"What about the players involved, Howard? Do we need to address their insurrection, or just let Archie's apology suffice?"

"I think less would be more, as is commonly the case. Archie apologizing should put it behind us."

"Okay, let's go ahead and let Gary and Archie know the plan and we can get to work on beating Boston."

"Very well, Donald. And thank you."

Howard knew he wouldn't want to have a beer with his colleague, but sometimes Donald wasn't entirely intolerable. Life in the NAFA could make for strange bedfellows; of that he was sure.

Lester Faber did not travel home with the team. He was kept overnight in St. Louis, where it was determined there was blockage in a couple arteries. Fortunately, he hadn't had a major heart attack; it was characterized as a "stress-induced cardiac episode." He was stabilized and flown to Buffalo the next morning and admitted to Buffalo General Hospital. He had a double by-pass procedure that same afternoon.

Jack went up to the hospital to see him the following evening. The team had been given three days off, as they didn't play again until the following Monday in Boston against the hated Revolution. Jack had given consideration to inviting some of his teammates to join him, but decided he preferred to visit Lester alone.

When he walked into the hospital room, Jack was shocked at the sight of his beloved mentor. Faber appeared old and vulnerable lying in the hospital bed wired up to a heart monitor with tubes running in and out of him. It seemed

Lester had aged several years overnight. Jack choked back his emotions, but before he could turn around to compose himself, Coach Faber noticed him.

"Hey, Coach."

"Jack Driftwood, my all-time favorite player." Coach Faber's voice was raspy from the tube they had forced down his throat during surgery.

"Right. They must have you on the good shit, huh," Jack said. "What I'm wondering is how they could do heart surgery on a man with no heart? What'd you do, go off to see the Wizard?"

"Come on, Jack. You know I am all heart. They could have done this surgery on my balls and got the job done."

"That would have been micro-surgery, Coach."

"Bullshit, they'd need a bigger scalpel."

"Seriously, though, how're you doing?" Jack asked.

Coach Faber shifted in the bed to get more comfortable and then coughed a little. He motioned to a lidded Styrofoam cup with a straw stuck in it sitting on the bedside table. Jack handed it to him. He took a sip and handed the cup back to Jack.

"Doc says I will be out of this damn place in a few days and then back to work another two weeks after that," Coach Faber said.

Joanne, his wife of thirty-two years, walked into the room. "Baloney, mister, you are going to take at least a month off, and even then you are only going back if I say so."

Lester rolled his eyes at her as Jack gave her a warm hug.

"Hey, Joanne," he said, "how are you holding up?"

"Okay, considering the circumstances, Jack. I heard you were the one who realized Lester was having some difficulties. Thank you so much. You probably saved his life."

"Ha!" Coach Faber said. "He's the reason I had the damn thing in the first place."

"You behave, Lester," Joanne said. "You know Jack is your favorite player. Honestly, Lester just raves about you, so don't let him try to fool you. He has told me many times if we had ever had a son he would want him to be just like Jack Driftwood."

The Fabers were the proud parents of six beautiful girls. Lester never did get his linebacker, but he did have a couple of young, rambunctious grandsons who appeared to have the makings.

"That's very sweet," Jack said. "I'll have to remind him of that the next time he tries to pick a fight with me on the sidelines."

Joanne laughed, putting her hands to her heart. "Oh my goodness, that was one of the funniest things I've ever seen. Poor Lester trying to fight through Gary Chuckles to throw a punch at you – right on national TV. Thank you for not killing him."

"I would have whipped his ass, Jo-Jo, and you know it," Coach Faber said.

"Thanks for sparing me, Coach," Jack said.

Lester just smiled and winked at him.

"Where are the girls?" Jack asked.

"They were all here this afternoon. Even Katie flew in from California. They're out to dinner right now, but they're coming back later to say good night."

"That's nice. Is everyone doing well?"

"Oh yes," Joanne said. "They are all worried about their grumpy, old father, but they are doing fine. I am going to run down to the nurse's station for a minute so I will let you boys chat. Thanks again, Jack. It was so nice to see you and for you to visit Lester."

Jack said his good byes to Joanne and gave her another hug and a peck on the cheek. She was such a dear, sweet lady. After she left there was a moment of awkward silence before Coach Faber spoke.

"You know, you guys were pretty hard on Archie."

"Yeah, I feel bad about that, but he was *way* out of line. You can't call out the guys up front like he did."

"Yep, he was way out of line. And you were right about the damned Dime. I wish I would have listened to you sooner. I heard Howie let you call that last blitz. Ballsy call – a good one, if only because it worked. But I need you to go in and talk with Archie. He is taking over for me while I am out and he needs your support. The guys follow your lead, and if you don't show him respect, none of them will, either. He already has a chip on his shoulder about never playing, but he is a good coach, Jack."

"I know, I know," Jack said. "But he needs to stand up in front of that room and apologize to those guys or it won't matter what I do, they still won't listen to him."

"I agree, I already talked to him about it. I also told him to listen to your suggestions rather than be threatened by them. Hopefully he will."

"Well, I'll try to be tactful in my own way, but we need you back before the playoffs. So you do what these people tell you and listen to Joanne. We'll be alright. You just get your ass better so we can go get us a ring."

"I heard that," Lester said as he weakly shook Jack's hand. "I definitely heard that."

Early that same afternoon Donald made a call to the Brogan residence. He was anxious to finish the contract extension for Billy Brogan for myriad reasons, the primary one being an ache set deep in his groin. Billy answered the phone.

"Hey, Billy, how are you feeling?" Donald asked.

"I'm a little sore but nothing a little rest won't take care of, Mr. Fegel."

Donald had given up on trying to get Billy to address him by his first name. The kid was just too polite.

"Good," he said. "Make sure you get that rest and we'll go beat Boston Monday night."

"Yes, sir."

"Is Nicole available? I want to set up a meeting to get this extension hammered out."

"Yeah, sure," Billy said. "Hold on, I'll get her."

Nicole Brogan took the phone and walked into her bedroom and closed the door. She and Billy had an agreement she would handle the business end of his career and he would get the job done on the field. So far the arrangement had served them quite well.

"Hello, Donald. Do you have the private jet fueled up and ready to go? I need to get out of here and get some sunshine. Let's go do this contract in Florida. You may find me much more agreeable."

"I wish," Donald said. "Although, I find you completely agreeable and adorable right here."

"I guess we will just have to do it in dreary, old Buffalo," she said.

"How about we get together tonight, knock the bottom out of this thing."

"What *thing* are you referring to?" she said.

"You know damn well what thing."

"Well, we will still have to do the contract, too," she said.

Damn, she pushed his buttons! Donald felt like he was going to explode when he talked with her and the flirting was almost more than he could handle.

"What contract?" he asked.

She giggled a little and said, "I don't know if I can wait until tomorrow night, but we will have to. We have plans for tonight, but then I am all yours."

"Good," Donald said. "I will be in my office late if you just want to swing by here and then we can take it from there?"

"Sounds scrumptious," Nicole said. "I will be over around seven."

"Just call my cell when you get close and I will come down and get you."

"Ta-ta."

Donald strutted into the private bathroom in his office and looked at himself in the mirror.

*Scrumptious, indeed!*

He shot both hands up like they were pistols and snapped his thumbs down, blasting both barrels. He brought each index finger to his lips and blew on them, one at a time, before giving them a spin and jamming them back into their holsters.

*Shoot-ah!*

He winked at his reflection and made a little clicking sound with his tongue. Things were lining up quite nicely for Donald Allen Fegel Jr.; quite nicely, indeed!

# Chapter Thirty-Four

Gerry Wainscott felt a little silly, but she was also enjoying her role in this bit of insider corporate espionage. She had left the Wigwam at six that evening making sure everyone knew of her plans for dinner and a movie. Donald had told her he was meeting Nicole Brogan for dinner so she knew he would be out of the office. Colin Meade would be gone as well. He had been leaving work early all week. Apparently he had some kind of remodeling project going on.

*Remodeling project, indeed.*

This presented a prime opportunity for her to head back to the Wigwam later that evening and poke around. She had already given Chaz all the official paperwork she could round up regarding the Wigwam project. Now she would attempt to sniff out something else; something hidden a little deeper under the surface.

The organization required access to all computers and collected all users' passwords, which were to remain confidential. Gerry felt a lingering guilt about using them, but she assuaged her moral compass by telling herself she was, after all, the owner of the company and, by extension, its computers. Thus she had every right to the passwords. Not to mention she was investigating a heinous, internal conspiracy in which a serious felony had been committed.

Donald was already camped at the door when Nicole Brogan screeched to a stop in the parking lot in front of the Blizzard offices in the Wigwam. Truth be told, he had been stationed in the lobby for the past fifteen minutes anticipating her call. He hustled out the doors and jogged over to her car before she could get out.

He opened the door for her and Nicole extended her hand. He gently kissed it, imagining sparks flying from his lips. They exchanged greetings, keeping everything aboveboard and professional, for now. Donald unlocked the doors letting them into the building and they rode the elevator to the fifth floor and walked through the mostly dark and empty hallway to his office.

"Business first," Nicole said as they entered his dimly lit office.

"Of course," Donald said.

He had dimmed the lights and lit several aromatic candles in a feeble attempt at creating a romantic ambience before going downstairs to get her. He felt a trifle foolish and dialed up the lights to their full capacity. They sat on a sofa, though not too close to each other, where he had laid out a Standard NAFA player contract on the coffee table in front of them. He had filled in the document with the most recent figures he and Nicole had discussed.

Nicole leaned in and concentrated on the numbers he had put into the deal. It was a five-year extension to Billy's current contract, which was set to expire after the season. The numbers were staggering. The entire deal was worth fifty million dollars plus incentives. There was an eight-million-dollar signing bonus and thirty-two million dollars of the total was guaranteed.

Donald watched her eyes get even bigger as she soaked in the numbers. Suddenly, tears were rolling down her cheeks, but they must have been happy ones because she smiled brightly at him when he offered a handkerchief. Donald didn't know what the hell to do. His palms were sweaty and he was afraid to talk as he sat dumbly on the couch and watched her. He didn't want to ruin everything, but what he didn't understand was he wasn't the one in control.

Nicole held power of attorney for Billy and signed the contract on his behalf. Donald handed her a check for eight million dollars. She stared at it, counting the zeroes over and again before carefully placing it into her clutch.

"I must say, I like the way you do business, Donald," she said in a husky voice, turning her full attention to him. "This calls for a toast! Do you have anything to drink?"

"I took the liberty of putting some champagne on ice," he said too quickly.

Donald was just happy to have something to do with himself. He hopped off the couch to fetch the ice bucket and a couple of flutes from behind his desk. In no time he popped the cork, which blasted off and thudded into the ceiling, leaving a mark.

The pressure released from the bottle seemed to have a similar effect on Donald, as he felt himself relax. It was his time to shine and he'd be damned if he was going to muck this one up.

"Does your cork always pop that fast?" she asked, taking a flute of the bubbly.

"The first one does," he said, "but the next couple take a lot longer."

"Ooh! I like the sound of that."

He held out his glass for a toast. "Here's to one deal hammered out."

"And another to come," she added, and they clinked the expensive flutes together before taking a long pull off of their glasses.

Donald came around the coffee table and sat down close to her on the sofa. Nicole put her hand on his leg and it was the only green light he needed. He leaned in and kissed her, slowly at first, but then hungrily. She responded in kind and soon they were all over each other scrambling to get out of their clothes.

He noticed the door to his office was slightly ajar. He didn't care, though, there was nobody left in the building except the coaches, and they were five floors below working in their basement enclave. As intended, he had Nicole Brogan and the fifth floor all to himself.

Gerry slipped through the front doors and into the lobby of the Wigwam. So far, so good, as she had yet to encounter a single soul. She hastily headed to the bank of elevators, got in, and punched up the fifth floor. The five lit up and instantly the elevator hummed to life, shutting the doors behind her before making the ascent.

Fortunately, there was no bell or other audible signal alerting the arrival of the elevator car, thus announcing her presence. She stepped carefully out of the car and scanned the horizon in each direction. With the coast all clear, she headed to her right, down the hall toward Donald Fegel's office, where she planned to begin her little raid.

It was extremely unlikely anybody was on the fifth floor at this late hour, but she still walked noiselessly, carefully tip-toeing on the balls of her feet in the exact manner Tree Spirit had taught her and Jack down in Mexico. As she started down the dimly lit hallway she noticed, for the first time, a shaft of light emanating from Fegel's office; her heart nearly stopped beating.

*Did that light just go on? I'm going to get caught. I just know it.*

Gerry froze like a statue upon noticing the light. She seriously considered turning right around and sneaking back out of there, but she hadn't yet willed herself to move. Her mind locked up in step with her body as she tried to think up a good alibi for being there, but she drew a blank. Time to abort.

When she turned halfway around, though, she thought she heard something like a low moan and froze again. She crept back closer to the sound and began to pick up a rhythmic, slapping sound and guttural groaning.

*What the hell is going on in there?*

As she racked her brain to figure out exactly what those noises were, she realized she had nearly reached the doorway to Fegel's office. That's when it clicked. Her hand flew to cover her mouth as she suppressed a gasp of shock.

*Little animal noises!* At least that is what Jack called the sweet sounds made while "doing the nasty."

Her curiosity got the best of her as she had to know just *who* was bumping uglies with Donald – in his office, no less. She had a pretty good idea, though, and wanted to confirm her suspicion. Hadn't Donald said he was meeting with Nicole Brogan tonight to work out Billy's contract extension? She decided to take a peek.

Despite seeing it with her own two eyes, Gerry couldn't believe it. Unfathomably, there in living color, right in front of God and everybody, was Donald

Fegel's bare, white ass pumping away like it was going out of style. Even more startling, the object of his affections was a half-naked Nicole Brogan, bent over the sofa.

In a mild state of shock, she leaned back out of the doorway and propped herself against the wall. The vulgar image was seared into her brain and would haunt her to her dying day. She breathed in deeply, intending to calm herself and gather the strength for one more gander, when she remembered the small camera she had purchased for the mission. Instinctively she fished it from her jacket pocket. Peeking around the doorway again, she raised the camera, took aim, and silently clicked off a smattering of shots.

Gerry was amped, bigtime, after gliding noiselessly back down the hall and into the elevator. Adrenaline rushed through her entire little body to the point where she felt she might puke once she got outside. She hugged herself as the elevator dropped toward the lobby, still not able to wrap her head around what she had just witnessed. Her hands were shaking almost uncontrollably on the steering wheel as she pulled out of the Wigwam's parking lot. There was no doubt where she was heading; Jack's place was just around the corner.

She punched in the access code to the garage and parked her car in one of Jack's spaces underneath the building and ran to the elevator, which seemed to take forever getting to the top floor. Ready to explode, she wailed on Driftwood's door like a wild woman, almost beating it down. She felt like she was going to pee her pants.

Jack was sitting at his desk watching Revolution game tape, occasionally nodding off in the process. He had had to roust himself a couple of times, as the Boston offense had a soporific effect on him. Hopefully, they would be equally boring come Monday night. He had seen their act so many times over the years he could practically call their plays for them, which was exactly what he intended to do.

The frantic pounding on his door rescued him from the tedium. He pulled himself from his desk chair and checked his watch on the way to the door. It was already after 10 p.m.

*What the hell? Who's beating down my damn door at this hour?*

"Hold on!" he hollered as the pounding became more persistent.

Driftwood swung the door open wide and Gerry Wainscott came flying at him. He raised his right arm and readied a clothesline but held up upon recognizing her. He caught her with his extended arm, effortlessly snatching her out of the air.

*Booty call. Yeah, baby!*

He was instantly turned on. Jack hoisted her up over his shoulder and headed toward his bedroom. She was yelling and kicking her legs and punching him across the back.

*Nice! Ain't she feisty tonight, I got me a live one.*

"Goddammit, Jack! Put me down! I'm not playing around!" she yelled, but it was no use.

She was trying to be serious but couldn't pull it off; she busted out laughing. Jack got her to his bedroom and flung her onto his bed. He jumped in after her and started nuzzling her neck. Seeing no other way out of it she pinched his nipple, hard.

Jack sprung up off of her and the bed and covered his nipple with one hand and his groin with the other. "What the hell is wrong with you?"

"I'm sorry," she said, struggling to control her laughter. "But it was the only way I could get you to stop and listen."

Jack hated anyone touching, and especially pinching, his nipples. Gerry had discovered this proclivity, and after a week or so of torturing him, she had promised she would stop.

"You promised! Goddammit, you know I hate that shit." Jack began to pout and sat back on the bed with his arms crossed, hands over nipples.

"I know, and I'm so sorry, honey, but I'm going to burst if I don't tell somebody right now."

"Okay, tell me. But I still say you didn't have to go all ape-shit and attack my nipples."

"I'm sorry but you have to hear this. Okay, so you know how I told you I was going to sneak back into the office tonight and do some internal espionage on Fegel and Meade?"

"Yeah, it rings a bell."

"Well, I went to the Wigwam, up to the fifth floor. I thought everybody was gone for the evening, but I saw a light coming out of Donald's office. I started slowly sneak-walking, just like Tree Spirit taught us down in Mexico. It works perfectly, by the way, even though I felt like an ass. But I'm glad I did it because as I got closer to his office, I started hearing 'funny little animal noises.'"

"No!" Jack sat up in the bed, suddenly keenly interested in her story.

"Yes," she said. "So I sneak-walked to the door to take a peek and there was Donald Fegel's flabby, white ass going to town. You are not going to believe who was catching."

"Who? Come on, tell me."

"One Nicole Brogan was bent over the couch taking it from the backside."

"No fucking way!" Jack shouted, punching a pillow. "Back door?"

"No, just backside."

"No fucking way, I do not believe it."

"Would you believe it if you saw it?" she asked coyly.

"No."

Gerry pulled the tiny spy camera from her pocket and held it under Jack's nose. "How about if I had pictures?"

"You didn't!"

He snatched at the camera but she pulled it back too quickly for him.

"Oh, I did!"

"Oh-my-God!" he said slowly as the full weight of Gerry's disclosure hit him.

He was initially gleeful at the thought of Fegel caught with his pants down, but the implications of the bigger picture also hit him. It hit him between the eyes like a hammer.

"Poor Billy, I can't believe it."

Talk about your instant buzzkill. Though they would never be best buds, Jack had come to like and respect Billy Brogan more and more as the season had worn on. The fun and excitement had been slightly diminished, but Jack was still chomping at the bit to see the pictures.

"C'mon, baby. Quit teasing me and hand over that camera so we download those pictures," he said.

They went into his office where he hooked the camera up to his desktop and down-loaded the photos Gerry had snapped. The images were more graphic than even Jack had imagined, which is saying something. All four pictures were perfectly framed and there was no mistaking the subjects or what they were doing. They had been taken from a side angle and Nicole had even turned toward the camera for the last one with her held tilted up and her eyes tightly closed.

"Damn, girl!" Jack said. "You've got a knack for this pornography shit. These shots are smoking hot."

"The shots or Nicole?"

"Both, actually."

"Yeah, but look at those rock-hard plastic boobs. That's just gross. They're so fake."

"We've talked about this before, sugar-britches. No such thing as a fake boob," Jack said in his most serious tone. "Let's be real."

"You're such an asshole."

# Chapter Thirty-Five

The flight home following the Monday Night Football game in Boston was not just an instant classic, it was in the top three best ever, and Jack couldn't remember the other two. He had partied hard at thirty-two thousand feet on numerous occasions but could not readily recall a bigger bash than their five-mile-high celebration after beating Boston. The flight home to Buffalo only lasted ninety minutes, which made it all the more remarkable. Jack hated to think what would have become of them if the game had been all the way out on the West coast.

The Blizzard had known going in to Boston a victory would clinch their first playoff berth in seventeen years. It was all anybody talked about all week long. Buffalo had lost to Boston earlier in the season and hadn't beaten them on the road for eight straight years. They were five-point underdogs in this one according to the Las Vegas oddsmakers. Buffalo must have known something the wise guys didn't.

They controlled the tempo from the opening kickoff and went on to dominate in every facet of the game. It was one of those rare nights where everything went according to plan as they scored an impressive 38-14 victory. Driftwood had earned his way back into the starting lineup due to his performance the previous week in St. Louis and took full advantage of the nod by recording his league-leading seventh interception on the opening drive.

Ben Brady and the BB-Gun Offense jumped on the opportunity, marching down the field on a 57-yard touchdown drive capped off by Anthony Petrucci's two-yard scoring grab. The Italian Stallion caught the ball in the flat and then flattened a pair of Revolution defenders on his way to pay dirt. The rout was on.

The postgame locker room was complete mayhem. In anticipation of their victory, Danny Steeley had iced down a dozen cases of semi-expensive champagne. Brady had a career game, tossing five touchdown passes, but his best play of the night was when he emptied two full bottles of bubbly on Howard Ivy's head while the old coach led the team in celebratory "Hip-Hip-Hoorays." Poured out alongside the champagne was over a decade and a half of frustration, heartbreak, and the embarrassment of failed season upon failed season. Rising from the outhouse to the penthouse never smelled better.

After a quick shower, Jack made his way to his new usual seat at the back of the fourth bus, and waited patiently for everyone to board. There was no airport in the immediate vicinity of the Revolution's stadium, so the team had to ride in a convoy of busses for over an hour to Providence, Rhode Island, and their chartered plane. Normally this was considered a pain in the ass, but nothing could spoil this grand occasion. Jack had a couple of Norco tablets burning a hole in his hand. As always, it had been a physical ballgame with Boston, leaving him all the worse for wear. He cracked the seal on the bottle of Crown to wash the pills down. He was daydreaming, gazing out the bus window basking in the glow of victory when a knee to the ribs jolted him from his quiet reverie.

"You got any extra juice for Thirsty Steven?" Stark inquired.

"Sure," Jack said. "You're one of *those* guys, huh? Just use me and abuse me for my body, good looks, and alcohol stash."

Stark laughed and slid into the seat next to Jack. "You're just the flavor of the week, bitch."

"What's the matter, Brogan didn't bring a bottle of Crown with him this week?"

"No, but he is on his way back here, too," Stark said. "The dude's on a mission. Says he wants to get drunk and celebrate. I guess him and Nicole are having some problems. The man needs a drink and I told him I know just the guy for that."

"Excellent. Do I get paid extra for babysitting you two freeloaders?"

"Nope, but you do get the honor and notoriety of hanging out with the cool kids again."

Moments later, Billy Brogan stumbled his way to the back of the bus. He was already noticeably tipsy, likely due to the contents of a nearly empty bottle of champagne he clutched to his chest.

"Goddamn, Billy," Jack said, "you ain't supposed to drink that shit, you're supposed to pour it on people."

Billy looked down at the bottle and then at Jack and Steven. "Oh," he said, before pouring the last dribble over the rookie's head.

"Geez, not on me, dumb ass!" Stark yelled.

He wiped at his mop of hair and bent over in his seat and shook his head like a wet dog before slicking his hair back with both hands. Billy plopped into the empty seat across the aisle from Stark and Jack passed him the bottle.

"Here you go, stud-hoss," he said. "This stuff will get it juicy for you."

"Huh?"

"Never mind, just hurry up so I can get a slug," Stark said.

Billy took a good nip from the bottle and then fought to keep it down. He coughed and hacked and made all manner of funny faces. His nose was running and his eyes welled up. When he finally did manage to speak, it was with a deep, raspy voice.

"This is the good stuff?"

"The best," Jack said. "But it's an acquired taste."

"How's about me fucking acquiring it, then," Stark said. He grabbed the bottle from Billy and dove into it.

They talked about the game, busted each other's balls, and passed the bottle around for the remainder of the bus ride to Providence. Generally, Jack hated bus rides. Most of the time they made him slightly nauseous, but not this one. This had to be the best damn bus ride he had ever taken.

The only negative was Jack found it tough to look at Billy without thinking about the pictures he had seen of Nicole and Donald. He didn't know what to do yet, but he wasn't going to ruin everything by bringing it up, or by dwelling on it. Perhaps another day, another way.

The team was loud and obnoxious boarding their chartered jet. The champagne and contraband bottles of booze had flowed freely on the bus ride to Providence. The first thing Jack did upon boarding the plane was pick up his favorite flight attendant, Sandy Thompson, and twirl her around before setting her back down in the aisle. Steven Stark, freshly back in the fold, followed suit grabbing Sandy's partner, Maryanne Comelia.

Young Steven had sat up front with Billy Brogan on the out-bound flight, but he had followed Jack and his bottle of whiskey through the plane to his old seat in the back row for the trip home. Jack had to give the kid a little credit; he knew where the party was. Brogan also worked his way to the back of the airplane, ready to endure several more rounds with the bottle of Crown.

Once they were airborne, the party intensified. Eric Sellars somehow managed to get his hands on a big bucket of fried chicken. Big E had removed his shirt and was dancing down the aisle of the plane, barebacked, singing about the barnyard pimp, vowing to eat the entire bucket.

Ben Brady hung tough for a while, but halfway through the flight he passed out, sprawling across an entire row of seats. He had been doing shots since boarding the bus and the heavy hits had taken their toll on the Blizzard QB. He was peacefully curled up in the fetal position, covered by an airplane blanket his center and primary caregiver, Nick Loney, had tenderly tucked around him.

Jack was still going strong in the back of the plane with a stout Stark keeping pace.

"I'm telling you, *mejo*," he said, "this is your big chance to join an elite group of travelers."

Jack animatedly jabbed his boy in the chest with the nearly empty bottle of Crown.

"I don't know," Stark said. "What if one of the coaches or Mr. Fegel comes back here and find out. I could be in big trouble."

"Ooooh! Not *big trouble*. C'mon, dude, this ain't junior-fucking-high. There's no such thing as big trouble. Besides, I'm the ultimate enabler, bro, I won't let anyone back near here. Just get your ass back there and ask her to help you with something in the bathroom. If she goes in there with you, it's for one thing and one thing only."

Stark took a deep breath, grabbed the bottle of Crown from Jack's outstretched hand and took a long pull of liquid courage. He stumbled up out of his seat and turned toward the galley. Jack, following closely behind, caught Sandy's eye and gave her a wink. She had been sitting on the rear jump seat counseling Maryanne.

Jack was pushing Stark forward like he was some bashful kid on a schoolyard playground building up to ask a girl to go with him for the first time. Stark stalled in front of Maryanne and started stuttering nonsense. They all laughed until Maryanne held out her hand, which Stark immediately grabbed with great relief. She led the horny, young lad into the bathroom and closed the door behind them.

Jack and Sandy high-fived before setting up watch. As members of the Mile-high Club themselves, they felt honor-bound to assist the attempt to join their esteemed company by providing as much peace and privacy as possible. The fanfare would come later.

Ten minutes had passed when Stark and Maryanne exited the airplane's restroom. They got a thunderous ovation from the back half of the plane. Stark took a bow, his goofy grin never goofier. Maryanne was much more humble and quickly hid in Sandy's comforting arms. The timing was perfect as the captain came on the plane's intercom and announced they were beginning their initial descent into Buffalo, thus it was time to prepare the cabin for landing.

Most of the players totally ignored the captain's warning and continued to party. Big E found himself a couple of the small food trays and made his way to the back of the plane.

"Cool-ass Drifty, clear the aisle for me, man. I'm bout to set me a new record," he said.

Jack went through the aisle picking up debris and clearing the way for Big E's record attempt at surfing the landing. The jet circled the Buffalo Niagara International Airport for its final approach just as Jack had cleared the aisle and the main cabin. Jack worked his way to the back of the plane and sat in the jump seat next to Sandy and strapped himself in.

"So just what is the record, Big E?" Jack asked.

"I made the ninth row after we beat the dog-ass Rough Riders back in 2009. But I got me a good feelin', Drifty. We in the playoffs now, homeboy. I'm a ride this bitch all the way to First Class."

Big E checked to make sure his size fourteen feet fit securely on the trays. The last thing he needed was a blowout to send him tumbling out of control up the aisle. The boys in the back began to chant for Big E as they came in for the landing.

"Barnyard Pimp! Barnyard Pimp! Barnyard Pimp!"

The landing was one of the smoothest Jack could remember. All five wheels of the DC-9 hit the runway together and she didn't bounce an inch. The captain reversed the thrusters and the plane decelerated at a high rate. Big E's massively strong hands were clamped to the chair backs like an angry crawfish's claws on a stick. He pulled on the seatbacks, launching himself forward down the aisle as the Jet's momentum shifted upon deceleration. He timed it perfectly and shot down the aisle.

The big man leaned forward in a crouch to maintain his balance and the trays held firmly to his feet as he skimmed over the carpeted aisle. He gained speed, sliding past the exit rows halfway through the plane's fuselage. The ride had record written all over it. The players were screaming and cheering over the roar of the jet engines. Amazingly, the big man held it together and cleared the coach cabin while still sliding at a decent clip. He threw his arms into the air triumphantly as he broached the First Class cabin barrier.

As the plane slowed, Big E burst into the First Class cabin, still sliding forward at a pretty good rate. He slid past the coaches and various front office personnel who were startled by the sight of the half-naked surfer gracefully skimming through the aisle. Finally, he ran out of runway and banged into the cockpit door. Bouncing of the door, he was flung onto the laps of Gerry and Gerald Wainscott, who were buckled into the first row. Everybody in the back of the plane was going nuts, cheering like they had just won the Mega Bowl.

Gerald Wainscott let out an "oomph" as the big man's elbow slammed into his mid-section. Sellars reached out his other hand to break his fall and it unintentionally landed on Gerry's right breast.

Big E looked into Gerry's eyes and gave her a little nod of approval and then a quick wink. She burst out laughing. Gerald Wainscott recovered his breath and clapped Sellars approvingly across his bare back. He had been on enough Buffalo Blizzard charter flights over the years to know all about surfing the landing.

"Congratulations, Eric, that has to be a record," the owner said.

Big E scrambled to his feet. "Yes, sir, Mr. Wainscott. I never made it to First Class before, so it's a new record, for sure. Sorry bout landing on top of y'all, though."

"That's okay, Eric. Well done! I'm proud of you," Wainscott said, followed by a cackling chuckle.

Donald Fegel jumped up out of his seat from across the aisle. "Jesus H. Christ! What the hell is wrong with you, Sellars? You could have killed somebody! Get your black ass to the back of the plane."

"Why it gotta to be black?" Big E asked.

"Donald!" Mr. Wainscott said. "That kind of talk will not be tolerated. Apologize to this man, immediately."

"Yes, sir, Mr. Wainscott. I am sorry, Eric. Now, could you please go take your seat?"

"Sure thing, boss."

Sellars skated his way to the back of the plane on his magic airplane-tray skis and was showered with everything that wasn't nailed down by his wildly cheering teammates. Big E had just set the world record for surfing a landing. At least the boys in the back and the Wainscott's appreciated the effort; Mr. Fegel sure as hell hadn't.

# Chapter Thirty-Six

A fierce wind whipped the falling snow into Neil Dadoska's red-raw face as he stood coatless outside the Buffalo Seneca Casino. He did have on a dingy, brown flannel shirt that helped cut the wind a trifle. He took one last long drag on his cigarette and then stubbed it out with his foot after throwing it to the ground. There was a receptacle for butts not two feet from him in the designated outdoor smoking area. Like he gave two shits. Call it his personal protest to the indoor smoking ban in the State of New York.

It appalled him that the State could tell a man where he could smoke. What the hell was happening to America? Before long you'd need permission to break wind. He lifted his right cheek and, in a silent but deadly protest, let one rip. On that bright note he headed back inside to his office. He was waiting for an email from Colin Meade which would contain the list of Jack Driftwood's pathetic friends and his new arch enemies.

Neil was not a football fan and didn't give a rat's ass about the Buffalo Blizzard and these so-called gridiron heroes. In his mind they were nothing but a bunch of overpaid, over-indulged pretty boys who thought the world owed them something. It would please him to no end to take one of them off the grid, or gridiron, if one preferred.

Upon returning to his office, he checked his email and, sure enough, there was the list of names and addresses from Meade. Dadoska printed it out immediately. He hated reading things on the computer screen. He was the tactile type; he needed to get things in his hands to get a feel for them.

Too much of the world was just floating through space these days. It wouldn't be long and everything would be done for you. You would just sit behind a desk all day and some machine would come by and wipe your ass. This was a bit hypocritical on Dadoska's part, as he spent much of his spare time at his computer playing online poker, but that irony was lost on him. That was different, that was poker. Poker was his life.

He looked the list over and his initial thought was this must be some kind of bad joke. He was obviously dealing with a bunch of know-nothing amateurs. Taking care of this crew would be like taking candy from a snot-nosed, howling, crying-ass little baby. However, one name intrigued him, if only because of the lack of information.

"Chaz. Address, unknown. Occupation, unknown. No photograph available."

The only other name on the list that was halfway interesting was Vinny Cappolla, a Buffalo Detective. Dadoska remembered meeting Cappolla on an earlier occasion. The fat tub of lard was running an investigation on a couple of grifters trying to run a scam on the slot machines at the Niagara Falls Casino several years back. Neil had considered the fat man a moron back then, even though Cappolla had made a collar in the case. The big boy must have stepped on his dick, fell in shit, and come up smelling like a rose, because he didn't have a clue when Dadoska had talked with him.

But this Chaz character was intriguing. Any guy who could maintain that low of a profile, to merely be known by a first name, which was likely an alias, had something on the ball. Hunting such a man down might even be fun, and possibly even be a challenge. He might even get to go into the old-school hunting mode to track this poor heathen down.

The more he thought about things, he vaguely remembered hearing the name Chaz before but couldn't recall from where. He was racking his brain and couldn't put a finger on it. On a whim he called Thomas Sargentoe, an old buddy who worked at the Erie County Holding Center. Sargentoe was the chief clerk and nothing happened outside his sphere of knowledge. After the usual exchange of familial insults, Dadoska cut to the chase.

"So has anybody by the name of Chaz ever come through there?" He asked. There was no immediate response. "Or maybe you heard somebody talking about this guy. Supposedly he's some kind of hard ass."

Neil was about to ask if Sarge had gone deaf when he spoke up.

"Yeah, you know what? I have heard the name. He's the dude who *really* caught those rednecks that took a tire iron to Earl Johnson. Not that fat, corpulent, human halitosis prick known as Vinny Cappolla."

"No shit. What else do you know about this Chaz, Sarge? I want to know everything."

"Well, that's the funny thing with this guy – that's all there is, the name: Chaz. I looked into it myself because I knew that sack of shit Cappolla couldn't have tracked down them boys by himself. All I could get was what you got, your dick in your hand."

"Hmm. Well, if you do hear anything more about this prick, let me know, post haste."

Neil hung up and began to pace across his office. This little investigation was heating up and he was getting caught up in the excitement. Perhaps he really had stumbled upon a worthy opponent in this Chaz son of a bitch. He also had learned not to underestimate Jack Driftwood. Anybody who had come out on top in a gunfight by throwing rocks was not to be taken lightly.

A foreign feeling had filled his expansive chest. Amazingly, Neil Dadoska was genuinely happy for the first time since he had ransacked Tree Spirit's house.

This was going to be some kind of old-fashioned fun! He would find out who this bastard Chaz was. And he would take great pleasure in nose-walking him out to the woodshed and beyond. Not only him but the rest of these pussies who were pissing in his pond.

The list contained eight names, including the mighty Chaz. Apparently, Driftwood didn't have that many friends. Dadoska studied the list a little more closely, trying to decide which of his operatives he would assign to investigate Driftwood's cronies. He had already called dibs on the creepy cop, Cappolla, and Chaz. He did not recognize any of the other names on the list.

| | | |
|---|---|---|
| **Joseppi "Cheese" Barcheezzi** | **510 Parkside Ave., Buffalo, NY** | **Occupation unknown** |
| **Vincenzo Cappolla** | **1222 Mile Strip Road, Hamburg, NY** | **Buffalo Detective** |
| **Melvin Quinni** | **3783 Sparrow Rd, Wheatfield, NY** | **Football Coach – Buffalo State** |
| **Steven Morris** | **119 Fair St., Buffalo, NY** | **Unemployed** |
| **Larry Blake** | **217 Market St., Buffalo, NY** | **School Teacher – Nichols High School** |
| **Jerry Monaco** | **11527 Stepping Stone Lane, Orchard Park, NY** | **Attorney** |
| **R.F. Harland** | **6721 Abbot Rd, West Seneca, NY** | **Medical Supplies Sales** |
| **Chaz** | **Address unknown** | **Occupation unknown** |

After looking at the list again, he decided calling his crew in for a face-to-face was the best way to work this investigation. Some of his guys may even know one of these douchebags. He got on the horn and called in his goon squad. Time for a little powwow.

It had become almost impossible for Colin Meade to sleep for more than a few hours at a time. He had slept like a baby the night the sanctity of his home had been violated, but that was due to the twenty-year-old bottle of scotch he had shared with his partners in crime.

Unfortunately, hitting the bottle again was definitely not an option. The entire next day had been a living hell for him. Colin, simply put, did not handle his booze very well. He had vomited until his guts nearly fell out and was convinced his head would explode if he had to endure that again. He tried sleeping pills, but they just made him drowsy. Colin would catch a few winks, but then he would wake up more tired than before he had dozed off and was still unable to sleep. He didn't know how much longer he could go on like this.

The nightmares, when he did sleep, were the worst of it. It was always a version of the same theme. He would arrive either at his house, his office, even his childhood home, and the place would be deathly quiet. He had a foreboding sense something was terribly wrong, but he couldn't quite put a finger on the danger. Compelled by some force beyond his control, he would venture inside, despite his instincts screaming at him to turn, run, and never look back. Though in the end, he would go in, every damn time.

Upon his entrance, the first thing he encountered was bloody writing oozing out of the walls. The place was always a mess, as if somebody had just tossed it, leaving everything scattered all over the place. The bloody writing seeped directly out of the walls and ran down in big streaks before pooling on the floor, obscuring things to the point where he could not clearly read the writing. But that didn't matter; he knew what it said. He knew damn good and well, because he had seen it before, in real life.

*TREE SPIRIT LIVES!!!*

Instinct told him to run; get the hell out of there, and fast! Then came the blood. It gushed from the wall now, spraying him from head to toe – it was all over him and he couldn't get it off. He would finally throw off the chains of his paralyzing fear and take off running. He had never run so fast in his life. He felt like he was faster than Shady Solomon. But when he slowed to a jog, he realized he wasn't going anywhere; he was still trapped in that bloody room, covered in the stuff. This is when he woke up, screaming, every time.

Colin knew he couldn't handle much more. It was time to make a move. A big move. He had known from the very beginning – since Mr. Fegel first approached him regarding the Wigwam Project – that one day he would have to make a quick, quiet exit. He was as prepared as he was scared. Had the time had come to set the wheels into motion?

The Buffalo Blizzard called a press conference for three o'clock the Tuesday afternoon following the monumental, playoff-clinching victory over the Boston Revolution. There were a couple of big announcements on the docket. The first of which concerned the all-important playoff ticket information. They assumed, after such a long drought, their fan base had forgotten or was otherwise unfamiliar with NAFA post-season ticket procedure and policy. They were correct. In spite of the fact the Blizzard was not even yet guaranteed a home playoff game, the NAFA had no problem taking the ticket money from the fans up front, in advance. The league itself handled all post-season tickets and it had turned into a very lucrative aspect of their business.

In the event Buffalo did not host a playoff game, the NAFA would simply return the money to the club, where, by rule, it had to be used for future game tickets or forfeited. The most highly recommended program was to have the money used as a down payment for the next year's season tickets. Of course, the NAFA took a ten percent handling fee right off the top, regardless of the outcome. It was good to be king.

The second announcement concerned the contract extension of inside linebacker Billy Brogan. The entire Brogan family was cooling their heels in the Blizzard Media Center slightly before three o'clock, right on time. They were heartily greeted by Donald Fegel, Howard Ivy, and Gerry Wainscott.

"Congratulations, Billy," Fegel said. "I must say, your wife drives an awfully hard bargain. But we are extremely excited about you and your family joining our family for years to come."

"Thank you, Mr. Fegel," Brogan said. "The best thing about it is I don't have to pay agent fees. Instead, I just turn the whole darn check over to her."

Fegel laughed a bit too loudly and assured Billy his precious Nicole was worth every penny. Gerry was sick to her stomach from watching him playing nice with the Brogan Family. She was disgusted all over again at the image instilled in her brain of him mounted on Nicole. She had to struggle to keep her smile up, hating herself all the while.

There was a huge media turn out as Blizzard fans could not get enough coverage of their team. The success of Blizzard Football was all anybody in Western New York cared to talk about. Several local TV and Radio stations carried the press conference live, interrupting their regular scheduled programming. They would not receive a single complaint for doing so.

The press conference began with David Blitzer, the Blizzard's vice-president of media relations, introducing the ticket policy. Blitzer then brought up Donald Fegel, who swaggered to the podium like John Wayne into a saloon to make a brief statement.

"It gives me great pleasure to announce the 2015 playoff-bound Buffalo Blizzard have agreed to terms on a five-year contract extension with Mr. Billy Brogan. Billy has quickly become an integral asset at the inside linebacker position, and with he and Steven Stark working in tandem, we now have the best pair of inside linebackers in the league for years to come. It is with great pleasure that we unite the Brogan family with the Buffalo Blizzard family. I want to especially thank Nicole Brogan, Billy's wife and agent, for her relentless efforts on her husband's behalf in hammering out the details of this deal. All I can say is, Billy, you are one lucky son of a gun."

The room broke into polite laughter and Gerry Wainscott dropped her head. Coach Ivy got up in front of the media next and spoke eloquently of Billy Brogan's hard work ethic and team-first attitude.

"I marvel at how fastidious Billy has been in his quest to integrate himself into the team with remarkably effortless cohesion. The man has already assumed the mantle of a leadership position both on the field and in the locker room. It is men like him who can manipulate events through the sheer force of their will and cause this franchise to turn the corner and reach the playoffs this season. However, there are several more rivers to cross, but I am proud to be in the company of this team and in that of Billy Brogan as we set out to achieve the ultimate goal."

Both Billy and Nicole Brogan took a turn at the podium parroting how welcome they were made to feel in Buffalo, by not only the Blizzard organization, but also the fans of the team and the community, in general. They also stated they were looking forward to a long and happy relationship, not only with the team, but also with the town.

Nicole ended her part by saying, "It has been a total pleasure hammering this deal out with Mr. Fegel at every turn. It was the most professional negotiation I have ever been a part of. If you are looking for a reason this long-dormant franchise has suddenly blossomed into a legitimate championship contender, look no further than your General Manager, Mr. Donald Allen Fegel Jr."

The room exploded into applause for Donald. He unconsciously puffed his chest out and tried to look humble as he nodded to the room. Gerry Wainscott puked in her mouth a little bit.

*What a joke! They "hammered" out the contract, all right.*

If she hadn't been on the verge of being sick she may have busted out laughing when Nicole had said it had been such a "professional negotiation." It made her wonder if Fegel had actually paid for Nicole's services. In a way, he had – with her father's money. It disgusted her.

The press asked a flurry of questions about the contract, which, of course, were answered with the usual company line that they had "No comment," thus leaving the details undisclosed. Another flurry of questions came about what it meant to have sewn up a spot in playoffs after such a long drought. These were answered with the same refrain Coach Ivy had espoused, "The team was proud of its accomplishments thus far but there was still much work to be done."

Finally, the media had their fill and the session came to an end. Everybody went back to work at the Wigwam as the reporters scrambled around the media center, working to meet their deadlines. Thoroughly repulsed by the entire charade, Gerry went to her office wondering what, if anything, she could do about the situation.

As she thought about it, her conscience asked her a simple question: *Am I doing the same thing with Jack Driftwood?*

Obviously, theirs was a different situation than Donald and Nicole. She and Jack were both single, consenting adults. It wasn't like they were cheating on anyone or anything. But if there was nothing wrong with it, then why did they have to sneak around? It just didn't sit right with her. The other issue was the last thing she wanted was to blindside her father; that was enough to tell her it was wrong. It would taint everything. She decided she was going to have to talk to him about it, and soon, because she didn't like the way she felt about herself.

Donald stomped out the doorway and down the hall towards Gerry Wainscott's office.

*How could she act like such a bitch? Is she jealous? Is it because Billy Brogan had usurped her man, basically taken his job? Is she that narrow-minded, petty, and selfish?*

He had seen the rage of jealousy on Gerry's face during the press conference, the way she sneered when he was introduced to a huge ovation. The way she grimaced when Nicole spoke. Her arrogance had forced his hand. Donald Allen Fegel Jr. was nobody to be trifled, with and, owner's daughter or not, Gerry needed to learn that little lesson, first hand.

Fegel didn't bother knocking on the partially ajar door to Gerry's office. He barged right in, startling her in the process, and closed the door behind him and stood in front of her desk, arms folded. They locked eyes for a moment before Fegel spoke.

"I've got to tell you, Gerry, I have noticed a big change in you lately – and it's not for the better, I might add."

"Really, because I've noticed the same thing about you."

Fegel totally ignored what she said and plowed forward with his accusations. "I think it all started when you began screwing one of our players. At first, I considered it a rookie mistake, a beginner's error, as it were. I figured it was a one-time mistake and things would run their course and you would come to your senses. But time has proven me wrong, and now, to make matters worse, your illicit affair has begun to cloud your judgment. I saw the faces you were making at the press conference – I was appalled. You've let your feelings for Jack Driftwood interfere with your job. You're actually jealous and green with envy that I signed a fine, young player like Billy Brogan to a long term deal and stole the spotlight from your beloved cowboy. That's taking it too far. In fact, it's embarrassing. I find myself wondering how your dear father would feel if he read about such a thing in, say, the Buffalo News."

Gerry was initially shocked at the way Fegel had come at her. Then she was fuming with anger. She decided she could no longer keep all of her cards close to the vest; it was time to flip a few of them over onto the table.

"I'll tell you what embarrassing is," she said. "Embarrassing is you having the nerve and the gall to get up there in front of Billy Brogan and his children and talk about *hammering* out a contract with Nicole when the only thing you hammered was her. I wonder what my dear father would think about that."

Now it was Fegel's turn to be shocked.

"Th-that, that is a ridiculous, baseless accusation," he stammered. "You, you don't know what you are even talking about or who you are messing with!"

"Oh, I know, and it makes me sick to my stomach. That's why you saw me making faces. I made the same faces when I came up here late one night last week and stopped by your office."

Fegel turned a bright shade of crimson and was shaking with anger and sweating profusely.

"That is a terrible, ugly lie, Gerry. That is low, even for you. I won't stand here and listen to such vile, false charges. All I know is that if Driftwood keeps visiting your penthouse, people are going to know about it."

Fegel turned to leave, but her hissing stopped him cold.

"My private life is none of your damn business or anyone else's, don't test me on this, Feegs. It will end up very bad for you. Very, very bad. I can promise you that much."

He huffed and stomped out of the office, leaving Gerry shaking with fury. She wanted so badly to call Jack, to have him hold her and tell her it would be all right. She realized she was becoming too dependent on him. She had to talk to her father; tell him the truth about her situation. She owed him that much. He would be disappointed, but he had always been understanding. Gerry decided she would tell him as soon as he arrived in Buffalo Saturday for Sunday's game against the South Florida Riptide. She also knew she could not see Jack until she came clean, if ever again. The thought of it made her burst into tears.

# Chapter Thirty-Seven

The city of Buffalo was getting ready for the biggest game of the season, which was saying something in a year replete with big games. Their arch rival and chief nemesis, the South Florida Riptide, were coming to town. If Buffalo managed to win the game they would win the Seaboard Division title outright, secure a bye in the first round of the playoffs, and have a chance to be the Eastern Conference's top seed. Their record would go to a sterling 13-3, good enough for at least a tie for the top mark in the entire NAFA.

South Florida was coming in to town with an 11-4 mark and a chance to surpass Buffalo in the division race with a win. Because the Riptide had beaten Buffalo earlier in the year, they would take the division title if they won this one due to their sweep in head-to-head matchups with the Blizzard. The winner of the game on Sunday would officially be the 2015 Seaboard Division Champions and receive the first-round bye. In essence, the matchup was the de facto Seaboard Division title game – winner take all.

The league's leading rusher, Scoop Brackett, was coming to town looking for another 2,000-yard season with 1,934 already to his credit. Much was being made of the altercation and personal battle between Brackett and Jack Driftwood from the first game. South Florida was talking trash in the press, calling Driftwood the dirtiest player in the league and making menacing threats that he had better not get caught standing around any piles Sunday or he would get his clock cleaned, free of charge.

Driftwood had refused to take the bait and was quoted in the press as saying he had great respect for South Florida and their outstanding running back. He did cause a little stir by adding he, "Had a heaping-helping of Brackett already this year and was looking forward to another Scoop."

The war of words escalated throughout the week. Buffalo put out an advisory warning their fans against fighting in the stands, even if their adversary was foolish enough to wear green and gold, South Florida's colors, or anything with a Riptide logo on it. All of those involved in such a fracas would be summarily expelled from the stadium and banished for the playoffs. Still, there were likely to be more fights in the stands than on the field, although it was considered to be a toss-up.

The main trepidation for Buffalo fans was the issue of the roof of the Wigwam. In years past, having South Florida visit late in the season was a significant advantage. The Riptide would habitually come up north and melt in the snow, much like Buffalo had melted earlier in the season in the South Florida heat. That was out of the question this year, however, as the roof over the Wigwam would undoubtedly be closed during the game. There was a small movement amongst a group of hardcore fans petitioning the organization to open the roof regardless of the weather.

Though this sentiment was understood and even sympathized with, there was no way the roof would be opened. The weekend forecast was typical for late December in Buffalo; it called for highs in the mid-twenties with steady winds bringing in lake-effect snow squalls off Lake Erie. As much as the brass would have liked the cold-weather advantage, they could not chance opening the roof and doing damage to the stadium with a Mega Bowl to host in six short weeks.

To end all arguments, Coach Ivy had come out in the papers and claimed, "Football is football, whether it is played in a palatial edifice or a dark alley. I have no preference. We will show up on Sunday, regardless."

Due to the excitement and magnitude of the game, Gerald Wainscott III decided to take his private jet from Cleveland to Buffalo in time for dinner Friday night rather than wait for Saturday morning. He was hoping to surprise Gerry with an early arrival and hoped to take her out to dinner. He wanted to catch up on things, having been away all week. He also missed his lovely daughter and relished the opportunity to spend some time alone with her.

Geraldine Marie Wainscott had been a complete surprise and total blessing to the Blizzard owner. He had lost his first wife, Mariam, to cancer when she, like him, was just fifty years old. Mariam had never been able to have children. Gerald figured it was just as well; he was an incurable workaholic and making time for a family would have been a tough task. A few years after his first wife had passed, he met Marie Henderson and fell in love all over again. Marie was forty-four when they had married, eight years Gerald's junior. They discussed having a family, but decided they were beyond the appropriate age to start such an enterprise.

Then a miracle transpired. Somehow, Marie conceived and Gerald became a first-time father at the age of fifty-five. The three of them had a wonderful run together until they lost Marie just five years earlier. She left this world peacefully in her sleep at the age of eighty. Gerald was alone again except for the apple of his eye, his one and only baby, Gerry. He felt incredibly fortunate she had been willing to pick up the family mantle, taking on the football business and keeping their team in Buffalo under the Wainscott name.

Gerald called Gerry as his private jet taxied after a smooth landing in Buffalo. He transferred into a limo on the tarmac and directed his driver to take him straight to the Buffalo Seneca Casino Hotel where he and his precious daughter would have a sumptuous dinner at his favorite local restaurant housed in the casino, the Bull's Horn.

Gerry hastily answered her cell phone after seeing it was her father calling.

"Hey, Dad," she said. "What are you up to?"

"I just landed in Buffalo and wanted to surprise my best girl by taking her out to dinner at the Bull's Horn."

"Ooh, that sounds like fun! Can I come along, too?"

"Don't be silly, young lady. You *are* my best girl. I will arrive in about twenty minutes, so get yourself ready. I will have somebody call up to your room when I get there. I want to hear all about what I missed this week and see how you are doing. You've almost made it through an entire season so you should have a good idea about things by now."

"That sounds perfect, I need to talk to you, too. See you in a few!"

She hung up the phone and immediately a wave of nervousness surged through her body. She felt like she did when she was younger and had gotten into some manner of trouble and was torturously awaiting sentencing. She was going to spill her guts about her relationship with Jack and wasn't sure how her father would react. The thought that scared her most was what if he told her she couldn't see Jack anymore and expect to keep her stake in the team. She wasn't prepared to make such a choice; she couldn't bear the thought of losing either.

One thing she didn't plan on mentioning was Donald Fegel and his antics. Not yet, anyway. That conversation would come soon enough. Once Chaz had finished building an airtight case against Fegel and company she would lay out the accusations to her dad first, and then the proper authorities. She couldn't wait to get the despicable thief thrown out and locked up in the pen; hopefully, for a very long time.

But she couldn't go off half-cocked. Her father would be prone to disbelieve such a story about his right-hand man. She needed a solid case buoyed by cold, hard facts. It wouldn't be long before Fegel's house of cards came tumbling down, the sooner the better.

The dinner had been nothing short of amazing in the elegant setting of the Bull's Horn. They had chatted away about what had happened while Gerald was in Cleveland all week and much of the conversation centered on the impending big game with the Riptide and the history of the rivalry. Gerry loved to listen to her father weave tales from the franchise's early days. He was still sharp as a tack and remembered the games and surrounding circumstances in great detail, reciting his players' names and even those of their opponents. His recall astounded her and also made her realize how much he loved his football team.

Finally, they got around to ordering dessert and Gerry decided the time was right to tell her story. Her father beat her to the punch.

"Gerry, I must say I couldn't help but notice you have been a little distracted this entire evening. I know something is bothering you. Care to tell your dear, old dad what is going on?"

"I'm sorry, Dad. I didn't mean to be rude. And you are right, I do have something I need to tell you."

Gerry fell silent and dabbed at her lips with her napkin before neatly folding it into her lap.

"Shoot," he said.

"I don't quite know how to say this so I guess I'll just spit it out," she said. "I have been secretly seeing one of your players for a while now."

Gerald's blinking of his eyes was the only sign of hurt he showed. He took the napkin from his lap and let the silent tension build while he cleaned his spectacles. After a deep breath he spoke.

"It's Jack Driftwood."

Gerry was shocked. "How…how did you know?"

"Call it a father's intuition, along with simple deduction," he said. "He's your age, he's a romantic, anti-establishment figure – which happens to be your type. And I recollect way back in training camp you had a little sparkle in your eyes when you spoke to him. I guess I shouldn't be surprised."

"I'm so sorry. I should have confided in you a long time ago and I know what a compromising position it puts you in. I also know how improper it is to sneak around behind your back on this thing. But please don't ask me to stop seeing him."

"Don't be foolish, young lady! I can't tell you who to like now any more than I could years ago when you went to the junior prom with that idiot, Bryan Malone."

Gerry cringed and then laughed, easing the tension. "Oh my God! That was awful. I should have listened to you back then."

"That was a disaster, if I recall," he said, laughing along with her. He reached his arthritic, liver-spotted hands across the table and took his daughter's fresh, perfectly-manicured hands into his own. "Do you love him, dear?"

"I don't know…maybe. He makes me laugh and treats me like his princess. We are so good together."

Gerald nodded. "I have always liked Jack very much. He's a bit old-school, a man of his word who knows the value of things. He would make for a wonderful son-in-law."

"Whoa, nobody is talking marriage, here."

"I'm just saying...you know I will always support you, Gerry, but I must make one request. I would ask you to keep this quiet until after the season. We are in the playoffs and have a real chance at winning. The last thing we need is a distraction such as this, even if it isn't a distraction, if you know what I mean."

"Yes. I know what you mean. I promise, nobody will hear it from me."

"Does anybody else know about this?" he asked.

"Yes, a few of Jack's friends and Donald. I wouldn't worry about Jack's friends, but Donald was upset about it. He thought it was very unprofessional and scolded me for it."

Wainscott laughed a little. "I think Donald was just worried about me if it were to get into the papers. He is always looking out for me in some manner. And he is right, it is unprofessional, but life is life and love is love. When I started dating your mother it was considered scandalous by many people around here. The press had a field day with it. But look what it brought me, the most beautiful, wonderful thing in my life – you. So don't you worry about Donald, I will have a talk with him. Everything will be okay."

"What about Jack?" she asked. "I have to tell him I told you."

Gerald raised his eyebrows. "So you do love him."

She remained silent at this, all but confirming his suspicion.

"Go ahead and tell him we talked and my only concern is keeping things quiet, for now. And tell him to keep doing whatever it is you two are doing because he is having a hell of a year."

"Dad!"

"I may be old and dumb, young lady, but I am not *that* old and dumb."

Gerry was on cloud nine. A great burden had been lifted from her heart. She was so blessed to have such great men in her life. She couldn't wait to tell Jack. She had been ignoring him the past few days and knew it was driving him crazy. But she couldn't help it, she was in over her head and hadn't known what to do. But that had just all changed. She would call him as soon as they finished dessert.

That same Friday night, a few miles away, Jack was pacing around his warehouse flat, brooding over his suddenly tumultuous love life. Gerry still steadfastly ignored his calls and texts. Even if she was dumping him, you would think she would at least have the decency to give him the courtesy of an explanation, in person. He deserved that much, didn't he? He didn't need this crap weighing on his mind while preparing for the biggest game of the year. The thought of barging into her office and throwing out a "What the fuck?" had crossed his mind, but that would be even more juvenile than her ignoring him.

Initially, he had reacted by contemplating another Hate List. His heart wasn't into it, though, because he realized he would have to put Gerry Wainscott at the top of such a list right now and couldn't handle that. Then he thought about flipping the process, coming up with a Love List. The problem was the same; she would top that list, too. There was no getting away from it…or her.

Cheese had come over to try cheer him up and calm him down at the same time. But he couldn't ease Jack's fear of the certainty of an impending heartbreak. Jack felt helplessly tied to the tracks with a speeding freight train bearing down on him. Getting any rest, relaxation, or respite was impossible, even for a second, as his mind was set on default. Default was Gerry Wainscott.

"Sit down and chill already, you fucking *mortadella*," Cheese said. "You're making me all jumpy and nervous with the pacing, already."

Jack ignored his friend and paced through the living room throwing an old baseball into the ancient mitt he had worn way back in Pony league when he was thirteen. Whenever he was extremely agitated, out of the closet came the mitt and ball. Smack! Having a catch, even if only with one's self, is effectively therapeutic and Jack found it the perfect distraction.

The Lou Brock autographed baseball his father had given him on his twelfth birthday hit the cracked leather of the old mitt that fit his hand quite snugly. Smack! The sting felt good and served to divert the pain in his heart.

"You know," Jack said, "I figured it wouldn't last. I mean, it was just too good to be true. But I thought it would end with a bang, not a whimper. I pictured some big blowout where she would just walk after seeing what an asshole I really am. But I never even got to be that asshole."

"Sure you did. Because you're being that asshole *right now*," Cheese said. "You don't even know what is going on with her."

"Dude, she hasn't talked to me or returned my calls or responded to my texts since I left her place Tuesday morning. It's Friday-fucking-night. Explain that."

"Maybe she's been busy," Cheese said.

"Yeah, or maybe she decided a washed-up, old-ass football player at the end of his rope wasn't her cup of tea. She had her dirty fun on the wrong side of the tracks, but now it's time to move on and step up. My mind keeps hashing over everything I've ever said to her, trying to figure out where the hell I went wrong. I ain't never had it like this, man. Back when I divorced Linda, I didn't even think about her for one second. I was just glad as hell to get that shit over with."

"That was different, man. She was cheating on you – plus, it was just a matter of time with her, anyway. But yeah, man, I don't get it either. You belong with her and she belongs with you, it's obvious. I've seen it, the way she looks at you. I want my future *goomah* to look at me that same way."

Smack! Jack pounded the ball into the mitt with extra force. "Are you trying to fuckin' help here, or are you just trying to make me *more* depressed?"

"I'm just saying, she's gotta be going through something, because the girl is obviously in love with you. Maybe the *Don* caught wind and shut it down," Cheese said.

"I thought of that, but Wainscott hasn't been in town all week. Plus, I don't think he would do that to her. He loves her too much."

"More than the team?"

"Way. Way fucking more."

Smack! Jack pounded the ball into the mitt one more time before his cell phone rang. He and Cheese froze, both eyeballing the phone lying on the table.

"You gonna answer it, dumb shit?"

Jack finally picked up the phone. It was Gerry Wainscott. He set it back down on the table and it stopped ringing.

"Was it her?"

"Yep"

"Are you out of your fucking mind? You better call her back right now!" Cheese said. He was as mad as Jack had ever seen him.

Jack mumbled something unintelligible and picked up the ball and mitt; he started pacing again, continuing his game of catch with himself. However, his throws had lost most of their sting.

"I'm out of here," Cheese said. He stopped at the door and turned to face Jack. "If you don't call her back right now you are the dumbest asshole I have ever met. You are supposed to be this big bad-ass, but you're such a pussy you won't even fight for the woman you love."

With that Cheese stormed out, not bothering to wait for a response. He slammed the door behind him for effect.

Jack had almost given up as he sat on the couch cradling his cell phone. He knew he was the one being a total dick now, but he didn't care. It didn't matter what her excuse was going to be, not calling him back and ignoring his texts for the past three days was inexcusable.

*What, does she think I'm just some goddamn flunky?*

It had been almost an hour since she had called and she hadn't called back. He wasn't sure if he was ready to answer if she did.

Suddenly, his phone vibrated, startling him so much he almost dropped the damn thing. The text was from Cheese.

**Cheese: Did u call her yet?**

He punched in a quick, one-word reply.

**Jack: Nope.**

**Cheese: Ur a douche. Now ur as bad as her. Call her ya DF.**

Jack didn't have to be a genius to know "DF" wasn't shorthand for "dear friend." He hit Cheese back.

**Jack: I can't do it just yet. She need 2 know how it feel 2.**

**Cheese: Real mature. Im gonna call her and tell her to come over to ur place.**

Jack knew Cheese was bluffing, but then again his friend was pretty pissed when he left. He may actually do it.

**Jack: U betta not. Im in no mood to c her.**

**Cheese: Just call her n B a man.**

**Jack: I will think about it. Don't call her. Please.**

Jack's resolve was beginning to crumble. Then his phone beeped at the same time the buzzer at his door rang. He quickly checked the phone.

**Cheese: 2 late.**

*You son of a bitch!*

Jack's heart was racing; he didn't know whether to kill Cheese or send him flowers. He was still mad and hurt and wanted to sulk for a while longer before getting over it, but that wasn't going to happen now. She was there, right outside his door. He knew it. Jack got up and walked over to the door and looked through the peephole.

Sure enough, there she was, pretty as a picture. He melted at the sight of her, even though his view was distorted by the peephole. He opened the door and Gerry rushed at him. She jumped up into the air and he intuitively caught her and they began to frantically kiss.

Gerry finally left Jack's warehouse flat at six o'clock the following morning. After she arrived, he carried her straight away to the bedroom and the make-up sex was the most intense they'd had. They talked for a long time afterwards.

She told him about her horrible conversation with Donald and Jack got up out of the bed, threatening to drive to Fegel's house and beat the dog piss out of him before she calmed him down. He solemnly vowed he was going to take that bastard out soon, one way or another.

Gerry apologized profusely for torturing him. That's what it was for him, plain and simple. She said she honestly didn't know he would be that hurt but admitted she should have. She swore she would never shut him out like that again. She told him what her father had said. Jack laughed until he had tears in his eyes when Gerry said he had guessed it was him.

*He's still one sharp sumbitch, no doubt.*

When she told him her father had suggested they keep on doing what they had been doing because Jack was having a great year it led to another love-making session. This one was much more tender and slow than the first go around.

Finally, Jack bared his heart and soul. He said it to her, out loud, for the first time.

"I love you, Gerry. I love you more than anything on this earth."

"I love you too, Jack," she said through tears.

That had led to round three. It was nearly three o'clock in the morning before they finally fell asleep, tightly intertwined. They mutually and emphatically agreed with Gerald Wainscott for the need to stay under the radar until after the season. Even though the clandestine nature of their relationship prevailed, they both felt a tremendous weight had been lifted from them, given Gerald's blessing. It almost made Jack wish the Blizzard wasn't heading to the playoffs. Almost, but not quite.

Jack woke up two hours after Gerry had left and he had never felt better. The first thing he did was get online and order a flower arrangement to be delivered to one Joseppi Barcheezzi. Then he began to contemplate his Love List he had decided to construct for the game. He had the perfect candidate for the top spot.

# Chapter Thirty-Eight

The Buffalo Blizzard's locker room in the bowels of the Wigwam was a luxurious combination of the best money could buy and what a football mind could conceive. The room itself was built in the shape of a football with spacious, individual lockers around the perimeter made from the finest cedar. There were thirty-seven-inch flat-screen monitors above each locker and a control panel built into the wall with a tethered remote so each player had control of his own media center. The monitors were hooked up to Wi-Fi, cable-TV, and the team's video library so they could – and did – watch film right at their lockers. There were no external speakers, though; if you wanted volume you had to plug in a set of headphones.

There was also a docking station for the tablets that were distributed to each player. The paper playbook had become obsolete. The new version programmed into the system not only had the X's and the O's, but also interfaced a video clip of each play accompanied by a voice-over from each position coach describing in detail what was expected of each respective position on every single play. Pro football had gone high-tech.

Brand new plays, of which there was no film, featured CGI animated video that was hauntingly real. Jack had suggested they just let them play the games and put that on TV. It would sure be easier on the body.

Scouting reports, game plans, and video of the upcoming opponent were downloadable to each tablet, making them invaluable. There was a five-thousand-dollar fine for losing one. The only player to ever get hit with that fine was Bo-Bo Karpinski. He had accidentally sat on his, and, rather than face the embarrassment of admitting he had squashed the thing, he claimed it was lost and paid the fine. Everyone found out he sat on it anyway and there was still the occasional crack about Bo-Bo shitting out off-brand tablets.

Regardless, it was amid this opulence the Blizzard players were getting ready to play the hated South Florida Riptide. Many of the TV's in the locker room tuned in to the early game featuring an inter-conference battle between the St. Louis Nighthawks and the Pittsburgh Brawlers. The Nighthawks' offense was shredding the Brawlers' Dime defense just like they had the Blizzard's. Jack shook his head. People never learned.

Normally, he would take such an example of stubborn idiocy and use it to fuel his own, thus getting his mind right for the game, but Jack was as relaxed as he had ever been before a game. He still had an ice ball melting away in his stomach, but it was only the size of a peach and it made him feel warm inside rather than giving him the usual chills. Maybe it was a lava ball, rather than an ice ball. Hell, he didn't know, neither did he care. He did know he liked it…a lot.

His focus for playing this game was all the things he loved; it was an utterly new experience for him. The Love List had replaced the Hate List. Thinking about all the good times he'd had while growing up had greatly boosted his spirits. It helped that his Uncle Jack had flown in for the game with Jack's cousins, Ed and James. The twins were twenty-five years old and thought they knew a thing or two regarding how to party. Jack was more than happy to extend their education. They were quite excited about the post-game shindig Ben Brady was hosting at the Longhouse.

Jack had sat around the night before the game reminiscing with his uncle and cousins about Big Ed and Erma Driftwood. It felt so good to hear and tell the old stories again. He had also visited Coach Faber, home from the hospital and chomping at the bit to get back to work. Lester was recovering nicely, and if things continued at the current pace he could be back in the saddle in as soon as two weeks – if he could convince Joanne. The transition elevating Archie Beatle to defensive coordinator had gone surprisingly smooth thus far. However, they were going to be severely tested by the South Florida offense. Scoop Brackett was no joke.

First and foremost on Jack's Love List had, of course, been Gerry Wainscott. He was embarrassingly giddy over their initial exchange of "I love yous." This one was for her and he could hardly wipe the smile off his face. He wasn't sure how well this love shit was going to mix with some old-fashioned, ass-kicking football, but he was excited to find out.

As kickoff got closer the Blizzard locker room grew unusually quiet. There were still occasional outbursts of encouragements laced with the usual creative string of profanities. And, as always, Leroy Clarkson made his rounds pounding everyone's hands with his trademark intensity. But as time ticked down toward kickoff, the locker room was noticeably more sedate than usual. Danny Steely gave the usual ten- and then five-minute warnings before it was time to go.

Finally, he hollered out, "Two minutes to kick-ass time!"

This was the signal to bring it up. Coach Ivy came out of the separate coach's locker room as everybody gathered together toward the middle of the room. Each man took hold of the man next to them and took a knee to recite the Lord's Prayer as one. Then, per usual, Coach Ivy had few, brief words to the wise.

"Men, this is a monumental game and an enormous task. But the truth is, they all count as only one in the standings. Just one. So our plan is to go out there and win just one, this one, as one. One game, one play at a time. We play together as one. Can we do that?"

The team roared in affirmation.

"However," Coach Ivy reeled them back in. "Before we go out there, there is one of our own who would like say a few things."

On cue, Lester Faber sauntered out of the coach's locker room chomping on a swizzle stick in place of his trademark cigar. He was greeted with a rousing ovation from the team.

*That old son of a gun! Just last night he said he wasn't coming to the game, doctors wouldn't let him. You can't trust anybody!*

Coach Faber was looking much better and stronger than he had since most of the guys had seen him. They loved him dearly and his presence gave them an immediate emotional bump. Hearing from him would have an even greater effect.

"Men, I believe it is time to play some football," Coach Faber hollered with great enthusiasm. "Now, we are playing the South Florida Riptide, and you have got to hate those communist cocksuckers! So let's get out there and kick ass and let them worry about taking names!"

The dam of pent up emotion burst as the team thundered its approval and stormed out the locker room doors. They were sky-high once again. Coach Faber headed up to the Owner's box, where he would attempt to calmly watch the game with Mr. Wainscott. Jack would have loved to witness that scene as Lester, who rarely showed emotion, was already excited as a two-peckered Billy goat in a rut.

Personally, Coach Ivy was overcome with emotion as he gave one of his favorite people on the planet, Lester Faber, a big hug before following the team out the doors. It appeared Coach Ivy was coaching this game out of a deep and abiding love as well. He had, once again, magically reached into his endless bag of motivational tricks to touch the hearts and minds of his men. Every so often, he reached in deep enough to touch his own.

Despite all of the love in the air, the game could not have started any worse for the Buffalo Blizzard. They fumbled the opening kickoff and South Florida recovered it and swiftly scored a touchdown on a Scoop Brackett one-yard plunge to go up 7-0. The Buffalo offense followed suit, going three-and-out, and following a short punt the Riptide took possession with great field position at the Buffalo 49. The Blizzard defense appeared to have stopped the Riptide on a third-down Scoop Brackett run, except a terrible spot by an official gave Miami a 1st and 10 at the Buffalo 39.

Coach Ivy had pulled the red challenge flag from his sock and considered giving it a toss. But it still would have only been fourth down if he'd have won it and South Florida could go for it. Not to mention, the spotting of the ball in the middle of the line was often too ambiguous to get a call overturned. Deciding to save the challenge for a better opportunity, Coach Ivy stuffed the flag back into his sock.

Inspired by their anger over the disputed spot, the Blizzard defense rose up and stopped the Riptide from converting another first down. South Florida ran the ball with Scoop Brackett on the subsequent three plays and the big back was held to a cumulative total of six yards. Driftwood and Stark had combined to stop Scoop for no gain on the third-down try. Those two were all over the field, getting in on nearly every tackle. South Florida had to settle for a field goal, which took their lead to 10-0 midway through the first quarter.

Finally, the Buffalo offense got in tune on the next drive. Ben Brady hooked up with his tight end, Delvin Simpson, for a 25-yard gainer on the first play from scrimmage. Simpson bowled over a couple of defenders, revving up the crowd, who had been sitting on their hands reeling from the dismal start. From there the offensive line took over, paving the way for Earl Johnson to burst, untouched, into the South Florida secondary where he made a couple of would-be tacklers look downright foolish. The Pearl broke off a 42-yard touchdown run and the home team was on the scoreboard. Tenudo split the uprights for the extra point, cutting the Riptide lead to three.

South Florida got the ball back and managed a couple of first downs before having to punt it away. The Blizzard defense was playing exceptionally stout against the run. Driftwood and Stark were still flying around out there like a couple of wildlings. After almost every play, they got up off the pile laughing and whooping it up like a couple of kids. Stark had seen Driftwood play this well before, but in those cases his face was a dark, twisted mask of hatred and violence. Today was wholly different. Driftwood had never been happier or looser on a football field.

"What the hell has gotten into you today?" Stark asked.

Driftwood had skipped to the sideline after the Blizzard defense forced another punt. "Love List, broham-brotherman."

"Seriously? What the fuck happened to the Hate List? Can't you make up your mind?"

"I flipped it. I'm getting too old for all the hatred, man. Plus, love is a way more powerful and enduring emotion."

"That is pretty close to being gay."

"If by gay, you mean happy, then you, sir, are correct," Driftwood said.

"I think I liked the hater-Jack better."

"Too bad, my boy, because love is in the air." Driftwood took in an exaggeratedly deep breathe. "And I just sucked me up a whole new batch."

"Now that's for sure gay, no question about it. Get the hell away from me."

"I love you, man," Driftwood said and skipped away, leaving young Steven alone, where he could contemplate the new Jack Driftwood in peace and quiet.

"It will never last," Stark yelled. "You're too big of an asshole."

Stark was right about Driftwood, but he couldn't have been more wrong about the enduring power of love.

The Buffalo offense marched right down the field with Brady zipping passes around the ball yard, hitting receivers as if they were ducks on a pond. The South Florida defense just couldn't keep up and Buffalo scored another touchdown on the final play of the first quarter to take the lead, 14-10. This tally came via a 17-yard toss from Brady to AC. The quarter came to a close, and, in a surprisingly offensive battle, Buffalo had taken control.

On the Buffalo sideline, during the network TV timeout, the Blizzard's special teams coach, William Siglar, casually strolled over and stood behind Coach Ivy.

"I think it is time for Red Storm," he said as inconspicuously as possible and without moving his lips.

Coach Ivy grunted his assent without turning around or showing any reaction, whatsoever.

"Lay it down," he coughed into his hand and walked away as if the exchange never took place.

Both men were extremely coy about the call. They didn't want to arouse the suspicion of any South Florida spies in the stadium. The Riptide undoubtedly had their best lip-readers behind a pair of binoculars trained on the Buffalo sidelines looking for anything they could find.

Coach Sig huddled up with his kickoff team on the sideline, as usual, to address them and make the call.

"I don't want anyone to show any abnormal emotion or reaction right now," he said, and then paused to let it sink in, "but we are going with Red Storm. Keep a straight face and just go about your normal business. Do your job and I'm telling you, we *will* get this thing. Put a hand in here. KBO on three. One. Two. Three…"

"KBO!"

The Buffalo kickoff team broke the sideline huddle in unison and took the field in their normal fashion, lining up as if they were going to kick it deep, per usual. But instead of driving the kick deep, Tenudo swung his leg down hard on top of the ball, which bounced off the ground and popped up short and high into the air. Billy Brogan was the designated recovery man and he ran under the ball and gathered it in 12 yards down the field. There wasn't a Riptide player within five yards of Billy when he reeled it in and downed the ball. South Florida was totally duped by the Red Storm call that Buffalo had executed to perfection.

The Wigwam erupted into a frenzy as the Blizzard offense retook the field. Brady called an audible at the line as South Florida showed an all-out blitz. They were pissed off at being hoodwinked and were manifesting their anger in the form of an aggressive defensive scheme. Big mistake. The protection for Brady was perfect and he launched a bomb down the sideline that hit Shady Solomon in stride for another Buffalo touchdown. The Blizzard quickly had a double-digit lead, 21-10.

This one was not turning out to be the kind of game the Riptide wanted to be in. They were a ground and pound type of outfit, relying heavily on the running game and consistently good defense. Shootouts took them into deep water, out of their comfort zone of handing the football to Bracket to scoop up yards and time from the clock. Buffalo scored again before the end of the half and took a somewhat insurmountable 28-10 lead into their locker room at halftime where the love was flowing.

South Florida tried to stick with the running game early in the third quarter, but Driftwood and company weren't having it. They shut down Scoop Brackett, forcing the Riptide to throw the ball. This led to several interceptions, including a diving one-hander by Driftwood, his NAFA-best eighth pick of the year. It also led to another Blizzard touchdown, one of many that fine afternoon. When the smoke had cleared, Buffalo had taken a decisive 48-17 victory, won the Seaboard Division, and clinched the top seed in the Eastern Conference, giving them home-field advantage throughout the playoffs and possibly for the Mega Bowl.

The Buffalo fans stormed the field after the game to celebrate their first Seaboard Division Title in seventeen years. It was a peaceful celebration that lasted long into the evening. Initially, security made a feeble attempt at stopping the fans from jumping over the wall and the six feet down to the field, but the tide of revelers became overwhelming. Leroy Clarkson and Eric Sellars commandeered the team's medical cart and drove laps around the perimeter of the field, high-fiving fans the entire way around. Driftwood and Stark headed for the tunnel to escape the chaos. But they sure did appreciate the love from the Blizzard faithful. They all did.

"That was the most fun I've had playing football since I was a little shiner," Stark said.

"Me too," Driftwood replied. "I had almost forgotten what playing for the love of the game is all about."

Stark sniffed a couple of times and then sobbed. "I love you too, man."

"Fuck you, you little shit."

Driftwood took a wild swing but Stark had slipped out of his reach. He wasn't worried, though, he knew right were the rookie was headed. There was cold beer awaiting them in Danny Steeley's office enclave. Who knew, maybe Coach Ivy would stop in again for a celebratory pop. Jack sure hoped so.

# Chapter Thirty-Nine

"Get your ass in here and close the door," Mr. Fegel yelled as Colin appeared in the doorway to his office.

"What's up your ass?" Colin asked, with uncharacteristic bravado.

"A red-hot poker, and I'm about to jam it up yours."

Colin stopped and examined Donald Fegel, blinking his eyes behind the Coke-bottle-bottom thick lenses of his black-framed nerd glasses. Mr. Fegel's eyes were hangover red with bags under them so big they wouldn't fit into the overhead storage bin of a 747. By appearances, the poor bastard must not have had a good night's rest for at least a week.

Mr. Fegel was slumped in his chair with his face in his hands, rubbing his poor, red eyes.

"Jesus, Donald. Are you okay? Can I get you something?" Colin asked.

"Nah. I'll be all right, it's just been a very, very long week. I got into it with that bitch Gerry and now she went and blabbed to the old man. The dumb bitch told him all about Jack Driftwood. How do I know this? Because Mr. Gerald Wainscott himself told me to basically mind my own damn business and keep my mouth shut about it. I have been walking on egg-shells around him all weekend. It tends to wear one out after a while."

Colin didn't know what to say so he just stood there in front of the boss's desk, blinking behind his heavy spectacles. Privately, he was alarmed. It appeared to him the boss was cracking under the pressure of the whole thing.

*This is not a good sign. Sure as shitting.*

Mr. Fegel let out a big sigh and got back to business. "The reason I called you in here is I have yet to hear anything from or about Neil Dadoska regarding his little investigation. Have you received any kind of progress report on that?"

"No, I haven't heard from him, either," Colin said. "The last time we spoke he was trying to figure out who that Chaz character is. He seemed to think he was the guy behind everything and the rest of Driftwood's friends were a bunch of quote unquote 'goddamn spineless idiots.'"

Mr. Fegel grunted. "What about your situation? Has anything suspicious occurred? Anybody following you or anything?"

"Not that I am aware of. I finally have the house cleaned up, had to get a new refrigerator. That damn red paint would not come off."

"Just send me the bill for it all. The Blizzard will pick up the tab on this one."

"Thanks," Colin said.

He started to turn to leave, assuming and hoping the session was over.

"One more thing," Mr. Fegel said. "When are we supposed to get those drug test results from the league? I need something to cheer me up and a Jack Driftwood suspension would certainly do the trick."

"I'm not exactly sure, but it should be any day now."

"Don't you have a connection in the NAFA offices? Why don't you drop a dime on your little bird and see when that bomb is scheduled to drop. I'd like to stay ahead of that, anyways."

"I'll get right on that, Mr. Fegel. I'll go call him right now and let you know."

With that Colin escaped the boss's clutches and bolted from the office. He wasn't sure the timing was very good for those test results to come in. Mr. Fegel appeared to be a wreck. Plus, he was worried about Gerry Wainscott. Getting rid of Driftwood would certainly set her off. Their position had weakened considerably, especially since the boss could no longer hold her tryst with Jack Driftwood over her head.

Colin didn't like where things appeared to be heading. It appeared to be merely a matter of time before Mr. Fegel crashed and burned. It was time to kick the last of his ducks into a row and blow this little pop stand.

The two-track leading into the highly camouflaged residence of the man known simply as Chaz was not easy to spot, even for the likes of an eagle-eyed, Border Collie super-sleuth such as Vinny Cappolla. Chaz had told him the entrance was just past the curve in the road to the south between a pair of big, old oak trees. Vinny had cruised around the corner too fast and had propelled right past his turn-off. He wasn't sure he had missed it until coming to a bridge an extra mile or so down the road. Chaz had said if he hit a bridge, he'd gone too far. He spun the Crown Vic around, fishtailing in the loose gravel and almost lost control, but he pulled it together and headed back up the road, cussing Chaz under his breath the entire time.

Given a second chance, he easily spotted the big, barren oaks covered with a light dusting of snow and turned off onto the road between them. The small two-track was minimally rutted and frozen as it wended down through a small ditch and then up onto a sandy trail. In some spots the hard shale that covered most of Western New York was raw and exposed. Chaz had told Vinny to go about a quarter of a mile and then take a right at the fork in the road at the top of the first hill and head down into a hollow that appeared to be a dead end. Chaz had said he would bring him in from there.

Vinny kept to the right and saw no sign of tracks in the hard, flat, frozen earth. The hills nearby were lightly dusted with fresh snow cover, but none had stuck to the ground anywhere in this low spot. He came as far as he could into the small valley and stopped at the base of a large hill, which rose almost straight up, cliff-like, to a large bluff some eighty-feet above him overlooking Hemlock Lake.

There was something not quite right about the side of the hill. As Vinny contemplated what was wrong with the picture, to his utter amazement, the hillside began to rise and fold up into itself, unveiling a three-stall garage. It was the first of many delightful surprises awaiting the big man at Chaz's underground lair.

*It's just like the son-of-a-bitching bat cave. Ha-ha! I love it. Fucking Chaz is out of control.*

"Cappolla, get your fat-ass in here! Someone followed you!" Chaz yelled at him from inside the garage.

Vinny pulled the Vic into the garage and the door behind him closed, immediately. He got out of the car and sidled up to Chaz, who was standing in front of a dozen monitors built into the back wall.

On the main screen, he recognized a blue Chevy Blazer that had just turned off the main road and was slowly starting down the two-track.

"Hey, I saw those fucks on the 90. I thought they looked suspicious. They looked at me funny."

"Looking at *you* funny in no way leads to suspicion. It is a perfectly normal response. You know either of these bastards?" Chaz asked.

Chaz hit the zoom and pointed the camera directly at the Blazer using a joy stick on the control panel built into a desk in front of him. Vinny checked out the wall of monitors as a close up of the vehicle's occupants appeared on every one of them.

"The driver is a local gumshoe, a private dick named Bernie Radowski. I don't know the other piece of shit."

"Fuckers followed you here," Chaz said.

"Sorry, I never even thought of that but now that I do, I did get that odd feeling."

"Right, they looked at you funny. Aren't you supposed to be a goddamn detective? Nobody can slip anything past you, my friend. You need to start listening to your gut, Lord knows it should be loud enough."

"Fuck you," Vinny said without teeth.

"If we get made I'm gonna have to take them out. And I do mean all the way out."

"Shit, I can't be party to that!"

"You won't have to be, but you will have to speak no evil. If he comes over the hill and down into the hollow I have a little surprise for him. See this button right here? It'll send a steel rod right through the block of his engine and that Blazer will never run again. Then I will have to get my guns out and take them hostage. I don't see no other way, pards."

Vinny couldn't believe what was happening. How could he have been so damn stupid to let them fuckers get the drop on him? Regardless of what Chaz said, this blood would be on his hands. This shit was getting too crazy.

"Radowski is a bit of a pussy, he ain't that smart and sure as hell ain't no hero. He will probably just sniff around and call off the dogs."

"I hope so, I really don't have time to mess around with hostages. And it don't fit the plan. Timing's all messed up, it's way too soon."

Chaz snapped open the cover of another control panel and flipped on a switch arming a pair of mounted, remote controlled, semi-automatic machine guns. They both watched intently as the blue Blazer crept closer to their bunker. The Blazer finally came to a halt at the bottom of the hill. Chaz zoomed the camera in so they could see both men's faces clearly on the HD monitor. The thugs were obviously engaged in some sort of an argument. It looked as if Radowski wanted to turn tail and get the hell out of there, but the other man wanted to continue.

Finally, the other man got out of the car and made his way up a path cut into the side of the hill. After a minute or so the man turned and slid back down the hill to the Blazer and jumped in. He was quite animated as he pointed up the hill and then back toward the main road. They headed back out the way they had come in, this time with a serious sense of urgency.

"The guy must've seen where the two-track winds around down by the lake and then heads back out to the main road. He thinks you gave him the slip," Chaz said. "Whew! That was way too close."

"No shit," said Vinny. "I guess we got to take this motherfucker to DEFCON Four if they are following *me* around."

"You think? So what's the story on this Bernie Radowski?"

"Poor-fucking-Bernie. He was a Buffalo cop with a notorious bitch of a wife. About ten years ago he divorced the cunt and left the force to become a private investigator. He does a lot of Kodak moments, you know – shooting pictures of adulterous bastards with their pants down. He ain't no fucking heavy hitter, he's mostly just a surveillance guy."

"What a cocksucker. The other guy was a heavy hitter, though. Looked to me like he wanted to mix it up a little bit." Chaz rubbed his hands together and smiled.

"I ain't never seen the asshole before, but if you can get me a picture I can run him through the computers downtown and see if we can get a match. If the fucker's got a record I'll find out who he is," Vinny said. He had puffed himself back up talking shop.

"You may be a cop after all," Chaz said. "No doubt a shitty one, though. I record these cameras on digital and it's all linked into my computer. I'll print you off a mug shot of that turd before you leave."

The tension built on the earlier drama finally broke and both men relaxed, noticeably. Vinny finally looked around to appreciate the detail that had gone into Chaz's subterranean hideaway.

"This bunker is unbelievable, man!" Vinny said. "When the world ends, I plan on being right here with you. This is a fucking fortress with style."

Chaz swelled a little with pride. "Shit, you ain't seen nothing yet, big 'un. Come on, let me show you around."

Once inside, the place was pretty much a normal, albeit plush, three-bedroom, three-bathroom ranch-style home. There was a nice-sized mud-room and laundry-room off the three-stall garage that led to the kitchen, which took up the corner of a large, open living-space. The bedrooms were down a hallway across the room and beyond that was what Chaz referred to as the "lab."

The lab was a long, rectangular room that had just about anything a mad scientist could ever need. The back end of it was a fully working machine metal shop on one side and a wood shop on the other. The room also served as his library; all four walls were covered by built-in book shelves that were chock full of books Chaz had been collecting since childhood. The books were organized from A to Z by author. Chaz could, and did, spend countless hours in the place tinkering and reading. He made all of his own furniture and many interesting, if not useful, contraptions. Because the bunker was built into the eighty-foot-high hill, it was essentially underground. The place was naturally insulated and pretty much stayed at sixty-five degrees Fahrenheit year-round.

"When can I move in?" Vinny asked, only half kidding.

"Never," Chaz said. "For one, I couldn't afford to feed your ass, not to mention I got a reputation to uphold. I can't have any Johnny Law dick-weeds hanging around my place. What would all my friends think?"

"Yeah, God forbid you associate with anybody but criminals. Asshole."

"Easy, big fella. I believe, although I don't know for the life of me why, I am associating with you. But quit fucking around. I gotta show you something."

Chaz pulled on a pair of rubber gloves and removed the file of papers from the strong box he had found under Colin Meade's bed and carefully laid them out on a long work table at the back of his lab.

"This here shit is radioactive. These are the original documents from the cooked books in the Wigwam building project. This is enough to put the whole bunch of them away for the rest of their lives or longer – whichever comes first."

Vinny inspected the papers with growing excitement.

"Holy hell! No wonder they are following me and tried to kill Tree Spirit."

"Well, the funny thing is, I don't think anybody else knows about this except for Meade. If Dadoska knew this type of intel had gone missing, believe me, heads would have rolled by now, with or without Fegel's consent. I mean, look at what he did to Tree Spirit just because the guy was snooping around. They had over ninety million bucks stashed in off-shore bank accounts, which I made a grab for. Unfortunately, Meade must've already moved it. I'm betting the little prick is planning to leave the country, and soon. I'm a little surprised he hasn't bolted yet. Something is keeping him here and I haven't figure out what it is yet."

"Maybe he is waiting for a new passport," Vinny said. He pointed to Meade's passport among the pile of documents.

"Hah! He isn't going as Colin Meade, I promise you that. He'll get his hands on a fake passport and a whole new identity, if he hasn't already."

A wide-eyed expression formed on the big Buffalo Detective's face. "I'll tell you what he's waiting for! The end of the fucking season. There is no way he's gonna fly the coop before the playoffs, especially the Mega Bowl, if we make it. As soon as they lose and the season is over the little prick will hit the road." Vinny sounded absolutely positive.

"Your gut telling you that, big boy?"

"Fuck you. I'm just saying, the chance to finally win a title and then ride out into the sunset is serious medicine, especially around these parts. People just ain't rational when it comes to Blizzard Football."

"Well then, my question to you, Mr. Detective, is how do we make this evidence admissible in a court of law? There is no way in hell I'm gonna testify. Even if I did, what do I do, get on the stand and say I broke into Meade's house and stole it?"

"Ah, Jesus. I got to think about that," Vinny said. "I got a prosecutor buddy of mine I can talk to, see what the story is. You were right though, this shit is definitely radioactive. If you think that big, ugly, Indian-fucker Dadoska is coming after us now, just imagine how desperate that prick is gonna get when he finds out we have the goods on him."

Chaz had a gleam in his eyes as he rubbed his hands together with the excitement of a small child about to get some ice cream. "Maybe we ought to tell him, then. That sounds like one helluva good time."

"Geesh, you don't have to be so fucking happy and excited about it," Vinny said, but he was pretty goddam jolly himself.

Chaz smiled his biggest smile. "You trying to tell me it ain't just a little hard, Mr. Holmes?"

"As a rock, brother. As a rock!"

# Chapter Forty

It's funny how things can change in an instant, as quickly as the sun leaps from behind dark clouds to brighten a day. A man could go from laying low to being on top of the world with a snap of the fingers. A morning tempest could dry up and blow out to sea, bringing warmth and sunny skies, almost as if it had never happened in the first place.

Janice Cole, Donald's longtime personal assistant, rushed into his office with tears streaming down her face. Her mascara had run in symmetrical lines leaving tear-streaks down her cheeks, making the poor woman look like Alice Cooper. She appeared to be in shock and could barely speak. Donald showed real concern for the dear lady. Rising from his chair, he scurried around his desk and put an arm around her, attempting to calm her down. Finally, she settled down enough to share her bad news through anguished sobs.

She had just received a phone call from Children's Hospital. Gerald Wainscott III had been rushed to their Emergency Room after collapsing at the downtown Buffalo Men's Club earlier that morning. As Donald understood it, Wainscott had been taking his daily walk around the track when he suddenly buckled, falling to the ground.

Fortunately, a doctor-friend of his was also doing laps at the time and revived him. An ambulance arrived within minutes and hurried him down the street to nearby Children's Hospital. The old man was stable and breathing, but he had not yet regained consciousness. The Buffalo Blizzard owner was comatose.

Donald consoled Janice briefly as he escorted her to the door of his office. He told her everything would be okay, but he needed to get busy handling the situation. He reminded her they must all be strong for Gerald and she had to pull herself together. He also requested she keep the news to herself until they found out exactly what was going on. His mind was racing one hundred miles per hour.

*This is exactly the kind of break I needed! How could I be so lucky!*

He closed the door behind her and danced his way back to his desk. He could hardly believe his sudden good fortune. Wainscott falling ill was the answer to all of his problems. There was a health clause in the team's legal charter giving him, Donald Fegel, control of the franchise if Gerald Wainscott III were incapacitated and unable to carry on the business of running the team due to health issues, at least until the Board of Directors could get together and determine a course of action. It just so happened he was held in high regard by the board, having several powerful allies amongst the group.

In addition, all of the team's assets were to be put into a Trust which Donald would ultimately control. The final papers ceding the team to Gerry Wainscott had yet to be signed. Her indecision would be her undoing, because the emergency provisions kicked in immediately upon Wainscott's incapacitation. Gerry could sign anything she wanted now because it was moot. The status quo would prevail.

With the way things were set up, Donald would be calling the shots for at least the foreseeable future, and with the Board in his back pocket, likely well beyond. The beauty of it was there wasn't a damn thing Gerry Wainscott or anybody else could do about it.

Donald and Colin Meade had discussed this scenario on multiple occasions, with Meade hinting it might behoove them to help the old man along in a potential health issue. They referred to the scenario as "Gerald's Game" after the Stephen King novel. Donald, though intrigued by Meade's plot, had not acted on it; he didn't quite have the stomach for it. And now his patience had paid off; he was large and in charge, with clean hands, no less.

This was an epic day that would set the course for the Blizzard franchise for years to come, certainly from Donald Fegel's perspective. He had often fantasized about this day, even going so far as to make a list of the things he would immediately do if a tragedy of this nature were to befall Wainscott. Even without knowing the details, he figured the odds of Wainscott pulling through a major incident like this were slim and none, and slim had just left town. He found the list in a folder stashed in the top drawer of his cluttered desk, though he didn't have to take a gander at it to know what topped that list: send Jack Driftwood packing.

He grabbed the phone and dialed Colin Meade's office extension. Meade picked up on the first ring.

"Go get the cowboy right now and bring him to my office, his time is up. Send up that special security detail we talked about as well."

"Now?" Meade asked. "Did someone from the NAFA call you? They were supposed to call me."

"It's time to play Gerald's Game."

"No kidding, I'm on the way!"

Donald had trouble concealing his excitement. Granted, he didn't even know the details of Wainscott's prognosis, although the man was in a coma and Janice Cole practically had him buried already. But the man was ninety-three years old. Odds of a quick recovery, if any at all, were stacked against him.

None of that would matter as soon as the word Jack Driftwood had failed a drug test hit the spotlight. It would even make Donald appear to be some kind of prophet. This was going down and it was going down now. His finger had long been poised on this trigger. With Steven Stark healthy now and Billy Brogan in the fold for the long term, Driftwood was a burden he no longer needed. He had been beyond patient with the renegade linebacker. The cowboy's time had finally come.

Donald leaned back into his chair and did his "shooter" routine. Drawing his hands from his pockets, he fired off his six-guns into the air. He didn't even realize how large of a smile had come to rest on his face. His foolish reverie was broken by a knock at the door.

A deep voice called out, "Security."

"Yep, come on in boys," he responded, consciously masking his delight.

The three-man, hand-picked security team that had been instructed to answer to him and him alone filed through the door. If Donald hadn't known better he would have thought it was the Blizzard offensive line standing at attention in front of him.

*These boys are serious customers, but then, isn't that why I hired them in the first place?*

"I'm having a player come up here who is not going to like what I have to say," Donald said. "It could get ugly, perhaps physical. You gentlemen are here to make sure things don't get out of control. Might I also remind you that you are under oath to not repeat anything you hear or see occur in this room. Are we good with that?"

He looked at each man separately and each responded with a nod.

*Geez, these jackals look like they hope it does get physical. That's good! That's real good!*

Moments later there was another knock at the door and Jack Driftwood entered the room, followed closely by Colin Meade.

"Good morning, jackass," Fegel said with a big fake smile.

Jack just grunted and looked around at the serious faces of Fegel's security men who had casually moved into formation, loosely surrounding him.

"What the fuck is up with the steroid security, Feegs?" Jack asked.

He moved into the middle of the room, closer to Fegel and farther from his trained freaks. It appeared things were going to get a little nasty. He knew an ambush when he stumbled into one. Jack was looking for as much room as possible to maneuver. Fegel had perched himself on the corner of his desk, his chest puffed out like a peacock.

"They're just here to keep the peace," Fegel said. "But don't worry about them, you have much bigger problems."

"Do I now?"

Fegel was way too confident; something must've happened to turn the tables, but exactly what, Jack didn't know. He figured he was about to be enlightened.

"Yes, you do," Fegel shot back. "You see, mister, you are being terminated from the Blizzard. Seems your bad habits have finally caught up to you. I have been informed by the league that you have tested positive for steroids, cocaine, and marijuana. The official announcement will be coming either later today or tomorrow. I am gravely disappointed in you, son, I thought you would have known better."

"I ain't your fucking son and that's a bunch of bullshit and you know it. I'm as clean as a whistle."

"Not according to the NAFA, buddy. But that doesn't really matter anyway. I'm in charge now and that's the real reason you're history. The dirty piss test just makes things easier for me."

Jack's mind was reeling. He had figured this day may come, but not two weeks before the playoffs.

*Something is fucked up here. What'd he say, he's in charge?*

"I'm going to take this up with Mr. Wainscott," Jack said.

"Good luck with that." Fegel chuckled before continuing. "You can go cry to the old buzzard all you want, but I don't think he'll hear you. He went into a coma this morning and he's hooked up to a shit bag. I run this team now, and my first order of business is to see you pack your bags and hit the trail, cowboy."

Jack felt like he had been sucker-punched in the gut, like he might have to puke.

"What the hell are you talking about?"

"Early this morning Wainscott had a stroke or something. They rushed him to Children's Hospital. Kind of ironic, huh, that old bastard in a children's hospital?" Fegel started to laugh now.

"I'm calling Gerry, she is still co-owner," Jack said.

Fegel's laughter stopped abruptly. A cold, ugly anger congealed in his feral eyes.

"That's another reason you are all done, son. She was all mine 'til you turned on your biker charm, but that shit won't play anymore. You see, she neglected to sign the papers giving her control of the team. With the old man out of the picture, you can bet she's going to be real nice to me now. *Real nice.* Eventually she'll come around and sign everything over to me. So, no matter how you look at it, this is my team now and you are no longer a part of it."

Jack was cut deeply by the news of Gerald Wainscott being in the hospital. It was no bluff. He sensed Fegel was telling the truth, at least about that. But to hear him make a mockery of it and then say those things about Gerry was too much. And what was this drug test bullshit? The only way he could have tested positive is if somebody had set him up or rigged the test. It was pretty obvious who that somebody was: the cocksucker was sitting right there in front of him.

He was trapped, backed into a corner. The thought dropped on him like a bomb. It was a seminal moment reduced to the most basic of human instincts – fight or flight was the issue. Jack Driftwood had never been one to run from a fight, and he wasn't about to start, even with the odds stacked so heavily against him.

*What the hell, I may lose but it ain't gonna be a shutout.*

He took two quick steps toward Fegel, loading his weight behind his hips, putting all the force he could muster into a vicious right cross. The magnitude of the blow knocked Fegel unconscious before he hit the floor behind the desk. A spray of blood splattered onto the wall as Fegel's nose exploded upon impact from Jack's balled-up fist of fury. Jack dove over the desk after Fegel and landed squarely on his limp form with a forearm to the ribs that had to break bone. He managed to land a couple of good shots upside Fegel's head before the beefy security boys could react. The last thing he remembered before fading to black was surprise at the malicious kick to his own ribs from none other than Colin Meade, who had joined the fray to extract his own personal pound of flesh.

Jack would have laughed if his lights hadn't gone out.

It took a few minutes before Donald Fegel regained consciousness. The first thing he saw was the four-eyed face of Colin Meade bent over him with a cold, wet handkerchief pinching his nose in a feeble attempt to stem the flow of blood.

"Get the fuck off of me!"

Donald's head was ringing and the pain in his nose was searing. He managed to sit up and survey the situation. Jack Driftwood was prone on the floor, face down, shackled and completely motionless.

"You didn't kill him, did you?" he asked. The memory of their brief fight was coming back to his mind.

"No, no, no," Meade said. "They hit him with a syringe of something. He will be out for a good while."

The security team was still there, standing by, awaiting further instructions.

"How long was I out?"

"Just a few minutes, sir," Rodney Pustay, one of the security guards, answered. "We knocked Drifty out, sir, cuffed him up just in case he regains consciousness. But I injected him with a good dose of sodium pentothal so he will be residing in dreamland for a couple of hours. What do you want us to do with the big galoot?"

"You assholes were supposed to be here to protect me," Fegel said.

His charge was left to hang in the air, unanswered by Pustay and the others. They were too busy trying not to laugh.

Donald was still shaking some cobwebs out of his brain and took another minute to sort it all out. He knew he needed to see a doctor to set his broken nose, and he knew he had better get his ass over to the hospital before too long to see how Mr. Wainscott was doing. He could kill two birds with one stone there. He also needed to put a viable story together and institute a plan.

"Alright," he said, "here's what's going to happen. I will forcibly admit Driftwood to Brylin Mental Hospital – he obviously went crazy and attacked me. The guy is a danger to himself, as well as everybody else. We have put players in there before on rehab stints. I will make a call and get it all set up. All you guys will have to do is bring him over there and drop him off."

Donald paused as another thought hit him. "Is there any way one of you can inject him with a highball of steroids, cocaine, and marijuana? Can we get that done?"

"Um, yeah. Sure, I guess, you're the boss," Pustay said. "I mean, if that's what you really want to do."

"Excellent, yes. He'll be so fucked up he won't even know what hit him."

Donald snorted, trying to suppress his laughter. The resulting pain from the air forcing its way through his mangled nasal passage nearly brought him to his knees.

Meade finally spoke up again. "Holy shit, did you see me kick his ass?"

"No, *unfortunately,* I was unconscious," Donald said. "I'm glad it was good for you, Colin, but can we get this train moving? You and I are heading to Children's Hospital to see the old man and get my nose back into joint. Nobody is to breathe a word about any of this to anybody until you hear from me. I will prepare a statement later today. Are we good?"

They all nodded in assent. The security boys picked up Driftwood and waited at the door as Donald went out to clear their path. To his good fortune, the fifth-floor lobby area and hallways were empty. He figured Janice Cole was off somewhere bawling her eyes out over the old man and did not question his luck. The security team dragged Driftwood to the stairwell and disappeared behind the door.

After stopping in the men's room to clean up as best as he could, Donald grabbed Meade and they set out for Children's Hospital. Despite his throbbing face, he was on top of the world. Not only was his personal albatross out of the picture, but Donald was running the ship. A ship whose course was locked onto the Mega Bowl.

He almost didn't mind his nose was spread all over his face. In fact, he was proud of his new red badge of courage. He had taken one for the team because he was man enough to do so. It also made him a walking exhibit of irrefutable evidence in the case against the maniacal Jack Driftwood. There should be little to no doubt he had done the right thing in admitting Driftwood to Brylin Mental Hospital. Obviously, the guy belonged locked up somewhere.

"Let's go, Mr. Meade. Chop! Chop! There's a new sheriff in town, and his name is Donald Fegel!"

For his part, Colin Meade felt like he had achieved a personal break through. He hadn't realized the depth of his own courage, jumping into the melee like that to defend the boss who lay unconscious on the office floor.

And to think, not too long ago, he had been plotting his escape from an inevitable trap, set to snare him and everyone else involved in the Wigwam scam. But now? Now, everything had flipped upside down!

It was true, Driftwood and his gang of losers had stolen his strongbox containing the cooked books, but with Mr. Fegel in charge and his own transformation into a man of courage, they could handle that little problem. They could handle anything!

The way he had gone after Driftwood not only surprised him but had awakened something deep inside of him. He had crossed a threshold in his mind. Thirty-nine years of pent up rage and anger at the way the world had treated him had manifested into one big kick into the ribs of Jack-fucking-Driftwood. Lord, did it feel good! So good, in fact, he wanted more. This was merely the beginning. If the boss was the new sheriff in town, then he had himself one bad-ass deputy, and his name is Colin Meade.

# Chapter Forty-One

It was one of those rare, unforgettable moments in life that Gerry Wainscott would always remember. She would be able to recall exactly where she was and what she was doing when she heard the news. She was in the ladies' room on the fifth floor of the Wigwam chatting with Cindy Chuckles peering into the mirror checking her make-up.

"So, how is Mr. Wonderful these days?" Cindy asked.

"Huh?"

"You know exactly what I mean. You have been walking around on cloud nine since Saturday."

Gerry couldn't help but smile. She trusted Cindy who, although also an employee, had become a dear friend. She was bursting to share her good news with somebody and Cindy fit the bill perfectly.

"Well, Mr. Wonderful is back in my greedy little clutches, but is it that obvious?"

"Probably just to me, since I see you every day. But come on, you know you are dying to tell somebody all about it," Cindy said. "You can trust me, Gerry. I won't say a word, if that's how you want it."

Gerry laughed at Cindy's sincerity and was ready to spill the beans and tell her the entire story, but before she could speak the door burst open and a Janice Cole rushed into the room crying. Janice shrieked something unintelligible and fell forward, collapsing into Gerry's arms.

"Janice! What's wrong? Are you okay?"

Janice forcefully grabbed Gerry's forearm with both hands. "You have to get to Children's Hospital."

"What is it, Janice? What happened?"

"It's your father, Gerald! He collapsed this morning and they took him there."

"What?" Gerry's mind was racing and her heart jumped into her throat. She had spoken with him the previous night and he was on cloud nine after their big victory and had never sounded better. "Janice, what is going on?"

"I just got a phone call from the hospital and they said he collapsed at the Men's Club while taking his morning walk. They rushed him to Children's Hospital." Janice started to sob again.

"Is he alive?"

"Yes, they said he was unconscious but breathing."

"Thank God!" Gerry said. "My dad is a fighter, he'll pull through this."

She was trying to reassure herself as much as Janice Cole. She pulled Janice close into a comforting hug. She found herself looking over the woman's shoulder at Cindy, who hadn't said a word and was obviously in shock.

"Cindy, can you stay here with Janice and help her hold things together here? I'm going over there right now. Are you going to be okay, Janice?"

"We'll be fine," Cindy said. "You go. But please call us with an update as soon as you can."

"I will," Gerry said. "I promise."

There was a tube stuffed down Gerald Wainscott III's throat through which his breathing was being regulated by a ventilator. Another tube, this one much smaller, snaked through his nasal passage down into his stomach to provide nutrition. There was an IV port sunk into the loose flesh of his upper arm that steadily dripped fluids and medications into his failing body. Several small patches were adhered to his chest and connected with electrical leads which led to a cardiac monitor tracking every beat of his heart. A catheter was inserted into his penis, draining into a collection bag that hung on the integrated hospital bed. The bed itself was set at a slightly upward angle to keep fluid from building up in his lungs. Several other monitors were set up in the private hospital room recording nearly every bodily function Gerald Wainscott III had left.

The man's only child had told herself she wouldn't cry no matter how dire the situation appeared, but upon entering her father's private room in the intensive care unit of Children's Hospital she broke down. Thinking about staying strong was one thing, however, seeing your father unconscious in a hospital bed with wires and tubes connected to him was quite another. The sight tore her heart out and she couldn't help herself. She wept.

With those tears streaming down her face, she held his hand and looked upon her dear, unconscious father. She spoke to him, convinced that somewhere deep down, at some level of consciousness, he could hear her. She expressed her love and encouraged her father to keep on fighting. She thanked him for everything he had ever done for her through a trickle of tears that wouldn't cease. She told him she wanted to own the Blizzard, but she wanted to do it with *him*. Finally, she begged him to wake up and to come back to her, they were just getting started again.

Gerry was still in the dark waiting to hear from her father's team of doctors as to what the diagnosis and, more importantly, the prognosis was. That was always the worst of it – not knowing what was going on. Where were his doctors, anyway?

She decided she was going to find out for herself. She took her compact from her purse and quickly fixed her makeup. Her moment of mourning had passed. Her father would expect her to be strong, not only for him, but for everybody in the organization. This was going to be her team sooner or later. Of that she was sure. It was time to act like it.

She realized she loved the Buffalo Blizzard and planned on signing the papers to take over for her father as the team's owner even before this incident. She just hoped her father would recover so she could share her decision and the team with him. It was essential to be strong and remain positive. She would not dishonor her father or herself by falling to pieces, no matter how difficult or dark the hour. Gerry gave her father a quick peck on the cheek and left the room. There had to be somebody around who could give her some answers and she was going to find them.

The plastic splint and shiny, white medical tape across Donald Allen Fegel Jr.'s nose only partially obscured what were quickly becoming two black eyes. We're talking a couple of world class shiners. It wouldn't be long and he would resemble a full-blown raccoon. He looked like he had finished a distant second in a face-pounding competition sitting in a chair in the hospital's Intensive Care waiting room.

"My goodness, what the hell happened to you, Fegel?"

Donald looked up, shocked to see Gerry Wainscott staring at him.

*Jesus, where in the hell did she come from?*

He shouldn't have been too surprised, although he hadn't known if Gerry was even aware of her father's condition yet. Word always traveled fast through the Wigwam.

"We have to talk," he said.

His beady eyes scanned the semi-crowded room. He had noticed a patient consulting room just down the hall when he and Meade had been escorted to the waiting area after getting his nose reset.

"Come with me."

He tried to take Gerry by the elbow, but she hastily recoiled from him as if a broken nose and two black eyes were contagious.

*What is her problem?*

Donald put up his hands, gesturing surrender. He got the message and moved ahead of her, opening the door and holding it for her.

"Please," he said, "there is a private room down the hall."

They walked the short distance down the hall in a silence lasting until they were seated on opposite sides of a small table in the consult room.

"How is Mr. Wainscott?"

"He's stable, according to his nurse, stable but unconscious," she answered flatly. "I have yet to hear from his doctors."

"I see, I'm very sorry, Gerry. He's a tough man. I'm sure he will be okay."

"Thank you, but what in God's name happened to you?"

Donald paused for a moment. He knew he had to play this out properly without tipping his hand.

"You are not going to like what I have to tell you…Jack Driftwood did this to me about an hour ago."

"Very funny. This is no time for stupid jokes."

"I'm not being funny," he said. "Let me explain. I got a call from the league office early this morning telling me Jack had failed a recent drug test. They said he tested positive for steroids, cocaine and—"

"Yeah, right, you are such an asshole!" She pushed herself back from the table and was ready to go for the door.

"Goddammit, Gerry! Sit down!"

Slowly she slid back into her seat.

"Thank you," he said and launched into his story. "Okay, here's what happened, I called Jack up to my office and told him of the drug test allegations. I told him I would keep it quiet and out of the news, but under the circumstances we were going to release him, effective immediately. He totally flipped out and attacked me. He sucker punched me – busted my nose."

She sat quietly trying to digest the information. Donald waited patiently, watching the emotion on her visage despite her attempts to conceal them. Sometimes women are so easy to read.

"So, then what happened?" she asked evenly. "Where is Jack now?"

"He totally lost it. He went totally off the rails, *exactly* like I had told you he would a long time ago."

"Where the fuck is he, Fegel?" she demanded.

"My security team subdued and tranquillized him and then I had him admitted him to the full security unit at Brylin Mental Hospital. It took all three of my guys to get him under control. He is a danger to himself right now – let alone the general public. He left me with no alternative. He is under sedation and under observation for the next seventy-two hours – doctor's orders. Then, once they do a full e-val, they will contact me."

Donald could see she was shaking with anger.

"Have you lost your fucking mind?"

"He left me no choice. The league's drug tests don't lie, Gerry. There is protocol, all I did was follow it."

"You locked up Jack Driftwood in a mental hospital." It was a statement, not a question.

"Yes, and he isn't getting out anytime soon. Look at what he did to me," Donald said, standing and motioning to his face.

"If you ask me that would only *prove* his sanity," she said. "You better be real careful about what you do, mister. I'll have your ass out the door before you know what hit you."

Donald just smiled. *Now I got you, little miss princess.*

"Actually, it's your ass that may be out the door. You see, you have yet to sign the papers taking over ownership, and according to the bylaws of the team's charter, everything goes immediately into a Trust if your father becomes incapacitated. Guess who controls that Trust?"

The big picture wound up and hit Gerry upside the head. She sank further into her seat. Donald was loving every second of it.

"You're a despicable bastard! If you had anything to do with my father's condition I will kill you myself!"

"What? No way! That's insane. I love that man and would never do anything to hurt him."

"I wouldn't put anything past a scumbag like you." She got up from the table and pointed a finger right at his face. "We will see about this, you just started a war you can't win. You're going down, asshole! You will never get away with this, that much I promise you!"

With that final salvo Gerry stormed out of the room. She was shaking and began to cry, this time out of anger. She quickly ducked into the ladies' room to compose herself and figure out what her next move should be. What she really needed was to be wrapped up in Jack's arms, but apparently Donald had them wrapped up in a strait jacket.

*And what is going on with Dad? Where are his damn doctors?*

She quickly brought up Chaz's number on her cell phone. If ever there was a time and place for his particular skills, this would be it. The gloves had come off.

Outside, snow had begun to fall. Gerry had been so preoccupied dealing with the storm of recent events she was oblivious to the storm brewing outside and heading their way.

## Chapter Forty-Two

Robert "Tree Spirit" Hansen was on the verge of drifting into a light slumber as he relaxed on the wicker sofa set on the front porch of Chaz's bungalow overlooking the Gulf of Mexico. The combination of the soft pounding of the light surf and the cool breeze out of the east had mesmerized him.

Tree Spirit was in this deep trance-like state when something triggered an alarm in his head. Immediately his senses went to full alert. The hair on the nape of his neck stood up; he wasn't sure exactly what had initiated his sudden heightened state of awareness, but he had learned long ago to trust such instincts. All was *not* right with the universe. In fact, something was terribly wrong; immediate danger lurked on the horizon.

Tree Spirit quickly and quietly slithered off the sofa into the house and directly to the bedroom he was occupying during their stay. He dug the nine-millimeter handgun from its hiding place in the bureau and moved silently back through the house. He set up watch outside on the same sofa on which he'd previously been sitting. His senses were hyper-tuned to every sound, sight, and smell in the immediate proximity. He was very glad Jack and Ms. Gerry were out for a walk and not present at the moment, although he expected them to return any moment.

Tree Spirit was positive he was being watched and unpleasant events were in the offing. He knew better than to put off his mostly unfounded alarm as a product of paranoia or an over-active imagination. Past experience had proven he possessed an internal early-warning system, an extra sensory perception regarding impending doom. This was not a drill.

He scanned the horizon to the north, up the beach toward where Jack and Gerry had embarked on their evening walk over half an hour ago when he heard the slight crackle of ground-up seashells under the foot of what he mentally calculated to be a two-hundred-pound man. The sound confirmed his suspicions and served as his cue.

He threw a leg over the couch and flipped behind it just as a masked and armed bandito appeared from the same side of the house where the noise had originated. A gunshot rang out as Tree Spirit disappeared behind the wicker sofa. He felt a sting high up on his left arm just below his shoulder. He had either just been shot or he had been bitten by some tropical pest. He returned fire from behind the sofa, blasting off a couple of rounds from his semi-automatic pistol in the general direction of where the attack had originated. He wasn't necessarily aiming at or trying to hit anybody, he was hoping his return fire might shoo them away.

Two more shots rang out, this time from the opposite side of the veranda. He distinctly heard two bullets whump into the furniture cushions in front of him. The sofa provided cover from sight but that's all – he was a sitting duck hiding behind that thing. He snapped off a couple more rounds to provide his own cover, dove to the ground, and proceeded to belly crawl into the house. Once inside the bungalow he quickly rose to his feet and ran through the house to the kitchen. He ducked behind the counter to take cover and have a look at his shoulder to assess the damage from the bullet.

Blood leaked from the torn flesh of his upper left arm onto the floor, forming a small puddle. Tree Spirit grabbed a towel off the counter and his first instinct was to wipe up the mess on the floor. But when he heard muffled voices and furniture being overturned on the deck, he snapped back to his senses and pressed the towel to the wound.

As noiselessly as possible, he hurried to the back door and opened and closed it with extreme care, so as not to make a sound. Sneaking out the back of the house might buy him the time to make it into the jungle south of the cottage and away from the driveway. Then he could double back and try to warn Jack and Gerry not to return to the villa.

The gunshot wound to the back of his upper arm was a bit of a bleeder but far from life-threatening. He was confident a proper cleaning and dressing of the wound would lead to a full recovery, barring any unforeseen infection. But there was no time for that now; he was worried to death Jack and Ms. Gerry would return at any moment, thus walking into an ambush completely unarmed and unaware of their present danger. If something happened to either one of them he would never forgive himself.

Tree Spirit ran to the edge of the jungle but stopped dead in his tracks when he heard Jack Driftwood yell out something about having the place surrounded.

*What the hell are you doing, Jack! Run! Get out of here!*

He paused to listen carefully and then pointed his pistol into the air and fired off a couple of rounds. The blasts may have taken some of the attention off Jack, but they put it squarely back on him; he couldn't just stand there like a stationary target at the edge of the jungle waiting to be shot again. He high-tailed it into the underbrush following an old, mostly overgrown path. He was halted again by the loud report of two more shots being fired. It sounded like they originated from farther up the driveway.

*Are they leaving?*

Standing, deep into the bush, he was holding his breath in the surreal silence when he heard a vehicle roar to life and spit gravel as it sped away, fleeing the scene. Jack Driftwood hollered out his name, calling him to come back to the bungalow, but he could not do that to his friends. His presence had already put their lives in grave danger. He had been foolish enough to think just because he was in Mexico Neil Dadoska could not find and reach him. It was a mistake he refused to repeat; he could no longer endanger the lives of his friends. Until Dadoska was locked up behind bars or incapacitated in some other fashion, he would go it alone, all on his own.

He trusted Jack Driftwood would gather up Ms. Gerry and get her out of there as fast as he could. He re-tied the towel tightly around his upper arm to stem the trickle of blood still lightly weeping from the wound. The Great Spirit would have to lead him now, he was in tune with that world.

His mantra, as he pushed further into the jungle, was a thankful one.

*Tree Spirit lives!!!*

The midday Mexican sun bore down on the Moon Over Cancun Cantina parking lot with the relentlessness of Scoop Brackett pounding the ball into the line in the fourth quarter. Juan Chavez had nearly finished the mundane task of sweeping the entire lot when he decided to take a break. He leaned on the broom to admire his work.

Physical labor was always good for the soul. He stared up into the sunny skies from under his straw hat as sweat poured off of his large, powerful body. It felt great to be alive and warm. He had been following the weather, like he always did, and noted a big winter storm brewing in the upper Midwest. He wondered how soon and how bad it would hit his friends in Buffalo. For some reason they always seemed to get the worst of it up there.

As the big man stretched his arms into the air in an attempt to loosen up his back muscles, he was distracted by a raspy whisper appearing to emanate from the undergrowth of jungle directly behind him at the back of the parking lot. He slowly turned his head and peered into the thicket of bushes and trees looking for the source. He saw nothing and was ready to dismiss the entire thing as paranoia brought on by a mild case of sunstroke when he heard it again.

He quickly grabbed the broom with both hands like it was some kind of ninja death stick. His instincts told him to run back into the Moon and grab one of his pistols, but his curiosity got the best of him. Slowly he edged closer to the jungle. He didn't feel as if he was in any immediate danger so he pressed on. The growth was relatively sparse for the first few yards and thickened up further in. He would need a machete if he was going to get very far.

Juan paused and took a look around before stepping into the thicket; his senses were on full alert. One could never be too careful in Mexico these days, even though this area was considered to be among the safest. Still, there were reports of kidnappings for ransom and random drug violence every day from all over the country. He still saw no sign of anything or anybody. He was ready to call it a fool's errand when a small, still voice spoke to him.

"Big Juan, it is I, Tree Spirit."

Juan wheeled around to face the source of the voice. He brandished the broom menacingly in front of him ready to fend off any potential attack. But there was no such attack forthcoming and the source of the voice was still a mystery.

"Please, put the broom down," whispered the voice, from behind him again. "I come in peace."

This time Juan slowly turned around, lowering the broom. Standing, in the shadow of the jungle, right there in front of him, was none other than Robert "Tree Spirit" Hansen.

"*Oh dios mio*, Tree, man. You scared the hell out of me! You are supposed to be dead, no?"

"Sorry for startling you, but I do not want to be seen," Tree Spirit said. "And yes, I was hoping I was considered dead. That makes me a much safer companion."

Juan shook his head and laughed. "You are a man of many surprises, Mr. Tree Spirit. Are you okay? Jack and Miss Gerry said you had been shot."

"Yes, but I am fine. I am completely healed now." He pulled his shirtsleeve up over his shoulder and did a half turn, revealing a fresh, pink scar covering what had been a nasty little bullet wound on the back of his upper left arm. "There are many effective healing herbs in the Mexican jungle."

"That is very good," Juan said. "And very good to know." He closed the gap between them and grabbed the rail-thin man, lifting him off the ground in a bearhug. "It is great to see you my friend and to know you are well. But we must get you some food. You have wasted away to nothing."

He set Tree Spirit back on the ground.

"Thank you," Tree Spirit said. "A little food would be very nice."

"So, what is going on, *amigo*? You didn't come out of hiding just for Big Juan to feed you."

"It is Jack Driftwood," Tree Spirit said, suddenly very worried. He clutched Juan's arm. "He is in serious danger, my friend. I have seen it in a vision. He has been locked away by some very bad people and we must go help him."

Big Juan Chavez looked deep into the eyes of the Seneca half-breed searching for truth and quickly found it.

"Then go, we must," he said.

Neil Dadoska was sitting in his underwear in his favorite chair playing in a five-dollar Texas Hold 'em tournament on his laptop. He always did his best thinking while mindlessly playing in small-stakes, online games such as these. It was still pissing him off he had gotten no further in his investigation into this "Chaz" character. But he had a feeling something was about to break his way. He had woken up that very morning with an uncomfortable feeling, almost like there was an ice ball in the pit of his stomach. The ice ball was slowly melting, giving Neil little jolts of energy and excitement. Something big was afoot.

The Seneca Security Chief was in what they call the calm before the storm. He had always had an extra sense about such things. Instinctively he knew when the shit was ready to hit the fan. This insight made him a very dangerous adversary. This innate feel for a call to action had served Dadoska well over the years. He always seemed to be a step ahead of the game. Something big was on the horizon and it was about damn time. Neil was a patient man, but this Tree Spirit shit was getting old; he was ready to go all in.

The wind had died outside of his four-bedroom ranch up in the town of Wheatfield on the edge of the Seneca Reservation. A light snow was falling, taking the edges off the horizon, giving an eerily soft and peaceful feel to the morning. Neil had been up with the sun and spent the bulk of his time intuitively getting himself battle-ready. He had located the chains for the tires of his pickup truck and thrown them into the bed before gassing it up. He had also gassed up his two snowmobiles and loaded them onto their trailer, which he hooked up to his truck. With his transportation ready, he had moved on to the task of cleaning and oiling his weapons. He had a pair of AK-47 semi-automatic rifles that were shined up and ready to roll, along with an assortment of smaller arms.

However, the bulk of his time had been spent with his precious baby, a .44 caliber Magnum six-shooter. He had disassembled, cleaned, oiled, and reassembled the sweet, sculpted revolver several times already that morning. It was his favorite and most reliable gun. He preferred a revolver because even if it misfired, as long as you had rounds left you could keep plugging away with it. He gave it a kiss for luck before a final wipe down with an oilcloth. That baby had served him well over the years and he had taken great care of it in return.

He also put together a small survival kit consisting of food and water, medical supplies, a compass, maps, field glasses, and several knives, all neatly packed into a backpack. He had called his right-hand man, Johnny Quest, and told him to round up Race Bannon and Hadji and clear their schedules; he would need them ready at a moment's notice once things got rolling. Something was brewing, something big. All that was left for the big man to do now was kill time. Neil was good at killing that, too.

He drew pocket rockets and matched the big blind. It was a little early in the game for a big raise; he didn't want to scare off the little fishes. Much to his delight, five players called with no raises. Just as the flop was about to come his cell phone rang. What do you know, Donald Fegel wanted to chat.

"You drop the dime, I'll do the crime," Dadoska said.

"Very funny," Fegel said.

"What's up?"

"Well, I just wanted to keep you up to date and in the loop on some breaking developments. I'm not sure how this will affect you, but I'm sure you will figure something out."

"I'm listening," Dadoska said.

The flop revealed an ace of spades, a deuce of clubs, and an eight of hearts on the screen. Dadoska silently congratulated himself for setting the trap and matched the small bet made by one of the other players.

"The old buzzard Wainscott almost croaked. He's in a coma up in Children's Hospital, so I'm running the ship because little Miss Wainscott hadn't signed the papers turning the team over to her yet and now it's too damn late. That cautious oversight cost her everything because the team automatically goes into a Trust run by yours truly. And you're going to like this - the first thing I did was send Jack Driftwood packing. The bastard took a swing at me so my security guys beat the piss out of him. The cowboy broke my nose, but it actually worked out quite well. It gave me reasonable cause to lock him up in the Brylin Mental Hospital. He's locked up for the next seventy-two hours and likely beyond."

Dadoska was silent on the other end, his mind worming its way around this new information. He absently wrote down "Driftwood-Brylin" on the blank tablet sitting on the end table next to his chair.

Fourth Street flipped up another eight onto the computer screen, this one a diamond. One of the players went all in. Then another. Neil flashed his nicotine-stained teeth at both the screen and the cell phone in a big ol' smile.

*Gotcha!*

He went all in. That was too fucking easy. Ha-ha! This was like taking candy from a snot-nosed, shitty-diapered, bawling-ass baby.

"You getting all this, hoss?" Fegel asked.

"Yep, did you talk to the fairy princess about the situation?"

"Oh yeah, that's the best part. The dumb bitch thinks I had something to do with her dear old daddy being put in the hospital."

Fegel guffawed into the phone and waited as Dadoska was slow to respond.

"And?" Dadoska finally said.

He doubted Fegel was that conniving but knew him well enough to not put anything past him.

Fegel started to chuckle. "No, I guess I'm not that bright. Honest, I had nothing to do with that."

Dadoska grunted. This much he believed.

The River brought the bitch herself, the Queen of Spades. The cards were revealed and Dadoska's aces over eights took the pot, knocking out the two other players who had gone all in.

"Dead man's hand," Dadoska marveled aloud, "and the bitch."

"What?"

"Nothing."

A shiver ran up his spine. People were going to die – soon, that much he knew. The cards didn't lie. And what the hell was the Queen of Spades doing, popping up like that, just as they were talking about Gerry Wainscott? These cards were talking! And Dadoska was listening hard, but he wasn't exactly sure what he was hearing. Not yet, anyways.

"So," Fegel continued, "she stormed out of here and immediately got on her phone. Not sure who she called, but I just thought I would let you know."

"Okay, good," Dadoska said.

There was something bouncing around in his mind. Something he couldn't quite put a finger on. It was some kind of call to action, but he couldn't quite pull it in.

"I'll call with an update, if needed," Fegel said. "But things are looking pretty good for the home team right now, chief."

"Here's to the new boss, same as the old boss. This is good, nice work, Donald," Dadoska said and hung up the phone.

He kicked his feet up onto the desk and began to process the new data. The thought of the rock-throwing linebacker locked up in a looney bin gave him enough pause to smile. The fairy princess must be one hot mess right about now. But somewhere tangled in this web was the answer Dadoska was searching for. Oh, he knew it was in there somewhere, probably right in front of him. He couldn't quite grasp it yet, but he wasn't concerned in the least. It was still plenty early. It was just a matter of time before it came to him. That's how things worked for Neil.

Meanwhile, he had just taken a substantial chip lead in the game of Hold 'em. He decided to play on, let his subconscious work on the riddle of his next move. He glanced out the window and noticed the snow had picked up considerably.

The nicotine smile spread across his visage once again. He was ready. With his nerves tingling, he knew something big was coming down the pike. Fegel had wrapped up his deal rather well, now it was his turn. The ice ball in his paunch kept melting away. *Drip, drip, drip…*

Weather-wise, it was the quintessential Christmas Eve. The snow was beginning to pick up and it covered the roads of Western New York. A significant lake-effect snow event was coming in off Lake Erie, dumping snow all the way north to Niagara Falls, through Buffalo, and down into the Southtowns. This snow was just a prelude to the storm on its merry way to town.

That beast was being fed by a low-pressure front packing added moisture siphoned from all the way down in the Gulf of Mexico. The storm had the potential of being the first blizzard of the season. The airport was still open, but most of the town was battening down the hatches. Chaos consumed the grocery stores, and the streets were full of people not only stocking up for the storm but also doing their last-minute Christmas shopping. It was perfect timing for Santa Claus weather. Rudolph was going to need his tweaker on full power to guide the fat man's sleigh through this one!

Chaz's truck, a four-wheel drive Dodge 3500 dually with a 6.1 Cummins diesel engine, handled the slick roads with ease, hauling one snowmobile in the bed and two more on a trailer behind it. He eased off the New York State Thruway onto the Transit Road exit. A couple of turns and he would promptly arrive at the Buffalo Niagara International Airport. He had gotten several bizarre phone calls that morning which had led him to take this course of action. The plan was fluid, but the objective steadfast. He was going to break Jack Driftwood out of Brylin Hospital and get him somewhere safe until they could figure out how to clear his good name.

Equally important was his desire to bring down Donald Fegel, Colin Meade, and this asshole Seneca Security Chief, Neil Dadoska, who had been harassing his friends and even tried to kill Tree Spirit. Fegel had fired off the initial volley, forcing Chaz to declare all-out war. It was time to roll on every front. He pulled to a stop at the curb in front of the arrival gates under the protection of the overhead canopy at the Buffalo airport.

When he pulled up, a large black man in a white parka strolled out of the airport escorting a tall, frail woman bundled up tightly against the cold. The wispy woman was wrapped in a white and turquoise blanket and had a white, knit winter hat pulled down on her head nearly covering her eyes. She hunched against the wind and blowing snow with her straight, dark hair shadowing her face. The big man held her at the elbow as she gingerly made her way to the curb and into the back seat of the awaiting truck. After nearly lifting the woman into the vehicle, the burly man nimbly jumped into the front seat. Instantly the truck sped away into the white, winter wonderland of Western New York.

# Chapter Forty-Three

The snow continued to pile up outside Buffalo General Hospital on Christmas Eve. Gerald Wainscott had been transferred there as they were much better equipped to care for him. Normally a Christmas Eve snowstorm would be a wonderful, spirit-lifting boost to Gerry, who loved nothing more than a magical, freshly-minted snowfall before Christmas. It reminded her of her childhood where a white Christmas made for a storybook setting. She would wake her parents up early to spend the entire day basking in the generosity of Old St. Nick. That seemed like a lifetime ago as she sat at her father's side in the critical care ward.

Gerry had met with Dr. Orlando Muscarro, the head of the team of physicians caring for her father. He had explained the situation to her as best he could. Apparently there had been a blockage in Gerald Wainscott's bowels which had backed up his entire system quite severely.

This had, in turn, caused a chain reaction leading to problems initially with his lungs and then his heart. The biggest issue, explained Dr. Muscarro, was that Gerald was just so old. When one system broke down it led to problems in other areas and the cumulative effect became too much for his body to keep up with. They had done an emergency surgery to relieve the bowel blockage and had stabilized Wainscott, who was still in a coma, and were monitoring him closely. Dr. Muscarro had put the odds of a full recovery at fifty-fifty. All they could do now was hope and wait.

Gerry had asked Dr. Muscarro if her father's condition could have been brought on by outside influences. He was confused, so she plainly asked if somebody could have done this to him. Dr. Muscarro carefully considered her question but told her no. Then he offered her some help if perhaps there was something going on that she could not handle for herself.

Gerry politely declined. If Chaz couldn't handle this thing, nobody could. She wasn't even concerned about how he would go about his business. First, they had to get Jack out of that horrible place where he didn't belong. Then they would worry about exonerating him and fingering Fegel and company. She clutched her cell phone trying to will it to ring.

There was really nothing else she could do. She felt lonely and helpless sitting by the window watching the blowing snow next to her dear father who lay unconscious in the bed.

The snow-covered streets of Buffalo were nearly empty by 8 p.m. The stores had all closed and people were making final preparations for Christmas Eve celebrations amidst the blizzard. Many parties planned for that evening had been cancelled due to the winter storm. It was a significant inconvenience to many, but the hearty folk of Western New York knew the drill: Stay home, stay warm, and hunker down to ride it out.

There were already ten inches of fresh snow covering Erie County and the winds were beginning to pick back up. The blowing and drifting had created white-out conditions and the major highways bisecting the city were already closed down by the State Police. The gale-force winds were coming out of the southwest, putting downtown Buffalo directly in the path of the bands of lake-enhanced snow. Forecasters predicted new snowfall at the rate of an inch per hour through midnight, when it would begin to taper off.

Chaz was thankful he had chosen the Dodge truck, because the brute could go through pretty much anything. He had taken his two passengers directly to Larry Blake's house on a side street off of Parkside Avenue, east of the Buffalo Zoo and Delaware Park, the Crown Jewel of the Buffalo Parks Department. Blake was out of town for the holidays but would be happy to hear they had used his place as the marshalling area for their planned raid on Brylin Hospital. He'd have been more than happy to lend a hand had he been around.

Chaz pulled the truck into the freshly plowed driveway. He had called Cheese to prep Blake's place and Cheese had it covered without another word. Chaz loved that about the wise guys; they were tight with their words and got shit done in a hurry.

"All righty, then," Chaz said. "Lets us girls head into the house and make some plans."

"Sounds good, *jefe*," Big Juan said.

"I know you fine gentlemen must be very hungry. Perhaps I can find something in Larry's kitchen in the way of sustenance before our mission," came the voice from the backseat of the truck.

"Good idea," Chaz said. "Now that you are back from the dead, perhaps an omelet would be in order."

Chaz cracked himself up; he was loose and playful, which is how he always got before a date with all hell breaking loose. It helped keep him relaxed before he locked into a laser-like focus. They piled out of the truck and rumbled into the house where they were greeted by Cheese. Tree Spirit took over the kitchen and whipped up some grub. They did some catching up over omelets and orange juice before planning their incursion. They had about three hours to kill before heading a few miles to the east to secure precious cargo. Chaz rubbed his beefy hands together, warming up to hatch the details of each of their roles in the upcoming mission.

*Nothing like a Christmas Eve raiding party to keep a man young, happy and alive!*

After winning the online Texas Hold 'em game, Neil Dadoska had nodded off to sleep in his favorite recliner. Apparently the glass or two (or was it three?) of the whiskey he had been sipping had eased him into a steady state of slumber. That is, until he awoke with a start from a reoccurring dream. He had had many variations of this dream where he was being chased through a burned-out section of downtown. He had made his way to the roof of a seven-story building where he was pinned down by his pursuers. He surveyed the situation and thought he could make the eighteen-foot jump to the roof of an adjacent building to make a clean escape. It was worth a shot.

He ran full speed and leapt, but as he launched himself the building disappeared and he plunged into the darkness of a seemingly bottomless pit. So far, anyways, he had always snapped awake before splattering onto an unknown surface.

*Goddamn, I hate that dream,* was Dadoska's first conscious thought as he bolted upright in his chair.

He checked his watch to see how long he had been out. It read 6:22 p.m. – not a bad nap. He stretched and his mind immediately went back to the conversation he had had with Donald Fegel earlier. There was something he was missing in the big picture. His eyes were randomly drawn to the words he had scribbled on a note pad.

**Driftwood-Brylin.**

His eyes blinked and he read the note again. Holy Shit! There it was right in front of him. What had his buddy over at County, Sarge, said? "Whenever Driftwood gets his ass in a bind this Chaz shows up out of nowhere to save the day." Those were his exact words.

*Well, there you go. Jack Driftwood ain't nothing but a big ol' hunk of cheese sitting in my Chaz trap.*

This Chaz character was going in to get Jack Driftwood. He was going to bust the cowboy out of the nuthouse. The answer was right there in front of him the whole damn time. He had even written it down!

*Sometimes I am as thick as a brick for being such a smart sumbitch. Ha-ha!*

That was it; that was what this whole thing had been about. He was sure the rescue mission was going down that night. The timing was perfect; Christmas Eve in the middle of a blizzard. All they had to do was swoop in, grab the dirtbag and get out the hell out of Dodge. But there was going to be one little problem with their plan, a little fly in the ointment. The Seneca Nation's Security Chief was going to be there laying in the weeds waiting for them.

He grabbed his cell phone and called Johnny Quest to round up the rest of the crew. They had a little ambush to plan and time was running low. There was, perhaps, a shot of amber liquid left in the tumbler sitting on the table next to him. To give himself a jump-start he quickly slugged down the contents. The alcohol mixed with the ice-ball drippings and other juices brewing in the big man's stomach. Dadoska felt alive! He would have his showdown with Chaz, of that he was convinced. He hopped up out of his chair feeling spry, like he could jump a fence right onto Pimp Street.

"That means you, too, superstar," the white-coated guard said as he moved up behind Jack.

A clinical sounding voice had come over the room's loudspeaker system telling all the patients it was time for "lights out" and to move into their private rooms. This new guard had just come on duty and Jack didn't like the way the man kept looking at him. He ignored the request and kept flipping cards. The guard sidled up next to him and looked over his shoulder at the spread of cards in Jack's game of solitaire.

"Move that three over there under the four," he said.

Jack grunted, pissed he hadn't seen the move. His head was still cloudy and he felt physically ill. He knew they had knocked him out with some kind of heavy-duty drug. He was still suffering from some of the aftereffects from the beating those security boys had laid on him. What he wouldn't give for a couple of Kappy's magic beans to take the edge off.

"It appears you have friends in high places, Mr. Driftwood."

"Is that so?" Jack asked. He was suddenly very interested in what the man had to say.

"Yes, sir, a man calling himself Chaz says he is coming by to get you at midnight. He mentioned you might be able to swing a couple of Mega Bowl tickets my way if I leave your door unlocked, along with the cage in front of the door to the stairwell."

"Are you serious?"

"He was serious enough to put five grand into my bank account this evening. I already checked, it's there."

"How does the fifty-fucking-yard line sound?"

"That'll do," the guard said, not able to suppress a smile.

"What's your name?" Jack asked. "I will leave them at the will-call window the day of the game."

"You can call me Race," the guard said, absently rubbing a scar on the back of his head. "Race Bannon. That's what the boss calls me."

Jack wasn't the least bit surprised Chaz had pulled some strings and was going about the business of his escape, but something about this security guard bothered him. He stood and faced the man, giving him a quick once-over. There was something familiar about him, but Jack couldn't quite place it. Plus, five grand seemed awfully steep.

"Do I know you?" he asked.

"Um, no, I don't think so, but you better get your ass in your room. I don't need people asking questions and neither do you."

He nodded and shuffled towards his room.

*Fucker is hiding something.*

He was still sore and stiff and wasn't moving very well yet. He needed to get loosened up with a good stretch, maybe a hot shower. A familiar feeling told him there stood a pretty good chance things would get physical just around midnight. The ice ball in the pit of his stomach was of the fast-melting variety and he was sure his juices would be ready. But something smelled rotten; this Race Bannon character was a bad actor.

# Chapter Forty-Four

The blizzard peaked as the clock wound down toward midnight. The snow was falling at a rate of nearly two inches per hour and the winds were blowing out of the southwest at a constant thirty miles per hour, gusting to fifty. Whiteout conditions prevailed. It wasn't fit outside for man nor beast. But it suited Vinny Cappolla just fine. He was sitting comfortably in a parking lot across the street from Brylin Mental Hospital in his city-owned Crown Vic.

He had heard about the extraction from Chaz and wasn't going to miss out on the fun, regardless of what Chaz had said.

*Stay home my ass! And let them fuckers botch the whole thing? I don't think so.*

Vinny was parked between a panel van and an old Ford Station Wagon in the front row of a small parking lot facing Delaware Avenue. He figured he was as inconspicuous as one could be smack dab in the middle of a blizzard. Plus, he had a great view of the entire area. If his boys needed any extra backup he was rough and ready sitting in the front row at the 50-yard line.

Vinny checked his watch for about the twentieth time since he had arrived at 11:28 p.m. sharp. It was only 11:42. Boy, was his wife ever pissed when he left the house at such a late hour on Christmas Eve. When he had explained, without much detail, his friends' lives could be in danger, Beverly had gotten even madder. He figured he might as well go ahead and go because the night was already ruined; she was going to bitch to high heaven the whole time now, regardless. Definitely not his idea of holiday cheer.

Vinny reached down and patted his ankle, making sure his throwaway piece was securely in its holster. He debated whether to unlatch it and take it out when his driver's side door was quickly yanked open.

"What the f—"

He looked up just in time to catch the butt of an AK-47 to the forehead.

Vinny's ticket was punched. Neil Dadoska quickly pulled the handcuffs off of the detective's belt and cuffed the big boy's chubby mitts behind him with Vinny's own iron. He fastened the seatbelt tightly around Vinny's girth so he couldn't lean forward and try to honk the horn. Not that there would be anyone around to hear him tonight, anyway, but why take chances? Before leaving, on a whim, Dadoska reached down and patted the cop's ankles.

*There you are. Come to papa. I knew it! Cappolla, you old bastard. Ha-ha!*

Dadoska snatched the untraceable .22 caliber revolver from an ankle holster affixed to the left leg of the heap of unconscious humanity known formally as Vincenzo Lewis Cappolla.

"Good looking out, fat man. You are definitely from the old-school."

He lightly tapped the butt of the gun on the side of Vinny's head as he spoke. With that bit of business complete, Dadoska slammed the door and disappeared into the blowing and drifting snow. He never would have found Cappolla except the dumb fuck had cleaned all of the snow off his windshield. His car stuck out like a sore thumb and Neil saw it when he first cased out the area on foot. Dadoska had figured Cappolla for half an idiot and he was not disappointed.

*Round one to me, Chaz. Make your next move.*

Exactly twenty minutes prior to midnight, Chaz, Tree Spirit, and Juan Chavez each hopped onto one of the three Ski-doo Renegade Backcountry snowmobiles Chaz had made ready. The posse roared out of Larry's driveway and headed toward Parkside Avenue where they would go north. They wore white, fur-lined parkas, goggles, and insulated boots. They were also heavily armed. The sleds were finely-tuned machines and handled like a dream in the deep, freshly-fallen snow. The posse quickly reached the railroad tracks that rose up before Linden Avenue. They veered off the road and cut between a few houses lead them to the tracks running through the backyards. They'd be following the railroad tracks for a good portion of the trip.

Under the prevalent conditions, the rails provided a wide-open superhighway for their snowmobiles, as the raised tracks ran in a gentle curve to the south. The sleds hurtling through the snow felt like were they gliding over and through puffy clouds. Unfortunately, they had to abandon the tracks once they reached the intersection of the Scajaquada and Kensington Expressways, as the tracks turned west for several miles, away from their target. The caravan of high-powered machines exited the rails and blazed a trail through the freshly-fallen snow, going west on East Delevan Street. From there it was a straight shot to Delaware Avenue.

Chaz anticipated a clean mission but had been ambushed enough times in his life to never take anything for granted. As they reached Gates Circle at the intersection of Lafayette and Delaware, about a block away from Brylin, they stopped and Chaz parked his sled behind a gas station. He was going in on foot while Tree Spirit and Juan drove ahead to survey the area, create a distraction, and act as backup, if needed. Once Chaz had Driftwood in hand they would each hop on the back of one of the sleds and hit the road running. If things were going smoothly they would stop and retrieve Chaz's sled on the way out. They also had Cheese in the truck around the corner for when things went to hell, like they always do.

The streets were completely deserted as the snow had rendered them nearly impassable. Only a fool or a man on a mission would be out at this hour in such conditions. Chaz began his trek past Millard Fillmore Hospital, which stood between him and Brylin. Juan and Tree Spirit revved up the snowmobiles and headed south on Delaware. They were in constant communications through voice-activated radios connected to hands-free headsets tucked under their fur-lined hoods. Chaz did love his toys.

Cheese was keeping an eye on the perimeter and listening in. He had parked facing north on Linwood Avenue, a one-way street running parallel with Delaware Avenue behind the hospital. If needed he could storm in with the truck and do an extraction or bring in some more firepower. He was instructed to maintain radio silence in case their frequency was being monitored. Chaz left nothing to chance.

He hadn't wanted Vinny Cappolla around simply because of plausible deniability. Plus, he needed Vinny to be clean, especially if he was going to be the one to finally put the collar on Fegel and his clan. As much as he hated to do it, he had asked the big man to stay at home.

The wind briefly abated as Tree Spirit and Juan roared down Delaware Avenue past the hospital and up the road another quarter of a mile. This gave them a great view as they surveyed the area on their drive by.

"Everything looks quiet, Obi-Wan," Juan said into the voice activated microphone.

He almost giggled. When Chaz had come up with the idea to use the Star Wars code names, he insisted on being Chewbacca. Chewy was the man! They turned their sleds around for another pass, taking this one much slower.

"Roger that, Chewy," Chaz said. "I am in position. Make another pass and let me know if the coast is still clear."

The sleds rumbled back northward and as they approached the hospital they came to nearly a complete standstill. Both riders scanned the area looking for anything seemingly out of order.

"We are a go, Jedi Master," Tree Spirit said.

"Roger that, C3PO. I'm going in. Take a lap, but don't get too far away."

The minutes passed excruciatingly slow for Jack Driftwood as he lay on the surprisingly firm mattress in his room on the seventh floor. The private room they had put him in wasn't all bad. It had its own restroom complete with a shower. He had taken a nice long, hot shower and afterwards stretched his stiff, beaten body as best he could. He had also clothed himself with every stitch of clothing he could find in his private room. This included three pairs of socks and three layers of the hospital gowns and pants that were provided to the inmates. He had taken another gown and had somehow fashioned it into a hat. He knew he was destined to be out in that blizzard at some point and didn't plan to bust out only to freeze to death.

At 11:57 p.m. he could wait no more. Quietly he went to his door to check to see if it was indeed unlocked. He was armed with the wooden leg he had broken off of the only chair in his room. After putting his ear to the door and hearing nothing, Jack slowly turned the door knob. It was unlocked!

Jack took a knee and pulled the door open slowly and carefully peeked out into the hall. He half expected to get jumped somewhere along the trail by his new friend, Race. The coast was clear so he padded down the corridor, away from the light coming from the guard station, and toward the padlocked, chain-link gate separating the patient's rooms from the emergency stairwell.

*This has got to be some kind of fire code violation,* he thought as he got to the gate.

As promised, the padlock on the chain looped through the chain-link door was also unlocked. Thus far, it appeared, the five grand had paid off. He upgraded his weapon to the chain by snapping the lock shut onto the end link of the two-foot length. Pushing the cage door open, he took five quick steps and was through the door and heading down the stairs. He forced himself to go slower after getting a head rush from zipping down the first flight of stairs.

*Easy, big fella.*

He held onto the metal railings until his bearings returned. Huge, glossy, translucent windows in the stairwell from waist level to the ceiling of each new floor provided scant, shadowy light. Jack's eyes had completely adjusted and he had no problem seeing, despite the stairwell lights being off. He proceeded at a much slower pace, carefully checking for company at each new level before descending down the next flight of steps. He still didn't trust that prick Race Bannon, or whatever his name really was.

The shadows of the Millard Fillmore Hospital had provided perfect cover for Chaz as he stole his way toward Brylin. Most of the snow had blown away from the area right next to the wall at the back of the building, so he made double-time until reaching the end of the building. A small parking lot was all that stood between Chaz and his targeted destination – the emergency stairwell exit at the back corner of the Brylin building. There weren't many cars in the lot, but there were enough to provide a modicum of cover. This is where Chaz knew he would be the most exposed, thus vulnerable, along his route. If somebody was out there waiting to snipe him this would be their best opportunity.

The wind kicked up causing almost total whiteout conditions. Chaz took it as a cue to initiate his approach through the snow. Following a serpentine route from car to car, he crossed the final thirty yards to the emergency stairwell doors.

He got to the doors and immediately put his back to the building. He was out of the wind and wanted to quickly survey the area before going to work on popping open the handle-less doors. He heard snowmobiles roaring in the background as he scanned the area. At first, he heard just the friendly hum of his own Renegades. But then he picked up the deeper growl of a couple more sleds. Those were definitely not his machines.

"What's up with the other sleds," he said into his headset.

"Not sure just yet," Juan said. "They just came roaring up Delaware on our tail."

"I'm at the doors," Chaz said. "I should be out with the package in five minutes, or less."

"We'll be here."

The sounds of the sleds grew louder as they passed by out in front of Brylin on Delaware Avenue. The sound faded as Chaz took one last look around. He turned and went to work on the double doors with a small pry bar. In a matter of seconds he popped open the doors.

Congratulating himself, Chaz stepped into the small vestibule at the bottom of the stairwell. Just as he crossed the threshold of the metal door he was pushed roughly from behind. The crowbar flew from his grasp and clattered to the cement floor. Chaz lost his balance but got his hands up before hitting the unpainted cinder-block wall on the far side of the tiny space. He slowly turned around and gradually raised both of his hands into the air. A man, covered in snow and wearing a full-faced ski mask, held him at gunpoint. It was at this exact moment when he heard the faraway spray of automatic gunfire coming from somewhere outside the building.

"Holy shit," came Juan's excited voice through the headset. "Those *pendejos* are shooting at us!"

Jack had been counting the floors on his way down, and by his count he was on the third floor. He peered down through the small space between the rails looking for the bottom of the stairwell when he thought he saw some movement in the shadows one floor directly below him. He froze and then sneak-walked to the door separating him from the third floor of the hospital. He tried it but the door was locked.

*Damn!*

He was stuck in the stairwell with someone lying in wait for him down on the next floor. There was literally nowhere to run and nowhere to hide.

Even though Jack was feeling much better, he continued wobbling down the steps holding the rail and shuffling slowly with a bent posture. He had tucked the chain into the side of the hospital pants with the lock hanging out, making it easily accessible. He labored down toward the second floor shuffling and groaning, taking one step at a time.

As Driftwood made the turn to go down the final flight of stairs, Race Bannon appeared in front of him. Bannon laughed in Jack's face.

"Wow, for a guy who is supposed to make the Star Bowl this year you can't even walk down a flight of stairs."

"You got your money and I'll get you the tickets. What the hell else do you want?" Jack asked.

Bannon pulled a Taser out of his belt and waved it at Jack.

"What I want is for you to slowly make your way down here so we can wait for the boss."

"There go your fuckin' Mega Bowl tickets," Jack said.

"Tough titty," Bannon said as he climbed a couple of steps, closing the distance between himself and Jack. "Now are you gonna be a good boy and walk down these steps, or do I have to shock the shit out of you?"

Jack slumped his shoulders and sighed. Then he looked up the stairwell. Bannon looked up as well, following Jack's gaze. The old head fake works every time! He yanked the chain from his hospital pants and swung it at the Taser in Bannon's hand before the man could react. The chain hit Race on the wrist and wrapped around it, knocking the Taser from his grasp. The man cried out in pain and surprise.

Jack launched himself down the few remaining steps, executing the perfect flying tackle. His practiced shoulder hit Bannon in the chest and sent him tumbling backward down the steps. His head cracked hard against the rigid cinderblock wall, knocking him out cold. Jack grabbed the Taser and, just to be sure, shocked the unconscious thug.

*Point this fucking thing at me? Huh, bitch! Huh!*

He was watching the bastard twitch when the doors one floor below him burst open and what sounded like a pry bar clattered onto the cold, hard cement floor. Was that the cavalry? He felt the cold draft of air blowing up the stairwell as he quietly crept down to see.

# Chapter Forty-Five

While unconscious, Vinny was having one of the best dreams of his life. He was a soldier in an unnamed army in a battle with his battalion and they had been assigned to take a hill. Vinny had charged forward up the hill fearlessly, screaming like a madman as men were dropping all around him from the enemy gunfire. Having advanced halfway up the hill, Private Cappolla had so far avoided attracting heavy enemy fire after resorting to a belly crawl. His platoon had taken out numerous enemy fighters and a couple of machine gun nests as they had slowly but surely worked their way up the hill.

There was another machine gun nest up to his left doing serious damage to his unit. He had managed to get within forty feet of the thing and off to the side, alive and undetected. He had just one grenade left and he rolled onto his back to pull the pin so he could lob his ordinance into the pesky nest and hopefully save not only lives, but the day as well.

Vinny was a southpaw. He was also the best damn pitcher Hamburg High School had ever seen. His fastball was straight smoke, but right now he had dialed up his Eephus pitch. With his right hand he pulled the pin out of the grenade, keeping pressure on the detonator with his left thumb. He extended his left arm and then rolled his body over towards the target. He let the grenade fly, rolling it off the palm of his hand.

The lobbed grenade floated in a perfect arc toward the dug-out nest housing the enemy's .50 caliber machine gun that had been ravaging his platoon. It was a direct hit. Vinny Cappolla was a bona fide war hero! Vinny was reinvigorated as he rolled back onto his stomach.

*By God and all that is good, we are taking this fucking hill!*

As he lumbered to his feet to lead the charge the big man woke up, handcuffed, sitting in his car in the midst of a raging blizzard. He strained against the handcuffs and could still hear the rat-a-tat-tat of automatic weapons firing.

*What the fuck?*

Suddenly, it all came back to the Buffalo detective. The dream and reality battled for control of his consciousness. Vinny vastly preferred the dream. But he knew the shit was real again when he saw the two Renegades fly down the road in front of him with two other sleds in hot pursuit. The second set of sleds was firing automatic weapons at the first two. That wasn't good.

As he began to wake up, he finally recognized the full scope of his predicament. The good news was he could get out of it. Vinny had been a New York

State Heavyweight Champion wrestler back in his Hamburg High days. He had won the title match by making an impossible escape by seemingly dislocating both shoulders. He had always been overweight and slow, but that didn't mean he wasn't quick and flexible. Or ornery as hell. His advantage was, despite his bulk, his joints were snake-like; he was as flexible as a circus freak. Both shoulders, elbows, and thumbs were double jointed, meaning he could dislocate them basically pain free. Because of this, there wasn't a pair of handcuffs on the planet that could hold him. He was a poor man's Houdini.

Vinny had won countless bets in bars and at various precinct buildings by wriggling his way out of a pair of hand cuffs. His reputation was such that it had become rare to find another sucker from whom to take twenty bucks. He could have gotten twice that for what he was about to do.

He worked himself sideways and first popped the seatbelt off. Once he had acquired this freedom he leaned forward and managed to wind-mill his arms all the way around so his hands were in front of him. Then he simply grabbed the key from his belt and the cuffs were off quicker than you could say "Jackie Robinson."

Vinny reached up and felt the bloody lump on his forehead. He checked out the wound in the mirror and decided he would be okay for now. He fired up the Crown Vic, backed it out of his spot, and pulled forward to the mouth of the parking lot exit, listening for the sound of the snowmobiles. Maybe he could still be a factor and take some of the heat off of his boys.

The cold draft rising up the stairwell ceased immediately once Neil Dadoska closed the double doors behind him. He did it blindly, keeping his eyes and his .44 Magnum trained on the man simply known as "Chaz." He was taking no chances. Dadoska carefully patted Chaz down, finding a gun stuffed into the large front pocket of Chaz's parka. He made a "tsk-tsk" sound and shook his head disapprovingly before throwing the gun out the door into the drifting and blowing snow. He slammed the door behind him again. Though they had not yet met, they both knew all too well who the other was.

"So, we finally meet," Dadoska said from under the ski-mask after a lengthy but oddly comfortable silence.

"Not really, Neil, since you don't have the courage to take off that mask," Chaz replied.

Dadoska laughed softly and shook his head. "Ah, Chaz, your little Jedi mind-tricks won't work on me. But it is a little warm in here under all these clothes."

Dadoska kept the revolver pointed at Chaz's chest and he flipped the ski mask up, revealing his face.

"Put it back on, you're a lot fucking uglier in person," Chaz said.

"So you're a funny guy, huh? You won't be near as funny when I pump some hot lead into your ass."

"You'd have to sneak up behind me and that'll never happen, again," Chaz said.

He was trying to buy time, hoping his backup outside was still listening and would come and save the day. Or maybe this clown would give him an opening to turn the tables. Dadoska had yet to notice the small earpiece and microphone under his hood and didn't know Chaz was broadcasting to his team.

"Enough of the bullshit," Dadoska said. "You have been a pain in my ass for far too long. I'm afraid you are going to have a tragic accident, Chaz."

"That so? Because either way you are going down, douche bag. Your boy, Colin Meade, saw to that. Didn't he tell you?"

Dadoska paused for a split second before taking the bait. "Tell me what?"

"He *didn't* tell you. I'm not surprised, I wouldn't have, either. What he failed to mention is when I raided his house, I found a small strongbox containing some very, shall we say, sensitive information regarding your stadium scam. It's all right there in black and white. You should have kept a better eye on that weasel. He fucked up real bad and he's bringing the whole ship down with him."

*This can't be true,* Dadoska thought.

And even if it was true he could take care of the aforementioned weasel. In fact, that was a part of his long range plan anyway. It would just have to happen a little sooner than he had anticipated.

"I see the gears turning in your ugly, fat head, Neil. So why don't you let me finish my business here and you can go take care of your business. What do you care if Jack gets out of this place? Unless you're taking orders from Fegel. *That* would surprise me."

"You don't get it, do you, dickhead? I don't give two shits about no Jack Driftwood or a fucking Fegel, for that matter. I came here for *you.* I thought we could tango, have a little fun, but I can see I overestimated you completely."

"Well, here I am," Chaz said. He nodded at the gun Dadoska had pointed at him. "You gonna use that thing or do you want a shot at the title?"

Dadoska busted out laughing at the challenge.

"How stupid you think I am?" he asked. "There may be a time and place for that, but it ain't now. As soon as my guy shows up with Driftwood, the two of you will be coming with me. The guard you made your little deal with happens to be on my payroll. He'll have him down here in a jiffy, and then the two of you are going for a long ride off a short pier."

Hiding around the corner on the stairwell, Jack Driftwood had listened with great interest to the exchange between the two bull geese. But the conversation had run its course and Jack decided it was time to make a move before Dadoska ran out of patience and actually used his gun.

Jack carefully came around the corner halfway up the first-floor stairs with the 50,000-volt Taser firmly clasped in both hands out in front of him. He pointed it directly at Neil Dadoska.

"Don't move a fuckin' muscle or you will be doing the chicken," Jack called down the steps.

The sound of his voice startled both Dadoska and Chaz. Neil turned and peered up into the dimly lit stairwell. He quickly surmised Jack Driftwood had the drop on him and muttered "Shit" as he slowly lowered his firearm.

"Put it on the floor. Now!"

Jack's hands were shaking. He almost pulled the trigger when Dadoska hesitated slightly. That was how people got shot!

"Shit, Driftwood, I had him right where I wanted him," Chaz said.

"Yeah, I could see that."

Dadoska slowly bent over and placed the gun down on the cement floor. Without pause, Jack bounded down the steps and scooped it up. He gave Chaz a fist-bump and then rushed back up the stairs to higher ground.

"Where the hell you going?" Chaz asked.

"I got one of his assholes up here unconscious and I'm just making sure he don't go all zombie on us."

Just as Jack vanished around the turn on the staircase to check on Bannon, Dadoska timed it out and flung himself at Chaz. He had seen Driftwood's hands shaking while holding the Taser and figured the linebacker lacked the gumption to take a shot at him, especially while he was tangling with Chaz. He might have been worried if the football star was armed with a rock, but it was obvious the pussy didn't have the stomach for guns.

*Damn few of us do,* Dadoska thought as he lowered his head to make his charge.

He wasn't afraid to die and had always promised himself he would go down swinging if the time ever came; perhaps it had.

"I'll take a shot at that title after all."

Chaz was more than happy to oblige.

Dadoska's initial charge had caught Chaz with his guard down, but only for a split second. Chaz was quite nimble on his feet for a big man and skirted sideways, taking only a glancing blow from the shoulder of the charging rhino of a man. As he slid out of the way, Chaz shot his right arm out and deftly caught

Dadoska under the elbow, turning him just enough to avoid most of the contact of the frontal assault. It was a dandy of a slip move.

With the grace of a ballerina, Chaz sidestepped the lumbering attack and used the man's momentum and the fulcrum of his hold on the elbow to slam Dadoska into the cement wall face first. Unfortunately, he had underestimated both his foe's strength and ability to take a blow. Dadoska bounced off the wall and came back swinging with a wild right hand that clipped Chaz just above the ear. The roundhouse punch knocked the earpiece device clean off of his head and it fell to the floor. Chaz wobbled a little bit from the instant vertigo brought on by the blow.

Dadoska was an inside fighter and ultimately intended to put Chaz into some sort of submission hold, taking advantage of his superior size and strength. He charged again, this time coming in low, looking to shoot the legs for a double or single-leg takedown. Chaz countered with a two-handed stiff arm and hopped backwards into a sprawl, putting his legs just out of Dadoska's frantic reach. Then he sidestepped the brute with a swift lateral move to keep from being pinned against the wall of the small vestibule.

Being much quicker than Dadoska, Chaz rained several blows down on the top and back of his head as he worked his way around to the side of his nearly prone opponent. Neil rolled away from the barrage and scrambled back to his feet. The two men squared off again, both now with their dukes up. The wrestling hadn't worked for Dadoska so he thought he'd try his hand at boxing.

Chaz assumed a southpaw stance and waded in. When in range, he rapidly pumped a couple of right handed jabs, each landing squarely on Dadoska's already red, bulbous, vein-laden beak. A trickle of blood appeared on his upper lip, but Dadoska swiped at it with his thumb the way boxers do, creating a cheesy, red mustache. Chaz flicked out another jab and then bent at the knees and threw a straight left hand into the paunch of the heavy-breathing and quickly tiring Dadoska.

"Harrumph!"

The air gushed involuntarily out of Dadoska. Chaz waited for the big man to crumble, but instead he surprisingly shook it off. With a guttural roar he charged Chaz again, this time engulfing him. Dadoska pinned him against the cement wall. He quickly brought up a knee, catching Chaz directly on the thigh, just missing his gonads in what could have been a decisively debilitating blow.

Neil wrapped his left arm around Chaz's head and put him in a headlock. Gaining control, he started throwing a series of right handed rabbit punches into the side and back of Chaz's skull. Things were not looking very good for the home team.

But Chaz possessed some inside fighting skills of his own. As if caught against the ropes in a boxing ring, he expertly horsed Dadoska around, reversing the tide. Dadoska's back was now to the wall. Chaz leaned in hard and tucked his chin and ducked under, breaking out of the headlock. He finished his amazing escape by extending both arms to push himself away and out of the clutches of the desperate brawler, once again.

Dadoska stayed on the offensive as Chaz tried to back away. He threw a short, quick, straight right hand that landed flush on Chaz's jaw. His knees buckled and he wobbled, but Chaz refused to go down.

Dadoska looked on in awe. No man alive had ever taken his best punch and stayed on his feet like that. He hesitated, waiting for Chaz to drop as the block of a man swayed, unsteady on his feet. But he never went down.

Dadoska charged in again, this time for the kill. Chaz instinctively shot out a jab, hitting a surprised, onrushing Dadoska flush on the nose, again. It wasn't a powerful punch, but it was well placed. Dadoska's nose busted all the way open this time as blood sprayed from his nostrils like a geyser.

The Seneca Security Chief stepped back and put a hand to his face, feeling for his nose. The damn thing was broken again and flattened off to one side of his face. He screamed with rage and, for the first time he could remember, fear.

The short break had allowed Chaz to recover slightly. At that point, he let his superior boxing skills take over. He waded into Dadoska with a sick five-punch combination, finishing with a jarring left hook that all but knocked the big man out.

Jack heard the commotion down below and hurried back to the top of the steps. He had just rounded the last corner when the crunch of knuckle on jawbone made him wince. The sweet science of the punch caused Dadoska's head to whiplash back against the wall, and when he hit the floor face first Jack could have sworn he felt the whole building shake.

Down goes Dadoska!

Down goes Dadoska!

Down goes Dadoska!

Chaz rolled the humongous heap of humanity over onto his back. The Seneca Nation Security Chief's eyes rolled up into his head and then closed. Unconsciously Chaz rubbed his meaty left hand, which was bloodied, cut, and beginning to swell.

Through heavy breaths, he let Jack have it. "Thanks a lot, ass-wipe. I could have used a hand there."

"You had it under control, champ. I would have shot the fucker if I was worried."

A big smile slowly spread over Chaz's face.

"Looks like I still own the title," he said, kicking Dadoska in the ribs for good measure.

Chaz and Jack shared a calm silence for a brief instant until the crackling sound of excited voices coming from the headset broke the spell. Chaz was still bent over, hands on his knees, trying to catch his breath as Jack scrambled down the steps and snatched up the headset.

"Hello? Hello? Is anybody out there? Hello…

# Chapter Forty-Six

The weather outside was frightful, but for anyone on a snowmobile it was delightful. Unless, of course, you were under fire from automatic weapons as you sped down the street. Such was the lot of Tree Spirit and Big Juan as they roared down Delaware Avenue on the Renegades. They had been heading north on Delaware Avenue towards Gates Circle when a couple of serious customers on sleds materialized out of the blizzard and were hot on their tails. Once they hit the roundabout they veered right onto Lafayette, and then hung another right when they reached Linwood Avenue. Their sleds were not only faster but handled the turns better, keeping them well ahead of the pursuers and thankfully out of the range of their gunfire.

They were hitting eighty miles per hour on the straightaway down Linwood and soon they could no longer hear the sleds chasing behind them. It appeared their pursuers had momentarily given up the chase. They flew by Brylin Hospital again, only this time they were on the back side of the complex.

"We have got to get back over there to pick up Obi-Wan and Skywalker," Juan yelled into the howling wind and snow as they continued at a slower pace up the snow-covered street.

"Yes," Tree Spirit said, "I think we lost them for now."

They came to a halt about five hundred yards from the next intersection, which was West Ferry Street. They had basically taken half a lap around the rectangular track of streets surrounding the hospital complex. They shut down their machines, listening closely in the ensuing silence for the sounds of any other snowmobiles. They heard nothing but the eerie howling of the wind.

"No doubt, they lie in wait to ambush us by the hospital," Tree Spirit said. "I think we need to bring in the Millennium Falcon for the extraction and then you and I will plow the road to keep those sleds away from Obi-Wan and young Skywalker."

The Dodge dually parked fifty feet in front of them on the east side of the one-way street flashed its lights.

"All right," Big Juan said, "but those banditos won't be the only ones spraying hot lead into the frosty night air!"

"You have a wonderful way with words, my friend," Tree Spirit said.

All Tree Spirit could see was the brilliant flash of teeth in the opening of Juan's dark ski mask. Even that mask could not conceal the effervescent smile of the big man.

The Dodge dually roared to life in front of them and they nodded to Cheese as they went by. It was up to Cheese to get the package now; the boys on the sleds were nothing more than a distraction.

Despite the snow being over a foot deep on Linwood Avenue, the dually plowed through it like the Italian Stallion bashing through the line. A huge parking structure was now the only obstacle separating Cheese from the Brylin Mental Hospital. He pulled the truck up to the curb right in front and threw it into park before killing the engine. He periodically rolled his window down to clear the snow so he could watch for any signs of both the bad and the good guys. Visibility wasn't the best, as the snow kept coming down hard and was being blown around by the steady wind whipping through the buildings.

Cheese cranked the volume on the CB radio he was using to monitor communications. Then he waited. He could hear the faint buzz of the snowmobiles across the way on Delaware Avenue. He also heard the gunfire. It sounded like the distant pop of firecrackers on the Fourth of July. Cheese crossed himself and said a quick prayer.

That prayer, unlike most, was answered immediately.

"Hello? Hello? Is anybody out there? Hello…"

Cheese grabbed the microphone of the CB radio and pushed in the talk button.

"This is the Millennium Falcon," he said. "I am at the pickup location, over."

"Cheese?" Jack said into Chaz's headset.

"Actually, it's Solo, Hans Solo."

"Quit fucking around and tell me where you are."

"Obi-Wan knows. Is he with you?"

"Yea but he's a tad bit winded after putting an ass-whipping on Darth Vader," Jack said.

"Well, get over here right now! There are a couple of bad guys on sleds shooting at Chewy and C3PO. They are going at it right now so you have got to move it, fast!"

Dadoska had started to moan and twitch a little as he lay in a heap against the far wall of the vestibule. Chaz was still recovering from his title bout but was ready to move.

"You ready to roll, champ?" Jack asked.

"Yep," Chaz said. "Gimmee that gun and go wait outside."

Jack was still shaking from the adrenaline rush and was ready to get the hell out of there. He looked hard into the Chaz's eyes, but the man wouldn't hold his gaze.

"No, we ain't killin' nobody." He said it with teeth.

"Goddammit, Jack. That's what they were going to do to us. I ain't happy about it neither, so just give me the damn gun and get your ass out of here!"

"I can't. I can't let you do it, Chaz."

"Look, man. They are going to keep coming after us until they do kill us. It's either us or them, that's the kind of assholes we are dealing with here. Don't make this harder on me than it already is."

Jack still held the Taser in his hands. He pointed it at Chaz.

"What the hell you doing?" Chaz asked.

"Where is Cheese with the truck?"

"Fuck you," Chaz replied and spat on the floor.

Jack didn't know what to do. He could not stand by and let Chaz kill the Seneca Security Chief in cold blood. That would be the same as him pulling the trigger himself, and he couldn't live with that. He knew Chaz wasn't one to back down either.

*Shit!*

There was only one thing he could do.

Jack fired the Taser. The cartridge hit the big man and his body did the chicken dance for a few seconds before going limp.

Vinny's car was shielded on the right side by a huge pile of snow left over from the previous plowing of the parking lot. The snow pile had nearly doubled in size to almost ten feet tall from the drifting and falling snow. It provided decent cover to the south, but the wind-breaking effect also allowed snow to gather on the vehicle's windshield. This limited Vinny's field of vision down the street.

He had already screwed up once and owed the fellas one. He rubbed the lump on his forehead where he had been thumped in the noggin and a scary thought occurred to him. Quickly he reached down to his ankle frantically searching for his .22 caliber pistol, which came up missing.

*That fucking Dadoska must've stolen it!*

If nothing else, Vinny Cappolla was a vengeful son of a bitch. And right now he wanted a heaping helping of the dish best served cold. That's why his police-issue Glock rested on the console by his right hand. He really didn't want to use the damn thing because he had to keep this whole incident off the radar. But if push came to shove, he wouldn't hesitate in taking down one of these fuckers. He'd deal with the consequences later.

Vinny couldn't see very far down the road to his right due to the huge snow bank, but he heard the rumbling of two sleds heading towards him at a high rate of speed. The sleds slowed a bit as they came upon the Brylin Mental Hospital.

From his vantage point Vinny saw two other sleds emerge from the parking lot across the street.

Those sleds roared out of the lot chasing the first two machines, which had fired back up and just blown by him. Shots rang out from both groups now; the chase was on once again. Vinny could see much better to the north, watching the taillights of the four sleds zoom down the street. He observed the chase intently, looking for an opening to help the lead riders, as four sets of red lights blinked off and on through the blowing snow.

Vinny was tempted to follow them, but under the current conditions his Crown Vic would be like a pig on skates compared to those sleds. So he waited, knowing they would be back. Maybe then he would have his shot at redemptive vengeance.

"What the hell did you do that for?" Chaz asked as they watched Neil Dadoska squirm on the floor with the metal probes from the Taser embedded into the front of his heavy winter coat.

"It was either you or him, and I didn't think I could carry your lard-ass all the way to the truck through this much snow. Let's just get the fuck out of here. What do you say, *mejo*?"

Chaz looked at him and sighed. "All right, you win. I just hope we don't regret this."

"As Coach Faber likes to say, we live to fight another down," Jack said.

He gave Chaz Dadoska's gun and followed him out the door. Once outside, they headed towards the parking structure. Running through the snow wrapped in hospital gowns with three pairs of socks covering his feet was one of the most surreal things Jack Driftwood had ever experienced. His body, which had been stiff and sore, loosened up dramatically from all of the adrenaline. He glided through the snow with the lightness of an angel, easily keeping pace with Chaz lumbering just ahead. It reminded him of running out onto the field during introductions at the Mega Bowl his rookie season, when his feet had scarcely touched the ground.

They made it around the parking structure and stopped at the street-side corner of the four-story edifice. Chaz carefully checked for any signs of the enemy before leading the way the final twenty yards to the truck awaiting them poised at the curb. There were no signs of bad guys anywhere and no telltale footprints breaking the surface of the fallen snow around them. Chaz nodded at Jack, signaling it was time.

As they approached the Dodge dually, they heard the buzz of the snowmobiles in the distance behind them. Jack and Chaz exchanged a knowing look of worry. They both knew Tree Spirit and Juan Chavez were still under fire and neither wanted to leave their boys behind. But that was just the way it was; they would have to make it out of there on their own now.

They piled into the dually; the package had been delivered. Obi-Wan and young Skywalker were safely tucked away in the Millennium Falcon and were about to make the jump to light speed. Cheese punched the accelerator as Chaz snapped up the microphone to the CB Radio.

"Get the hell out of Dodge! We have the package! I repeat, we have the package. Get the fuck out of there, now!"

There was no response. Cheese revved the engine and they were underway down Linwood Avenue, easily cutting through the foot and a half of snow blanketing the road. It was as quiet as church inside the truck. Each man entertained his own thoughts, centering on their friends still out in the blizzard fighting for their lives.

"They will be okay," Cheese said. "I said a prayer for them."

Vinny sat and continued to monitor the humming of the snowmobiles. They had been following the same pattern, for the most part, and he was waiting for his opportunity to intervene. The sound started to break up, and Vinny wasn't sure what was happening.

*Divide and conquer?*

One of the machines was at full throttle and had to be approaching one hundred miles per hour when it blew past the Crown Vic crouched at the curb in the parking lot across the street from Brylin. Vinny recognized the blur of the yellow Renegade and knew it was one of the good guys. He quickly threw the Crown Vic into drive and punched the gas pedal. The rear tires of the big boy's city-issued car spun for an instant before grabbing some traction. The car lurched out onto the street and into the rooster tail of snow left behind by the passing snowmobile.

Vinny hit the brakes but couldn't stop his momentum. The front end of the car slammed into the snow bank on the other side of the street and was stuck. Oh well, at least he had effectively blocked off half of the roadway. He took a gander out of his driver's side window and saw the snowmobile in hot pursuit coming right at him. The sled was on a direct collision course with the driver's side door. Vinny nearly shit his pants. He ducked his head in preparation for a catastrophic impact.

The driver of the snowmobile in hot pursuit was an Iranian known simply as Hadji to his comrades. He was an expert snowmobile driver and raced on weekends up in Watertown. Hadji saw the car cross the street, coming from out of nowhere, and thump into the snow bank directly in front of him. He leaned to his right and pumped the brakes. By turning the sled hard to the right at the last instant and leaning as far as he could, he miraculously avoided smashing into it. The sled nearly tipped but it held on, staying upright due to a combination of deep snow, skillful driving, and blind luck. Hadji had narrowly missed the back bumper of the Buffalo detective's vehicle.

After clearing the vehicle, Hadji tried to lean and turn back to his left to right the ship but failed miserably. The centrifugal force was too much for him. He did manage to straighten out the machine as it barreled up and into the huge pile of snow across the road.

The snow pile acted as a natural ramp which the sled hit at close to seventy miles per hour, launching it into the frosty, snow-filled night air, rider and all. Hadji had gamely held on for a brief instant but eventually lost it midair. He was catapulted off the machine. The sled crash-landed, embedding into the windshield of a mini-van before bursting into flames. The man called Hadji was equally unfortunate. Landing head first into the bed of a small truck, he rattled around the small box like a pinball before coming to a standstill in an awkward position. He was DOI; dead on impact.

Tree Spirit had tapped into the Over-soul, becoming one with his snowmobile, if not the universe. Using the snow banks to maintain his speed on some of the turns, he put some distance between himself and his pursuer. The man chasing him was pretty nifty on a sled as well, but he was no match for an in-tune Tree Spirit and his superior machine. The only potential equalizer was the machine gun the man kept firing in Tree Spirit's general direction.

Weaving through the parking lot, Tree Spirit heard a tremendous crash of fractured metal and broken glass from up the street. As he banked a corner, cutting around a trio of parked cars, a plume of smoke rising above a fireball came into view from over on Delaware Street. His heart leapt into his throat and he silently prayed it was not his dear friend Juan who had crashed. He made one more loop through the parking lot and then decided he would do a flyby past the stairwell door from which Jack and Chaz had recently escaped.

He needed to stay a safe distance ahead of his tracker, who was steadily firing off live rounds in his direction. Some of the shots were getting close, as Tree Spirit could hear bullets piercing some of the automobiles parked in the lot, buried under the mounting snow. He was thankful nobody else was out in this storm;

he would hate for some poor, unfortunate, innocent bystander to get hit by a stray bullet or mowed down by one of the fast-moving sleds. At the speeds they were hitting, if somebody stepped out in front of him there was no way he could scuttle his sled fast enough to keep from running them right over.

*I knew dumb-ass Driftwood was soft and stupid,* Dadoska thought as he pulled himself up slowly from the vestibule floor. *But I didn't think his asshole buddy Chaz was. Should've killed me. I'd have killed the both of them, sure as shitting.*

The thought made Dadoska chuckle for an instant until a sharp dagger of pain stabbed his ribs, buckling him at the knees. He had taken a hellish beating. However, the shock from the Taser had been partially mitigated, as his thick winter coat had somewhat insulated him from the electrical current. He had felt it, sure enough, but it wasn't debilitating in the long term. To some extent, he figured it had only served to juice him back up.

But now was the time to get the hell out of there. He had to regroup and cook up some new plans. He also wanted to see how his guys on the sleds had faired. Maybe one of those yahoos had saved the day.

Dadoska once again raised his hulking frame off the floor. He did a quick check to see if all his parts were working properly. He swung his arms around in big circles and then stood on each foot while shaking the opposite leg. He moved his neck around and winced at the pain, again.

*That fucking Chaz hits like a mule.*

All things considered, Neil felt pretty good, although he was going to be as sore as a honeymoon virgin the morning after. He would get his paybacks on the man named Chaz if it was the last thing he did. Paybacks were a bitch and this shit was far from over. Those things he knew.

Neil climbed the flight of stairs and found Race Bannon conscious but sitting against the wall in a mental haze. The man had a concussion and had been zapped with a 50,000-volt Taser; other than that he appeared just fine.

"Looks like we lost round two, partner," Dadoska said. "But this battle isn't over just yet. Come on, we need to vacate the premises."

He managed to help Race up onto his feet and by the time they reached the bottom floor the man was almost supporting himself.

They could hear the approaching roar of snowmobiles right outside the door. Dadoska reached down and pulled Vinny Cappolla's .22 caliber from his boot and held it up for Bannon to see.

"I told you this battle ain't over yet. I'm going out there to get me some!"

He howled and shook the pistol in the air to punctuate his resolve. He gave Race a wild-eyed look and barreled out the door and back into the fray.

Tree Spirit slowed down before he hopped the snow bank at the curb and tapped the breaks again to maintain control of his sled. He was on the sidewalk that ran right in front of the emergency stairwell doors of Brylin. He had slowed enough to identify two sets of tracks in the snow heading toward the Linden Avenue pick-up point. He knew who had made those tracks and his heart swelled with joy. Satisfied, he rolled his right wrist forward, punching the sled to full power as he blasted up the sidewalk. He was going back to Delaware Avenue to see how Juan Chavez had faired.

Johnny Quest watched Tree spirit slow down in front of the doors and took advantage of the situation.

*I got you now you son of a bitch!*

He hit the gas and roared up to the curb at almost full-throttle, closing the gap with Tree Spirit significantly. He caught some big air as he flew the snow bank and saw the sled in front of him tap the brakes. What he hadn't seen was the doors to his right fly open and the boss come rambling out directly in the path of his airborne sled.

Dadoska never knew what hit him. He hurried out the door hoping to surprise somebody and maybe riddle their ass with bullets. He turned to his left with the pistol raised, but the sled flying over the snow bank was on top of him before he could say "Jackie Robinson."

Instinctively Neil blasted off a couple of rounds just as the razor sharp, custom-built spoiler on the front end of the airborne sled hit him above the shoulders, completely shearing off his head. One of the shots he had fired found its mark, hitting the rider right between the eyes and sending him sprawling backwards off the sled. Johnny Quest landed on his back like a sack of potatoes on the snow-covered sidewalk, dead as a doornail, right at the feet of the boss, Neil Dadoska.

Race Bannon was still huddled in the vestibule trying to get it together when he heard the mayhem occurring just outside the door. The sled had veered to the right on impact and crashed into the building, killing the engine. Everything went eerily quiet. Bannon wondered if the boss had pulled it off after all. That would be just like Dadoska; the guy somehow always kept his head on straight in the darkest of times. Bannon felt a surge of hope as he pushed open the door to check things out.

The first thing he saw as he stepped out into the storm was the headless corpse of the big boss-man lying in the snow nearly foot-to-foot with the bloody body of Johnny Quest. It took a moment for the scene to fully register in his hazy head.

The carnage was too much for his reptilian brain to process. He screamed bloody murder before passing out again, doing a face plant into the soft bed of falling snow.

After hearing the crash behind him, Tree Spirit shut off the Renegade and crept quietly back towards the corner of the building to take a peek. The snow did not even crunch under his nimble feet. He ducked to his knees and stole a glance. The wreck of the snowmobile was the first thing to catch his eye, but as he looked further down the snow covered walk he saw two bodies lying foot-to-foot like they were doing mirror-image snow angels.

There was something wrong with the picture, though. Then Tree Spirit's eyes came to rest on an oblong shape sitting in his sled's tracks, about twenty feet up the sidewalk from the bodies. It was partially covered in snow and sat in what Tree Spirit knew to be a dark pool of blood. It eerily looked like a football. Just as the big picture dawned on the half-blooded Seneca Indian the door to the stairwell swung open. A man limped out, looked at the carnage, and screamed and dropped face first into the snow.

Tree Spirit could relate, he felt like screaming, too. Wasting no more time, he jumped back on his sled and fired it up. He pulled out onto Delaware Avenue just as Juan was pushing Vinny's vehicle out of the snow bank.

"There you go, *amigo*," Juan said. "Think you can get this war barge home?"

"Does a chicken have lips?" Vinny asked through the open driver's side window.

The car sagged on the driver's side under his massive weight but was free and clear of the snowbank.

Juan bellowed a big laugh. "Make sure you go get your head looked at, Vinny, you took a nasty bump."

"Fuck that, none of this shit ever happened."

Tree Spirit came along side and popped off his helmet. His pale face was as white as the falling snow.

"What the fuck's wrong with you, Tree Spirit?" Vinny asked. "You look like you saw a goddamn ghost."

"More like the Headless Horseman, but I'm okay, let's just get out of here."

Sirens began to wail in the distance as Vinny put the over-sized sedan into gear and headed down Delaware Street on his way home to Beverly. Juan and Tree Spirit wasted no time hopping back on their sleds and getting the hell out of there – safe and mostly sound.

# Chapter Forty-Seven

On Christmas day the city of Buffalo wore the postcard-picture perfect look of a pristine winter wonderland. The lake-effect snow machine had shifted and was currently pummeling the area to the south, while the sun made a cameo appearance over the city. It was just like Santa Claus to leave a parting gift, as if to make up for the previous night's punishing storm. Buffalo sparkled in all of her fading glory like a priceless piece of heirloom jewelry buffed and polished to a shine in the rare, effervescent winter sunlight.

This beauty was totally lost on Donald Fegel as he made his way from the Buffalo Seneca Casino Hotel to the Wigwam through the second-floor, glass-covered walkway. Due to the storm, Donald had spent the night in the casino hotel. It would have been foolish to try to drive home given the conditions when the hotel was just a walk across the street – he didn't even have to go outside to get there. Besides, it wasn't like there was anybody at the Fegel house to celebrate the holiday with; Donald was pretty much alone in the big, old world.

He happily whistled his way to a small but thriving retail center on the second level of the stadium concourse. He hoped it was open this early on a holiday. He needed to pick up a few basic toiletries and wanted to grab the morning paper on his way to the office. It was his lucky day as the small shop had just opened for business. He paid for the toothbrush, toothpaste, deodorant, and the Christmas morning edition of the Buffalo News, which he blindly picked up and shoved under his arm on his way out the door.

He meandered through the concourse towards the Blizzard office complex continuing to whistle a happy tune. Surprisingly, there was a handful of people meandering through the Wigwam walkway and Donald found himself waving and nodding to them just a little past 8:30 that Christmas morning. As he approached the doors to the Wigwam office building, he casually unfolded the newspaper and glanced at the front page headlines.

He about shit a brick.

**Driftwood Escapes Mental Hospital?**
***Three Found Dead at Brylin***
By Budd Kilmer
Buffalo News Sports Editor

(Buffalo, NY) Buffalo Blizzard inside linebacker Jack Driftwood has apparently gone AWOL from a Buffalo area mental hospital. The Blizzard star was involuntarily admitted to the Brylin Hospital Thursday by the Blizzard's General Manager, Donald Fegel. The organization has yet to comment regarding the player's admittance to Brylin, but unidentified sources say Driftwood had tested positive for more than one illegal substance banned by the North American Football Association.

This anonymous source went on to say Driftwood, an 18-year NAFA veteran, "flipped out" when informed of the positive test and attacked Mr. Fegel, who was treated for a broken nose at Children's Hospital Thursday, the same day as Driftwood's admittance to the mental health facility. Mr. Fegel, who was unavailable to comment for this story, is also reportedly sporting two black eyes, obviously part of his injuries suffered in the Driftwood assault.

Officials at Brylin Hospital refused to officially comment on the situation, but an off the record source indicated Jack Driftwood was admitted to the hospital yesterday, shortly before noon. However, he was conspicuously absent during the patient count early Friday morning. The source claimed Brylin Hospital authorities had "no idea" how Driftwood might have escaped from the facility. Currently Jack Driftwood is at large, as neither the police, hospital, nor team can confirm his whereabouts.

In addition, the unidentified source claims one of the security guards, Roger Abercrombie of Medina, who was working security on the seventh floor Monday night, was also notably missing this morning. Mr. Abercrombie's family has filed a missing person's report with the Buffalo Police as the man did not come home after work as expected and is currently unaccounted for.

The seventh floor of the Brylin Hospital is a secure area of the building which houses psychiatric patients admitted involuntarily. The floor is locked off from the rest of the hospital and routinely guarded at all hours by at least three security guards armed with 50,000-volt Tasers.

In what may be just a bizarre coincidence, three area men were found dead outside Brylin early this morning. The Seneca Nation Security Chief, Neil H. Dadoska of Wheatfield, was apparently killed in a snowmobile accident along with Stanley R. Atkinson, also of Wheatfield. Omar Abdullah, a Cheektowaga resident, was found dead in a different location outside the hospital. He, too, was the apparent victim of a snowmobile accident.

Buffalo Police Chief Billy Tunney said the incidents are "likely unrelated but under investigation." He went on to say there were no "overtly apparent indications of foul play," though he did not rule out such a possibility.

Jack Driftwood, who led the Blizzard in tackles during the regular season with 169 and tied for the league lead with eight interceptions, was placed on the team's Non-Injured Reserve List on Thursday. The NAFA has a non-disclosure confidentiality policy regarding first time offenders to its illegal substance abuse program, however, performance enhancing drug violators do not share this protection. League sources reported Driftwood did recently submit to a random test for PEDS, but those results have not yet been returned from the lab.

The Blizzard have reached the playoffs for the first time since 1998, Driftwood's rookie season, and has a bye this weekend in the first round of the playoffs before hosting a game at the Wigwam the following weekend.

Donald Allen Fegel Jr. was sitting, head in his hands, on a bench on the second-floor concourse of the Wigwam when his phone rang. The buzzing device shook him from a deep malaise. He reached into his suit coat and plucked the annoying phone from his pocket. It was Colin Meade. Just. Fucking. Perfect.

"Where in the hell have you been?"

"Roasting chestnuts over an open-fucking-fire," Meade replied with equal venom.

Donald pulled the phone away from his ear and looked at it in disbelief. Had the whole world gone nuts?

"Listen," Donald said in a much more civil tone, "I am about to walk into my office. How about you meet me up here so we can make some plans before our whole world completely goes to hell?"

"Too late for that shit now."

"Huh? What do you mean too late?"

"What I mean is, our little world is already in hell. It's over, Fegel. And I'm not going to be the poor bastard left holding the bag, here. I don't even want to talk to you."

"Listen to me, you little prick," Donald yelled, "I made you a very rich man. Maybe you forgot who pulled your lame ass out of the gutter, boy. You are going to talk to me whether you like it or not. You owe me that much!"

Meade was silent on the other end of the phone. Donald knew Meade didn't feel any great sense of loyalty to him – the guy wasn't built that way – it was more like a subservient fealty. He knew he intimidated the mousy man, wielding some sort of power or mystical sway even he didn't fully comprehend.

"Well?" Donald asked.

"Alright, I'm not coming over there, but I'll tell you what I know."

"Fair enough."

He was relieved he hadn't lost his touch completely. However, he wasn't sure if he really wanted to hear what Meade had to say. All he really wanted was for this shit-storm to pass.

"What happened at Brylin last night?" Donald asked.

"Basically, Jack Driftwood escaped from—"

"Jesus H. Christ! I know that already, Colin. So does everybody else who can read – it's on the front page of the morning paper. I need to know what happened to Dadoska and his crew."

"I swear if you interrupt me one more time, I will hang up and you will never hear from me again, you got that?"

Donald pulled the phone off of his ear and looked at it, again.

*This can't be Colin Meade. Who does this little rat-bastard think he's talking to?*

He took a deep breath to calm him down. Apparently he was going to have to eat a load of crow in order to get Meade to play ball.

"Sorry Colin, it won't happen again. Please continue."

Meade proceeded with a little snot in his voice. "As I was about to say, I got a call in the middle of the night from one of the chief's guys. They call him Race Bannon, but that isn't his real name. Anyway, he was totally freaking out. He said Dadoska knew the Brylin Security boss and got him in as an overnight guard. They set up an ambush for Driftwood's pals who were coming to rescue him at midnight. Neil said he was going to take down the whole bunch of them once and for all – 'make 'em all disappear,' as he put it."

Meade paused to catch his breath, which Donald interpreted as a lame attempt at melodrama. The pause stretched the limits of what remained of his patience. Meade had him on a string, slinging him up and down like he was a yo-yo attached to Colin's middle finger. As galling as it was, Donald managed to remain mum.

"The whole thing blew up in their faces, literally," Meade said. "Bannon said he was bringing Driftwood down to Neil when that mysterious Chaz guy showed up. He beat the piss out Dadoska at the bottom of the stairwell. They both got knocked out cold, and when Bannon woke up Driftwood and Chaz whoever-the-fuck were gone. They heard snowmobiles outside so Dadoska went out there with a gun. Shots were fired and then there was a big crash. He went outside and found both the chief and another one of his guys lying dead in the snow. And get this, Dadoska got hit by a snowmobile and it cut his head clean off."

Donald's knees nearly buckled. His mind was reeling and he felt like he was going to be sick. He sat back down on the bench.

*How am I supposed to clean that up?*

Personally, he didn't care for Dadoska. The man wasn't pleasant to deal with on any level; but he was a partner in crime, and therein lay the problem. Under any circumstances, a dead Dadoska would bring scrutiny. But getting beheaded in a snowstorm in the middle of the night on Christmas Eve? That was national news.

"H-h-how can this be? How could this happen?"

"That's not all. Another one of Neil's guys was killed in a separate snowmobile crash across the street."

"Sweet Jesus," was all Donald could manage to say. His mind was racing.

*Could they trace this thing back to me in any way? What do the cops think? Would they tie it to Driftwood? Can I pin this on him somehow?*

"Hello… Donald… you still there?"

"Yes, I'm here," Donald said. It was the voice of defeat.

"Well, what are you going to do now?"

"Let me think about it, Colin. Let me think about it and I will call you back. Let's just keep cool in the meantime. It's Christmas so not a lot should happen today. That buys us a little bit of time to figure something out."

"Okay," Meade replied. "Oh, and Merry Christmas, boss."

"Yeah, and a Happy-Fucking-New-Year."

# Chapter Forty-Eight

Gerry flopped around non-stop on the cot next to her father's bed trying to get comfortable. Worrying about her father and waiting to hear from Jack had made her a bundle of nerves. Her mind focused on the myriad things that could go wrong in either scenario. She knew firsthand from her trip down to Mexico how dangerous things were likely to be over at Brylin.

The negative thoughts were eating away at her and finally became too much. She rolled off the cot and slipped into her shoes. After unplugging her cell phone from the charger, Gerry dropped it in the front pocket of her sweater and slipped out of the room. The cafeteria down on the second floor would be open; maybe she could get some hot chocolate to help her settle down and sleep. Anything was better than laying there flipping around on that cot, sick with worry.

It was just past three o'clock in the morning when she was making her way back up to the fifth floor to her father's room. As she stepped off the elevator, she felt her phone vibrate in her pocket. She quickly pulled it out hoping it would be Jack. A chill of dread and anticipation coursed through her body.

It was Cheese. She looked up to the heavens and then slid her finger across the screen.

"Jack?"

"None other."

"Jack! Is it really you?"

"Live and in person, sweetheart."

"You are the most careless, reckless, hurtful man I have ever known! Don't you ever do this to me again!" she said, trying to sound angry.

"Whoa, whoa, whoa, settle down there. You make it sound like I tried to get beat up and tossed into the nuthouse."

"I've been worried to death about you. Are you okay? What happened?"

"I got roughed up a touch, but it wasn't anything I couldn't handle. I take beatings for a living, you know. I also dish them out from time to time."

She was so happy to hear his voice she was giddy. "I saw what you did to Donald. You broke his nose, you know."

"Sweet," Jack said, "I was hoping to snap a couple of his ribs, too."

"Where are you?"

"I am in the subterranean lair of a fuckin' madman, which, ironically enough, is a substantial distance from the Brylin Mental Hospital. A few good old boys made sure of that."

"Thank God. What happened? Is everybody all right?"

"It's a long, crazy story that I can't get into right now, but yes, everybody is cool, on our side anyway. But how about you? How are you doing? Is your father any better?"

"I'm hanging in there, I guess. I'd really like for you to hold me, though."

"I'd really like that myself."

"He's about the same, Jack. He's still in a coma. He had a blockage in his bowels and they did surgery to clear it, but there are issues with his lungs and heart. They don't know if he will wake up, and even if he does, they don't know the extent of the damage. They are mainly worried because he is just so old."

"I'm so sorry, Gerry. I've known him a long time and he is one tough old man, you know that. My money is on him. It's going to be okay, you just hang in there."

"I know, I'll be all right," she said.

Gerry had told herself she wasn't going to cry but was fighting back tears. She didn't want Jack to worry about her, Lord knows he had enough on his own plate.

"I know you weren't using any of those drugs they said—"

"Hell no! Those test results are bogus; Fegel faked that shit, somehow."

"That's what I thought," she replied, "but he thinks he has an airtight case. I spoke to Commissioner Goldman and he looked into it himself. He said he has every confidence the chain of custody on your samples was not compromised. The samples were properly sealed and they have your signature and initials on all the paperwork. I saw it myself, he emailed me pictures and it's definitely your handwriting, Jack. Everything else appears to be in order. It's pretty damning evidence."

"Holy shit!" Jack said. "I don't fucking believe it."

"What? Believe what?"

"It was the Pissman. I *thought* he was acting weird. When I took my piss test the Pissman had me sign two sets of the forms, said he screwed up the first one. He must have given it to Feegs and he took it from there."

"I thought you said he was a good guy?"

"Yeah, well I must be a horseshit judge of character – have you met my friends?"

She actually laughed for the first time in days. "Do you think we can talk to him? I mean, at least we have something to go on."

"We're gonna do more than talk to him, I can promise you that. The bastard will tell the truth one way or another. Chaz could make a mute go on a filibuster. But I have a hard time believing the guy would do this to me. Hell, he even had the balls to ask me to sign a football card for his neighbor kid after he did it. Feegs must have paid him a shit-ton of money for it."

"I knew they had to have done something. I didn't believe you were on those drugs for one second."

"They ain't gonna get away with this shit, Gerry. We're going to nail their asses to the wall."

"I know," she said. "Will I get to see you soon?"

"It won't be much longer, I promise. I love you, Gerry. You hang in there, we'll get through this."

"I love you, too." Just hearing him say it and saying it herself made her feel so much better.

The ride out to Hemlock Lake was a thing of beauty for a fan of pastoral, rural settings after an apocalyptic snowstorm. The trees were covered in a white veneer outlining the intricate weave of every branch. Light-gray, puffy smoke signals poured from the chimneys of snow-covered country homesteads. The normally gruff and profane Vinny Cappolla was struck by the natural beauty left in the wake of the storm. The scenery made him sadly nostalgic, reminding Vinny of his childhood growing up on a farm in Western New York's Snow Belt, south of Buffalo near Lakeshore.

The snow fall totals diminished the further east he travelled, but the splendor of the landscape remained. Vinny was nearly in a trance cruising alone along the I-90. The roads weren't that bad, having been freshly plowed, thus he was making good time on his way to the bunker home of Chaz Davenport for a "team meeting," as the man had referred to it. The article in that morning's Buffalo News had cranked up the urgency of the situation. There were plenty of ducks needing to be quickly put in a row if the reputation and innocence of Jack was going to be properly restored and demonstrated in a timely fashion.

So far Vinny had been able to monitor the Buffalo Police Department's investigation into what had been dubbed the "Cuckoo's Nest Nightmare." The acronym CNN was born to refer to the incident, which had quickly become the second most popular topic of discussion in all of Buffalo, right behind the closely related topic of the Blizzard's playoff chances. Nearly every cop in the area had a theory on how things had gone down at Brylin. Vinny had listened intently to the wild ideas and witless theories his shield-toting brethren dreamed up to account for three dead and two missing. What unnerved him was every single one of these scenarios tied Jack Driftwood's disappearance to the body count. Vinny's mood had darkened with worry by the time he reached Chaz's hideout. One way or another, Jack would have to tell his story; and it had better be a good one.

He purposely drove past the entrance and doubled back but didn't encounter any other vehicles. No tail on this whale. He rolled down the incline, and as he reached the bottom, the side of the hill opened up to swallow him. He drove into the hidden garage and walked back into the workshop as the hillside closed behind him.

"We can get started now," Chaz hollered, "Kojack is here."

Vinny grabbed his groin with a meaty mitt. "I got a *Ko* you can jack, right here."

"That is some messed up stuff, *amigo*," Big Juan said.

He jumped out of his chair to give the fellow burly man a bear-hug.

"Now there's a coupling I would pay to see," Cheese said. "It'd be like watching a sperm whale mate with a wild boar."

"Which is which? And who's gonna suckle the baby Sperm Boars?" Jack asked.

He was sitting with his legs up in a leather Lazy-boy recliner re-reading Budd Kilmer's article about the carnage at Brylin.

"Well, if it isn't the most wanted fucking man in Western New York," Vinny said. "I saw your ugly-ass picture on the post office wall this morning: Wanted, dead or alive. I voted for dead."

"You mean like your pecker?"

Vinny just laughed and gave Jack, who was too lazy to get up, a fist-bump.

Chaz was rubbing his stubby-fingered hands together. "Gentlemen – and I use the term loosely – if I may, I would like to bring this meeting to order."

The room hushed as the assembled team of Vinny, Cheese, Driftwood, Juan and Tree Spirit were anxious to hear what their fearless leader had come up with. They had been relentless in parsing out a plan amongst themselves as to how to clean up this mess and get Jack Driftwood back into a Blizzard uniform for the playoffs. It was time to crank up the machine again. Chaz was ready to present Phase II of his master plan. Phase I was a *fete accompli.*

Gerry had arranged for her attorney, Millard Steinman, to meet her at the hospital. She preferred not to leave her father alone at this stage. The doctors said it was possible he could wake up at any given moment – you never knew in these cases. She could tell as soon as she saw Millard things were not going all that well. Millard confirmed as much, telling her unless some new information came to light Fegel had a strong legal case for control of the team.

She pounded her small fist on the table. "I cannot believe this, how can this be, Millard? The Blizzard is my father's team and I am his only heir. How can they give it to a bastard like Fegel?"

"I am extremely sorry, Gerry," Millard said. "But as I previously stated, you had not yet executed the paperwork and unfortunately the Team Charter has an explicit policy regarding this situation. Our only recourse is to prove Mr. Fegel has done something unethical or illegal, which could possibly disqualify him from his position."

Gerry bit her lip until it nearly bled. She had proof of both, but Chaz had asked her to hold on for just a little longer. They had to be sure the case against Fegel would stand up in court, that Meade's cooked books would be admissible evidence. She just had to be patient for a little longer. If that meant keeping quiet while that smug, little bastard whistled his way through the halls of the Wigwam for a few days, so be it. It wouldn't be easy, but she could do it.

"It's just hard to swallow. But I'm okay." Gerry said.

"Are you sure? Is there anything else I should know?"

Gerry wasn't able to look the man in the eye. "No. Nothing right now, anyway. What about Jack, how do we get him reinstated?"

"I've been working the phones on that, and am waiting a call back from the Commissioner. It looks like we may get a hearing on Monday. From what I hear, the league office is not very happy with Mr. Fegel, either. Goldman was none too pleased to find out about this whole mess through the papers."

"Is there anything I can do to help on Jack's behalf?"

"Well," Millard said, "we do need cooperating witnesses on Jack's behalf."

Gerry shot him a quick look. She didn't know Chaz's entire plan, but she did know the gang was up to something. Hopefully, they were rounding up some additional help.

"I will see what I can do."

"All right then, Gerry, let me know if you think of anything else. Until then, I wish you and your father the best, dear."

"Thank you," Gerry said. "If anything changes I will let you know."

Millard Steinman looked at her for what seemed like an eternity. There was obviously another question on his lips, but he shook his head and walked out the door.

The fresh blanket of snow, if only for a short time, disguised the usual dirt and garbage strewn across the landscape outside of Walter Keating's humble one-bedroom apartment in the Fighting Village housing development in Rochester, New York. Walter had wrapped himself in an old army blanket and was slumped down in a well-worn recliner to watch the EFC Wildcard game starting at 1 p.m. There wasn't anyone left Walter called family, thus there were neither any cheery Christmas decorations nor a beautifully decorated tree to bring any holiday joy to the drab apartment. There were no stockings hung by the chimney with care awaiting Keating when he had risen the previous morning. He thought briefly about cranking the thermostat up to seventy as a gift to himself, but the sobering reality of having to pay the heat bill made him wrap up in the old blanket instead; he left the dial at sixty-two.

Walter had settled in for kick-off to a long day of NAFA football on the tube. He could live with that. An official sounding knock on his second-floor apartment door put an instant damper on those plans. Walter reluctantly extricated himself from the warmth of the blanket and shuffled to the door.

*Who the hell wants to kick me in the pants, now?*

Through the peep-hole in the door he saw a squat, thick-shouldered, late to middle-aged man with his long, carrot-colored hair pulled back into a ponytail. The guy had a NAFA credential hanging around his neck on a lanyard.

"Who is it and what the hell do you want?" He hollered through the door.

"Mr. Keating, my name is Charles Johnson. I'm from the league office, and we need to talk."

Walter had seen the Budd Kilmer article and had been watching the local television stations have a field day speculating about Jack Driftwood's disappearance from some mental hospital. He was surprised the NAFA already had somebody at his door, but only a little.

"Are you serious? It's the day after Christmas, a Saturday afternoon, for chrissakes. Don't you people ever rest?"

"I'll only take a moment of your time, but this is a very important matter."

"Alright, hold your horses." He removed the chain-lock and slid the bolt to open the door. "Come on in, then, don't mind the mess. The maid is off for the holidays."

Johnson laughed politely and shook hands with Walter, obviously scoping out the apartment as he entered.

"Pleased to meet you Walter – may I call you Walter?"

"That's what my whore of a mother named me," Walter replied. "Here, sit down, Mr. Johnson. Tell me what this is all about."

He pointed to a small, janky dinette set crammed into a corner of the room. Johnson took a seat across from Walter at the grimy, linoleum-covered dining table.

"Thanks, but I think you already know exactly what this is about."

Johnson's face changed in an instant from warm and friendly to menacing and threatening like the sun dipping behind a dark cloud. Uncertainty crept into Walter's mind; he did not like the sudden change of tone from his guest.

"What the hell you say?" Walter said.

"This is about what you did to Jack Driftwood," Johnson said. "This is about how you made up some bullshit story to get him to sign an extra copy of the drug sample collection paperwork, and then gave it to Donald Fegel so he could falsify a positive test and suspend Jack. Ring a bell?"

"N-N-Now, you just wait a minute here, pal."

"No, you wait a fucking minute!" The veins in Johnson's neck bulged and his face had taken on a red hue as his emotions rose. "I'm here to help you, Walter, God knows why. But I'm not one to stand idly by while an innocent man gets railroaded by a bunch of criminals. I'm giving you one chance to come clean, and if you do, I'll help you. But if you want to sit here and play games and jack me off things will get ugly."

Walter looked silently at the invader, weighing his options. He wasn't sure who this character was, but he didn't look like anybody he'd want to tangle with, and he sure as hell wasn't from the NAFA offices.

"Okay, I'm listening."

"Good," Johnson said. "Here's what going to happen. You're going to throw some clothes into an overnight bag and you're coming with me. I'm putting you under my personal protection until you can testify at Driftwood's hearing Monday morning. Then all you have to do is tell the truth. Think you can handle that, Pissman?"

Walter shook his head. "That'll cost me my job, and as you can see, I can't likely afford for that to happen."

"You will have a lot bigger problems than unemployment if you refuse to cooperate. Of that, I can assure you. However, I know a lot of people, and if you play ball, I will see to it you get a job and a fair shake. But it's up to you to tell the truth, and the truth, Mr. Keating, shall set you free."

"That's real easy for you to say, Mr. Johnson, or whoever you are. But in case you weren't aware, I'm a sixty-two-year-old registered nurse who hasn't had a nursing job in over three years. Nope, I've been watching grown men piss the whole time. Ain't nobody hiring me. On top of that, everybody I ever gave two shits about is either dead or refuses to talk to me. So don't come in here thinking you can sprinkle magic fairy dust around and shit out a few rainbows and solve all my problems. Threats don't mean much to a man with nothing left to lose."

"Oh, I am aware, Walter. More aware than you know. Frankly, I don't get it. What the hell happened to you, man? You were a damn-fine family man, an important part of the community. You were a solid citizen who cared about people. You had a heart. Where did that Walter Keating go? He didn't just up and disappear. He's still here, right in front of me.

"It ain't too late. Sure, somewhere along the line you got kicked around. Well, life does that to all of us. You just have to fight it, fight it every fucking day! I know that good man, that fighter with the big heart, is still in there. I don't believe that man would just shrug his shoulders while an innocent Jack Driftwood gets hung out to dry by the same kind of assholes that ran you into the ground. That ain't you, Walter, that ain't you, and you know it. It's time to come back. To come back and fight."

Walter met Johnson's gaze briefly and then looked away. He leaned forward in his chair and put his head into his hands. What had happened to him? Whoever this bastard Johnson was, the man was right. Walter did have a heart – that is, until it had been ripped out five years prior when his only son passed away from cancer.

The medical bills had ruined him financially; he was still making payments and would be for the rest of his life. The entire nightmare had caused a bitter fight with the rest of his family. He could no longer recall exactly what started the whole thing, only that he had washed his hands of the lot of them. But it wasn't working for him anymore. Giving up on life and wallowing in his bitterness was not the answer. Maybe this could be a start. Maybe he could turn this thing around.

"God, I never meant to hurt Jack Driftwood. He's one of the few of them Blizzard that's a decent man. But they paid me ten thousand dollars, and ain't no money tree growing around here. I'm making peanuts watching millionaire assholes piss into a cup while I'm up to my ass in debt. How would you like to be known as the Pissman?"

"I hear you, Walter. But it's time to man up. You can either be the guy who helped an asshole like Fegel kick an honorable man like Jack Driftwood to the curb, or you can be the man that stood up and told the truth when it mattered."

Tears welled up in Walter's eyes as he marveled at how far off track he had gotten. Enough was enough. Johnson was right; it was time to man up.

"All right, Mr. Johnson," Walter said. "I'll come with you. And I will tell the truth at Driftwood's hearing. He deserves as much."

"He'll be glad to hear that. He is out there in my truck waiting for us right now. Pack up your shit and let's go."

"Jack Driftwood is here? At Fighting Village?" Walter looked toward the windows. "No shit. I'll bet he's the first Blizzard to ever set foot in this hell-hole."

Walter Keating shook his head in amazement as he headed into the bedroom to throw some things into an old Blizzard duffel bag. He already felt a hundred pounds lighter. And Jack Driftwood was right there at Fighting Village.

*Nobody is gonna believe this one*, he thought. *Nobody*!

The Crown Vic pulled up the driveway to the old farmhouse in the sleepy town of Medina, just off the southern shore of Lake Ontario, early Saturday afternoon. Despite the snow and cold, Cheese, the unfortunate passenger on this long ride, had his window open and his head was hanging outside like man's best friend. When the vehicle stopped he scrambled out of the torture chamber as fast as he could. Vinny, apparently immune and totally unaffected, shook his head and took his sweet time getting out. Then he had to wait for the passenger side window to roll up.

"You are such a fucking baby," Vinny said after pulling his significant mass from the car.

"I don't know what you ate," Cheese said, "but I'm thinking it was a skunk's ass."

Cheese vigorously rubbed his nose up and down between his forefinger and thumb. He bent over and gagged, dry heaving a little before a coughing attack ravaged him.

"You sick fucker. You literally painted the inside of my nose. I can't get it off me."

"Special vintage, partner. Two bottles of a nice merlot blended with Beverly's special sauce over a plate of kielbasa and sauerkraut."

"Sauerkraut! I knew it – hell, I tasted it! You really need to get that thing checked, although I can't imagine being your doctor. I could have you killed for this, you know," Cheese said.

"Right. What you gonna do, call Luca Brasi and make me swim with the fishes?"

"Don't tempt me," Cheese said. "And quit screwing around. We need to get this done. The guy supposedly is staying in an apartment above the garage. Hey, I got an idea. If he gives us a hard time you could open up another can of ass – sit on his face and let it rip and he'll sing like a canary, unless he dies first."

"Now, that is some forward thinking right there," Vinny said.

They climbed the steps attached to the garage sitting twenty yards behind the old farmhouse. There were several cars parked around the place, so the assumption was somebody was home. Cheese led the way and had to wait for a huffing and puffing Vinny at the top of the steps.

"Jesus, you gonna make it, big guy?"

Vinny gasped and grabbed the rail. "Fu…fuck you, you little horse prick. Knock on the goddamn door."

"Ok, if you say so. Looks like I will be doing the talking, huh? At least until you catch your breath."

With that parting shot Cheese rapped on the door. They waited a moment and then Cheese banged on the door again, this time with authority.

"Geez, why don't you just knock the damn door down," Vinny said.

Cheese was about to give it back when the door opened. A man stood mute in the doorway and looked Cheese up and down before turning his attention to Vinny without a hint of recognition.

"Yes," he said, "what can I do for you?"

Cheese was about to speak when Vinny's massive left arm bumped him aside as it shot out past his shoulder to display his police badge.

"Buffalo Police, homicide," Vinny said in his official-police-business voice. "May we come in." It wasn't a request.

The man looked past Vinny out into the driveway, obviously scanning the area for other visitors, perhaps some backup for the two men at his door. A nervous smile and a look of recognition registered on his face.

"Ah, yeah. Sure, come on in officers," he said.

Vinny was tempted to set the record straight, that Cheese was no cop, but figured this petty criminal didn't need to know that. Let Officer Cheese have his moment of glory.

"Thank you," Cheese said. "I'm Detective Barcheezzi and this here is Officer Cappolla."

Vinny instantly regretted his decision and jumped into the conversation. "Mr. Abercrombie, I presume. Roger Abercrombie?"

The man nodded.

"Also known as Race Bannon?" Vinny asked.

Abercrombie didn't even try to hide the surprise on his face. "H-How, how did you know that?"

"I know everything, asshole," Vinny said. "I know you worked for Neil Dadoska. I know you shot Tree Spirit Hansen down in Mexico, where Jack Driftwood beaned you with a rock. I know you were at Brylin Hospital on Christmas Eve where this same Mr. Driftwood beat the shit out of you and zapped you with your own Taser, stupid ass. I know a lot of other shit, but it isn't relevant to this discussion. So sit the fuck down."

Abercrombie had backed into the room absorbing each new accusation from Vinny like a body blow. His eyes had grown big and wild. When he took a seat, he did so in silence.

"Looks to me like you hit a nerve there, officer," Cheese said.

Vinny ignored the jab; he was all business now, police business.

"Here's how you are going to stay out of trouble for a little while. You are going to show up at the Blizzard offices Monday afternoon at one o'clock to testify at a hearing being held by the NAFA to determine the fate of Mr. Driftwood. You are going to tell them Neil Dadoska hired you and got you into the building as an overnight security guard in order to break Driftwood out and bring him downstairs to Dadoska. You have no idea why Dadoska wanted Mr. Driftwood because you learned long ago not to pry into Mr. Dadoska's business. As you were escorting Driftwood down the stairs, he got the jump on you and lit your dumbass up with your own Taser. When you regained consciousness Driftwood was gone and you got your lame ass out of there. You got all that?"

Abercrombie sat there in stunned silence.

Vinny took a menacing step towards him and yelled, "I said, do you got all that?"

"Yes, yes, sir, I got it. That's almost what happened."

"No, Mr. Abercrombie, that is *exactly* what happened." Vinny let that resonate in the air for a moment.

"And don't go getting any bright ideas like trying to run or hide," Cheese said. "I will have eyes on you until you show up at the Wigwam, Monday at one."

Cheese pointed two fingers at his own eyes and then jabbed them into the air at Abercrombie before holding up one finger, perfectly miming his words.

"N-No, I wouldn't do that. I will be there," Abercrombie said.

With that Vinny nodded at Cheese and they left without another word until they reached the car and Vinny's phone rang. It was Jack.

"Cappolla," he answered.

"How'd it go, big boy?"

"It went fine except for the felony Cheese committed by impersonating a police officer."

"Well, you've been getting away with it for years so it shouldn't be too big of an issue."

"Very funny. So where we at?" Vinny asked.

"We're pretty much all good. The Pissman is in and the security guard is not a big Fegel fan, so he's on board as well. So, unless you two fucked it up somehow, we should be ready."

"Us two? Let me tell you something, I am a true profess—"

The line went dead.

"Can you believe that shit, Detective Barcheezzi?" Vinny said. "Your good friend Mr. Driftwood just hung up on me again."

"Wow, officer, that's *really* hard to believe," Cheese replied.

"Somebody is going to have to pay for that," Vinny said as he got into the car.

The first button he pushed was the window lock. The new Detective was going to be the one to pay. And pay he did, the entire long, odoriferous ride back down to Buffalo.

# Chapter Forty-Nine

The opening round of the NAFA playoffs began the weekend following Christmas. After the busy weekend schedule of exciting action, the NAFA Commissioner, Bob Goldman, made a stop in Buffalo, catching an early flight out of Chicago Monday morning. The Commissioner's ambitious plan to attend three of the four weekend games was a rousing success and a relaxing good time. Goldman knew how to have fun on the road. And now he was off to Buffalo because there were some issues to settle in the Mega Bowl host city.

National headlines trumpeting a player being admitted to a mental facility, only to break out and leave in his wake a pile of dead bodies, all while the team owner was in a coma at a local hospital and the franchise was embroiled in an internal battle for control, all made for one hell of a soap opera, but it added up to bad business for the NAFA. Goldman intended to head this off at the pass and set a precedence of swift justice under his regime. One of the primary reasons he had been hired the previous summer was to put to an end to the mayhem that had transpired throughout the league under his predecessor's watch; this was a golden opportunity to show his leadership ability and display a firm hand in quelling such nonsense. And that is exactly what the Commissioner intended to do.

The hearing was set for one o'clock Monday afternoon in the Wigwam. The agenda was to determine the status of Jack Driftwood for the playoffs, but while Goldman was in town he also planned to hear from both parties involved in the fight for control of the franchise. He had initially ruled in Donald Fegel's favor, but Gerry Wainscott and her attorney Millard Steinman had appealed that decision. The hope was, given Goldman's presence, both issues could be settled, or at least moved in that direction, allowing the fervor to die down and for the focus to be put back on the playoffs where it belonged.

The hearing began with opening statements from each side. Bob Goldman sat as judge, jury, and executioner on all discipline matters in the league, per the NAFA's collective bargaining agreement with the Players Union. He sat at the head of the immense table in the Blizzard boardroom. Like teams on their respective sidelines, each side flanked the mahogany slab clearly dividing the room.

The Blizzard led off the examination by calling Donald Allen Fegel Jr. to the stand. A separate table and chair had been set up on risers to the right of the commissioner as an impromptu witness stand, the proverbial hot seat for those called to testify. Fegel ambled up onto the platform and swore to tell the truth, the whole truth, and then told anything but the truth.

His story went like this: He was given a heads up by a friend at the league offices Jack Driftwood had failed his recent drug test for PEDs. This type of courtesy call was not uncommon to the NAFA. The official lab results would be released by the NAFA in due time. For Fegel, this was the final straw for Jack Driftwood. He explained Driftwood had already faced internal discipline for various infractions, including drinking on the team bus, fighting a coach on the sidelines during a game, and getting in trouble in the city's nightclubs. Driftwood had a long track record of violent transgressions.

Compounding matters was the timing of Mr. Wainscott's health issues. The news of Driftwood dishonoring himself had come mere moments after hearing of Mr. Wainscott's condition. Poor Mr. Wainscott had enough to worry about, and Donald swore to himself Jack Driftwood wouldn't be one of them. He would see to that personally, and with immediacy.

Knowing Mr. Driftwood's history of violent actions, he called in a few select members of his security staff to hopefully deter the man from resorting to his usual methods. It had obviously been a fruitless precaution, as one look at his face testified; Mr. Driftwood actively resented authority of any kind. However, it was a good thing he had made the call, or chances were, he wouldn't even be there to testify. The implications were ominous.

He had bluntly told Driftwood it was over; he was letting him go. That's when the guy got predictably belligerent and ultimately violent, hitting him with a sucker punch that shattered his nose. Two of Fegel's ribs had also been broken in the process, so he claimed.

In the aftermath, Fegel realized how badly off Jack Driftwood really was; the man was clearly a danger to himself and, demonstratively, to others. Just take a gander at Donald's face. It was a brutal blow, Fegel knew, to not only have been fired but also to have just heard the news about Mr. Wainscott. On top of this, his body was coursing with steroids and God only knew what else. 'Roid rage was real; the guy needed some serious help.

Fegel theorized Jack had also become institutionalized to a large extent, having been in the NAFA for the past eighteen years, being told what to do and when to do it. No doubt, he was frightened and desperate at the prospect of life without the structure of the daily routine of football. With the drugs involved, who was Donald Fegel to take a chance with another man's life? He committed him to Brylin Hospital for seventy-two hours of observation in maximum security. It was the only humane thing to do.

There wasn't much else to it, so with that the Blizzard wrapped up their case. They called no other witnesses. Their attorney, Marcus Badger, summed things up by requesting the Commissioner respectfully permit the Blizzard to handle their own personnel matters with regards to who they do or do not carry on their roster, as per the NAFA Charter and league rules, the same as he does with the league's other thirty-five franchises. The team had violated no league statutes when making the decision to release Driftwood, or when they committed him to Brylin.

They had, in fact, done Driftwood a favor far above and beyond their normal responsibilities to a player. He cited precedence of several other NAFA team's taking similar actions with their players. Ultimately, Badger argued, as damning as the drug test results were to Mr. Driftwood, even they were a moot point. The bottom line was Donald Fegel, as the General Manager and legal head of the Blizzard franchise, was perfectly within his rights to release any player he so desired. And thus, he did so in regards to Mr. Driftwood. In light of Mr. Driftwood's track record, it was downright shameful Mr. Fegel was even called to defend this action.

Bob Goldman sat listening intently to the summation, often nodding in agreement and clearly empathizing with the team's stance. After the rundown from Badger, the Commissioner called for a half-hour recess. The defense was up next, and by appearances they had better have one hell of a case or Jack Driftwood's days as a Blizzard player were history.

Millard Steinman had Gerry's assurance Jack would appear at the hearing. She had also briefed him on the witnesses available to appear on Jack's behalf, along with their stories. Steinman was outraged at the behavior of Donald Fegel on a professional level; personally he despised the man. He never fully understood Gerald Wainscott's tolerance of the vermin, let alone the position of power Fegel had weaseled his way into.

Millard planned to call his witnesses in an order similar to a big rock concert – a few warm-up acts before the main-headliner, Jack Driftwood, hit the stage. But right before Jack was called, he planned on dropping a bomb in the form of Walter Keating on Fegel's case. He relished the thought. He had heard through the grapevine Fegel had had people desperately searching for the man all weekend. However, they never thought to look in a bunker out on the north end of Hemlock Lake. Millard couldn't wait to see the look on Fegel's face when he brought Keating in from his hiding place in Gerry's office.

Steinman got the ball rolling by calling one of Donald Fegel's security guards, Rodney Pustay, to the stand. Pustay was sworn in and began his testimony with how he was selected to Mr. Fegel's security team, in order to establish his background and his role in the affair. After Steinman established the foundation, he got to the meat of things.

"So tell us, Mr. Pustay, What happened when Jack Driftwood came into Mr. Fegel's office?"

Pustay shook his head. "It was bogus, man, right off the bat Fegel was like, it's time for you to hit the trail, cowboy. You tested positive for steroids, coke, and weed but that ain't what this is about. You're gone because I'm running this ship now. So Drifty was like, okay, then I'm gonna talk to Mr. Wainscott about this because you're trippin' dude. So Fegel goes, you can cry to the old bastard all you want but he ain't gonna hear you. He had a stroke and is hooked up to a shit bag over at Children's Hospital so this team is mine now, boy. Then Fegel says, 'Imagine that, an old bastard like that at a children's hospital.' And he starts laughing this crazy, whack laugh.

"You could see it hit Drifty hard, man, like he was shook for a second, but then he says he's gonna talk to Gerry, Ms. Wainscott. That's when Fegel got really hot and was like yeah, that's another reason your ass is grass. Me and her was gonna hook up 'til you turned on your biker charm. But that shit won't fly no more. Then he's all like, yeah, and Gerry's gonna be real nice to me with the old man out of the picture. She's gonna sign everything over to me, it's all mine and you ain't part of it no more."

Steinman was a little shocked both by Pustay's candor and his vernacular, as was most of the room. However, there was little doubt he passionately believed every word coming out of his own mouth. And the man had a remarkable memory, as his story matched what Jack had told him with uncanny accuracy. He wasn't sure if Pustay's delivery detracted from his testimony or damaged his credibility, but this cat was out of the bag. He looked over at Gerry with his eyebrows slightly raised, but she kept her head down looking at her notepad as if it were the most interesting thing on the planet. Jack was fighting to keep a straight face as was most everybody else in the room.

"Then what happened?" Millard asked.

"Well, that was when Drifty lost it, man. Fegel was sittin' on the edge of the desk all cocky, stickin' his chest out, you know, almost like he was daring Drifty to do something; kinda eggin' him on like that. So Drifty obliged him. He snapped off a tight right cross and pop! He hit ol' boy flush on the button. I mean he knocked Fegel's ass clean over the desk and into next week. Then Drifty dove after him, punching and swinging and that's when me and those other boys had to go to work. I mean, that was our job, you know what I'm sayin'? We was getting paid to protect the dude, but I'm telling you if I wasn't on the clock, I would have been cheering Drifty on. Fegel had it comin' to him, no doubt. So we jumped in and pulled Drifty off of him and one of the other dudes, Kim Welch, roughed him up a little bit to make it look good."

At that point Pustay looked over at Jack and said, "Sorry about that, man. It wasn't nothin' personal – just doing the job, you know?"

Jack nodded but kept quiet, so Pustay continued.

"Everybody knows Jack Driftwood is one bad-ass hombre who won't quit. I knew we would have to do some serious damage to the cat to make him stop so I stuck him – injected him with a sedative to knock him out. Fegel had told us it might get a little rough so I came prepared, per usual. That's why I am the best at what I do."

"I see," Millard said. "And what did Mr. Fegel do at that point?"

"Well, Fegel was out like a light for a minute – Drifty had knocked his ass out cold, one-punched him. But he came around pretty quick-like and told us to take Drifty over to that mental hospital to admit him. He said he would call and set it all up. Then he asks us to shoot Drifty up, you know, inject him with steroids, coke, and weed before we took him over to Brylin. I was like, sure dude, whatever you say. But I promise you, we did not stick no pins in him, man. I mean, I don't care what anybody does to their own body, but dosing cats just ain't cool, man. I could never do nothin' like that."

He looked directly at Jack as he said it.

"One last question, Mr. Pustay, and I just want to thank you for testimony here today."

Pustay nodded eagerly, obviously pleased with himself and the way things were unfolding.

"What, if anything, did Mr. Fegel say to you after you returned from Brylin Hospital?"

"Well, see, that's the thing. I never returned. I ain't said word one to the dude. After bringing Drifty over there, I headed straight back to the crib. Life is too short to work around such a negative vibe, you know? For all I knew I could be next on Fegel's hit list. And that whole business bout shooting Drifty up with all those drugs; that's just evil, man. What kind of freak would do that? So, I quit and I ain't darkened these doorways since, until today. And to tell you the truth, I can't wait to get the hell outta here, right now. This whole place creeps me out."

"Let's take care of that for you then, Mr. Pustay. You are dismissed," Millard said.

"That's it?" Pustay asked. "I can go now?"

Commissioner Goldman nodded his assent.

"Yes, I believe it is. You are free to leave," Millard said.

Next up was Roger Abercrombie, aka Race Bannon. Abercrombie was a lot less colorful than Rodney Pustay but equally effective. He told his story efficiently, though it was obvious he was no fan of Jack. He described how he worked security for the Seneca Nation under the direct supervision of the late Neil Dadoska. The boss had called him and told him he was needed to work the overnight shift, seventh-floor security at Brylin Hospital, where he was to bring Jack down the emergency stairs at midnight and Neil would take it from there.

If there was a problem the plan was to remove Driftwood themselves, take him to a safer, more secure location. However, Driftwood suckered him, too, limping and acting all beat up and then jumping him in the stairwell. He knocked him out and then zapped him with his own Taser. When he came to, Driftwood was long gone, so he hightailed it out of there.

He never mentioned Dadoska's decapitation nor the mayhem he regrettably witnessed in the aftermath; he never planned on speaking of any of that ever again, not for as long as he lived. He also never referred to the five grand he had been paid by Chaz to assist in Driftwood's escape. No sense in making things any messier than they already were.

Bob Goldman called for a fifteen-minute recess so everybody could stretch their legs or use the facilities. Next up for the defense was a mystery to all but a few; the Pissman, Walter Keating, would be called to the stand. Steinman had strategically kept Keating on ice in Gerry's office down the hall and he personally went to retrieve him. He did not want Fegel to know if the man was even alive, let alone right there in the building.

Donald's face went completely ashen when Keating entered the room. He had frantically tried to find Keating himself, to make sure he had his story straight, but nobody could find the guy. He was Colin Meade's connection, but that little prick was incommunicado, too. And now this man, Keating, a veritable pawn in the scheme of things, was going to testify and take down a king. This could not be!

Keating was sworn in and looked imminently uncomfortable sitting up on the risers as the room focused in on him. Jack winked at him and stuck his thumb up, which seemed to brighten Walter's spirits.

After Steinman established Keating's credentials he got right to the heart of the matter.

"Mr. Keating, on November thirtieth, did you come to the Wigwam to collect urine samples for the NAFA random steroid testing program?"

"Well, yeah," Keating said. "That's my job, as I stated. I come here every Monday and Friday during the football season."

Steinman nodded. "And on that date do you recall Jack Driftwood arriving on the sixth floor of this very building to produce a urine sample?"

"Yes. He was the first one to come up. It was early, before their meetings. Usually guys come up during their lunch hour or after practice, but I get here early in case anybody wants to get it out of the way before their meetings start."

Donald was getting more and more nervous as he sat listening to Keating's testimony. How had Driftwood tracked him down? This did not look good. He wondered if he should run. Just take off and get as far away from this room as possible. But then what? It was no good.

"And after you witnessed Driftwood producing the sample, did you have him sign an extra set of forms that accompany these samples to testify as to their validity?"

Keating looked down at his hands and sweat broke out on his brow. "Yes, I did. See here's what the deal was, Colin Meade came to me the previous Friday and offered me ten grand if I were to tell Jack Driftwood I had screwed up the original forms and needed him to sign another set."

There was an outburst of gasping and murmuring in the room, causing Bob Goldman to slap his hand down on the table like a makeshift gavel. It had the desired effect.

"People, please!" he bellowed. "Let's let the man talk here! Please continue, Mr. Keating."

Walter looked around the room before once again focusing on Jack – for some reason it calmed him down. "I can tell you this much, being the Pissman don't pay shit. I lost my nursing job three years ago and I got medical bills up the wahzoo. So it was an easy yet regrettable decision to take the money. I did what they wanted – I told Jack I screwed up the first form and had him sign and initial a fresh batch. I'm damn sorry I did, now."

"Did anyone mention you what those forms were for?"

"Didn't have to, I ain't no dumbass. They needed signed forms for the league to legitimize the sample. It was obvious the plan was to use some dirty urine to frame Driftwood with a positive test."

"What did you do with the forms after you were done?" Steinman asked.

"I brought them down to Colin Meade's office. I gave him an envelope and he gave me one and that was that."

"What did Mr. Fegel have to say?"

"Mr. Fegel? I guess I wouldn't know that. See, I did all my dealings with Colin Meade. I never talked to no Fegel, not once."

Donald exhaled and took a big gulp of air. He hadn't realized he had been holding his breathe while Keating testified. He relaxed several notches, and quickly his breathing was back under control. There it was, his golden ticket! His claim of ignorance was entirely feasible, he could pin this whole thing on Meade. He'd had no idea the man was up to such chicanery. It was perfect! It was no wonder Meade hadn't shown up for work the past two days and wouldn't answer his calls. It all made impeccable sense.

He looked over at Millard Steinman, who was seldom, if ever, blind-sided in a courtroom. Steinman did an expert job of hiding his surprise and dismay, but Donald knew it was there. Sure, Jack Driftwood would get reinstated, but Donald Fegel would get off scot-free. Steinman had to make a split-second decision on whether to pursue him or close up Keating's testimony in hopes of limiting the damage. He couldn't help himself and chose the former.

"Well, did Colin Meade mention Mr. Fegel in any of your conversations?" Steinman asked.

Keating thought about that for a second. "Not that I recall. I mean he said 'we' a lot but he never mentioned any Fegel by name."

Swing and a miss! Steinman's lips formed a tight line and he quickly wrapped up the questioning.

"Finally, Mr. Keating, is anybody paying you for your testimony here today in front of this tribunal?"

"No. No, sir. Is that an offer?"

The courtroom tension was lanced by the round of laughter that followed. Even Judge Goldman cracked a semblance of a smile.

"I'm sorry, I'm afraid not, but thank you, Mr. Keating."

After Keating left the room, Donald cleared his throat to make his play. "Excuse me, Bob, I swear to you and everybody else in this room that this is the first I have heard of any this and I am as disgusted by it as the rest of you. Colin Meade acted entirely independent from me on this scam. It's obvious now why he has skipped work the past two days and won't return anybody's phone calls. I believe he saw the writing on the wall regarding this hearing today and likely skipped town. He is officially suspended as assistant general manager of this franchise, effective immediately. I will not tolerate such deception or scheming around here.

"Furthermore, if Jack Driftwood can pass another drug screening, I will reinstate him immediately to the team. I'm willing to forgive and forget. Obviously, Driftwood knew he was being railroaded by this false positive drug test and came to the erroneous yet somewhat understandable conclusion that I had orchestrated this whole fiasco. Although this does not forgive his attack on me, it does make it a bit more palatable."

He paused to let that sink in amidst the excited whispering and undercurrent of susurrating rampant in the boardroom. "Also, effective immediately, Walter Keating is no longer employed by this franchise. Millard?"

Millard was infuriated by Fegel's air of superiority and torn by the bittersweetness of his proclamation. The bastard had deftly put the whole thing on Colin Meade and then magnanimously reinstated his client pending a clean drug test. Sure, Steinman had achieved his primary objective, but to expose the slimy General Manager and take him down was a close second. It appeared that ship had just sailed out of the harbor. The slippery son of a bitch had slithered through his grasp unscathed.

"I need a moment with my client," he said, directing his comment at the commissioner.

"Fair enough," Goldman said. "We will take a ten-minute recess. Will that suffice?"

"Yes, sir, it shouldn't take that long," Millard said.

"Very well," said Goldman. "We will just sit here and await your return."

Millard and Jack left the room. Both were fuming mad Fegel had managed to dodge the bullet with his name on it, though they remained stone-faced until safely behind Gerry's office door. Millard was even more upset with himself. He had never seen the sleight of hand coming, having assumed Keating had dealt directly with Fegel. It hadn't occurred to him to ask Keating about it while briefing him prior to the hearing. It was a rookie mistake for which he would be a long time in forgiving himself.

"Sorry, Jack," he said, "I just assumed Fegel was in on this thing with Mr. Keating."

"I know, it caught us all off guard. Fegel didn't even see it coming, I saw it in his eyes. But don't sweat it, he will get his, and believe me, it won't be long."

He said it with such conviction Millard knew something was afoot. He had figured Gerry Wainscott wasn't entirely leveling with him and Jack had just confirmed it. But this was not the time to get into that.

"Sorry, but I have to ask. Are you clean?" Millard inquired.

"As a whistle, unless that hipster Pustay is lying and they shot me up."

"We have a deal then?"

"That we do," Jack said. "That we do."

They immediately went back into the room to wrap things up. The place was humming with conversation but went silent upon their re-entry.

"Mr. Driftwood is willing to submit a new urine sample with the understanding that if such is deemed clean, he will be reinstated to the team with a clean slate and no other disciplinary action shall be taken against Mr. Driftwood regarding this matter," Millard said.

"Do we have an agreement, Mr. Fegel?" Goldman asked.

"Yes, we do," Fegel said. "And if Driftwood passes that drug test, I will publicly apologize for these heinous actions of Colin Meade under my watch."

"Very well," Goldman said. "However, as the commissioner of this great league, it is my job to mete out discipline for violent and unlawful behavior. This being the case, I will agree to these terms but am imposing a ten thousand dollar fine on Mr. Driftwood for his attack on Mr. Fegel and I am putting him on probation for six months. Any further incidents of violence from you, sir, will result in an immediate one-year suspension from the NAFA."

Millard looked at Jack, who nodded.

"We agree to your terms, Mr. Commissioner."

"Thank you all for your diligence and professionalism in settling this matter. I will arrange for a NAFA representative to administer the drug screening for Mr.

Driftwood immediately, and we will have the results available in twenty-four hours. If there is no problem with that, Jack Driftwood will be reinstated to the Blizzard fifty-five-man roster. That is all."

# Chapter Fifty

After pulling through the hearing earlier that afternoon virtually unscathed, Donald was feeling as close to invincible as he thought possible. With the Driftwood mess resolved it was pretty obvious he was meant to own the Buffalo Blizzard. With the way things had fallen in place for him, who could argue? Colin Meade going missing was turning into a personal bonanza. He was going to take another look at the Wigwam scam and see if he couldn't pin that whole thing on Meade and Dadoska, too. Then he would not only have the cash to fall back on, but he would be free and clear from any possible repercussions.

Life was pretty damn good as Donald stood at his office window overlooking the partially frozen easternmost tip of Lake Erie; king of all he could see. So this is what it felt like to be at the very top. He nearly started beating on his chest like some modern day Tarzan, smiling at the thought. Gazing out over his kingdom, it struck him there was still one very important detail missing.

*What is a mighty king without a beautiful queen?*

He knew how to fix that. Donald pulled out the B-phone and punched up Nicole Brogan's number. She answered on the first ring.

"You are not going to believe this one," he said.

"What? Tell me, Donald, I've been dying over here. What happened? Did you win?"

"Yes…and no. It's complicated and a bit of a long story. I need to see you. Right now!"

"First, you have to tell me what happened."

"Okay, okay. Long story short, they brought in the drug sample collector and he claimed Meade paid him ten grand to trick Driftwood into signing an extra copy of paperwork so Meade could fake a positive test. I thought my goose was cooked but then I realized I had never personally talked to the guy, so the way it worked out, I pinned the whole thing on little Colin Meade. It helped greatly that the little twerp skipped town, played right into my story. Some things are just meant to be, Nicole. They bought it hook, line, and sinker.

"The only downside is I have to reinstate Driftwood if he passes a new drug test. But my meetings with the commissioner couldn't have gone any better. He is supporting me the whole way. He said if I can get the Board of Directors to back me I will control the Trust that owns the team. Essentially I own the team because I own the Board."

"Oh, Donald, that is wonderful. We need to celebrate, immediately!"

Donald felt himself becoming aroused. "That's what I've been trying to tell you! Can you pick me up at the usual spot?"

"I'll be there in fifteen minutes. You better be ready, mister."

He looked down at the bulge in his otherwise neatly pressed dress pants. He was already ready.

The security line at the Buffalo Niagara International airport was longer than Colin Meade expected, but at least it was moving along at a fairly decent clip. He checked his watch: 4:22 p.m.

His flight to Montreal didn't depart until 6:15 p.m. – no problem. From Montreal he would fly directly to Frankfurt, Germany. From there a train would bring him to Bern, Switzerland, where he would clean out his bank accounts, taking a load of cash and wiring the rest to a bank in Bangkok, Thailand, his final destination. Meade had researched the place and was very interested in the illegal sex trading done in that country. He was going to have to find some way to make it up to himself for missing out on the Buffalo Blizzard playoff run. Perhaps he'd find something in Bangkok to fill that void.

He hated having to flee the country but had been honest with himself, knowing the day would surely come. He was toast if he stayed. He sensed the noose tightening around their collective necks, even if Donald Fegel was too deluded and power drunk to realize their current situation. Colin was nervous even he had cut it too close; that strong box stolen from under his bed had been a time-bomb destined to blow. He couldn't believe it hadn't detonated already, sending him and Mr. Fegel up the river to the big house. There was no way he would survive in prison; he would be low-hanging fruit in one of those places. Colin Meade refused to be somebody's bitch for the rest of his life, to run was a no-brainer.

He handed his passport and boarding pass to the TSA Agent.

"Hello, Mr. Schenkel. Traveling alone today?"

"Huh? Oh, yes." Dammit, he had better get used to hearing his new name. "I'm off to Germany to visit relatives."

The Agent cocked his head a bit to the side and gave Schenkel the once over. He made a few marks on the boarding pass before handing it back along with his passport.

"Well, safe travels. You're all set."

"Thank you."

So far so good. He lowered his eyes and headed for his gate. His heart was mixed about leaving Buffalo for the last time. It had been his home for most of his thirty-nine years on the planet, other than a brief stint running a scam out East. Would he miss it? Maybe, but probably not; it wasn't like he was leaving much behind, other than the Blizzard. He was confident he was ready for his new life as Paul William Schenkel, just another filthy-rich, ugly American living abroad. It had a certain appeal, especially the filthy-rich part.

As he sat at the gate waiting for the boarding call, his cell phone beeped, alerting him to a new text message. He had almost forgotten about that damn thing. He pulled it from his suitcoat pocket.

**Call me u little prick.**

It was from Donald Fegel, an asshole to the end. Paul Schenkel powered down the phone and discreetly dropped it into a nearby trash can. That was the last "little prick" he would ever be.

Nobody noticed Donald slip out of his office into the stairwell, not that he really gave a shit. As the captain of this ship, he'd do as he pleased, when he pleased. But he did find a singular, naughty pleasure in sneaking out of the place. That pleasure stemmed from whom he was sneaking out to meet as much as anything.

Donald reached the bottom of the stairwell just in time to see the sleek, late-model Mercedes SL600 Roadster slide to an abrupt stop by banging into the curb. He exited the building with his head on a swivel scanning the surrounding area. All Clear. Fortunately, there was nobody around to see Nicole smash into the curb or him hop into the car. Nicole climbed over the console into the passenger seat as Donald slid into the driver's seat. He had no sooner hopped into the car and Nicole was all over him like white on rice. They embraced, mashing lips in a deep, lascivious kiss. Donald wanted to take her right there but quickly came back to his senses.

"Damn, Nicole," he said. "We better get away from here before it's too late."

"Too late for what?" she asked with a predatory look in her eyes.

"Too late for me to just take you right here."

He put the car into gear and pulled away from the curb.

"Sounds like a plan to me," Nicole said. "You're the owner now, you can do whatever you please."

"Yes, I suppose I can."

Donald shook his smiling head in wonder. He was the owner – kind of. He was calling the shots, that much was for sure. If he said it, people did it. Nicole leaned over and began undoing his belt.

"Jesus, Nicole! You're going to make me crash."

"I don't care, I need you in me – right now."

Nicole had climbed on top of the console and was trying to hike her leg over him, but he managed to push her back into her own seat. She was not to be denied and reached over and began to fumble with his belt again. Donald was fully aroused by now and he let her do what she would. She giggled as she finally managed to get his pants undone and pulled slightly down. She liberated his cock and eagerly took it into her mouth all the way to the hilt. Donald gasped and clutched the steering wheel with both hands.

"Oh, oh shit."

Nicole greedily worked him up and down. She reached one of her hands down between her legs and began to pleasure herself at the same time. Donald took one hand off the wheel and hungrily searched for her breasts. They easily tumbled out of her dress and skimpy lace bra.

*So this is what road-head feels like!*

But the road was miles from his head. Unconsciously he accelerated and decelerated the expensive automobile in rhythm with Nicole as she continued to expertly do her thing. Donald was lost somewhere between reality and the transcendent world of extreme sexual pleasure. He was building up past the point of no return.

"Arghh!"

Donald was sure he was going to blow the back of her head off with the force of his ejaculation. When she reached under his balls and pushed his magic button it was all but over. He arched his hips and let it go. It was the most glorious sensation he had ever experienced.

Great God Almighty!

The girl knew what to do! It was as close to an out-of-body experience Donald Allen Fegel Jr. had ever achieved; he was in the netherworld. Bright colors and inexplicable images beautiful beyond description filtered through his mind. If there was a heaven, he had just had a glimpse. He no longer saw through a glass darkly. At the core of his very being, he had broken on through to the other side.

Nicole had simultaneously brought herself to a climax. Donald instinctively squeezed her breast, pinching and twisting one of her nipples between his forefinger and thumb. It sent Nicole up another level and then over the top as her entire body contracted in a simultaneous paroxysm with his.

This mutual bliss seemed to stretch for an eternity until it ended in sudden, raw violence. The transcendental trip through wonderland abruptly stopped. He reverted back to reality, opening his eyes. For a second, Donald could not clearly recall where he was. All he could see was the full moon radiating in the northern sky at dusk on this cold, clear evening. What an odd sensation.

*Why are we flying?*

The call came in at 6:15 in the evening, just after the sun had set and darkness was descending over Western New York. Vinny Cappolla's shift had just started and he was patrolling the Buffalo streets in the area around Riverside Park. Because of manpower issues he was stuck doing a shift in a squad car to help in filling out the schedule. He was hoping to take advantage of the situation and scout around for some of his underworld contacts who hung around the park. Word on the street was a new crystal meth dealer had set up shop in the area. Vinny was following a loose and mostly cold trail attempting to track the guy down.

Vinny's police radio crackled to life with the voice of the dispatcher.

"David 235 investigate motor vehicle accident, corner of Niagara and Vulcan. Possible personal injury. Late model black Mercedes flipped on shoulder of the road. Ambulance in route. Over."

"This is David 242. I'm right around the corner at Riverside Park. Be on the scene in two minutes. Over and out."

He sped up Tonawanda Street and took a left onto Vulcan. As he approached Niagara Street he saw the overturned vehicle a few hundred yards up the road to his right. It looked like a big, black turtle flipped on its back, unable to right itself. As Vinny pulled up he saw the passenger side had taken the brunt of things; it was completely caved in. It wasn't likely the passenger had survived this one.

"This is David 242. I'm on the scene. Send Fire and Rescue. Injuries yet unknown. Over."

Vinny came to a stop and rocked his gigantic mass twice to gain the inertia to pop out of the squad car. He was the first responder on the scene and quickly made his way to the driver's side of the vehicle and dropped to a knee to have a look inside. He nearly fell over backwards in shock when he recognized the driver of the car.

Fegel was alive but unconscious, bleeding from a laceration on his forehead. There was a female passenger draped across his lap face down. She was also unconscious but showed no signs of breathing. The driver's side window had been smashed in the accident so Vinny quickly took his flashlight and knocked away the jagged pieces of glass protruding from around the window frame. He reached in and pulled her shoulder back, exposing her face.

*Holy fuck! Nicole Brogan. Aw shit!*

There was an obvious obstruction in her air passage with copious amounts of blood around her mouth running down the front of her. Her breasts were exposed and bloody as well, but something wasn't right, it wasn't her blood. Vinny got down on both knees, reached into the car and pulled her out through the window. Without thinking, he tried to pry her mouth open with one hand while pushing on a pressure point under her jaw with the other. Vinny found the right spot and her mouth popped open like he had hit a button. He slid his thumb and forefinger into her mouth and pulled out a fleshy mass. Straightaway, Nicole coughed and sputtered and spit blood; but at least she was breathing again.

Vinny instantly turned his attention to the fleshy lump that lay in his hand. At the moment of realization he nearly slipped into shock himself. He was holding, in his beefy, bare hand, what was unmistakably Donald Fegel's penis. Or what was left of it, anyway.

Vinny Cappolla had pretty much seen it all; very little affected him. But this was hard medicine, even for him. He fought the urge to throw the thing into a snowbank and instead he tossed it back into the bloody lap of Fegel from whence it came. He stepped back and turned, stumbling away from the scene wanting to laugh but having to puke. The big boy lost his lunch right there on the side of the road. He wiped his hands off unconsciously on his pant legs before wiping at his mouth with the back of his hand. An ambulance pulled up onto the shoulder of Niagara Street next to the totaled Mercedes. A medic jumped out.

"You're not gonna fucking believe this one," Vinny said, a twisted smile spreading across his face.

He was bursting at the seams to tell somebody about what he had just seen with his own two beady eyes. It was amazing how things worked themselves out. Vinny turned the investigation over to the next arriving officer and headed back to the cruiser to have a seat. Once he was comfortably settled in, he grabbed his cell phone off the dash. He punched up Jack Driftwood.

"You're not gonna fucking believe this one, bro."

"What? You finally get laid?" Driftwood said.

"Better than that, I am sitting at an accident scene where one of the victims got beheaded."

"You shittin' me? You're a sick fuck, you know that?"

"No, listen to me. I took a call on this car accident and low and behold, I arrive at the scene and I recognize the guy right away. He flipped his Mercedes and there was an older, hot-ass MILF riding shotgun. So I check it out and the bitch ain't breathing. She's covered in blood all around her mouth and her tits, which had somehow manage to wiggle their way out of her dress. She ain't breathing when I pull her out of the car so I whack her on the back and she spits out this lump of flesh. She totally 'Garped' the fucker: Bit his fucking cock off right at the nub."

Driftwood groaned. "Aww man, I don't want to hear this shit."

"Yes, you do. Because the driver was Donald Fegel and the chick was Nicole Brogan."

"Fuck you. You're a big, fat liar."

"I may be big and fat but I ain't lying, pal. It just happened. I'm still at the scene of the crime."

"No way," Driftwood said.

"Way."

"Is he dead?"

"No, he lost some blood, probably broke a few bones and got a concussion," Vinny said. "He obviously lost an appendage, but he'll pull through. Nicole is gonna have some bumps and bruises but she was shit-faced – probably saved her life because she didn't tense up, you know, rolled with the flow."

"If you are fuckin' making this up I will never talk to you again."

"Scouts honor, dude."

"Wow."

Driftwood was speechless on the other end. Vinny was overjoyed by the karmic turn of events. That bastard Fegel got what was coming to him. He would soon be on his way to prison, totally dick-less. He was going to make some Bubba a perfect partner in a federal pen.

"What the fuck, Driftwood? I thought this would make you at least a little jovial."

"Yeah, yeah, I was just thinking about Billy, that's all."

"Speaking of which, where is the poor bastard?"

"He's gotta be over at the Wigwam, probably watching film."

"All right. I'm heading down there to talk to him."

"Go easy on him, Vinny. He's a good man."

"Hey, douche bag, I'm a professional. This ain't my first rodeo." It sounded like ro-day-o.

"Whatever."

Vinny looked at this phone as the line went dead. The fucker hung up on him, yet again. Jack was too damn sensitive. This was poetic justice and Vinny was going to enjoy it. He knew someone else who would enjoy the news as much, if not more, than himself.

"Come on, tell the truth. I won't say nothing, I promise," Chaz said. He tried to sound as innocuous as possible.

"I am telling the fucking truth," Vinny said.

"Dude, there is no shame in it. You saved a woman's life. That's your job. It was in the line of duty. You did what you had to do."

The silence on the other end of the line told Chaz Vinny's defenses were weakening.

"I won't tell a soul, brother. I swear. But you know me. I get off on the fucked up details of shit like this. I've seen and heard a lot of sick shit, but you got one humdinger of a tale here. You gonna deprive your boy of something like this?"

Vinny finally relented. "All right, goddammit, but you gotta swear you won't say anything to anybody, I'll never hear the end of it."

"I already swore," Chaz replied. "But if it makes you feel better, I swear again."

Tree Spirit and Juan Chavez had gathered around Chaz when he danced into the room waiving them over pointing at his phone. Chaz had been holding a finger to his lips trying to hush the boys, who were chomping at the bit to find out what was going on. As soon as Vinny started talking again Chaz hit the speakerphone button so they could all hear the big boy spill his guts.

"Okay, the chick, Nicole, was lying across the Fegel's lap and I could see she wasn't fucking breathing and she had blood and what looked like drool all over her face and her tits – which were fine as hell by the way – and they were popped out of her dress. So I grabbed her by the arms and pulled her out of the car. She wasn't breathing and I could see she was choking on something so I dug my hand into her mouth without even thinking and yanked out the obstruction. She started coughing up blood and phlegm and shit. That's when I looked at my hand and realized what the fuck she was choking on. I almost threw the thing into the snow bank I was so fucking disgusted. I chucked it back into the car right onto Fegel's lap where it came from. There, you happy?"

All three of them busted out laughing uncontrollably. They could no longer hold it in.

"You the new meat man!" Juan hollered.

"That wasn't drool, you tool. It was jizz!" Chaz said amidst a fit of laughter.

"I hope you have washed your hands," Tree Spirit said.

"You motherfuckers!" Vinny yelled. "If you tell anybody I will kill you all, slowly."

"You're already killing me," Chaz said. "How was it handling another man's meat? Did you like it?"

"Did it move?" Juan asked.

"Fuck you guys."

Vinny hung up the phone. But he had to laugh at himself. It was funny after all, in a sick and twisted way. Just the way he liked it.

# Chapter Fifty-One

It had been decades since anybody had gotten the drop on Chaz Davenport. That shit just *did not* happen. But Chaz was lost in thought as he turned into the Main and Jewett branch of First Niagara Bank. He pulled into the empty parking lot, and before he could shut off his car two State Of New York vehicles roared into the lot and shimmied up tight along either side of him. He quickly threw it in reverse, but a Limo pulled up behind him, blocking any possible retreat.

*Interesting. I wondered if these turd-burglars might show up…*

A man wearing a dark suit with matching shades had rolled down the window in the vehicle to his left and was motioning for Chaz to do the same. He obliged. The guy fit the stereotypical government agent to a tee.

"Sorry to box you in like this, Mr. Davenport, but Senator Blutarsky would like a word with you…if that's ok?"

"Why?" Chaz asked. "Is he still pissed I didn't vote for him?"

The agent broke character and smiled a rare smile. Chaz's response had broken through his thick veneer.

"I don't think it's that serious."

"Oh, good," Chaz replied.

The sedan backed up just far enough for Chaz to open his door. Two other agents had scrambled out of the other car and were waiting to escort him back to Blutarsky's limo. They opened the door for him and Chaz slid into the back where he found himself face to face with the Senator, alone in the back of the expansive vehicle.

Jack couldn't believe he was going to go through with it, but the more he thought about it, it made sense. He dialed the number Chaz had scrawled on the back of a matchbook for him.

*Who even does that anymore? Chaz is one analog dude in a brave, new, digital world.*

The phone rang half a dozen times and nobody answered. Jack was about to hang up when he heard a click.

"Who the hell is this? This is a private line."

"This is Jack. Jack Driftwood."

"Real funny, asshole. How'd you get this number?"

"No, I'm serious, this is Jack Driftwood."

"You don't give up easy do you, douchebag. I'm going to ask you one last time, how did you get this number? This is a private number – *nobody* has this number."

"Well, apparently *somebody* does because I just called it. But I think you are going to want to quit fucking around and listen to what this old, washed-up lumber has to say, Mr. Kilmer."

"Is this really you, Jack?"

"Yes. And I have some information that you most definitely want to see. This shit is so hot even a hack like you might win a Pulitzer with it."

"Ha-ha! If that's true then I am all ears. And Jack?"

"Yeah, Budd?"

"Sorry about all the earlier stuff. I get crackpots calling me all the time."

"I bet you do. And don't worry about the name calling. I've called you a whole lot worse."

"I bet you have. So what's going on, Jack?"

"You know that burger joint, Zorba's, over on Transit? How about you meet me there at say, five o'clock this afternoon."

"I love their red-hots, but the burgers are even better."

"Well, you ain't so full of shit after all, Budd. I feel the same way."

"Hello, Chaz," Senator Blutarsky said, extending his hand.

Chaz shook the man's hand and nodded.

"Sorry to jump on you like this, but I really needed a word with you before I leave the country tonight. I'm sure you know what this is all about."

"Enlighten me."

"That little Wigwam project issue wherein you seem to have acquired egregiously erroneous and potentially damaging information. Ring a bell?"

"Ah, yes," Chaz said. "I was wondering whether I might hear from you regarding this, shall we say, delicate situation."

Blutarsky nodded. "Delicate indeed. I wish you had just come to me in the first place, but I understand. I'm not one to beat around the bush, so here's the deal. I recently received a phone call from a low-life by the name of Colin Meade. I think you did some refrigerator art for him a while back, if I'm not mistaken."

Blutarsky raised his eyebrows at him, but Chaz remained stone-faced. The Senator's expression betrayed his mild disappointment; he had obviously been expecting at least some type of reaction from his guest. Chaz refused to give the man any such satisfaction.

"Well, anyways, Mr. Meade has been on my radar for years. Word has it, he tried to rip off a big furniture manufacturer's pension fund out East before being run out of town. He came back home to Buffalo and took up with Donald Fegel here, some five years ago. Armed with this knowledge, I was especially careful handling the State's end of the business on the Wigwam and casino building projects. Thank goodness I was, but it still hasn't prevented the two-bit thief from trying to run a sting on me.

"Those three stooges, Meade, Fegel, and that recently deceased, crazy Indian Security Chief apparently robbed the project blind. To protect themselves, they cooked up bogus documentation which implicates me as an equal partner in their heist. As I said, Meade called me and threatened that if they go down, I go down with them, so I had better do what I could to protect them and cover this mess up. He said he planted a set of books in his house, which have evidently found their way into your hands, that he claims was exactly as he planned. And now, of course, he is trying to blackmail me for protection, to stop that sensitive information from becoming public."

The Senator paused again for effect, closely watching Chaz's reaction to see if the man was buying his story. Still nothing. Chaz's expression hadn't changed through the entire course of their mostly one-sided conversation.

"I have had my people keeping tabs on Meade and Fegel, as well as the Chief, at least until he lost his head, so to speak. Meade must've bugged out, probably left the country a couple days ago. No doubt from there he cleaned out several off-shore bank accounts – his own, the chief's, Fegel's, and another that was supposedly mine. It has also come to my attention a meeting will be held later today where an anonymous source is going to sing into Budd Kilmer's ear."

Blutarsky thought he saw a flicker of surprise in Chaz's eyes.

*That's right, Mr. Davenport. I've got you wired!*

"So here's the deal." Blutarsky opened the briefcase sitting on the seat next to him. He pulled out a fairly thick file folder and set it teasingly upon his lap. "These are the *real* cooked books, not the garbage Meade concocted to implicate me. You will see the numbers match what you've uncovered, except things are divvied up only three ways, rather than four. There is no need for my name to be dragged through the mud or for tens of thousands of taxpayer dollars to be burned up defending my obvious innocence. Nobody needs another scandal.

"So all I am asking, Chaz, is that when your canary sings to Mr. Kilmer, it be the right song. Thus, we avoid all that nonsense I just mentioned. I won't insult you by offering any money, but I do have a little incentive you may find of interest. You see, my friend, I am privy to the whereabouts of Colin Meade. As a gesture of goodwill, I will provide you that information, with which you can do as you please. What do you say, Mr. Davenport? You do want to get this thing right the first time, do you not?"

Chaz looked down at his hands, examining his fingernails as if he had not a care in the world. He had to admire Blutarsky. The man had invented a viable, nearly plausible smokescreen to obscure his involvement. On the one hand, he hated to see the slimy politician get away with swindling the Wainscott's, but it appeared the Senator got hoodwinked himself, that is if Meade had, indeed, taken all of the money. If he made the deal he could track the little prick Meade down and retrieve the money; at least what the little bastard hadn't spent. There was also the added incentive of old-fashioned, vigilante justice, which he would, no doubt, exact from Colin Meade. Not to mention it was never a bad thing to have a State Senator on the hook – a rather big hook, at that.

He reached out his hand and Blutarsky placed the folder into it.

"The information on the whereabouts of Colin Meade is in there as well," Blutarsky said. Then he flashed an evil smile. "Oh, and say hello to our mutual friend, Vinny Cappolla, for me. I owe him one and I've got a feeling he is due for a promotion."

Finally, the shady Senator solicited a reaction from Chaz, whose head snapped back to look at him with fire in his eyes.

*That motherfucking Cappolla! He tipped this son of a bitch off!*

Chaz got out of the limo without a word and headed into the bank, followed only by the Senator's laughter.

**Fegel Fleeces Blizzard and Seneca Nation in Wigwam Scam?**
***Blizzard GM Investigated for Skimming Stadium/Casino Project***
By Budd Kilmer
Buffalo News Sports Editor

(Buffalo, NY) It's not all champagne and roses at One Wigwam Way, despite the Buffalo Blizzard, who qualified with the top seed, advancing to the NAFA playoffs for the first time in 17 seasons. Blizzard General Manager Donald Allen Fegel Jr. is under investigation for allegedly bilking millions from the stadium and casino construction projects. Fegel is formally running the franchise because the only owner in franchise history, Gerald Wainscott III, lies incapacitated in a Buffalo hospital. Fegel won the first round of a battle for control of the team with Gerry Wainscott, Mr. Wainscott's daughter and only heir, just last week, although Ms. Wainscott has appealed the decision made by NAFA Commissioner Bob Goldman.

Fegel managed the massive building project of the Wigwam and the Buffalo Seneca Casino, completed this past September, in conjunction with the Seneca Nation of Indians. According to an anonymous source, Fegel, along with Blizzard assistant general manager Colin Meade and the late Seneca Nation Security Chief, Neil Dadoska, combined to form an illicit partnership, which reportedly stole as much as 90 million dollars from the 1.2-billion-dollar construction project.

Dadoska was recently killed in a bizarre snowmobiling accident in the early morning hours of Christmas Day outside Brylin Hospital. Dadoska's death is currently under investigation by the Buffalo Police Department. It is unknown whether Blizzard linebacker Jack Driftwood is involved, but Driftwood did break out of the Brylin Facility earlier that same night.

Driftwood had been involuntarily admitted to the facility the previous morning after attacking Fegel in his Wigwam office over a disputed positive drug test result. While Driftwood has been cleared of any wrongdoing, the Buffalo Police Department refused to comment on their ongoing investigation for this story.

Fegel and company reportedly used a kick-back program with multiple construction companies, accepting bids with under the table agreements to receive cash back from the companies in exchange for winning bids for work done on the projects. Also, the group allegedly used substandard building materials in the building of the structures, pocketing the difference in the price for top of the line materials.

Purportedly they went so far as to change the labels on some of the materials in order to pass inspection. Of particular concern is the possible use of inferior heating filaments in the Wigwam's glass roof. The roof was not built to hold up under the weight of any substantial accumulation of snow and ice. The implementation of the heating filaments in the glass panels were intended to eliminate any such buildup by melting the ice and snow.

The building passed State of New York building inspections, and thus is considered up to code. New York State Senator William F. Blutarsky represented the state in all of the proceedings, including arranging the inspections. However, it is believed Senator Blutarsky and company were duped along with everybody else and is in no way complicit in the scam. His office stated he was unavailable for comment as the Senator left the country yesterday on a fact finding mission to Africa.

Fegel, who was involved in an apparently unrelated single-car accident Monday, was unavailable for comment. He is currently in Buffalo General Hospital in stable but serious condition. However, he is expected to make a full recovery. Attempts to contact Colin Meade were unsuccessful. According to David Blitzer, VP of media relations for the Blizzard, Meade has not shown up to work since Christmas Eve.

NAFA Commissioner Bob Goldman assured me the league had no intentions to alter the location of the league's annual title game, the Mega Bowl, which is scheduled for Sunday, January 24, 2016, at the Wigwam here in Buffalo. No host team has ever played in a Mega Bowl in their own stadium in the 49 previous years of league history.

Millard Steinman carefully picked up the note from amongst the documents spread across his antique walnut desk with a pair of tweezers and dropped it into a large plastic Ziploc bag. He continued the process with each of the pages covering the finely polished surface. He had already contaminated them slightly upon opening the envelope, but he quickly realized what he held in his possession was potentially seriously damning evidence. He doubted if the documents he was examining were the originals. He wasn't one to take chances, though. He would let the cops worry about that. Regardless of whether they were the originals or not, they were exactly what the note said they were – the crooked accounting of the Wigwam construction project.

If the documents were legit, Donald Fegel was going away for a long, long time. The evidence was right there in black and white, incriminating as anything he had seen in his career as a practicing attorney. They were a blueprint for an investigation and easily verifiable. Somebody's hand was caught elbow deep in the cookie jar.

Millard couldn't wait to show it all to an old friend, the city's District Attorney. He had read the Budd Kilmer article online and was looking at the same information that old hack must've been privy to. A good day just got a whole lot better. Millard had just one request from his friend. He wanted to be there when they read Fegel his rights. That request was honored the following afternoon just down the road in a private room in Buffalo General Hospital.

Donald Fegel was comfortably stretched out on the lounge chair poolside, close enough to where he could easily reach his hand into the sun-warmed water. He did so, cupping a handful and playfully tossing it onto Nicole's red-hot, sunburnt back. Even though the water was warm by any standard, it was vastly colder than her steamy back under the blazing Florida sun. She popped up off the chaise lounge, but her bikini top didn't make the trip. Donald threw his head back in laughter as she screamed and scrambled to cover herself up, giving the late-afternoon pool crowd a sight to behold and a story to tell.

"Donald Fegel! Somebody needs to teach you a lesson, mister."

"Yeah, you know anybody smart enough?"

He got up to help her tie the bikini top back on. It wasn't like the garment left much to the imagination, anyway.

"I think I can teach you a thing or two myself," Nicole said, wiggling her backside into Donald as he stood behind her tying her top.

He pressed back against her. "Perhaps we should take this lesson up to the room."

"Oh, Donald. Donald. Donald!"

He woke from the dream and for a moment wasn't entirely sure what was real and what was merely a product of his drug-induced haze. But somebody kept calling his name. And it wasn't Nicole. His room was full of people, but she wasn't among them.

He had been out of surgery for a while now, and the doctor had been by to check on him, saying things had gone very well. The man had mentioned a penis transplant as a possibility further down the line, but Donald was in no condition to even consider such a thing, let alone comprehend what he meant. This surgery had been the second attempt to clean up and make functional the remaining mangled nub of flesh protruding from his groin. The procedure was designed to enable him to urinate, but any other normal function would require a transplant or reconstruction.

A breathing tube had just been removed from his throat, making it too irritated for him to comfortably speak. Donald closed his eyes hoping the scene was merely a mirage, and he could transport himself back to his poolside triste with Nicole. But when he opened them again, his hospital room was still crowded with cops and lawyerly types.

"Donald. Donald! Oh, good, you're awake," Millard Steinman said. "There is some business that needs tending to here, Mr. Fegel, and it won't wait. Do you understand?"

Donald's eyes darted around the room and fear settled into his heart. He had harbored hopes of figuring a way out of this mess, but by the looks of things, it was going to be more complicated than he had imagined. He nodded his head, affirmatively.

"Good. There is somebody who would like to speak to you briefly before we proceed," Millard said.

Gerry Wainscott stepped out from behind a couple of burly police offers. He winced at the sight of her and shrunk back into the bed.

"Hello, Feegs. You look, uh, well. I insisted on being here on behalf of my father. Remember him? The man who took you from sniffing dirty jocks as a locker room attendant and put you in charge of his franchise? The man you stabbed in the back, stole millions from, and, for all we know, put into in a coma? I wanted to be here to watch your freedom officially end and wish you the best rotting in jail, and then in hell. My dad *will* wake up, and when he does it will be my pleasure to tell him how you cowered in your bed, dick-less, while being handcuffed like the criminal you most certainly are." She wiggled her little pinky at him. "Good bye, Feegs. Rot in hell, you little prick."

One of the cops read him his rights while another handcuffed him to the bed. The District Attorney read the charges and Donald tried to protest, but when he opened his mouth nothing came out but a raspy wheeze.

*It can't end this way! The team is mine!*

He had earned it, worked his ass off. That little bitch couldn't lock him up like this. He was Donald Allen Fegel Jr! It wasn't fair. A lone tear rolled down his face as the only visitors he would receive during his entire stay in the hospital happily exited the room.

# Chapter Fifty-Two

This night would forever live in Jack Driftwood's memory like a snapshot of one of the happiest occasions of his life. He figured it could only be topped by winning a Mega Bowl, or maybe if he were to marry and have kids one day. He was finally going to see her again. It felt like it had been weeks rather than the actual few days since they were last together. He was sitting at the bar in the Bull's Horn, nursing a beer, waiting for his princess to arrive.

Jack saw her coming through the door. She was an earth-angel, a vision of beauty. Her dark hair glistened, even in the dim light, as it framed her aristocratic face. Her skin glowed, highlighting her high cheek bones that shone despite the fact she wasn't caked in make-up like the other lady warriors battle-clad in the dingy bar. She was dressed conservatively in a blue jacket and pants with a white lacy blouse that ruffled at the collar. She was obviously a damsel in distress, dangerously out of her element at the Bull's Horn.

Jack wove through the crowd to the rescue without taking his eyes off of her. She spotted him coming a mile away and flashed a faint smile before looking around as if plotting her escape.

*Too late, princess. Jack Driftwood's in the house.*

"Excuse me, Cinderella, but aren't you a little late for the ball?"

"I like to make an entrance," she said. She gazed around the crowded saloon looking for somebody – anybody – to rescue her from what was bound to be a lame come on from the quintessential meathead. Then she stared Driftwood straight in the eyes and said with unmistakable disdain, "I can see Prince Charming isn't here yet, either." It sounded like eye-thur.

They both cracked up.

"Let's me and you get out of here before midnight strikes," Jack said. "I don't want to turn into a pumpkin or some such shit."

"I think you'd look lovely in orange."

There was no golden carriage awaiting to whisk the storybook couple away to live happily ever after; rather, it was a black Limo. They buzzed around town for a while sharing champagne and snuggling closely together in the back of the long car before ending up at Jack's warehouse-flat in the Downtown Casino District. There, they spent the night getting reacquainted. It was a rendezvous long overdue, but they made up for any lost time.

It was hard to explain. Driftwood could not imagine a much greater thrill even under normal circumstances, let alone after the turmoil he had so recently endured. His very life had been snatched from his control, but miraculously eve-rything came back better than ever. It was almost more than he could handle emotionally. He couldn't help himself; when "the voice" of the Blizzard, Dodge Brophy, called his name during pregame introductions he was crying like a baby. He burst from the Wigwam tunnel like an Olympic sprinter and dashed to the Blizzard logo painted in the near end zone and raised his arms to the rousing applause of the Blizzard faithful who impulsively sprang to their feet and roared, welcoming their hero's return.

They honored Driftwood with an extended standing ovation fit for a king returning home after a successful campaign. Tears streaked down his face as he blazed through the gauntlet of teammates all slapping his hands, helmet, shoulder pads, or ass. They all wanted to touch him to demonstrate their love as their defensive leader ran past. There was no question he was the heart and soul of this closely-knit group that had come together, and he was back.

The home crowd loved him now more than ever. They had breathlessly fol-lowed his exploits the entire exciting season, both on and off the field, and ad-mired his stout perseverance and reveled in his ultimate redemption. He was re-turning just in time to lead them through the playoffs and hopefully all the way to a Mega Bowl victory. That was pure Hollywood stuff right there, and it was happening in Buffalo. Who could believe that? They were downright giddy!

Waiting at midfield was his rookie, Steven Stark, who had been introduced just prior. When he finally made it to Stark, Driftwood collapsed gratefully into his prodigy's thick, open arms.

"Jesus, you're crying." Stark laughed and gave him a bear-hug, lifting him into the air and turning around to display him to the adoring crowd which had offi-cially gone ape-shit.

"Fuck you," Driftwood said through his tears, and then he started laughing.

He was laughing at himself and at all he had been through and where he was. It was surreal being in the middle of the Wigwam hosting its inaugural playoff game considering his career had nearly ended with him locked tidily away in a mental hospital. The ovation was the highlight of his career and he was over-whelmed. Thank God he would have a few minutes to compose himself before kickoff; he needed it.

They were playing the Minnesota Northmen in the Divisional round of the NAFA playoffs. Minnesota had gone down to South Florida and upset the Rip-tide in the wildcard round the previous weekend on a last-second field goal to earn their trip to Buffalo.

One of the big concerns expressed prior to the game was whether or not all of the off-field issues would distract the team. Budd Kilmer had written a column predicting as much and had placed Jack Driftwood's neck firmly in the noose as the primary problem. To be fair, though, he had also called their "imminent collapse" Donald Fegel's "parting gift" to the franchise.

As an unintended consequence, Kilmer's commentary had galvanized the team. The article had been pinned to the training room bulletin board and received its proper due. They were determined to shut the man up – hard. There was also a great sense of emancipation throughout the organization, a new-found freedom that led to a healthy looseness. They were all too happy to be out from under the thumb of the volatile reign of their former General Manager, Donald Allen Fegel Jr. The prevailing sentiment amongst the players and coaches was good riddance to bad garbage.

A brilliant sun glared through the clear, sparkling roof of the monolithic stadium. There wasn't a cloud in the sky in the Queen City on the Niagara, a rarity for early January. The temperature outside was a frigid twenty-eight degrees; inside the Wigwam it was a cozy seventy-two. There had even been pregame talk amongst the usual diehards about how the roof should be opened, but that was mostly a product of false bravado and contrarianism. It didn't matter either way, because this was the day Blizzard Nation had been anticipating for nearly two decades. They were back in the Mega Bowl hunt and nothing was going to spoil this party.

The game officials signaled for the captains of each team to meet at midfield for the coin toss. Coach Ivy always selected his captains on a week-to-week basis and it was his esteemed pleasure to name Jack Driftwood and Nick Loney for the honor against Minnesota. Driftwood took Loney's gloved, heavily-taped hand and strode to the middle of the field for the ceremony. He had settled down and was ready to play some ball. Less than ten days ago he was a fugitive from justice, on the lam hiding out in an underground bunker wondering if he would ever play football again. And now here he was, geared up for battle in this over-sized greenhouse in front of over ninety thousand screaming devotees. It felt like a dream.

But it was true. Oh, it was true. He raised his eyes to the glass roof where he could see all the way into heaven and gave thanks. A smile every bit as goofy as Steven Stark's spread across his face. He knew Big Ed and Erma Driftwood had a perfect bird's-eye view through the transparent glass into the stadium to watch the action. Their only son Jack and fifty-four of his closest pals intended to put on a show for them and anybody else who cared to watch.

Before any football would be played the public address announcer had one final request; he called for a moment of silence. That gesture was an extremely emotional one for every Blizzard fan, player, coach, and employee in the building. Collectively they paused to honor the fallen Blizzard owner, Gerald Wainscott III.

The old man was hanging in there, although he was still in a coma in the ICU of Buffalo General Hospital. His doctors were far from giving up hope, but things were beginning to get a little dicey. They desperately needed Gerald to come out of it soon if he was ever going to have a normal life again. His body, though still strong enough, especially given his age, was beginning to atrophy and his chances of a full recovery lessened with each day he remained unconscious. Driftwood had never heard such an overwhelming silence from so many people and found himself in tears for the second time since taking the field.

The communal display of respect not only touched his heart, but it girded his resolve. This one was going to be played for the old man. That sentiment carried through the entire Blizzard team. Coach Ivy had reminded them before the game of the vow they had made to Mr. Wainscott way back in training camp. To a man they were resolute to give it all they had, all day long on this sunny Sunday afternoon. Of that, there was no doubt.

To be honest, Minnesota never really stood a chance. Indubitably, they gave a valiant effort, attempting to pull out all the stops. They even executed a surprise onside-kick to perfection on the opening kickoff, recovering the ball on their own 43-yard line. In effect, they stole a possession from Buffalo, although it didn't turn out all that well for them. All it did was put the Buffalo defense on the field first.

Driftwood couldn't have been happier. He slapped Coach Ivy on the ass much harder than he intended as he headed onto the field.

"I told you we should have deferred," he said laughing.

Coach Ivy was nearly apoplectic in his search for Coach Sig, his special teams coach. He was still unconsciously rubbing his own backside while chewing on Coach Sig's when the roar of the crowd drowned him out. Big E had beat his man with an inside pass-rush move on the game's first play from scrimmage and sacked the Northmen's quarterback before the guy knew what hit him.

The next two plays resulted in another negative eight yards combined. First, Stark made a tackle for a loss of three, which Driftwood followed by sniffing out a draw for a loss of five. The only gear the Minnesota offense had found was reverse and were forced to punt. Ben Brady and the BB-Gun Offense came out at warp speed with their high-tempo attack and covered 80-yards for a touchdown in just four plays.

The Blizzard defenders were flying around the field with their hair on fire and forced another three-and-out on the next series. Not to be outdone, the Buffalo offense mounted another touchdown drive and the rout was formally on. The Buffalo lead climbed to 35-3 at halftime and there was no doubt who would be hosting the NAFA's Eastern Conference Championship Game the following Sunday afternoon. The final score ended up 45-3. By all appearances the Blizzard was healthy and peaking at the right time. A sense of destiny had taken a strong foothold in their collective mindset. Their performance against the Northmen only reinforced this confidence; they left the Wigwam one win away from the Mega Bowl.

Tree Spirit held up a spatula in the wonderful aroma-filled air, politely pontificating the intricate virtues of his special marinara sauce. An impromptu spaghetti-fest had busted out in Chaz's underground bunker and had quickly morphed into a sauce-cooking contest. Chaz's kitchen looked like a war zone as the three chefs each worked their own brand of sauce magic; Tree Spirit's "Mysterious Sauce" was going up against Cheese's "Old-World Marinara" and Vinny's "Grandma Cappolla's Super Sauce." The best anybody could get was even odds.

They had all headed out to Chaz's bunker to celebrate the victory from earlier in the day. The Buffalo Blizzard had advanced to play in Mega Bowl 50 on the merits of a 52-37 shootout victory over the Great Lakes Division Champs, the Detroit Muscle, in the Eastern Conference Championship Game at the Wigwam.

The game was incredible. Detroit had come out firing and had the Buffalo defense on the run most of the afternoon. But the Blizzard D had hung tough. They scrambled around, dug deep, kept fighting, and came up with several decisively key stops late in the ballgame.

Their offense was unstoppable. Earl "the Pearl" Johnson was a one-man gang all by himself. He tallied a NAFA Playoff record six touchdowns; four on the ground and two receiving. He ran for 217 yards and added another 104 receiving. He also threw for a touchdown, hitting Ben Brady with a strike on the Reverse Throwback Pass out of shotgun. A case could be made the Pearl had put the Blizzard on his back and carried them into the Mega Bowl. Earl had playfully been busy making such a case since the final gun sounded.

He might have pulled it off, too, except too many others had made a multitude of timely, significant contributions. It was as complete a team effort as Buffalo had put together the entire season. Giving up so many points was a concern regarding their defense, but the Detroit offense deserved some credit. They had played extremely well in defeat, and were an exceptionally talented outfit, especially at the skill positions. But in the end, Buffalo was too strong for the Muscle; they were going to the Mega Bowl, and the Mega Bowl was in Buffalo.

After the game Jack and company headed for Hemlock Lake for a private party. Chaz had approached Jack with the idea and they agreed a nice low-key affair tucked away in the underground privacy of the bunker was the ticket. It was also the only way Jack and Gerry could celebrate the momentous victory together with their friends. This was Jack's idea of a good party, anyway. He was beat up and dog-ass tired, yet euphoric from the victory. A cleated kick to his right quad had left a golf ball-sized knot a few inches above his kneecap which was beginning to color up nicely. He knew if he stopped moving it would stiffen up, making it a struggle just to walk. It was a good thing the Mega Bowl was two weeks down the road. He would need the time to recover.

The spaghetti celebration was steeped in tradition, as it turned out. Cheese had asked Jack if it had hit him yet, that he was going to the Mega Bowl again. Jack remembered the exact moment the realization hit home when he toiled as a rookie linebacker for the Blizzard seventeen years earlier. He had been out to dinner with Big Ed and Erma at Ugi's Italian Ristorante in Orchard Park in the shadow of their old stadium. Much of the team would hit Ugi's for dinner after games back in the day, bringing their family and friends to celebrate in lavish hospitality.

The proprietor himself, Ugi Vitale, would greet them at the door with warm hugs and kisses and handshakes up to your elbow. Ugi had been blessed with the biggest hands Jack had ever shook. The cheerful, fun-loving man had played for the Blizzard their first two seasons in the CFL and was still a big part of the extended family.

Jack had been quietly taking in the scene of the celebration seated at a table at Ugi's in front of a plate of spaghetti. Many of the team's veteran players were already rip-roaring drunk, toasting anything and everything. This was their fourth-straight trip to the big game and they were used to it. This would be young Jack's first bite at the apple. Jack had only had a couple of beers, taking it slow. Although he fully intended to catch up to his teammates, he just couldn't take his eyes off the spaghetti, nor lift his fork off the table. He wanted to eat, but he couldn't make himself move. The whole experience was overwhelming and the magnitude of what had happened seemed to have jammed him up.

Erma Driftwood, ever the mother, prodded her son to eat his food. "It's getting cold, Jack. Don't you think you ought to eat?"

"We are going to the Mega Bowl, Mom." Jack said it as if the concept had just dawned on him as a sensible enough reason for his inability to consume the pasta.

"No shit, Sherlock." Big Ed always had a way with words.

Jack smiled stupidly at them both and leaned his head back and rather forcefully smacked his face down onto the plate of noodles covered in Ugi's secret sauce. He took a big mouthful and then slurped it all in and swallowed before slamming his face into the pasta again. Big Ed roared in laughter; Erma put a hand to her mouth, totally appalled.

"Jack! Where are your manners?"

Jack just laughed and rolled his face through the plate of noodles and secret sauce, moaning with pleasure.

In his mind it was the perfect expression of how it felt to be going to the Mega Bowl. Big Ed reached over and added a little force to the equation, mashing and rolling his son's face into the plate of pasta. Erma Driftwood was horror-struck. This behavior was inexplicable, if not childish, but they ignored her and laughed heartily, whooping it up, as Jack slurped up every last piece of spaghetti and lapped up every drop of Ugi sauce, leaving his plate completely empty with a spit-shine.

They had crowded into Chaz's kitchen to determine an early leader in the sauce competition. Vinny, who rarely drank, was well into his cups and holding court.

"Stand back, boys. You're sucking up all my oxygen. Both me and my Granma-sauce need to breathe."

Vinny sprinkled cinnamon over his pot of sweet-smelling sauce as a finishing touch. He turned his back to the group and semi-stealthily reached under a short stack of napkins and stole the final bite of the third brownie he had pilfered from the pantry. He figured there were enough of them that nobody would be the wiser, so he snuck a few of the chocolatey delights. They were a little chalkier than usual, but the flavor couldn't be beat.

Vinny cranked up the burner under his sauce. "All I gotta do is bring this fucker to a boil, let 'er cool off and set-up, and you bitches will be in Granma-sauce heaven."

Vinny's boast was followed by a deep, resounding burp and his massive stomach gurgled loudly, then heaved. Vinny's concern grew with each gurgle of his stomach which continued to growl in protest.

"I think something else is about to boil, big man," Jack said. "You alright, or are you gonna shit yourself right here in the kitchen?"

"Just a little gas," Vinny said. "You'll know when it works its way out, believe me."

At that Vinny hiked up his left check and grunted. The look on his face was priceless. He had terribly misjudged his situation and obviously sharted in his pants. He looked at Jack wide-eyed.

"I'm pretty sure our boy, here, just shat his didies," Jack said.

Adapting a tight, quick, Chaplin-esque waddle, Vinny hurried as best as he could for the bathroom around the corner. Everybody was caught between laughter and fighting their gag reflex as they quickly scattered out of the panic-stricken big boy's way. They followed him to the bathroom door.

"How many of them brownies did you steal, fat-man?" Chaz asked through the door.

"Why? What'd you do to them, you fuckers?"

"You know, you really should have asked first, man," Chaz said. "Those are my ex-lax brownies for when things get a little backed up. How many?"

"Three," Vinny said from behind the door.

They roared in laughter and exchanged high-fives all around. Vinny had fooled nobody and had fallen right into the trap.

"Ah, shit…literally. I usually only need a half of one them bad boys to get my butter churning," Chaz said, failing to suppress his laughter. "I guess the next time you set me up for your new master, the Senator, you may want to think about this shit. This shit and the next thirty or so you are about to take. Paybacks are a shitty bitch, huh, Cappolla?"

"When I get out of here, I'm gonna kill all of you cocksuckers," Vinny said between groans.

"Good," Chaz replied, "that'll give us a good three-hour head start. I'll leave you a fresh pair of bloomers and some sweatpants at the door. I don't need you mucking up the whole damn place."

Their laughter filled the bunker through the night, most of which Vinny spent in a little bathroom off the kitchen. He never did get to see Jack and company face-dive into his winning sauce entry. The newly crowned Mega-Sauce King had super-sauce problems all his own with which to deal.

# Chapter Fifty-Three

The Mega Bowl is a different kind of animal. It is the ultimate game in the ultimate sport. The entire world is watching. There are so many moving parts it boggles the mind. The sheer magnitude of the event is overwhelming. The players are pulled in so many directions leading up to the game from media and ticket requests to well-wishing, ego-boosting fans, one could easily lose perspective. Coach Ivy had been through it four times in his illustrious career. And though he had lost all four of those games, the experience was invaluable.

It was with these thoughts and doubts that he spoke to his football team. He also had the novel consideration that this game was ultimately a home game. This could be a huge advantage as the crowd would, no doubt, be behind them. They would enjoy the comforts of home for the two weeks prior to the game, although the league mandated the team check-in and stay at the Buffalo Seneca Casino Hotel for the entire week of the game.

However, Coach Ivy, as coaches tend to do, worried about the possible negatives of playing in Buffalo. The distractions at home, away from the Wigwam, would be much greater with family, friends, fans, and media types coming out of the woodwork. Every person his players meet on the streets would want a piece of them. They would want to talk about the game, offer them something for free while trying to garner a small piece of glory for themselves. Amidst all the chaos, the team still needed to prepare to play their opponent, the St. Louis Nighthawks. It was a lot to deal with. The key was to keep things as simple as possible. With all of this weighing heavily on his mind, Howard Ivy was still charged with excitement as he stood before his team in the bowels of the Wigwam in their first official meeting of Mega Bowl Week.

"Men, let me begin by extoling some of our virtues; we are indubitably a mentally strong entity. You have kept your focus and ascended to the top. This is a very difficult thing to achieve. Now I have been around the block a few times…"

Coach Ivy paused to allow for the polite laughter from his team. "Alright, perhaps more than a few, but I can honestly say I have never had a more committed, hard-working, selfless group of men take that walk with me. This will be the fifth time I will have led a football team into a Mega Bowl. As the saying goes, the fifth time is the charm."

Again the room was moved to polite laughter. The coach was keeping things light. He knew from experience there was no cause for rousing, over the top motivational speeches with the game still a full five days away. He also knew the battle, the game itself, would be enough to make them tense. The intensity level would build on its own until it was off the charts. The trick was to keep things calm and take the pressure off his players during their preparation.

"As you know, we, or I, have come up short in all four of those previous encounters. I have done my share of soul-searching regarding those losses, believe me. Many a person has inquired as to what I would have done differently, or for that matter, do differently if given another chance. I've pondered that same query many a late night struggling to find rest for my body and soul. But the answer is a simple one: Nothing! Not one damned thing. There is a saying you hear all the time from people around this great game. The saying goes, 'It is what it is.'

"Yes, it is what it is. Well, of course, it is. This saying is redundant and incredibly self-evident. Therein, however, lies its genius. It is what it is. Think about it…it is what it is…so what is it? I'll tell you what *it* is to me, it is Bo-Bo Karpinski eating up a double team to free up Driftwood, Stark, or Brogan to make a tackle. It is Earl Johnson fighting for extra yards. It is Jeremy Patton and his battalion knocking people off the ball. It is Leroy Clarkson executing bump and run coverage to perfection. It is Eric Sellars getting to the quarterback. It is Ben Brady throwing a perfect pass to Shady or AC. It is Killings making a tackle on kickoff coverage."

The coach's voice rose and was packed with emotion as he named off his players doing the very things they had done throughout the entire season.

"Gentleman, it is what it is! And what it is, is exactly what we have been doing this entire season. The point is we don't require anything extraordinary or monumental to win this game. All we need to do is exactly what we have been doing all year long. Don't situate any extra pressure on yourselves to do something spectacular or different than what you have been doing. We will prepare precisely the way we have all year, and then we will go out and execute in the same fashion. And when we do that, we will win, just as we won all year. Because it is what it is, men. It is what it is."

The big news broke in time to be the lead story on every area evening newscast the Wednesday prior to the big game. There were no fewer than a half dozen satellite trucks parked outside in the light evening snow dusting the main parking lot of Buffalo General Hospital. Jillian Pierce of Channel Four News Buffalo had broken the story an hour earlier. She had gotten a call from her old friend Jack Driftwood tipping her off. Channel Four had interrupted regularly scheduled programming to make the announcement, setting off the media feeding frenzy. The buffet was in full gear by 6 p.m. as an overlapping, continuous stream of live-hits were orchestrated for the swarm that had descended on the hospital campus.

The Channel Four News Buffalo anchor, Craig Herbstman, began the six o'clock newscast with an update throwing it live to Jillian standing outside of Buffalo General Hospital for a special report.

"Thanks, Herbie," Jillian began as light snowflakes fell onto her pretty face, "Channel Four broke this major news story about an hour ago and has confirmation from a reliable source inside the Buffalo Blizzard organization that team owner, Gerald Wainscott III, at the age of ninety-three, awoke from a coma earlier today and is alert and communicating with his doctors and family. Mr. Wainscott fell ill twenty-three days ago while exercising at an area health club. He subsequently underwent surgery to repair an obstructed bowel, but he lapsed into a coma as a result of complications from the surgery. I have it from a reliable source that Mr. Wainscott is miraculously awake and fully aware of his surroundings.

"The team has undergone momentous change off the field while Mr. Wainscott has been comatose. Former Blizzard General Manager Donald Fegel is awaiting trial on multiple felony embezzlement charges as he recovers from injuries suffered in an automobile accident. His assistant, Colin Meade, is missing and the subject of a nationwide manhunt. Meanwhile, Gerry Wainscott, the owner's daughter, has taken control of the team following Mr. Fegel's arrest.

"While this was all occurring the Blizzard continued to win on the field and will play the St. Louis Nighthawks in the Mega Bowl at six p.m. this Sunday at the Wigwam. Channel Four News Buffalo will have all the pregame coverage you need starting at noon. Reporting live from Buffalo General Hospital, I'm Jillian Pierce."

"Jillian, how aware is Mr. Wainscott? Does he know the Blizzard will be playing in the Mega Bowl on Sunday?" Herbstman asked.

"Doctors are taking things slowly, but it is my understanding it was one of the first things Mr. Wainscott inquired about. I was told he was overcome with emotion and shed tears of joy upon hearing his team had qualified for the game."

"That's incredible! Any chance he will be able to make it to the game Sunday?"

"Nobody is even talking about that right now, but this is an extraordinarily resilient man we are talking about. If anyone could recover in such a short amount of time, I would have to believe it would be the iron-willed Gerald Wainscott III."

The Buffalo Blizzard security team had taken control of both the ninth and tenth floors of the Buffalo Seneca Casino Hotel. They had men posted outside and in each elevator and several more patrolling the hallways and stairwells. Their explicit instructions were to not allow any non-Blizzard personnel onto the floor under any circumstances unless they were accompanied by team personnel. Security staff also escorted the team's security chief, Eddie Stinson, to the players' rooms to perform bed check each night.

The Friday night curfew had been established at 11 p.m. – no exceptions. Coach Ivy had warned the team a good night sleep two nights before an athletic contest was more important than the night before the game. The coach had researched the issue and was adamant about the point. He needn't have worried. The veterans on the team had established this policy early in the year. The unwritten rule was stay off the streets Friday and Saturday night, which is why, in part, the team had carried on the tradition of Thursday Night Out.

There were a couple of schools of thought that came to light in the impromptu players-only meeting held after Thursday's practice. Some of the more conservative members of the squad had spoken out on the subject. The team's clean-living, hard-hitting, bible-toting free safety, Dave Gaston, had stated it in the simplest of terms.

"Guys, this is the biggest game of our lives. We need to be as ready to go as possible, which includes taking care of not only our bodies, but our spirits and souls as well," he argued. "I don't think it's an unreasonable sacrifice to stay off the streets tonight."

"Dave is right," added one of his disciples, Matt Peters. "Y'all can party after we win the game."

There were immediate protests amongst the group, but Earl Johnson's voice rose above the noise.

"That's a bunch a bullshit, right there," Earl Johnson said. "It's been a long standin' tradition round here that we get turnt up Thursday nights. Y'all know that. My black-ass needs to go to the Longhouse and chill, have a few pops, and holla at my biddies. That's how I take care of my spirit and soul."

There was laughter but it didn't lift the weight of the palpable tension permeating the air. If anything, it drew a line in the sand; the issue was far from settled. The last thing they needed was dissension in the ranks, especially at this late hour. Jack Driftwood stood up amidst the clamor and the room grew quiet. He had the ear of the team, if only because he was the oldest thing in the Wigwam, dead or alive.

"Hold up, now. Hold up. Let's talk about this a minute," Jack said, moving his arms in the air like Ben Brady trying to quiet the crowd. "This is what, our nineteenth game of the season? We got one game left. Is this one game any different than the others? I mean, it is what it is, right? Isn't that what coach told us at the beginning of the week? I've been to a Mega Bowl, although it was so damn long ago I can barely remember it."

The team responded with a polite round of laughter but without the usual catcalls regarding Driftwood's old jockstraps and leather helmets. They wanted to hear him out.

"But one thing I do remember is what we did during the week back then. We had lost the previous three Mega Bowls and had been accused of partying too hard. Maybe rightly so, at least from some of the stories I heard. Regardless, we all got together at the beginning of the week and made a vow to stay clean all week. Nobody on the streets, no drinking, no hollerin' at the biddies. No nothing. We kept that vow, too, but we still got our asses kicked."

Driftwood paused to let that sink in. "The point is, it doesn't mean shit what we do on Thursday night. Thursday night doesn't have a goddamn thing to do with what we are going to do on Sunday. It ain't about Thursday night, it's about Sunday, because on Sunday we are going to come out and play the best damn game of our lives. We're gonna get after that ass. Now, whatever we have been doing has worked pretty well up to this point. So to me, you go out and do what you have to do, but keep one thing in mind. When we come in here Sunday, we come as one. We come in here together, ready to lay it all on the line – for each other. Don't try to fool yourselves or sell yourselves no wolf tickets. Do what you got to do, but come Sunday, we walk out that tunnel together – as one."

Jack paused again, then without thinking, shouted one last thing. "As one big, badass motherfucker!"

The whole team jumped up out of their seats hollering and screaming, high-fiving and chest bumping. They sent desks and chairs scattering all over the place as they scrambled into a big huddle in the center of the room. Leroy Clarkson was smack dab in the middle of the chaos. He raised his hand in a fist over his head and yelled above the ruckus.

"Yeah, baby, on three. One, two, three…"

"Yeah, baby!"

That settled the issue and the meeting broke up; the boys were together. Thursday night at the Longhouse had been completely off the hook, but that was another story for another time.

It was certainly of no concern to Jack as he stuck his head out the door of his hotel room at 11:30 that Friday night. He had another fish to fry, higher up in the building, if not the food chain. In what Jack considered a true sign from above and a fortuitous stroke of good fortune, he saw Eddie Stinson down the hallway holding court with his security team in front of the elevators.

Driftwood gave a low whistle and stepped into the hallway. Several members of the highly strung security team turned towards him, breaking ranks. Two of them took off, on the hop, in Jack's direction. Eddie Stinson ran a tight ship. But when he saw who it was, he let out a whistle of his own, freezing his rambunctious soldiers in their tracks.

"I'll handle this one, gentlemen," Stinson commanded. "You all have your assignments, let's get cracking!"

The security team quickly dispersed to tend to their business as Stinson strode down the hall to greet Jack.

"Hey, homeboy," Jack said, reaching out to shake hands.

Stinson grabbed Jack's outstretched hand and pulled him into a man-hug like he was a long-lost friend not seen in years. Hell, he had just seen Jack half an hour earlier during bed check.

"Can you believe it, Jackie boy? We are back in the Bowl, Mega, that is!"

"It's been awhile hasn't it?"

"Gosh, I remember you were just a peach-fuzzed, know-nothing rookie," Stinson said.

Jack self-consciously stroked the multi-colored three-week beard that covered his face, which featured much more gray than he had hoped.

Stinson was one of the few people who had been with the Blizzard organization longer than Jack. He was a short man who resembled a leprechaun, except his hair had whitened entirely. The same was true for his bushy eyebrows and sideburns that blended with his hairy ears. He had an irrepressible gleam in his eye.

"You know, Eddie," Jack said, "back then, I thought we would be going to the Bowl, Mega, that is, every year. Like it was a goddam birthright or something."

"Me too," Stinson replied. "After four in a row you just put it on your calendar. But here we are again and it only took seventeen years. I was wondering if it would happen again before I retired."

"I know, right? But we made it back, which is a good thing, because I ain't gonna be around here much longer my damn self."

Stinson chuckled, shaking again like a bowl of walking Jell-O as they ambled down the hall toward the elevator in lock-step.

"So, what can I do you for, Jack?"

"I need a hall pass, Mr. Stinson. There is a little fish-fry going on upstairs, if you know what I'm sayin'."

"Ha-ha! I knew it. No problem, I've got you covered. Just do me one thing. Win it this time. I got a great-grandson on the way and I want to give him the ring."

"That's the plan," Jack said, stepping onto the elevator after hitting Stinson with a fist-bump.

"Take Mr. Driftwood wherever he wants to go. You never saw him or heard it from me," Eddie told the guard operating the elevator.

"Yes, sir," the security guard replied.

"Thanks, Eddie. We'll get your little guy that ring." Jack said.

The sweet leprechaun of a man winked a twinkling eye at Jack as the elevator doors closed. And in the blink of that eye, Jack was catching a jumping Gerry Wainscott in the doorway of her eighteenth-floor penthouse suite. He carried her, kicking and giggling, all the way into the bedroom where he dumped her onto the king-sized bed. It felt like the first time all over again.

# Chapter Fifty-Four

Jack woke up early Mega Sunday in the Buffalo Seneca Casino Hotel with a mega ice ball in his gut. He tried to roll over and go back to sleep but his brain kicked in as soon as his eyes had opened. And his brain would not let him forget the Mega Bowl would be played in approximately eleven hours. The countdown was on and the titanic melon filling his abdominal cavity continued melting like an internal timing device, set to go off later that evening. He tried to put it out of his mind but soon discovered it was impossible. He felt like he was eight months pregnant. Trying to stay low key and breathe easy while waiting around for the game would be the day's biggest challenge.

He rubbed his hand through the rugged beard that had incrementally consumed his face over the past few weeks. The offensive line had taken a vow not to shave until after a Mega Bowl victory once the playoffs had begun. Jack had put away his razor upon rejoining the team in solidarity with the offensive line and in honor of the playoff beard tradition.

*Damn, I need me a good, clean shave.*

Many of his teammate's wives and girlfriends were counting down the hours as well.

Jack showered and threw on a brand-new sweat suit before making his way down to the team brunch in the Tomahawk Room on the third floor of the hotel. It seemed every time he returned to his hotel room during the week he'd find a new bag of goodies awaiting him. Sponsors from across the spectrum put together gift bags for the players in hopes they would wear the heavily logo-laden items in front of the ubiquitous media cameras covering the week-long festivities. It was all about the exposure.

The meal was optional for the team so the room was barely half full when Jack arrived. He grabbed a plate of food from the extravagant buffet and sat down next to Nick Loney. As his career had advanced, he found himself naturally gravitate toward the offensive linemen. He had discovered the behemoths who played on that side of the trenches often made the best company. These gigantic men were usually among the most intelligent, eloquent, and interesting members of the team. Jack found this to be delightfully ironic given the stereotype of the big, dumb lineman.

Loney had finished eating and was sipping coffee, working on the New York Times Sunday crossword puzzle. It had become something of a tradition for Jack to sit with Loney and complete the puzzle on game days. Loney was extremely superstitious about the ceremony and would not leave the table until the puzzle was completed. He would not hesitate to use his option to phone a friend or even cheat by using his phone to look for answers online; but only as a last resort. As long as the puzzle was completed by the end of their meal, the source of the answers was irrelevant.

"Hey, Looney-tunes. Thanks for waiting for me, dick. Did you knock that bitch out yet?"

"Good morning, Jack. It's Loney, not Looney. You know I never wait for the likes of you and I'm about halfway through it. So, as usual, I do all the heavy lifting and you arrive in time to steal the glory."

"Good, then I'm not too late. It's also your lucky day, because I gotta tell you, bro, I'm feeling smart as a whip this morning – on top of my game."

"Really? To what do you attribute the sudden change?"

"You do realize nobody really likes you and I am pretty much your only friend on the whole damn team, right?"

"Lucky me," Loney replied without looking up from the carefully folded newspaper.

With the formalities out of the way they began to work on the puzzle together.

"You see a big storm is about to hit the fan?" Loney asked.

Jack hadn't even considered the weather, given the game was under a huge, glass dome. He took a long look out the big window, scanning the western horizon. The sky out over Lake Erie was dark and ominous and a light snow had begun to fall outside.

"Too bad we're playing in an oversized greenhouse," Jack said. "I would love to see them St. Louie boys try to throw the ball in a good old-fashioned blizzard."

"Indeed, that would be optimal. They should just open the roof. Those poor saps would turn groundhog after popping their heads out of the locker room. Shut it down and declare six more weeks of winter."

"Looney!" Jack hollered with sudden excitement.

Loney put the puzzle down and shot Jack a look of exasperation. He hated that nickname with a passion.

"No," Jack responded, reaching over and tapping the crossword puzzle. "Check it out, sixty-eight across. Blank bin. It's looney. Fucking looney bin."

Loney shot Jack another dubious glance and then hunched over the paper to read the clue. He laughed and quickly filled in the answer.

"Of course, you would figure that one out. Didn't you just spend a holiday weekend locked away in one of those places?"

"More like twelve hours, dipshit, but it was a helluva holiday. I celebrated with your mother. After I banged her, she told me to tell you she was still crazier than a shit-house rat."

"Wow," Loney said, shaking his head sadly. "Really? A lame 'momma' joke? You weren't kidding, you really *are* on top of your game."

"Dude, check it out! It's a sign! You're number sixty-eight and the answer is your real name, Looney."

A slow smile spread across the wide, white face of Nick Loney.

"Maybe it is a sign," he said. "But that isn't my real name, dude."

"It is now," Jack said, pleased as pie.

"Let's check your number out, smart guy. I bet the clue is 'asshole.' Now that truly would be a sign."

They checked out the clue for fifty-seven across. It read, "Washed up lumber." It was a nine letter word. They looked at each other with wide eyes as the realization hit them simultaneously.

"Driftwood!"

Loney yelled the answer and started laughing as he filled it in, the ruckus drawing attention from around the otherwise placid room. It fit perfectly.

"No-fucking-way," Jack said.

"There's your sign! Plus, it is the perfect clue for you. You are washed up lumber incarnate!" Loney was loving every minute of it.

Several players gathered around as Loney proudly showed them the clues and the answers. Soon the entire room was abuzz. Maybe it was a sign, maybe it wasn't. But to a bunch of generally superstitious professional athletes on the morning of the biggest game of their lives, it was as close as they would get. It gave them all a boost of confidence, taking it as a harbinger of great fortune destined to come to fruition later that day.

Looney and Driftwood! They finished the puzzle in a jiffy after that, and word of the amazing coincidence spread through the team. Sometime late that afternoon, the rumpled newsprint puzzle was pinned to the bulletin board in the training room underneath the Wigwam.

Jack didn't know what to think about it. Initially, it gave him a shot of confidence, but then he wondered if it wasn't a curse. As he dwelled on the possibilities, the ice ball in his paunch swelled and then melted, almost as if it were breathing, sending electric shocks of juice into his system. Waiting for the game was torturous. Everything was a damned sign.

*It's just a stupid crossword puzzle… isn't it?*

Nearly the entire western coastline of Lake Erie was under a blizzard watch, with both a high-wind advisory and a heavy snowfall warning. Despite the forecast, the possibility of postponing the game was never considered. The authorities made several announcements warning everybody attending the game to get to the

Wigwam as early as possible. Of primary concern was not if, but when the major roads going in and out of Buffalo would be shut down.

The snow that had begun falling early that morning picked up in intensity and had accumulated into a fresh white coat that blanketed the city by midafternoon. The winds were expected to pick up later that evening when the low-pressure front arrived, bringing the main thrust of the storm. The prelude was mostly lake-effect snow being sucked up from the open waters of Lake Erie before being spit back out onto the city.

The Nighthawks had cancelled their plans to spend the night an hour northeast of town in Rochester, New York, at a hide-away hotel because they were worried about making it back into town due to the impending bad weather. They had simply stayed at the Buffalo Hyatt overnight and had to put up with the noise from revelers who had partied until all hours. It was a good decision, as they may not have made it back to town in time – if at all – had they ventured east across the Thruway. The Blizzard had no such problem; they simply had to saunter through the indoor walkway connecting their hotel to the huge monolith of a stadium.

Despite the snowstorm, the downtown streets of Buffalo were packed with Blizzard fans, most of whom did not have tickets to the game. This was a once in a lifetime prospect and nobody wanted to say they had missed it. The city's snow removal crews were doing their best to keep up with the storm, paying special attention to the Casino District and the Downtown area. They had their hands full, but removing snow in Buffalo had been elevated to an art form over the years and they kept ahead of it, for the most part. All of the townies considered the snowstorm to be a great, wondrous sign. After all, they were the Blizzard.

Fans began arriving downtown early that morning and the Wigwam was rocking four hours before kickoff. To accommodate the early arriving crowd the stadium gates had been opened at noon. Fans poured into the building early and were entertained by watching the pregame programming on the stadium's big-screen monitors. Concessions opened a couple of hours early as well, and the food and alcohol were flowing the whole time.

Across the street, the Buffalo Seneca Casino was packed and doing record business as fans were plugging the slot machines and Seneca Nation dealers were hitting soft seventeens. There was also legal wagering on the game for the first time in the history of the State of New York. The Seneca Nation had received special dispensation to do so after withdrawing their threat to take the matter to court. Both the NAFA and the state of New York were able to negotiate for a piece of the pie and suddenly the solid moral ground upon which they had so firmly stood caved. Funny how that worked.

The casino posted just about anything you could think of to wager on relating to the game, from who won the opening coin toss to the normal point spread, which anointed Buffalo as a three-point favorite – the standard amount given for home-field advantage. There was even a play regarding whether or not Jack Driftwood would get an interception. The prop bet was paying out ten-to-one.

Chaz put ten grand on his boy and thought about doubling it. Tree Spirit, who would normally never wager, put one thousand down on it. However, the mysterious half-breed Seneca did not consider it a bet. It was a sure thing, akin to robbery, as he claimed to have had a vision while standing over the stove steaming fresh vegetables. Cheese bought in with more cash and enthusiasm than the rest of the group as he threw twenty-five large on the prop bet. Even Juan Chavez put a grand on it, but only after making everybody swear they wouldn't tell his wife, especially if he won.

They honestly felt like it was a done deal and were even more confident after Jack had called with the story about the crossword puzzle. They didn't tell him about their side bets; the man had enough pressure on him as it was.

Gerald Wainscott III had made remarkable progress since coming out of a coma just five days earlier. His doctors were dumbfounded and considered it nothing short of miraculous. However, there was no way they were giving the cantankerous, old codger the green light to go to the game. That was unthinkable and an option that was not even on the table. Wainscott had put up a tremendous stink about it but in the end conceded. He had a seventy-inch flat-screen TV brought into his room as part of a compromise.

Wainscott had been walking the halls of the hospital with the assistance of a walker the past three days and was rapidly regaining his strength. He did still tire rather quickly, but he felt like he could move on his own. The metal contraption mostly got in his way, though it did give him security in preventing a fall. He was now using it as a form of resistance exercise, carrying it for stretches on his walks.

If only the game were the following weekend, then he would be able to waltz into the Wigwam, no problem.

"You have to be there, Gerry," Wainscott insisted to his daughter. "Somebody has to represent the ownership of the team."

"I know, but I don't want to leave you here all alone. I want to watch the game with you," she said.

"Are you whining, young lady? Shame on you," Wainscott chided. "You need to be there for Jack, too. So you better get along. The weather isn't going to get any better and I don't need to worry about you stuck out there in a raging blizzard."

"Okay, okay. I'm going. I love you, Dad. I will have my phone with me so call or text if you need anything."

"I love you too, dear. Now, get on over there and tell them to win one for the Gipper."

"Win one for the what?"

"Never mind," Gerald said. He smiled at her as she walked out the door.

*Damn kids these days. They know nothing.*

# Chapter Fifty-Five

The beginning of the game was one big blur in Driftwood's mind. How could something that was supposed to be so good begin so badly? He had tried to remain loose and calm in the locker room leading up to kickoff, but that was like expecting a goose not to crap indiscriminately; it wasn't going to happen. Leroy Clarkson had circled the room a record five times giving intensity laden high-fives to anyone not smart enough to hide. Driftwood took his medicine and endured the full handful of Leroy's whacks. His mitts felt like he had been running a jackhammer. He wised up and put on his custom-fit sheepskin gloves for the last three of Leroy's blasts. That took the edge off the sting.

Coach Ivy's pregame speech had been short and sweet. After gathering the team up for the Lord's Prayer he appealed to their hearts.

"Men, there is a kindly, old gentleman who would love to be here amongst us today, where he most assuredly belongs. However, circumstances dictate he watch us from a hospital bed a few miles away. And believe me, he will be watching – closely. It is what it is. So I say let's go out there and put on a show for him – a show he will not soon forget. Let's go out there and win one for the Gipper!"

Driftwood was sure half the team didn't even know who the damn Gipper was, or what it even meant. Not that it mattered: They all knew the kindly, old gentleman. Ultimately, it hadn't mattered what words Coach Ivy chose, they still would have charged out of that locker room as if their hair was on fire. The energy had been tangible, nearly visible, as the players roamed around and roared like caged beasts.

The offense had been selected to be introduced, but when the public address announcer called out the first name, the entire Blizzard squad stormed the field. The red-hat who was in charge of making sure the right player ran onto the field at the right time got knocked to the ground by the Buffalo stampede. Pure bedlam erupted! The house was rocking and shaking as the Blizzard faithful lost it in a fit of screaming and stomping. The TV people were pissed.

Driftwood goose-stepped onto the playing surface, kicking his legs out like a drum majorette all the while screaming incoherencies. He was zonked out of his mind along with the rest of his teammates. The scene was incredible and the glass roof seemed to vibrate under the audio assault from the crowd.

St. Louis won the coin toss and took the ball. Bennie Tenudo was so jacked up with adrenaline he kicked the pigskin through the uprights and into the stands, leaving the Nighthawks to start the drive from the own 20.

Mega Bowl 50 was underway!

The Blizzard defense was gathered tightly around Coach Faber for their traditional opening drive sendoff. They had learned their lesson from the earlier loss to the Nighthawks and the game plan called for primarily using their Base package. The Dime would be used sparingly, only in specific situations.

Coach Faber smiled like he knew the punchline before the joke even started. "You know the drill by now, so get out there and let's kick some ass and let them worry about taking names!"

Driftwood could tell by the gleam in Coach Faber's eyes the old boy would give his left nut to suit up and play in this one. Hadn't he always claimed he had one left in him?

Driftwood took a minor detour on his way to the field to slap Coach Ivy smartly on the ass. "That's a good omen, Coach. Defense is up first!"

"Don't sit here chapping *my* ass, Jack," a jubilant Coach Ivy yelled. "Get out there and hit somebody!"

Unfortunately, Driftwood and company failed miserably on that account. The Nighthawks rolled out their underrated running game, pounding the ground on five of their first six plays, shoving it down the Blizzard's collective throat. Buffalo had expected to see the Wigwam air riddled with footballs and were caught off guard. Driftwood missed an assignment and a tackle in the series and St. Louis quickly pierced the Buffalo red zone. The nose of the ball rested at the Blizzard 17 yard-line with the Nighthawks facing a 3rd and 2.

The call came in from Coach Faber; it was an all-out blitz putting Driftwood in man-to-man coverage on the lone back in the backfield, Javon Steamer. Steamer was barely five foot seven but weighed 210 pounds and ran like a possessed land crab. Coach Faber had referred to him for the past two weeks as a, "Goddamned rolling ball of butcher knives."

Driftwood sugared up the blitz, dancing around before the snap, and deployed a Green-dog technique, cautiously joining the blitz in hopes of keeping Steamer in the backfield for pass protection. At the snap, he attacked the open B-gap in front of him, and, sure enough, the running back stayed in to pick him up.

The crowd roared as the Nighthawks' Star-Bowl quarterback, John Tillison, had nowhere to go with the football. The Blizzard secondary had locked down the St. Louis receivers across the board. Driftwood somehow got under the diminutive Steamer's pads and rolled his hips, lifting him back into Tillison's lap, giving the QB a quick case of happy feet. Driftwood was close enough to where he could reach over the top of Steamer and grab the tap-dancing Tillison. He went for it; tossing Steamer aside, he lunged for the QB. He whacked him across the chest and was bringing him down, but at the last second Tillison managed to dump the ball over Driftwood's head into the hands of a surprised Javon Steamer.

Steamer wasn't the only one surprised; the Buffalo defense was caught with their pants down.

Steamer took off running like a scalded dog as Driftwood hammered Tillison to the turf. The middle of the field parted like the Red Sea as the Blizzard secondary was plastered to their men; nobody could react soon enough to make the play. Seventeen yards later Steamer was dancing in the end zone and St. Louis was up 6-0 with the extra point to come.

The St. Louis contingent went bananas. The NAFA's top scoring offense had shredded the Blizzard defense, making it look easy in their opening drive. Moreover, they did it on the ground, rushing the football seemingly at will. The extra point was good and the Nighthawks soared to an early 7-0 lead.

Buffalo's offense didn't fare much better, managing just a single first down before having to punt the football away. The Buffalo defense took the field intending to show the initial drive was a fluke. Driftwood stomped in front of the huddle as the world waited for play to resume during an extended TV timeout.

"Hey, we're okay, boys," Driftwood said. "We just gotta settle our asses down and play our game. We got the bad shit out of our system. Run to the ball and good things will happen. C'mon now!"

He was right, kind of. Good things did happen – for St. Louis. The Nighthawks took a deep shot on first down from their own 42-yard line. Tillison faked a handoff and took a five-step drop. Driftwood came on a delayed blitz and got tripped by the turf monster and fell down face first with nobody around him. He would have had a clean sack if he hadn't stumbled on the tacky surface.

He never saw the play, but he didn't have to; he knew by the crowd noise it wasn't good. Tillison spun a beautiful, high-arching bomb that floated softly into the hands of his favorite target, Jeremy Hinton, 50 yards down the field. Leroy Clarkson had the coverage, but he tripped too, leaving Hinton wide open. Apparently the blizzard was falling both in and outside the Wigwam.

When Jack finally did get his eyes down the field he saw his worst nightmare. It was Hinton's turn to dance in the end zone. Halfway through the first quarter the Nighthawks had a 14-0 lead; Buffalo was in trouble.

Outside the Wigwam the snowstorm had picked up in intensity. The Western New York sky had turned a menacing greenish-blue color and intermittent lightning lit the firmament. In a rare occurrence thunder snow was raging over the city. An uncommon, frozen brand of snow, actual marble-sized ice pellets began tumbling ominously from the sky at an alarming rate. All of the fans who had gathered in the streets around the stadium ran for cover. It felt like an omen portending the end of the world.

The heating filaments in the glass roof covering the Wigwam had been cranked up to full bore since the storm began. When the snow fell at a moderate to even heavy rate they had been effective, keeping the white stuff from piling up on top of the structure. However, several of the substandard heating filaments Fegel had installed were beginning to fail, allowing the ice and snow to gain a foothold in several spots. The barrage of miniature ice balls pelted the glass roof like mini-meteorites. During a lull in the action on the field the fans inside were unnerved by the volume of them pinging off the glass.

Bolts of lightning flashing directly overhead drew "oohs" and "aahs" from the spectators. The resulting light show from inside the Wigwam was quite spectacular. The bright flashes of light refracted through the ice crystals, giving the appearance of millions of tiny rainbows in the ice beginning to form on sections of the roof. Mother Nature's display blew away the hokey pregame pyrotechnics show, by far.

A tremendous flash of lightning, followed immediately by a fantastic boom of thunder, silenced the Wigwam. Had lightning just struck the building? Even the Western New Yorkers, who had previously experienced this type of winter storm, were awed. Murmuring regarding concern for safety ran rampant inside the domed structure. The question was twofold. What was more impressive, the storm or the St. Louis offense, and who pissed off Mother Nature?

The Buffalo offense had the ball in excellent field position after a nice kick return by Shady Solomon, who had taken over return duties for the playoffs. The ball was resting near midfield and Brady was in the shotgun with four receivers spread evenly across the field. He picked up his right leg like he was kick-starting a motorcycle. This was the signal for Nick Loney to snap the ball. Loney snapped it all right, but the results were disastrous.

The ball had started to slip from Loney's grasp so he put a little extra mustard on the snap to make sure it got safely into Brady's hands. Instead, the ball had zipped over his quarterback's head. A mad scramble ensued and St. Louis came up with it on the Buffalo 32-yard line. The home crowd began booing.

"Some fucking sign, huh, Jack?" Loney said as he passed Driftwood coming off the field.

Driftwood shrugged. "No shit. Just keep sawin' wood, bro."

That proved to be a daunting task as St. Louis seemed to get every possible break in the first half. Driftwood and the Blizzard defense held this time, though. They forced the Nighthawks to kick a field goal, putting St. Louis ahead 17-0. That's how the first quarter ended mercifully for the Blizzard and their fans that made up approximately sixty percent of the capacity crowd.

The second quarter wasn't much better as St. Louis continued to pour it on. They scored two more touchdowns to make it 31-0 and were driving again just before the first half was coming to a close. They had matriculated to the Buffalo 25-yard line with only 13 seconds left before the halftime break. Another touchdown and you could piss on the fire and call off the dogs.

John Tillison brought the St. Louis offense to the line. With one timeout remaining he could use the entire field and still stop the clock to trot out the field goal unit, if necessary. The red-hot Nighthawk QB surveyed the defense before dropping under center. Javon Steamer was lined up directly behind him. As Tillison belted out the cadence, Driftwood remembered seeing this same formation on film from an earlier game the Nighthawks had played against Minnesota. Driftwood knew in an instant what was coming.

The defense Coach Faber had sent in called for a four-man rush with the linebackers dropping into the underneath zones, protected over the top by a cover-two shell and the corners man-to-man on the edges. Trusting his instincts, Driftwood ignored his zone and tracked Steamer from behind the Blizzard pass rush. A seam opened as Tillison back pedaled, drawing the pass rushers up the field. With the trap properly set, the Nighthawks' QB flipped the ball over the top of the onrushing Eric Sellars and into the waiting hands of Javon Steamer.

Crack!

The violent sound of the collision reverberated through the entire building. It was so fierce fans out in the mezzanine hustled back into the arena to see what had happened. Just as Steamer turned up field, Driftwood showed up from the shadows in a very bad humor. He whacked Steamer so hard some of the fans thought the thunder snow had returned. Incredibly, Steamer held onto the football, but his helmet flew off and landed five yards away. Driftwood scampered to his feet and kicked at the ground, displaying his fury. His teammates raced to him, jumping on and around him like they had fire ants in their pants.

The Public Address system immediately blared the old House of Pain song, "Jump Around." The entire Blizzard sideline picked up on the tune and did just that. Their supporters, who had been sitting on their hands for most of the first half, began hopping around like millennials in a mosh pit. They had been waiting for something to cheer about and they finally got it in a big way. The Wigwam erupted into a human zoo.

The Nighthawks burned their final timeout. They had hoped things would calm down before they had to kick the field goal, but they weren't that fortunate. The Buffalo crowd continued pounding their feet on the bleachers, screaming as loud as possible for the duration of the timeout. Finally, the party had started!

The field goal block unit danced onto the field, bringing the cacophony up another notch. Buffalo's special teams coach, William Siglar, had been harping all week about how he was putting, "the two widest asses in the northern hemisphere over the skinniest ass on Nighthawks' roster." Bo-Bo and Loney, the designated wide-asses, lined up on opposite shoulders of the Ram's long-snapper, a 235-pound rookie linebacker by the name of Randy Kirkendahl. Coach Sig had guaranteed Coach Ivy a blocked place-kick in the ball game due to the mismatch.

At the snap, Kirkendahl fired a laser-guided rocket to the holder and then tried to make himself wide. Bo-Bo mowed through him like a stoner through a bag of potato chips, but the guard on his side leaned in to help slow down the charging rhino of a man. The result was a huge hole right up the gut for Nick Loney. Loney timed it perfectly and stretched his six-foot-six-inch frame to its full height, casting an immense shadow over both the holder and the kicker.

Thump-thump!

The dreaded double thump. The first thump was the right foot of the Nighthawks' kicker, Bovo Oblouf, striking the ball; the second thump was the ball hitting Nick Loney in the chest. The ball ricocheted straight back past the Star-Bowl kicker like a line drive base hit. It bounced twice before Leroy Clarkson scooped it up in full stride. Nobody was going to catch Leroy. Not today. The game clock flashed all zeros as Clarkson high-stepped his way into the end zone.

Touchdown Buffalo!

The Wigwam was up for grabs. The Teepee in the far end zone sent out smoke signals and fake snow fell from the rafters. Fireworks blasted from the perimeter of the upper rim of the stadium. The Blizzard fans felt a titanic shift in momentum and were screaming for all they were worth. Bennie Tenudo tacked on the extra point amid the ruckus and hope was alive in Buffalo!

The Blizzard players danced their way around the stadium, reluctant to head into the locker room for halftime. They finally had cause to do a little dancing of their own. They slapped the hands of overjoyed fans leaning over the railings. You would have thought they had just won the game rather than closing the gap to a still daunting 24 points. Finally, the last member of the Blizzard team made it to the tunnel leading to the locker room. They were down 31-7, but there was hope. After getting their collective ass kicked for 29 minutes and 47 seconds, Buffalo had thoroughly dominated the last 13 seconds of the half. Hey, it was a start. Ironically, their fans were overjoyed. The building was afire.

The private helicopter descended toward the freshly shoveled helipad outside Buffalo General Hospital through the falling snow. The quick descent was perfectly executed despite the weather. The pilot kept the whirlybird engine running, as he didn't plan to be on the ground for long. The mission had nearly been scuttled, but the weather had eased up significantly. Radar showed a break in the slow-moving storm, providing a perfect window of opportunity for the flight.

Mere seconds after touching down the double doors to the side entrance of the hospital opened and several orderlies pushed the austere gentleman in a wheelchair immediately and directly up to the whirling machine. They slid the door open and helped their patient up and into the back seat. The man was decked out in a tuxedo, but you could barely tell since he was wrapped in several blankets heisted from the hospital.

They strapped him securely into his seat then quickly folded up the wheelchair and loaded it behind the seat. As requested, they carefully put a headset onto the kindly, old gentleman's head. The local broadcast of the game immediately filled his ears. Two of the orderlies jumped into the helicopter, one up front and the other in the back. They strapped themselves in and gave the thumbs up signal to the pilot.

The entire process took less than three minutes. The pilot grabbed the stick and pulled it gently backwards. The helicopter lifted off the ground, its precious cargo in the fold. They climbed straight up in a perfect vertical ascent and soon were safely above the building. The pilot eased the stick forward, starting the short journey across the city.

The man in the back got on his radio to inform the ground crew at their destination they were airborne and would be arriving stat. That crew had already shoveled off a makeshift landing pad. They were ready and waiting.

In less than five minutes the helicopter made its descent. The pilot had easily spotted the impromptu landing area and hit it dead center. Speedily the ground crew at the landing site peeled open the doors, unloaded the wheelchair, and helped the austere gentleman out of the aircraft and into the wheelchair.

They wheeled the man down a shoveled path into a loading dock. The entire process took less than ten minutes from start to finish. Gerald Wainscott III was going to the Mega Bowl game, come hell or high water. What were they going to do, ground him?

The Blizzard stormed into their locker room riding the high of their last-second touchdown that hopefully had put them back into the game. But that adrenaline quickly wore off and they had to face the reality of the situation. They had gotten their asses handed to them for nearly 30 minutes on the field. Soon a quiet pall was cast over the room as small pockets of players talked quietly amongst themselves, killing the extra time.

Coach Ivy stepped into the room. "Take care of your business, men. As we discussed, we have an extra fifteen minutes, so relax, but make sure you keep your focus. Your coaches will get with you in twenty minutes so we can get this all sorted out."

The Mega Bowl halftime is an endurance contest. They last twice as long as normal because of all the entertainment and commercials the NAFA and TV networks crammed into the event. Driftwood remembered this well from his previous Mega Bowl experience.

He immediately stripped down to a pair of shorts and headed for the hot tub. After a nice, quick soak, he planned on getting a good stretch, and a short but sweet massage. It was an abbreviated version of his normal pregame routine. He knew if he didn't take care of his old carcass it would stiffen during the extended break. As he walked by the training room, he noticed somebody had ripped the crossword puzzle off the bulletin board. Maybe that was a fucking sign, too.

## Chapter Fifty-Six

The luxury boxes in the Wigwam were top of the line in both comfort and decor. Each suite featured a modern kitchenette, plush carpet, and fine cherry cabinetry. Granite countertops cascaded into a large double sink centered on the inside back wall. Above the sink was a window with one-way glass so occupants could look out into the wide hallways without being gawked at themselves. Flat-screen TV monitors hung on each of the walls so revelers would never miss a play, even while fetching refreshments.

There was a TV monitor in the bathroom, which featured two sinks, a urinal, and a separate closet for the commode. The expansive main room was split in half by an oak bar surrounded by a dozen custom built stools featuring the Blizzard logo. Opposite the bar, a wraparound leather sofa with elegant end tables and lamps created a homey feel.

Sliding glass doors separated the inner chamber from an open terrace overlooking the field. The outside seating area featured five graduated rows, each with swiveling leather recliners so the fans could turn to follow the action. The NAFA Commissioner, Bob Goldman, was relaxing in one of those recliners in Gerald Wainscott's suite, excitedly anticipating the halftime mini-concert when Gerry Wainscott tapped him on the shoulder.

"Oh, hey, Gerry," Goldman said, barely taking his eyes off the stage at midfield. "Sorry about the way your team is playing. Let's hope they can get it together in the second half. Nobody likes a blowout."

Gerry smiled her best "blow me" smile before leaning in so the Commissioner could hear her above the music. "We may have bigger problems than how my team is playing, Commissioner. Could you please come with me?"

The serious nature of Gerry Wainscott's tone and demeanor finally pulled Goldman's attention from the festivities on the field. He hoped it was something he could quickly assign to one of his many underlings hovering about so he could get back to watching the show. Gerry led him out of the suite and into the hallway where two overtly nervous gentlemen were awaiting them.

"Commissioner Goldman," Gerry said, "you've met our head of security, Eddie Stinson, and this is Artie Gonzalez, the building's chief engineer."

Goldman nodded. He didn't bother to hide his impatience as he stole a glance back over his shoulder towards the ongoing halftime spectacle and then checked his watch.

*This damn well better be important, this is my favorite part of the show.*

"Mr. Gonzalez, will you please repeat what you just told me to the Commissioner?" Gerry asked.

"Yes, ma'am," Gonzalez said.

He was clearly agitated and the worrisome look on his face made Goldman a little nervous. This obviously wasn't about a toilet paper or hot dog shortage; something serious was afoot.

"We have a grave problem with the snow and ice accumulating on the building's roof, sir. The snowmelt system has been overloaded due to the magnitude of this storm. The ice pellets that fell earlier did not melt fast enough, creating a base upon which the snow is piling. If we do not open the roof immediately, I am certain it will fail. It was not designed to handle this heavy of a load."

Goldman went blank. *Did this guy just say the roof was going to fail? What the hell does he mean fail?*

If this was somebody's idea of a joke it sure as hell wasn't funny. He glared at Gerry waiting for the punch line. None was forthcoming.

"Excuse me," Goldman finally said, "what do you mean *fail*?"

"By fail, I mean the roof will fail, sir," Gonzalez replied. "As in it will collapse under the weight of the snow and ice and fall on top of the field, players and fans. It will be catastrophic."

A horrifying image of the Wigwam's roof collapsing, crushing both teams and tens of thousands of fans under a mountain of ice, glass, and snow metastasized in Goldman's mind's eye. Suddenly, he had a terrific urge to pee his pants.

Goldman had been appointed as the NAFA Commissioner prior to the season but had yet to encounter any truly difficult situations. He was mainly hired to clean up the NAFA's battered image due to a major class-action concussion lawsuit brought by former players and myriad off-field issues. That he could handle, but nobody had mentioned anything regarding mitigating disasters of epic proportions in the league's showcase event when he took the job. Nope, he could not recall that being anywhere in the job description.

Such a calamity would forever stain his tenure with the league and would be witnessed by the entire world on live television during his watch. Of course, he wasn't the guy who screwed up the roof, but that wouldn't matter, the buck stopped with him and he knew it. The gist of exactly what they wanted from him dawned on him. They wanted him to evacuate the stadium and call off the Mega Bowl. No. No way. No way in hell!

"We can't just call off the game and evacuate the stadium," he shouted at Gerry. "That's insane!"

"There is another alternative, Commissioner," Gerry said calmly, almost with a hint of a smile.

Goldman didn't like look on her face or her tone, not one bit. *What the hell is this woman up to?*

"And just what would that be, Ms. Wainscott?" Goldman said, managing to whine snottily.

"We can open the roof."

"Are you out of your fucking mind? There's a raging blizzard going on out there!"

Goldman roared incredulously, flapping his arms with an escalated anger directed at Gerry Wainscott, as if she was personally responsible for this blatant attempt to piss on his parade.

Artie Gonzalez shrunk away from the man's angry outburst, but it had the opposite effect on Eddie Stinson. He was hot. He stepped in between Gerry and Goldman and got right up in the Commissioner's grill.

"Listen here, Mr. Big Britches, you don't need to be talking to the lady in that manner. You better get down off your high horse and get ahold of yourself, or I will do it for you. You have two very clear choices. Either call off the game and evacuate this building immediately, or we open that roof. Because if we don't do one or the other, a lot of people will get hurt here tonight, and that will be on your head, buddy-boy. Not to mention I will make it my business to see to it that you are among them."

Goldman stepped back and raised both hands in surrender. The haranguing from Stinson, as a challenge often does to bullies, took all the air out of him and he settled down.

"Easy big fella, certainly nobody wants anybody to get hurt here tonight, especially me."

"Well, Bobby, what's it going to be?" Gerry pressed. "We are running out of time."

Goldman hated to be called Bobby, but that was the least of his problems at that point. He took a deep breath and looked up at the roof.

"Well, we aren't going to cancel the game," he said adamantly. "So, I guess we will have to open the goddamn roof. Now if that is all, I'd like to watch the halftime show so I can die happy. It's sure to be a much better performance than what your Blizzard have put on thus far."

With that he turned and abruptly walked back into the Owner's box to watch the rest of the halftime show.

The mood in the Buffalo locker room had gone from an adrenaline-fueled high to a sobering low as time slowly ticked off the extended halftime clock. Their collective confidence had been thoroughly shaken by their shoddy first-half performance, but slowly they began to pick up the pieces and steadily build themselves back up emotionally. The extra time they had was proving to be a blessing, as they began to flush away the disappointment of the first 30 minutes and clear their minds of their abject failure. It felt like they were getting ready for the start of an entirely new ballgame.

Yells of encouragement began to fill the air as guys were girding their minds for the second half of the battle. By the time Danny Steeley hollered out the usual five-minute warning, they were collectively chomping at the bit to get back out there and play Blizzard Football. The usual meetings with their coaches had helped rebuild their fragile psyche. The coaches had come up with few, if any, adjustments to their original game plan. The plain and simple truth was they needed to execute better. That was crystal clear to everybody in the room.

Usually Coach Ivy wouldn't bring the team up until Steeley gave the two-minute warning, so it was a bit surprising when he hurried into the locker room and blew his whistle before climbing up onto one of the wood-topped canvass hampers used to collect dirty laundry so everybody could see him.

"Men, let me have your attention," Coach Ivy yelled above the general chatter.

The team sensed something big was up; the room went instantly silent.

"I have just been informed, due to the magnitude of the storm, the snow-melt system built into the roof is failing. Snow and ice continues to accumulate on the roof, which was not designed to support that heavy of a load."

Murmurs ran through the room. Everyone in town knew Fegel had fudged the building project and had stolen a bunch of money, but they weren't privy to all the details. However, they had all read the Budd Kilmer story mentioning issues with the glass roof. Was this going to screw up their shot at a comeback attempt?

"Due to the imminent threat of the roof collapsing," Coach Ivy continued, "a decision has been made to open the roof before the game will resume. Therefore, halftime will be extended another five to ten minutes or so while they open it up and then clean off the field from the snow that falls during the process. Now, I don't know about you, but this is the best damn news I've heard all night. It appears as if Donald Fegel has, albeit unknowingly, bequeathed to us the parting gift of resurrecting our historical home-field advantage. We are going to play the second half in an all-out blizzard!"

The team erupted into a tremendous roar – they were the Blizzard! It took Coach Ivy a little longer to get them settled down and regain their attention this time. He tried yelling over the commotion but that was fruitless; most of the guys thought Coach Ivy was cheering along with them. Seeing no alternative, he blew a long blast on his trusty whistle, the one sure method of gaining any football team's attention. The rigorously shrill blast quieted down his spirited charges.

"Get whatever cold-weather gear you need from Danny and the equipment staff, including the proper footwear as the field's surface is sure to be wet and slippery. Let's get prepared to play the old-school brand of Buffalo Blizzard football!"

Coach Ivy punctuated his last few words by pumping his fist repeatedly into the air. He was as fired up as they had ever seen him. The primary catalyst for his resurgent intensity was the thought of how this same announcement was indubitably received with a small fraction of the same gusto across the way in the St. Louis locker room.

Things were chaotic for the next several minutes as each man geared up to face the elements. When Danny Steeley gave the final two-minute warning, the team once again assembled around Coach Ivy, who was standing in front of the locker room doors leading to the tunnel and the field.

"Men," Coach Ivy began, with a reclaimed and unmistakable twinkle in his eyes. "A couple of hours ago, prior to the kickoff, I stood here before you and I spoke of a kindly, old gentleman who would be watching us play from a hospital bed a few miles from here. Well, many things have changed tonight, including that."

Coach Ivy paused and peered around the room for effect, catching as many eyes as possible. "Because that kindly, old gentleman is no longer in a hospital bed. He is right here, right now!"

On cue, the double doors to the locker room popped open and Gerald Wainscott III, looking exceptionally dapper in a black tuxedo complete with a Blizzard-blue bow tie, walked into the room with men flanking each elbow. The players began to whistle, laugh, cheer, and even cry at the sight of their owner.

The spectacle of Mr. Wainscott, walking under his own power, dressed to the nines, gave Jack chills and his eyes welled up. He wasn't alone. It was the single most inspirational thing Jack had ever seen. There was no way they were going to lose this game now; no matter the score. They'd sooner die.

Wainscott, battling his own emotions with tears of joy filling his eyes, came to a halt in the center of the room. He embraced Coach Ivy. Neither man spoke; they didn't have to. Having endured so much together over the years, an unbreakable bond had forged between the two aged men. This palpable connection passed from them into the heart of every man in that room. There wasn't a dry eye in the house as they poetically embraced smack dab in the middle of the team's logo woven into the carpet at the center of the locker room. If they hadn't come together prior to this moment, they certainly did now.

Slowly Gerald Wainscott turned a complete circle, eyeballing every single one of them. "Fellas, forget that first half," he said. "It doesn't count because I wasn't here."

There was some soft laughter but the room quieted quickly; they were mesmerized. Wainscott's presence had cast a spell on the room.

"I couldn't take it anymore watching on that damned TV, so I called a friend of mine who happens to own a helicopter and owed me one. I can tell you right now, he and I are even. Miraculously, the weather cleared long enough for him to fly me over here after breaking me out of the hospital. It probably wasn't as exciting as your escape, Jack, but it was equally effective."

They laughed again, louder this time. Just like that, Wainscott had managed to raise his team's emotions to a crescendo, yet loosen them up at the same time. The man had a gift. He went in for the kill.

"When I brought this team to Buffalo fifty-five years ago, the only thing I knew for sure was we would have a decided home-field advantage when winter came along. And it was true, we did. Nobody wanted to come up here and play us late in the season. But of course, genius that I am, I went and spoiled our only inherent advantage by building this damned Wigwam with its big glass roof. Well, the good Lord has seen fit to overrule me on that count and bring back that advantage. But as Coach Ivy has taught me over the years, there *is* no advantage unless you *take* advantage. So, I ask you for one last favor, I am asking that you go out there and take advantage. Take full advantage and let's go out there and kick their asses!"

An unparalleled explosion of emotion erupted in the bowels of the Wigwam. Born of the moment, a raw, undeniable determination to finish their quest congealed within the ranks of this exceptional brotherhood. Their owner had fundamentally put his life on the line to come be with them and see them through to the end. They were ready to do the same for him. The raging Blizzard charged out of the room, down the tunnel, and out onto the field, where they were met by another raging blizzard. It was pure poetry.

That blizzard was the most beautiful thing this Blizzard had ever seen.

The impromptu plan was to wait for the halftime show to conclude before making an announcement to the crowd, giving them a five-minute warning before the attempt to open the roof. Arturo Gonzalez had hurried from the unpleasant meeting with the distasteful Commissioner to the control room in the basement of the building.

Artie had been involved with the Wigwam construction venture from day one. He was among the many whom Donald Fegel had conned throughout the development of the great structure. Artie considered his inability to see through Mr. Fegel's deception as a personal failing and felt responsible for the potential impending catastrophe.

His primary concern was the damage may have already been done; the weight of the snow and ice collecting on the roof likely had already disabled the machinery, meaning the roof wouldn't open. The system supporting the rails upon which the roof rested wasn't built to handle the current load amassed atop the building. It was possible the whole shebang could come crashing down once the motor engaged and the roof began to separate. Unfortunately, there was only one way to find out.

Artie monitored the situation via twenty-seven different HD display screens fed from live cameras situated strategically around the facility. Of particular concern was a line of snow drifts already a couple feet high along the eastern edge of the stadium roof. Fortunately, these white ridges would be the first of the snow to slide off the building when the roof ambulated. Another monitor showed stadium personnel marshalling people away from the area along the outside of the stadium where the snow would drop once the process was initiated. Another series of monitors showed stadium personnel ushering the fans out of their seats and onto the concourse to get them from harm's way once the process began.

An LED clock on the panel told him the time had come. After crossing himself and saying a quick prayer, Artie Gonzalez was as ready as he would ever be. He pushed the all-call button activating the communication system and began the countdown, which was broadcast over the stadium's public address system and live on TV to a worldwide audience. A camera crew had made their way into the control room and they were rolling live.

"Initiating opening sequence in ten…nine…eight…"

The fans in the upper deck had the best view of what may be their apocryphal demise. Many of them had ignored the requests to move into the concourse. They weren't going to miss the fun of watching the roof slide open. If it worked, they would be the first to know; if not, they would be the first to go. They went silent upon hearing the initial whir of the electric motors that drove the system. The rest of crowd picked up their cue and a silent, anticipatory pall was cast over the entire stadium.

Every eye in the building was trained on the seam splitting the massive expanse right down the middle, where the glass would hopefully soon separate, revealing the black night sky filled with contrasting falling snow. There was an excessive pause that seemed to last an eternity, which further quieted the crowd and ratcheted up the suspense. The ninety-two-thousand-plus in attendance inhaled in unison and held their collective breath as the motors spewed forth a petrifying, high-pitched whine. All other noise in the cavernous structure ceased as the crowd seemed to grasp the gravity of its peril, en masse, for the first time.

Thuwwwaaack!

The resounding crack sucked any remaining air from the crowd, as the ice bond sealing the roof gave way. Instinctively, most of the onlookers ducked, as if that would save them from a collapsing roof. A barrage of ice chunks and heavy snow plummeted down in a straight line, effectively skunking the field, fans, and stands below with a relatively wide white stripe square down the middle, dividing the field into equal halves.

The roof had separated and began to slowly slide apart, splitting perfectly in two. The silence was replaced by a raucous response, rising up and building momentum from the much relieved crowd. Somewhere in the basement of the Wigwam, Arturo Gonzalez howled at the moon with a great victory whoop.

The roof never wobbled and parted without incident, functioning exactly as it had been designed despite the encumbrance of ice and snow. An avalanche of snow falling off the edge of the building outside looked like a waterfall cascading to the ground, shaking the building when it hit the earth. Television cameras captured the sight for the record TV audience from all over the world. The video was simultaneously shown on the Jumbotrons inside, captivating both audiences. The TV commentators were having a field day building the initial drama and describing the desperate nature of the situation before rejoicing after all went well.

Disaster had been averted; the most momentous Mega Bowl in NAFA history would go on. If the second half of the game held merely a fraction of the halftime drama, it would be one whale of a show.

## Chapter Fifty-Seven

Buffalo took the field to receive the second-half kickoff. Driftwood was watching the Nighthawks' sideline in an attempt to gage their reaction to the sudden change in the playing conditions. A handful of them were jumping up and down trying to get loose and stay warm. Many had put on the light blue Blizzard overcoats provided by Danny Steeley and his staff. To a man, they were stealing looks upwards into the snowy night sky through the cavernous black hole at the top of the stadium. A few of them appeared to be in shock; no doubt, their focus had switched from the game to the prevailing conditions.

Driftwood had thought the days of the opposition sky-watching had passed with the opening of the Wigwam, but he was being proven wrong. What Mr. Wainscott had just told them in the locker room was no joke – Buffalo had enjoyed a distinct advantage due to foul weather over the years. The snow and cold had ultimately been the undoing of many a good football team venturing north to play them late in the season over the years. If their fans were the twelfth man, then Old Man Winter was the thirteenth. And old number thirteen was alive and kicking!

The storm had re-intensified and the big, fat snowflakes were quickly gaining a foothold on the Field turf surface inside the Wigwam. Any heat in the building was pouring out through the open roof, causing the temperature inside to plummet. It was seventeen degrees outside and wouldn't be long before the Wigwam transformed into a giant refrigerator.

It had already transformed into a gigantic snow globe that appeared to have just been violently shaken. Large, fluffy flakes were coming down fast and furious, making accumulation inside the building inevitable. If it kept falling at the current pace, Driftwood figured there would easily be more than a half a foot covering the field before the game's end. His heart swelled inside of him; talk about your signs! If this wasn't a good omen, he didn't know what was.

Bovo Oblouf, teed the ball up for St. Louis in preparation for the second half kickoff. Jumping up and down and flapping his arms, Bovo tried to get himself loose and the St. Louis crowd riled up for the kick at the same time. His actions elicited the opposite effect from the partisan Blizzard fans. A rousing chorus of boos rained down on the Nighthawks' kicker, which only spurred him to more theatrics. Buffalo followers remembered well Bovo's ridiculous celebration after hitting the 54-yard game-winner when the teams had met during the regular season. He had spread his arms like some kind of human airplane and run all over the field dipping and turning. The cocky kicker was more hated than most of the Nighthawks and took pride in the fact.

He strutted around like a banty rooster before finally lining himself up to kick the ball. His taunting of the crowd had led to the play clock nearly running out and Oblouf, realizing it, hurried his approach to the ball. He may have gotten away with it on a dry field, but his plant foot slipped out from under him on the wet surface as he swung his mighty right leg at the football. He nearly missed the football, just grazing the tip.

The pigskin rolled briefly and came to a stop roughly five yards in front of where it had been teed up. Bovo slid on his backside along the wet turf and laid there trying to decide if he was hurt. Everybody else froze. They just stopped, laughed, and gawked at the ball, clearly anticipating a whistle and a re-kick; everybody except Jerry Killings, that is. From his center spot on the front line of the return team, the Blizzard's top special-teamer darted to the ball. Killings dove on it and slid another few yards right into the legs of Bovo, who had jumped up off the ground, deciding he was unhurt. However, that didn't last very long, as Bovo's legs twisted awkwardly upon contact and he went down in a heap, draped awkwardly over top Killings. Whistles blew and both teams took it as a signal to start the arguing that immediately ensued.

After getting an earful from both sidelines, the referee huddled up with his crew. A short discussion preceded his announcement as he clicked on his field mic to give the verdict.

"The St. Louis kicker made contact with the ball, thus making it an official kick. Buffalo legally recovered the ball on the St. Louis thirty-five-yard line. NAFA rules state the ball must travel at least ten yards or the kicking team is penalized for an illegal kick. That penalty will be marked off making it Buffalo ball, first and ten, at the St. Louis thirty-yard line. Please put fourteen minutes and fifty-four seconds on the clock."

The Wigwam erupted. Replays on the huge video boards clearly showed Bovo had made contact with the ball. St. Louis did not even challenge the play. Throughout the heated discussion, hardly anybody noticed Bovo was still down on the field, collecting falling snow. Eventually, the St. Louis' medical staff detected their supine kicker and rushed onto the field to attend to him. He had to exit the field on the cart with his broken left leg engulfed in an air cast, propped up on his helmet. Just like that, St. Louis no longer had the services of their angry little kicker.

Once things settled down the long overdue Buffalo offense came to life. They took advantage of the excellent field position with Ben Brady working from the shotgun, despite the snowy conditions. He sent AC deep on a play-action pass on the very first play from scrimmage and lobbed the ball up for grabs in the corner of the end zone. With perfect timing, AC went up and muscled the ball away from a pair of St. Louis defenders for the touchdown. Buffalo scored their second touchdown in three plays going back to the first half and had closed the gap further, trailing now by 17, 31-14, with 14:47 left in the third quarter.

It was during the TV timeout following that touchdown when critical mass was achieved and the snow began to stick to and cover the field. The grounds crew was working feverishly clearing the sidelines and yard lines so the officials, players, fans, and worldwide TV audience could see the field's markings. It didn't matter how hard they worked, they were simply overmatched by the astronomical rate at which the snow was falling.

Just as the telecast came out of commercial break and the game was ready to begin again, a deep rumble began emanating from the tunnel behind the south end zone. People were already nervous from the roof incident. What now?

Suddenly, several large tractors with big brushes rigged to the front of them came roaring out of the south end zone tunnel, drawing an enthusiastic ovation from the relieved crowd. These old-time football Zambonis had been mothballed in a storage area in the basement of the Wigwam and were earmarked for the new Blizzard museum set to open in the stadium come springtime. Thus, the stadium operations crew had them tuned up and ready to go. They swiftly cleaned the boundaries delineating the field with great efficiency and it was time to play ball again.

The Nighthawks returned the kickoff out to their own 26-yard line and their offense returned to the field for the first time in over an hour. Driftwood and company hoped the long interlude had dulled their sharpness. The Blizzard was sky high as they took the field riding the wave of emotion fed by the unlikely turn of events. Driftwood stood in front of the huddle alongside his rookie, Steven Stark.

"This is how we did it back in the day, son," he hollered directly at Stark.

"Hey, old-timer, I grew up around here. I've played in snow way more than you have, ass-muncher. This is my world!"

"You just ran out of ass-munchers," Driftwood replied, "because I ain't gonna be any more of 'em."

"Shut the fuck up and make the huddle call, ass-muncher!" Stark said through his goofy grin.

Things were definitely back to normal in the Blizzard huddle. St. Louis attempted to recapture the recipe from their opening touchdown drive glory and ran the ball on three consecutive downs. But they failed miserably gaining a grand total of three yards on the drive. Their play calling was ultraconservative; they were afraid of turning the ball over amidst the snowy conditions. Driftwood and Stark combined for the tackle on all three St. Louis runs. This was how things were supposed to go from the very beginning. Driftwood just hoped they hadn't pulled their heads out too late.

St. Louis punted and Buffalo took possession at their own 38-yard line. Brady engineered a methodical drive featuring a quiver of short passes, mixed in with the tough inside running of both backs: the Pearl and the Stallion. Earl Johnson thrived in wintry conditions, owning a long and storied history of running rampant through Buffalo snow. His bow-legged, slashing style enabled him to maintain his balance where other backs would slip and fall attempting to cut on a slick, snow-covered surface. He would have made one hell of a lead dog in the Iditarod. As for Petrucci, he wasn't smart enough to slip. Additionally, the bulk of his weight was in his lower body, making him churn through the snow like a Sherman tank.

Johnson finished off the nearly eight-minute drive by taking a toss sweep the final seven yards in for the score. Through the heavy snow the huge scoreboard at the north end of the stadium now read: St. Louis 31, Buffalo 21.

The Buffalo crowd was euphoric. The whole thing seemed like a dream. They were sitting in what was supposed to be an indoor stadium tossing snowballs at Nighthawks' fans as their team was storming back in the Mega Bowl. They had no doubt they were going to catch up with St. Louis, the only question was whether they would run out of time.

The fans watching at home were also captivated by the incredible and unlikely turn of events. Nobody could have predicted this. What had been a pristine, indoor environment in the first half had transformed into a snowy winter-fest in the second. Word spread quickly and the world stopped to watch one the wildest scenes imaginable playing out on the stage of the biggest sporting event in the known universe. The record for the largest television audience in the history of the medium was being shattered.

During each timeout the army of groundskeepers continued to effectively clear the sidelines, goal lines, end lines, and yard lines of snow, although it continued to pile up everywhere else in the stadium. It reminded Driftwood of his youth when just about any time it snowed, he and the neighborhood kids would venture out to play football. The first thing they would do, even before picking teams, was mark off the field by shuffling through the snow, creating their own customized gridiron. The Wigwam's grounds crew was essentially doing the same thing, albeit on a much larger scale with superior equipment, but the effect was identical.

The Blizzard kicked off again and this time St. Louis broke off a decent return, bringing the ball all the way out to their own 47-yard line. The Nighthawks were beginning to get desperate, knowing they had to do something to stem the tide and wrest back the momentum. On the very first play they ran a flea-flicker, totally catching the Buffalo secondary off guard.

Tillison took the snap and handed it to Steamer, who crashed towards the line of scrimmage only to stop, wheel, and pitch the ball back to his QB. The play worked to perfection as a Nighthawks' receiver slipped behind the Buffalo secondary unnoticed. Tillison heaved the ball up into the heavy, snow-laden air. The pass was underthrown or the play would have surely gone for a touchdown. Like a baseball outfielder, the St. Louis receiver camped under the ball for what seemed like an eternity. The time the ball spent spiraling through the air allowed free safety Dave Gaston to make up enough ground to catch up to him and drag him down at the Buffalo 12. It was now the Nighthawks' fans turn to throw the snowballs.

However, the Blizzard defense dug in and stopped St. Louis from advancing the ball any further. Facing a 4th and 10 from the Buffalo 12-yard line, St. Louis was forced to attempt a field goal using their punter, Phillip Cunningham, as Oblouf's replacement. In a stroke of luck for the Nighthawks, time ran out in the third quarter before they could snap the ball and get the kick off.

The stoppage in play to switch ends of the field allowed the grounds crew time to clear the snow from where Cunningham would attempt the kick. The Blizzard faithful mercilessly booed the driver of one of the tractors as he took a pass over the area where the placement for the kick would occur. The poor guy was just doing his job but would be lucky to get out of the stadium alive if recognized. A hail of snowballs peppered him as he wheeled his tractor back up the tunnel.

Cunningham was a one-step kicker with limited range, but he did get the kick off quickly. It was a good thing, too, as Bo-Bo and Loney got great penetration again and nearly blocked another one. However, the 29-yard field goal attempt was good and St. Louis extended their precarious lead to 13 points, 34-21, early in the final stanza.

Cunningham followed up his vital field goal by shanking the ensuing kickoff out of bounds, giving Buffalo great field position at their own 40 to start the drive. The BB-Gun Offense had cranked it into high gear in the second half and took the field brimming with confidence. But rather than go full speed in their fast-break no-huddle offense, they choked it down, resetting and controlling the tempo of the game. They converted a pair of fourth downs along the way in culminating a clock-eating, 17-play drive with yet another touchdown. This one came via a 13-yard pass from Brady to Earl Johnson, who had snuck out of the backfield into the left flat.

The Pearl executed one of the prettiest spin moves ever perpetrated on a field sheathed in a couple inches of snow. Hemmed in by two Nighthawks near the sidelines, he slid to an abrupt halt before pirouetting back to the inside like a Juilliard graduate. The Pearl made for one hell of an ice dancer. The fluidity and poetry of motion displayed by the graceful back was mesmerizing. After coming to an almost complete stop, he used his momentum to transition into the spin, appearing to change directions midair, defying gravity and all logic. He landed lightly on both feet and accelerated on a straight course to the goal line. It was one of the most athletic moves Driftwood had ever witnessed.

The would-be tacklers smashed into one another as if Earl had magically disappeared in the haze of snow-dust being kicked up. When Earl reached the goal line he dove emphatically into the end zone and slid nearly to the end line. When he finally came to a stop, he flipped onto his back and made the prettiest, most perfect snow angel any Blizzard fan had ever seen.

Bennie Tenudo came on and split the uprights and with 7:12 left to play the Blizzard trailed St. Louis by only six points, 34-28. The Wigwam was off the hook in what was later coined "Fandamonium" by Budd Kilmer in the Buffalo News. The place had never been louder, even with the roof closed. Hundreds of the male faithful seated in the lower bowl – and occasionally a few of the ladies – took their shirts off, making a mockery of the Nighthawks players huddled on their sideline around several old, propane-fueled heaters the stadium ops crew had also dug out of the museum collection. It took a special kind of deranged individual to go shirtless in sub-freezing temperatures during one of the biggest snowstorms to ever hit Western New York. Buffalo was rife with them.

The worsening conditions began to take a toll on both offenses as they each went three-and-out in their following possessions. After trading punts, the Nighthawks got the ball back with 3:13 left in regulation. All St. Louis needed was to churn out a couple of first downs and they would win what was fast becoming the greatest, if not most bizarre, Mega Bowl on record.

St. Louis started the drive backed up on their own 13-yard line after Billy Brogan made a diving, shoestring tackle on the punt coverage. On the very first play of the series, they ran a screen pass and it worked to perfection. Javon Steamer caught the ball, slipped a tackle, and gained 12 yards, moving the chains. The clock ticked down under 2:30 when they snapped the ball again from their own 25.

On a simple, inside zone run, Driftwood met Steamer, stopping him in the hole for no gain. He frantically called for the timeout from the bottom of the pile as Buffalo used their second of three timeouts with 2:25 showing on the game clock. The Blizzard had burned their first timeout in an earlier drive to discuss the prudence of going for it on a fourth down.

Driftwood and Stark headed over to the sidelines to confer with Coach Faber, who was mindlessly chewing the piss out of a swizzle stick to calm his nerves. His face was red and chapped from the unexpected cold but gave away no emotion as he looked intently at the rumpled call sheet in his hands, as if it were somehow a great oracle holding all of the answers. Finally, he spoke.

"They are going to run the son of a bitch right at you again. Let's go with 'Dog the Set.' Tell Stillwaters to get his ass up to linebacker depth and play run first. If the clock doesn't stop we gotta burn the last timeout."

"You got it, Coach," Driftwood responded. He turned to head back onto the field but then wheeled around. "Goddamn, Lester, give that swizzle stick a break."

Coach Faber smiled at Driftwood. "I'd give *your* left nut for a good cigar right now."

"Shit, ol' Lefty is worth at least a box of good cigars, Coach."

"You always did have an over-inflated opinion of yourself. Now get your ass out there and get us a stop!"

The Nighthawks did try to run it right at them again, going with a lead draw out of an offset Pro I formation. Eric Sellars tripped up the ball carrier at the line, but he stumbled forward for five yards before Driftwood and Stillwaters finished him off, bringing him down at the Nighthawk 30-yard line. Driftwood screamed for Buffalo's final timeout from the bottom of the pile. It was 3rd and 5 with 2:21 left to play and Buffalo was fresh out of timeouts. The Mega Bowl title was riding on the next play.

Once again, the two Buffalo linebackers trotted to the sideline on the snow-covered field. Driftwood took his helmet off and steam rose from his sweaty skull. He looked around the stadium, taking it all in. Everybody in the place was on their feet screaming as loudly as they could. The once pristine, immaculate, state-of-the-art facility was completely blanketed with several inches of freshly fallen snow. Not in a million years could Driftwood have dreamed up this scenario. It truly inspired awe. He looked skyward past the heavily falling flakes of snow and through the hole in Wigwam, all the way up into heaven itself.

*Must be the good Lord didn't want to watch this one through the glass. No doubt, Mom and Dad are enjoying it, too.*

"Don't worry," Coach Faber said, "they're watching."

Driftwood nodded. A big smile spread over his entire visage. He and Coach Faber had been through a lot together, but it still amazed him when his coach read his mind.

"Run or pass?" Stark asked, completely oblivious to the moment.

"Well, now," Coach Faber said, chomping on the swizzle stick like a chicken on a June bug, "that *is* the million dollar question."

"Tillison's gonna want to throw it," Driftwood said. "Sumbitch thinks he's a hero."

"Yeah, but he may get overruled. We got to cover both."

"Hey," Stark said. "Let's play that Bear thing. Remember, we put it in early last week. We press the corners; put Jack on the tight end, bring Stillwaters up into the box and we are still strong for the run. We haven't shown it all night."

Driftwood and Coach Faber looked at each other in disbelief. The kid had just come up with the call of a lifetime.

"What?" Stark asked.

"Son, I'm gonna have to take away your rookie card - that is the perfect call, the call of a fucking lifetime," Coach Faber said with a Cheshire grin.

"Looks like all my hard work polishing up this blue-chip turd has finally paid off," Driftwood added.

"Do it," Coach Faber said, "then let's go dancing!"

St. Louis came out in a balanced pro-set with split backs. The tight end was to the left, the wide side of the field, with a receiver flanked out wide to each side. Tillison got up under the center and surveyed the defense. Driftwood yelled "Move!" and Buffalo shifted into the "Bear" front. The strong safety, Eric Stillwaters, moved up into Driftwood's linebacker spot and Driftwood slid down onto the line over the tight end, bumping Sam Beeson out wide to rush off the edge, while both corners rolled up into a press. Both defensive ends closed down next to the Bo-Bo, getting into three techniques covering the outside shoulders of the guards. In his peripheral vision, Driftwood saw Tillison's eyes widen as he recognized the defensive set.

Tillison excitedly barked out an audible, checking the play at the line of scrimmage and flashing hand signals to his receivers. Driftwood knew right then, in his heart, exactly what the play was. Tillison was coming right after him! He wanted to get the ball to his tight end on a little option route. It all played out in his mind, in the instant that lasts an eternity, occurring immediately prior to every snap.

The tight end was going to run exactly six steps up the field to a depth of approximately eight yards, depending on his release. From there he would stem the route inside, hoping to lean in on Driftwood and make contact with as much of his body as possible. After selling the inside cut, he would plant the inside foot before breaking the route back to the outside away from coverage. The ball would be delivered a split second before he made his break, anticipating more than enough separation to complete the pass. It was an easy throw, nothing more than a little pitch and catch, really. It was a basic play the Nighthawks had been running since the first day of off-season workouts. It was as effective as it was simple; simple and yet it could win them the Mega Bowl.

Driftwood snapped back into the moment at the snap of the ball. He let the tight end off the line without too much of a struggle. Wanting to bait the trap rather than disrupt the timing of the pattern, he was going for it all. He wanted the tight end to think he had a fish on the line who had swallowed the bait – hook, line, and sinker. He was going for broke; he was tapped in to the Over-soul and had already visualized the outcome. He needed only to maintain his patience. He got on the man's inside hip in a slight trailing position, turning his back completely to the quarterback.

As the tight end leaned inside, Driftwood supplied some resistance, but only with his arms so when the guy pushed off it wouldn't be enough to jar him from his planned course. When the tight end planted his inside foot and quickly gave a head and shoulder fake to the inside, Driftwood made his first move – a similar head fake to the inside, hoping to give the impression he had bit on the tight end's fake. At that point, Driftwood knew it was too late for Tillison to pull the ball back; it was likely already in the air.

Driftwood had also planted his inside foot and he broke to the outside, half a step ahead of his man, effectively undercutting the route. If the tight end had continued over the middle the guy would have been wide-assed open and the Nighthawks would claim the title. But he hadn't. Driftwood had guessed correctly and whipped his head back around to pick up the flight of the ball just after it left Tillison's hand.

Driftwood continued outside but also on a slight angle back toward the line of scrimmage and right in front of the Nighthawks' tight end. He plucked the ball out of the snowy night air and ran like never before. He was 35 yards from the end zone when he had made the interception. The only one with half a chance to catch him was the tight end. Normally Tillison would have had a shot, but Big E had creamed him as he let the ball fly.

But nobody was going to catch him. Not on this night. Jack Driftwood ran his way into the end zone, the history books, Mega Bowl lore, and NAFA immortality. His first and only career touchdown capped off the biggest comeback in Mega Bowl history amidst the most bizarre and unusual circumstances the game had ever seen.

He sprinted into the end zone untouched. Going to his knees as he crossed the goal line, Driftwood raised the ball triumphantly over his head. He nearly slid all the way to the back of the end zone on the slippery, snowy surface. Knowing what was coming he tucked the ball into his gut and curled up in the fetal position waiting for his teammates, who shortly would pile onto him from all directions.

Once the pile broke up they half carried Driftwood off the field. Bennie Tenudo came on to kick the most important extra point of his life. It was right down Main Street! Buffalo took their first and only lead of the game, 35-34.

Driftwood grabbed Stark and started singing his own version of the lad's touchdown song.

"I scored a touchdown, I scored a touchdown, we're gonna win the Mega Bowl. We're gonna—"

Driftwood and Stark were singing, holding hands and dancing along the sideline when Coach Faber clubbed the both of them, harnessing their attention real quick like.

"You dumbasses," he yelled, "there are still two minutes left in this game and all they need is a field goal. Quit acting like jackasses and let's finish this thing!"

The Nighthawks still had one timeout remaining and two minutes left on the clock to play with. But they were devastated, their spirit was heavily damaged and taking on water. Their return man couldn't handle the kickoff, and after dropping it twice, he just laid on the ball at his own five-yard line; not the most enviable place to begin an all or nothing drive.

John Tillison brought St. Louis to the line with a steely glint of determination in his eyes. There was no quarter given, none taken. Both sides had fought valiantly and weren't about to give up now.

He took the snap, faked a hand-off to Steamer, and back pedaled, setting up a screen pass. Steamer tried to hide amongst the tall trees in the forest of linemen before turning back to his QB for the little dump pass. The throw came out high as Tillison had to clear the outstretched hands of the onrushing Bo-Bo Karpinski. The pass bounced off of Steamer's outstretched fingers and popped up into the air.

The ball seemed to drift for an eternity outlined against the black sky by the falling snow, but gravity would not be denied. It appeared the ball would float harmlessly to the ground, stopping the clock and keeping the Nighthawks' hopes alive. But Steven Stark had been playing screen the whole way.

The rookie linebacker dove and slid face first through the snow towards the spot he had calculated the ball would land. At the last second, he gracefully flipped over onto his back, mid-slide, and extended his arms above his head. The ball came nestling down into his awaiting hands like a gift from heaven.

Interception!

Game, set, and match!

The Buffalo offense took the field after Driftwood had carried Stark off of it and took a knee on three consecutive snaps until the clock finally wound down to all zeroes.

Finally, Buffalo had won the Mega Bowl and the Mega Bowl was in Buffalo!

**Jack Driftwood Wants a Word with You, Buffalo**
***Blizzard Linebacker Retires After 18 Seasons***
By Budd Kilmer
Buffalo News Sports Editor

(Buffalo, NY) I got some bad news, sports fans. There is no easy way to say it and no sense beating around the bushes about it: Jack Driftwood has officially retired.

Talk about going out on top. He played in Mega Bowl 33 as a rookie and hung around the interim 16 years before not only winning Mega Bowl 50 right here in Buffalo, but was also named the MVP of the game. But that is history, and now, so is Jack Driftwood.

I know, you'd think I'd be celebrating considering the way I have ridden him hard over the years, even calling for his head on a platter on several, in retrospect, dubious occasions. I have been hard on Jack Driftwood and I don't take that back, nor do I necessarily regret it.

Admittedly, he was a pretty easy target, being one of the few common denominators of 16 years of ineptitude from the Blizzard. I also confess to holding him to a higher standard, but such is the price of being the elder statesman on the team for nearly the past decade. However, I am not too proud to give credit when credit is due.

And, folks, Mr. Driftwood has earned himself a whole heaping helping of praise. I was one of many who believed the entire Donald Fegel fiasco would distract and ultimately doom this team. Think about it; the Blizzard had every excuse in the world to fall apart when the going got tough, and the going did get tough multiple times throughout their historic run to the Mega Bowl Title.

But as the saying goes, "that's when the tough get going." And I don't care what anybody says, Jack Driftwood is as tough as they come. He had a Star-Bowl season while playing the last half of the year with basically one arm after separating his shoulder week nine. His intensity carried this team of champions through the valley of death, time after time, during this special season. He was the heart and soul of this football team.

He will not be easily replaced, especially in the locker room, where his 18 years of experience kept this team calm yet laser-focused on the task at hand. His performance in the Mega Bowl itself was one for the ages. Not only did he score the winning touchdown, astonishingly his first trip to the end zone in his unlikely career, but he was all over the field making big hits and tallying 15 tackles.

I spoke with Jack yesterday when he called me. He said, “Budd, I know you don’t owe me any favors, but I would appreciate it if you would do me this one thing.”

At that point, I have to admit, I thought he would tell me to “pound salt,” or some such other colorful metaphor. I wouldn’t have blamed him – much.

“I’m retiring,” he said, “and I want to make sure every Blizzard fan and all of the Buffalo people know how much they have meant to me over the years. You know, I have seen them all, Budd. I’ve played in every NAFA Stadium at least twice and nobody even comes close. Blizzard fans are the best in the land because Buffalo people are the salt of the earth. Can you tell them all I said thank you from the bottom of my heart and could you tell them I love them?”

There you go, Jack. I got a pretty good feeling they love you, too.

It occurred to me, the NAFA is renovating its Hall of Fame this summer to mark the 50th anniversary of the league. Perhaps they could use a piece of driftwood in a display as an example of endurance, fortitude, resilience, heart, determination, and toughness. We have the perfect driftwood for them right here in Buffalo.

His name is Jack Driftwood.

# NAFA Divisional Alignment

## Eastern Conference

Seaboard
Buffalo Blizzard
Boston Revolution
Montreal Mayhem
Toronto Gladiators
New York Rough Riders
South Florida Riptide

Atlantic
Philadelphia Liberty
Baltimore Avengers
D.C. Stars
Cincinnati Wildcats
Pittsburgh Brawlers
Nashville Cougars

Great Lakes
Detroit Muscle
Chicago Predators
Cleveland Greyhounds
Wisconsin Knights
Minnesota Northmen
Indianapolis Drive

## Western Conference

Southern
Georgia Wild Hogs
New Orleans Outlaws
Charlotte Speed
Orlando Rage
Houston Space Invaders
Mexico City Dragons

Heartland
Colorado Mountaineers
Dallas Stampede
Omaha Meadowlarks
St. Louis Nighthawks
San Antonio Defenders
Kansas City Demolition

Pacific Coast
Seattle Stealth
San Francisco Miners
L.A. Firebirds
Arizona Roadrunners
San Diego Cadets
Las Vegas Gamblers

# Buffalo Blizzard 2015 Schedule

**Preseason**

Gm 1: @ Cincinnati Wildcats
Gm 2: @ Dallas Stampede
Gm 3: @ Detroit Muscle

**Regular Season**

| Wk. | Date | Opponent | Home/Away |
|---|---|---|---|
| 1 | Sunday, Aug 30 | Georgia Wild Hogs | Away |
| 2 | Sunday, Sept 6 | Pittsburgh Brawlers | Home |
| 3 | Sunday, Sept 13 | New York Rough Riders | Home |
| 4 | Sunday, Sept 20 | Baltimore Avengers | Away |
| 5 | Sunday, Sept 27 | South Florida Riptide | Away |
| 6 | Sunday, Oct 4 | Cleveland Greyhounds | Home |
| 7 | Sunday, Oct 11 | Toronto Gladiators | Away |
| 8 | Sunday, Oct 18 | Montreal Mayhem | Home |
| 9 | Sunday, Oct 25 | Arizona Roadrunners | Home |
| 10 | Sunday, Nov 1 | Boston Revolution | Home |
| 11 | Sunday, Nov 8 | New York Rough Riders | Away |
| 12 | | Bye Week | |
| 13 | Monday, Nov 23 | Toronto Gladiators | Home |
| 14 | Sunday, Nov 29 | Montreal Mayhem | Away |
| 15 | Sunday, Dec 6 | St. Louis Nighthawks | Away |
| 16 | Monday, Dec 14 | Boston Revolution | Away |
| 17 | Sunday, Dec 20 | South Florida Riptide | Home |

**Playoffs**

Wildcard round games: Dec 26 & 27
Conference Semifinals: Jan 2 & 3
Conference Finals: Jan 10
Mega Bowl 50: Sunday, Jan 24th, 2016

# Check out these great children's books written by Ray Bentley

Darby the Dinosaur Series
Illustrated by Mike Hamby

Shopping with Darby
Naptime for Darby
Darby's Christmas Adventure

Bubba Gator & the Gator Family Series
Illustrated by Tim Gordon

No More Hiccups!
The Great Gator Princess
Nobody Said…Happy Birthday!

Books available to order online at www.fivecountpub.com.

# Ray Bentley

Ray Bentley was born and raised in the Grand Rapids, Michigan area. He graduated from Hudsonville High School in 1979 and attended Central Michigan University on a full-ride football scholarship. While at Central Michigan, Ray majored in English and accomplished many feats on the football field. He broke the all-time career tackles record while playing linebacker for the Chippewas and still holds the record for most tackles in a single season. He was the first defensive player ever to receive of the Mid-American Conference Player of the Year award in 1982.

After leaving Central Michigan, Ray began his professional football career in the USFL, winning the league's inaugural championship in1983 with the Michigan Panthers and playing in the title game with the Oakland Invaders in 1985. In 1986, Ray signed with the Buffalo Bills of the NFL. He played in Buffalo for six seasons, including the first two of the four historic consecutive Super Bowl appearances. After suffering a knee injury with the Cincinnati Bengals in 1992, Ray retired from professional football after a 10-year career.

Once retired, Ray began a media career hosting a local morning radio show in Grand Rapids and working Mid-American Conference football games on television as a game-analyst. He expanded that role into play-by-play and called games for the NFL on FOX. In 2000, he became the Head Coach and General Manager of the Buffalo Destroyers, an Arena Football League team. After resigning in 2003, he made his way back to television, becoming the lead analyst on NBC's coverage of Arena Football. He also began working for ABC and ESPN covering college football games, the job he still holds today. Ray also worked Buffalo Bill's preseason telecasts as their play-by-play announcer for seven years ending after the 2014 season.

In the late 1980's and early 1990's, Ray wrote and published seven children's books. Ray is the father of five children with his wife of 33 years, Jodi, and the grandfather of two boys. He currently resides in New Hampshire just down the street from those grandsons.